STATS™ 1993 BASEBALL SCOREBOARD

John Dewan, Don Zminda, and STATS, Inc.

Foreword by Vin Scully

Illustrations by John Grimwade

 HarperPerennial

A Division of HarperCollinsPublishers

STATS is a registered trademark of Sports Team Analysis and Tracking Systems, Inc.

FIRST EDITION

Cover Design by John Grimwade

ISBN 0-06-273138-6

93 94 RRD 3 2 1

ACKNOWLEDGEMENTS

There is no way that I can adequately describe for you the heart and soul put into this book by the staff here at STATS. I'm sure you can feel the creativity, effort and dedication just oozing out of the pages. Never has so much been done by so many! Let me try to give you a rundown of our lineup and roster.

Bob Mecca is one of the key men in our batting order, batting leadoff. Bob sets the table for the rest of the lineup by coaxing our computer to produce the marvelous reports that address the questions posed in this book.

We have the ideal number-two hitter in Pat Quinn. Pat showed he can really hit behind the runner by typesetting most of the book's essays.

John Grimwade bats third. John hits 1.000 in clutch situations; his artistic talents bring the Scoreboard to life.

In the cleanup spot, Don Zminda. Don can do it all: hit for average, hit for power, get on-base, and even steal a few bases when they're needed. His analytical and writing skills form the centerpiece of this book.

Chuck Miller is in the number-five slot. Chuck's power hitting is awesome as shown by his work in statistical editing and art coordination.

The rest of the starting lineup is rounded out by the programming talents of Dave Pinto, Dick Cramer, Rob McQuown and Mike Canter. Their contribution to the team (and this book) is immeasurable.

Steve Moyer is on the mound. His work as proofreader/editor/writer put the finishing touches on this complete game effort. Art Ashley, Sue Dewan and Ross Schaufelberger form the rest of our rock-solid starting rotation. Every effort of theirs is a quality start; their contributions to this book were top notch.

Finally, our championship team boasts the deepest bench in the world of baseball analysis. Rob Neyer, our bullpen closer, wrapped up this Scoreboard with his summary of our previous Scoreboards. Mike Hammer, defensive specialist, assured our victory with some clutch programming work. Marge Morra, Jim Musso, Suzy Neily, Allan Spear, Michael Coulter, Alissa Hudson, Deb Pokres and Jules Aquino are all major contributors to the STATS team.

The bat boy is two-year-old Jason Dewan, who patiently waits for his dad to finish his turn at bat. The fan club is led by seven-month-old Christopher Mecca, who cheers from his playpen in his dad's office during weekend games. The trainer is Sharon Zminda, who always has the right prescriptions to keep her husband in the lineup.

Thanks, gang! Nobody does it better.

— John Dewan

Table of Contents

II. GENERAL BASEBALL QUESTIONS 73

FOREWORD

By **Vin Scully**

When I look at statistics I try to read past the numbers on the page. I look at what the numbers are telling me, conclusions from the stats that will be interesting to the listener or viewer. The **Baseball Scoreboard** takes an unconventional look at various aspects of the game and forms succinct conclusions based on statistical analysis.

The conclusions are what I enjoy about this book. I offer you this aphorism that sums up my feelings. I don't know who said it, but it basically goes like this: "I don't ever want to use numbers like a drunk uses a lamp post — for support, not illumination." The **Baseball Scoreboard** uses statistics to enlighten the reader.

I have always been a butter and egg man as far as statistics are concerned. When I talk about statistics, I am more interested in home runs, RBI, batting average and stolen bases for everyday players and wins, losses, saves and maybe ERA for pitchers. Ironically, that is why I like this book. It analyzes the statistics for me so I can use the information to make a point.

You can't just read statistics on the air. Imagine a radio show where all they did was read the stock market price quotations; who would want to listen to that? I try to soften the numbers. For example, if the statistics say a player is hitting .326 over the last 20 games, I may say that he is hitting close to .330 for the last three weeks. It's a lot easier on the ear. I am trying to use statistics and topics in the **Baseball Scoreboard** to supplement a thought. This book looks at unique, detailed statistics, and is somehow able to form pointed conclusions and provide witty analysis of the numbers.

There are plenty of numbers in this publication, yet it doesn't read like a stat book. The **Baseball Scoreboard** is more of a narrative of the issues not normally addressed among baseball fans. Issues that you may think about but can't find the answer to. Topics like who has the best heart of the order, which players drove in the most runs per opportunity and who had the most infield hits are dissected and made interesting for the baseball fan.

In my business you have to be interesting. Instead of just regurgitating numbers, I will make a syllogism — a major statement and a minor statement which leads to a conclusion. The statistics help you do that and, combined with the inferences, make an interesting point. Just to babble is a killer.

I won't use some of the statistical deductions in the **Baseball Scoreboard**. When I look through this book I have a myriad of information that I can use to second guess a manager and that's not my style. I never want to give a stat where the listener says, "why would Lasorda do that or why would Leyland pitch him?" With this book I have too much ammunition. The manager has his own reasons for making the moves that he makes. I can't just sit up in the booth shooting bullets from the **Baseball Scoreboard**. You'll have to read this book for yourself and form your own opinions if you want to be an arm-chair manager.

You may think it odd that someone who does not live and die by statistics would recommend a STATS, Inc. publication. My philosophy on statistics is summed up by an old cliche that I believe was credited to Disraeli. He said, "There are lies, damn lies, and statistics." The **Baseball Scoreboard** is a lot more than just statistics.

INTRODUCTION

This is the fourth edition of **The STATS Baseball Scoreboard**, and our first for HarperPerennial. Some of you are probably familiar with what we try to do in this book, but many of you are not. So let's explain what the **Baseball Scoreboard** is all about.

Imagine that you, a die-hard baseball fan, had access to an unlimited amount of statistical information. What kinds of things would you want to learn? You already have the basic information — which teams had the best records, who were the leaders in the basic statistical categories, that sort of thing. This is your chance to probe deeper, to unlock some of the hidden secrets of the game. Doesn't that sound like fun?

We thought so, too, and that's the premise behind the **Baseball Scoreboard**. We start with the information, mountains and mountains of it. Throughout the baseball season, STATS reporters are stationed in every major league press box, using a computerized scoring system to record virtually everything that happens on the field. And we do mean everything: we log every pitch, every foul ball, the direction and distance of every ball in play. We even keep track of such supposedly "meaningless" things as pitchers' throws to first. As veteran fans of this book well know, it turns out that they're anything but meaningless.

Much of the information we gather is used to provide information to STATS clients: box scores for the Associated Press and **USA Today**, numbers for the ESPN baseball broadcasts, information for major league teams. We also produce several books of our own during the off-season, in addition to this one. But those outlets, thorough as they are, merely scratch the surface of our database. What we do in the **Baseball Scoreboard** is what you, as a fan, would do if you had the chance: probe the data more completely, to try to get some of your wildest questions answered — and, always, to have some fun along the way.

Say you're a student of relief pitching. You know who the save leaders are, but you also know that all save opportunities are not equally difficult.

Some relievers always seem to come in with the tying runs on base, and have to pitch out of a jam. Others always seem to get the call at the start the ninth inning, with the luxury of a three-run lead. Is that an accurate perception? We probe the issue in "Do Saves Come Easy for Dennis Eckersley?"

Or say you're a fan of the new Colorado Rockies. You know that thanks to the altitude, Denver is likely to be a very friendly place for hitters. Just how much of a boost will the hitters get at Mile High Stadium, and which hitters are likely to benefit the most? We investigate that issue in our Rockies essay, "Will the Hitters Have a Mile-High Season?"

Or say you appreciate the importance of good defense, and want to know which second basemen are best at turning the double play. We provide the answers in "Who Are the Prime Pivot Men?" We also answer a number of other questions on the often-neglected defensive facet of the game.

We think you get the idea. Every year we pick 101 questions, the most interesting stuff we can find, and answer them — with full discussion of the issues involved — in two- or three-page essays. Some of the questions are perennial favorites, like "Who'll Be the Next to Reach 3,000?" — our projection of the players, young and old with the best chances to reach 3,000 hits (or 500 home runs) in their careers. We know a lot of you love the old Bill James stats, like runs created and secondary average, so we include essays each year on some of those fascinating numbers. But most of the questions this year are completely new: questions like, "Do Emotional Wins Fire Up a Team?"; "What Happens to Rookie Pitchers the Second Time Around the League?"; and "Do They Steal With a Big Lead These Days?" Those are just a few examples.

We know most of you follow a particular team, and this year, for the first time, we've specifically geared one question to each major league club, including the new franchises in Colorado and Florida. For the Dodgers we ask, "How Costly Were All Those Errors?" For the Brewers, we wonder, "Does the Running Game Also Distract the Hitter?" Usually the discussions will include the other clubs as well, so (for example) you don't have to be a Red Sox fan to enjoy the Red Sox essay.

While these are serious discussions, you don't have to be a numbers cruncher to enjoy or understand them. Many of the articles, as usual, include easy-to-follow illustrations by the talented John Grimwade. And, as usual, most of the articles include more detailed statistics in the Appendix.

Enjoy!

John Dewan and Don Zminda

I. TEAM QUESTIONS

BALTIMORE ORIOLES: WILL THEY UNLOAD THE BASES AGAIN IN 1993?

One of the Orioles' hidden talents in 1992 was their uncanny ability to come through with the bases loaded. Mike Devereaux, in particular, was deadly, pounding out 13 hits in 25 bags-full at-bats for a .520 average. Devereaux drove in 107 runs in 1992; more than one-third of them, 38 to be exact, came out of bases-loaded situations.

It wasn't just Devereaux. The O's as a team were outstanding in this regard. They batted .351 with the sacks full, best in the majors and 82 points above the major league average for this situation (.269). They had 135 bases-loaded RBI, one less than the Twins, who were similarly excellent. Here are the major league figures for 1992:

Batting with the Bases Loaded — 1992

Team	AB	H	HR	RBI	Avg
Baltimore Orioles	131	46	5	135	.351
Minnesota Twins	138	48	5	136	.348
Detroit Tigers	147	46	5	130	.313
New York Yankees	117	35	4	105	.299
Montreal Expos	109	32	1	90	.294
New York Mets	134	39	3	122	.291
Atlanta Braves	111	32	2	88	.288
Los Angeles Dodgers	119	34	2	90	.286
Boston Red Sox	158	45	7	130	.285
St. Louis Cardinals	134	38	3	102	.284
Cleveland Indians	117	33	4	89	.282
Pittsburgh Pirates	134	37	4	94	.276
Oakland Athletics	140	37	4	111	.264
San Diego Padres	95	25	4	79	.263
Milwaukee Brewers	122	32	2	107	.262
Chicago Cubs	88	23	3	66	.261
California Angels	78	20	1	69	.256
Chicago White Sox	131	33	4	114	.252
Toronto Blue Jays	123	31	2	99	.252
Philadelphia Phillies	136	34	5	97	.250
Houston Astros	133	31	2	87	.233
Seattle Mariners	113	26	5	82	.230
Cincinnati Reds	144	32	2	98	.222
Texas Rangers	123	26	3	82	.211

San Francisco Giants	97	20	1	55	.206
Kansas City Royals	86	15	1	61	.174
MLB Totals	3,158	850	84	2,518	.269

In terms of runs per opportunity, the O's again ranked near the top. They scored an average of 0.82 runs for each one of their bases-loaded opportunities last year; only the Twins, their rivals for bases-full supremacy, did better (0.85 runs/opportunity). The average major league club got 0.69 runs, on average, out of a bags-full situation.

This might seem like a relatively unimportant skill; after all, how often does a club get an opportunity to come up with the bags full? The answer is, a lot more than you might think. The average major league club had 154 plate appearances with the bases full last year, or nearly one a game. The Boston Red Sox had an even 200, and the Orioles 171.

Cashing in on those opportunities is important, in good part, because if you fail, you give up a chance to have a big inning . . . and a terrific chance to win the game. Last year major league teams had a .408 winning percentage in games in which they had no bases-loaded opportunities. If they had one or more and failed to score, their winning percentage was only marginally better, .430. But if they came through and cashed in the opportunity with even one run, they wound up winning the game almost 70 percent of the time. Here are the figures:

1992 MLB — Game Results with Bases Loaded

Situation	Wins	Loss	Pct
No Bases Loaded During Game	910	1,322	.408
Team Loads Bases — Doesn't Score	299	396	.430
Team Scores After Loading Bases	897	388	.698

The Orioles, not surprisingly one of the top clubs, had a total of 58 games in which they scored at least one run with the bags full. They won 46 of the 58, for a winning percentage of .793. Only the Pirates (.818), Athletics (.814), and White Sox (.800) had higher winning percentages in such games.

No wonder Mike Devereaux is such an important guy in the Baltimore scheme of things.

A complete listing for this category can be found on page 245.

BOSTON RED SOX: WAS IT THE LACK OF THE BIG TWO-OUT HIT?

When a club finishes last for the first time in 60 years, as the Red Sox did in 1992, it obviously had more than a few problems. Boston's primary trouble last year was its offense. Despite playing in Fenway Park, which is still a fine park for scoring and batting average (though no longer a great park for home runs, due to architectural changes), the Sox ranked next-to-last in the American League in both team batting and runs scored.

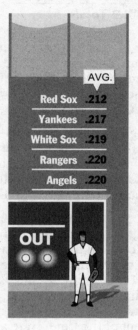

But Boston's problems were compounded by the fact that they also struggled in the clutch: they ranked next-to-last in the AL in batting with runners in scoring postion (.245), and dead last with runners in scoring position and two out (.212). It's the latter figure which concerns us here. What kind of teams struggle with men in scoring position and two out — obviously a high-pressure, do-or-die situation? Is it merely a function of having a weak offense, or the sign of some deeper problem (choking, we mean)? Here are the 1992 figures for all major league teams:

Batting With Runners in Scoring Position
Two Out, 1992

American League

Team	Avg	OBP	Slg	AB	HR	RBI
Blue Jays	.257	.362	.425	685	21	233
Royals	.247	.331	.353	677	11	193
Tigers	.246	.343	.416	658	24	229
Orioles	.243	.344	.390	667	17	213
Brewers	.241	.342	.335	701	9	216
Athletics	.233	.365	.357	678	18	213
Twins	.230	.345	.317	682	9	196
Indians	.230	.314	.328	643	13	185

Batting With Runners in Scoring Position
Two Out, 1992

American League

Team	Avg	OBP	Slg	AB	HR	RBI
Mariners	.221	.306	.361	628	15	175
Angels	.220	.310	.307	567	8	153
Rangers	.220	.323	.348	676	16	198
White Sox	.219	.332	.327	648	12	180
Yankees	.217	.335	.343	607	17	195
Red Sox	.212	.325	.299	636	6	182
League Avg.	.231	.334	.349	653	14	197

National League

Team	Avg	OBP	Slg	AB	HR	RBI
Cubs	.235	.329	.318	622	8	175
Cardinals	.234	.342	.332	743	5	211
Expos	.231	.333	.320	653	6	171
Phillies	.228	.341	.332	671	11	184
Pirates	.228	.349	.322	658	8	181
Braves	.222	.322	.360	653	16	179
Giants	.221	.312	.333	637	11	167
Reds	.221	.336	.327	675	11	179
Dodgers	.219	.321	.312	648	6	157
Padres	.214	.330	.352	585	17	145
Astros	.199	.323	.288	649	10	157
Mets	.189	.318	.305	604	11	162
League Avg.	.220	.329	.322	649	10	172

As you can see, hardly anyone hits in this situation. The major league average with runners in scoring position and two outs last year was a somewhat sobering .226. And only one club could hit more than .250 in this situation — the world champion Toronto Blue Jays, at .257.

But as you can also see, a low average in this situation is not merely a function of a weak overall offense. The White Sox, Yankees and Padres, all of whom had decent offensive numbers, struggled terribly in this situation — a major reason why all three clubs had disappointing seasons.

On the other hand, the Royals and Cubs, both of whom had offenses nearly as weak as Boston's, did very well for themselves.

Most of the Red Sox hitters were absolutely pathetic with runners in scoring position and two outs. Jack Clark was 4-for-32, .125, with 14 strikeouts. Phil Plantier was 6-for-39, .154, and Jody Reed 8-for-47, .170. The only good hitters were Bob Zupcic (14-for-46, .304) and Wade Boggs (12-for-40, .300).

So what was it — the Red Sox choked in the clutch? Let's not get too carried away. Since the average major league club gets around 5,500 at-bats over the course of a season, it's a little silly to single out these 650 or so as the only ones that are really important.

If you look at another set of numbers — ones that are easily as valid — you get a more flattering picture of the Red Sox offense under pressure. In the late innings of close games, Boston batted a very healthy .262, the fourth-best figure in the league, and 16 points better than their overall average. So let's not say Boston choked; it's more than enough to say they had a very weak offense.

Why are batting averages with runners in scoring position and two outs so low — around 30 points lower than the overall major league average? One big reason is that the pitchers often refuse to give the batter anything good to hit. In the American League last year, the overall walk rate was about one base on balls per 10 at-bats. But with runners in scoring position and two outs, the rate was one per 6.8 at-bats — almost 50 percent higher. In the National League, they pitched around the hitters even more — one walk per 11 at-bats normally, one per 6.4 ABs with runners in scoring position and two outs. The problem is that a lot of hitters simply refuse to take a walk in this situation; they think they have to drive the run in. As a result, they swing at bad pitches, and get themselves out.

A complete listing for this category can be found on page 246.

CALIFORNIA ANGELS: WERE THEY TRAPPED BY THE TRAPPERS?

For the last decade, the California Angels have been building up their fans' hopes with a series of "can't miss" prospects, all of whom came up through their AAA farm club at Edmonton. It's partially Southern California hype that builds players like Dick Schofield and Lee Stevens into potential superstars, but there's been more than that at work: the deceptive quality of those Edmonton numbers.

Edmonton is in the hit-happy Pacific Coast League, and it's easy to compile impressive numbers there. Last year the Trappers' team batting average was .290, the year before .286. Our "major league equivalencies," which adjust minor league figures for park and league, show how deceptive such numbers can be. Here are the raw minor league totals at Edmonton, the major league equivalencies (MLE), and the actual numbers posted by California prospects with the Angels, based on 18,453 Trapper at-bats over the last five seasons:

Major League Equivalencies — Edmonton Players (1988-92)

	Avg	OBP	Slg
Edmonton	.279	.357	.415
MLE	.226	.281	.311
California	.236	.290	.329

The MLEs are right on. In fact, the slightly better performance with California is expected because, on average, it's a couple of seasons after the corresponding MLEs. MLEs would have removed a lot of the hype; instead, the Angels kept building up their prospects, and getting disappointed. Here's a brief rundown of a decade of inflated expectations:

Dick Schofield	AB	H	HR	RBI	Avg
1983 Edmonton	521	148	16	94	.284

Future All-Star, said the Angels about Ducky Schofield. We could have told the Angels that these numbers transferred to nothing special at the major league level: maybe .230 with 10 homers. But would they have believed us? Never.

Gary Pettis	AB	H	HR	RBI	Avg
1983 Edmonton	529	151	11	52	.285

Pettis actually fashioned a decent major league career: five Gold Gloves, some useful seasons with steals and some walks. "But he could have been a contender," say the Angels. No, he could have been a .236 hitter, which is what he was.

Jack Howell	AB	H	HR	RBI	Avg
1985 Edmonton	284	106	13	48	.373
1986 Edmonton	156	56	3	28	.359

We'll admit that even we were fooled by Jack Howell. .373! .359! Superstar! Howell wasn't all that bad: a decent glove, two 20-homer seasons. But he could never hit lefties, and the Angels kept expecting .373! .359! Howell finally did become a star . . . in the Japanese League.

Devon White	AB	H	HR	RBI	Avg
1985 Edmonton	277	70	4	39	.253
1986 Edmonton	461	134	14	60	.291

Another useful player: Gary Pettis with less patience, but more power. The Angels expected more, though, especially after White hit 24 homers in that fooler of all years, 1987 (see essay on p. 116) The Angels sent him back to Canada, where expectations are a little lower, eh?

Mark McLemore	AB	H	HR	RBI	Avg
1986 Edmonton	286	79	0	23	.276

He was going to be Ducky Schofield's double play partner "for the next decade." Yeah, right. Now 28, he's still a "prospect," with a .229 lifetime average, for the Orioles.

Dante Bichette	AB	H	HR	RBI	Avg
1987 Edmonton	360	108	13	50	.300
1988 Edmonton	509	136	14	81	.267

Overall, not a bad player, but not as good as the Angels expected; what else is new? Could have a better year, now that he's back in the Pacific Coast League, sort of, with the Rockies.

Gary DiSarcina	AB	H	HR	RBI	Avg
1990 Edmonton	330	70	4	37	.212
1991 Edmonton	390	121	4	58	.310

A sign of lowered expectations: they're just hoping he'll be better than

Dick Schofield. It's possible.

Lee Stevens	AB	H	HR	RBI	Avg
1989 Edmonton	446	110	14	74	.247
1990 Edmonton	338	99	16	66	.293
1991 Edmonton	481	151	19	96	.314

The Angels expected Stevens to be a star, then gave up on him after not giving him much of a chance. The Montreal Expos think they're wrong, and so do we.

This season brings us Damion Easley and Tim Salmon. We're optimistic about Salmon, but what can we say except this: don't believe all the hype. The Halos, meanwhile, have left Edmonton for Vancouver. Don't they know the fun they'll miss?

A complete listing for this category can be found on page 247.

CHICAGO WHITE SOX: HOW IMPORTANT IS A SLUGGING OUTFIELD?

One reason the White Sox finished a disappointing third last year was that they had a very underpowered outfield. Underpowered? The Sox received only 19 homers from their outfielders in 1992, an average of six measly home runs from each of the three positions. No major league club had fewer. Even more importantly, the Sox had only 169 outfield RBI, a total matched in futility only by the "pre-Barry" San Francisco Giants.

To get an idea what kind of handicap the Sox were working under, let's look at the total number of home runs and RBI produced by each major league outfield last year, ranking them by total RBI. For purposes of comparison, we'll show the number of home runs and RBI produced by the non-outfielders on each club:

1992 HR & RBI
Outfielders and Non-Outfielders

A.L. Team	Outfield		Non-Outfield	
	HR	RBI	HR	RBI
Twins	51	274	53	427
Blue Jays	71	266	92	471
Mariners	63	254	86	384
Yankees	57	254	106	449
Orioles	53	254	95	426
Rangers	73	250	86	396
Brewers	39	245	43	438
Athletics	46	214	96	479
Tigers	53	200	129	546
Red Sox	31	195	53	372
Indians	44	190	83	447
Angels	26	178	62	359
Royals	23	176	52	392
WHITE SOX	19	169	91	517
Lg. Avg.	46	222	81	437

N.L. Team	Outfield		Non-Outfield	
	HR	RBI	HR	RBI
Expos	57	265	45	336
Pirates	60	258	46	398
Cardinals	49	250	45	349
Astros	45	233	51	349
Braves	52	225	86	416
Cubs	45	219	59	347

1992 HR & RBI
Outfielders and Non-Outfielders

Mets	44	204	49	360
Phillies	34	204	84	434
Reds	41	196	58	410
Padres	37	181	98	395
Dodgers	26	175	46	324
Giants	27	169	78	363
Lg. Avg.	43	214	62	374

In terms of outfield power production, the Sox rank at the bottom of the major league list. But everywhere else, they were well above average. Look at the top RBI totals from non-outfielders:

Most RBI, Non-Outfielders

Tigers	546
WHITE SOX	517
Athletics	479
Blue Jays	471
Yankees	449

At the non-outfield positions, the Sox received more RBI than any major league club except for the Tigers, who led the majors in both runs scored and RBI. The White Sox ranked a little lower in non-outfield home runs, but they were still a very respectable seventh. It was the outfield which dragged the Sox offense down to a mediocre sixth in team RBI.

Or to be more precise, it was right field. The club considers Lance Johnson's speed and defense in center field a vital factor to their success, so they're not expecting offensive production there; Sox center fielders drove home only 49 runs, 26 below the league average. Similarly, Tim Raines is in left field for his speed and on-base ability. Though Raines and his helpers were surprisingly productive, the Sox did well to get an average number of RBI from their left fielders (73; the league average was 72). So what they need to make up for left and center is above-average production from right. With Dan Pasqua slumping last year and no one available to take up the slack, Sox right fielders drove in only 47 runs, the fewest in the league and 27 fewer than the league norm.

Now compare that with 1991, when Pasqua had a good year and got some help from several other right fielders. The Sox received a very respectable 84 RBI from right field in '91, almost twice as many as they received in 1992. The position simply killed them last year.

As long as Raines and Johnson remain regulars, the White Sox will probably continue to have a below-average outfield in terms of homers and RBI. But 1991-style production from right would vastly improve their offense; the 37 RBI they lost from the position last year probably meant about four fewer wins.

No wonder finding a solid right fielder was one of the club's top priorities over the winter. They hope Ellis Burks, signed to an incentive laden contract in January, can fill the bill.

A complete listing for this category can be found on page 248.

CLEVELAND INDIANS: DO YOUNG CLUBS CONTINUE TO IMPROVE?

According to our weighted measuring system, which we'll explain in a minute, the Cleveland Indians had one of the two youngest clubs in the major leagues in 1991. After losing 105 games in '91, the Tribe improved greatly in 1992, winning 19 more games. The other young team, which had a weighted age identical to that of the Indians, was the Houston Astros. Houston, 65-97 in 1991, improved nearly as much as the Tribe did last year, winning 16 more games. Here are the figures:

Youngest Clubs in the Majors — 1991-92

	1991			1992		
Team	Avg Age	W	L	Avg Age	W	L
Cleveland Indians	26.61	57	105	26.84	76	86
Houston Astros	26.61	65	97	26.90	81	81

That's obviously a hopeful sign: both clubs were young in '91, and got a lot better in '92. But does it follow that such improvement will continue? We decided to use our historical database to find the answer. We calculated a weighted average age for every team since 1920, looking for clubs that were similar in age to the 1991 Astros and Indians. "Weighted average" simply means that the more heavily a player is used, the more he counts toward his club's average. Thus a 29 year old who plays every day is given more weight than a 21 year old who sits on the bench. It's based on plate appearances for hitters, and batters faced for pitchers.

Since the average age of the 1991 Astros and Indians was 26.61, we looked for clubs whose average age was between 26.4 and 26.8 years. We also wanted teams that were big losers like the '91 Indians and Astros, so any club with a winning percentage above .410 was eliminated. We recorded the clubs' winning percentage in Year 1 (1991 for the Astros and Indians), and then their winning percentages during the next three seasons. Here are the clubs:

Team, Year	Ave Age	Year 1	Year 2	Year 3	Year 4
Senators, 1956	26.42	.383	.357	.396	.409
Mets, 1967	26.48	.377	.451	.617	.512
Athletics, 1965	26.49	.364	.463	.385	.506
Cubs, 1962	26.52	.364	.506	.469	.444
Pirates, 1955	26.58	.390	.429	.403	.545

White Sox, 1976	26.62	.398	.556	.441	.459
Padres, 1971	26.65	.379	.379	.379	.370
Royals, 1970	26.69	.401	.528	.494	.543
Expos, 1976	26.72	.340	.463	.469	.594
Blue Jays, 1979	26.74	.327	.414	.349	.481
Browns, 1950	26.76	.377	.338	.416	.351
Rangers, 1973	26.77	.352	.522	.488	.469
Average	26.62	.371	.451	.444	.474

In general, most of these clubs were like the Astros and Indians in 1991: they played in small markets, they had thrifty ownerships, and they used younger players, at least in part, because it was cheaper than using veterans. Some of them, like the Senators, Padres and Browns, were lousy to begin with, and they stayed lousy. However, the general pattern was one of improvement. By itself, that isn't very startling: bad clubs generally get better, and so do young clubs.

The question is whether there was improvement toward a pennant by Year 3 or 4. In several cases there was good progress, but a pennant was still a couple of years away, even by Year 4. The '65 Athletics were a winning club by 1968, but it would take three more years of careful building by Charles O. Finley before they would win their first division crown. The Pirates wouldn't win a flag until 1960 (Year 6), the Royals not until 1976 (Year 7), the Expos not until 1981 (Year 6), the Blue Jays not until 1985 (Year 7). In all these cases the ownership had a long-race plan, nurtured their good young players, and stuck it out until they finally achieved success. That gives the Indians and Astros some hope, but not necessarily for 1993.

Unless, of course, they have some sort of . . . miracle. The club we haven't mentioned was the 1967 Mets, who were bad that year, improved significantly in Year Two (just like the Tribe!), and then circumvented that "long-range building" stuff by rushing all the way to a World Championship in 1969.

The "Miracle Indians"? They can always dream.

DETROIT TIGERS: HOW MANY RUNS DO THEY NEED TO WIN?

The Tigers are not exactly a finesse team. With them, it's strictly kill or be killed: they led the American League in runs scored with 791, and their pitchers nearly did the same thing, as only the Seattle Mariners permitted more than the Detroit staff's yield of 794. No, every Tiger game didn't end up 794 to 791; it just seemed that way.

When a club has a great offense but poor pitching, it would seem likely that they'd need to score a lot of runs in order to post a victory. Is that true of the Tigers, or were they able to win some low-scoring games last year when their pitchers came through? Let's see how the Tigers fared last year according to how many runs they scored in a game:

Zero Runs: The Tigers didn't win a single game last year in which they scored no runs . . . but then neither did anyone else. Detroit was shut out nine times last year, a surprisingly high number of times for a club with the majors' best offense. But then, the Cubs were shut out 20 times.

One Run: With their bad pitching staff and strong hitting, the Tigers wouldn't be expected to win many 1-0 games last year. They didn't win any; they were 0-16 in games in which scored one run. On the other hand, the Pittsburgh Pirates won four 1-0 games last year (their 4-12 record when they scored one run was the best in the majors). The Kansas City Royals were 0-25 when they scored one.

Two Runs: Want to see a contrast? Well, here's one. Last year the Atlanta Braves, with the best pitching staff in the majors, were 13-14 in games in which their offense scored a measly two runs, the best record in the majors. The Tigers, on the other hand, were 1-14, the worst. Let's add this up: when their offense scored two runs or less, which happened in nearly one-fourth of their games, the Tigers were 1-39. The Braves were 16-32, the Pirates 13-35.

Three Runs: When their offense scored three runs last year, the Tigers were 5-13, the fourth-worst record in the majors. The Cardinals, though, were 12-4, the Pirates 20-11. Now go back to the running total. When the offenses scored three runs or less, the Pirates were 33-46 (.418); the Tigers were 6-52 (.103).

Four Runs: Even when their offense scored four times in 1992, the Tigers were just 12-12, the fourth-worst record in either league. The Pirates, for once, weren't a lot better at 12-9, but the Cincinnati Reds were 18-6. The running total: the Tigers were 18-64 (.220) when they scored four runs or less last year. That's more than half their games. But the Tigers' innings are coming.

Five Runs: So, is **this** their inning? No, it isn't. The Tigers couldn't even win half their games when they scored five times last year, going 9-12. They were the only club in the majors with a losing record when they scored five runs last year. The Brewers were 16-0 when they scored five times last year.

Six runs: Okay, Detroit has finally scored a touchdown; they missed the extra point, but can they win? Yes, they can: they were 13-6 when they scored six times last year. Even that percentage was seventh from the bottom (.684), but most clubs don't score six runs 19 times, so volume was on their side. The Orioles and Cubs were both 11-0 when they scored six times, the Expos 17-2.

Seven or more runs Now, it's their turn. The Tigers played 40 games in which they scored at least seven times — even that wasn't the highest total, as the White Sox scored at least seven 42 times (going 40-2) and the Blue Jays 41 (they were 39-2). But the Tigers did well enough, going 35-5 when they scored at least seven. Even then, they had their adventures. Once they scored nine times against the Jays and lost, 10-9; another time they scored 11 against Toronto but lost 15-11. What a team.

So our perceptions about the Tigers were correct: they basically had to bludgeon their opponents to death to win. When they scored six runs or more, they were 48-11; when they scored fewer — even five runs! — their record was 27-76. How many runs do they need to win? Six, based on last year. Think how far a little pitching would go.

W-L Records by Runs Scored

1992 Runs Scored	Detroit			Rest of ML		
	W	L	Pct	W	L	Pct
0	0	9	.000	0	289	.000
1	0	16	.000	58	418	.122
2	1	14	.067	148	443	.250
3	5	13	.278	266	343	.437
4	12	12	.500	317	217	.594
5	9	12	.429	312	143	.686
6	13	6	.684	254	89	.741
7+	35	5	.875	676	77	.898

A complete listing for this category can be found on page 249.

KANSAS CITY ROYALS: ARE ONE-CLUB PLAYERS A THING OF THE PAST?

One of the more nostalgic stories of 1992 was the simultaneous quest by Robin Yount of the Brewers and George Brett of the Royals to reach 3,000 hits. Adding greatly to the sentiment, of course, was the fact that each player had played his entire career with the home nine: Brett with Kansas City since 1973, Yount since 1974 with Milwaukee.

We often hear that the "one-club player" like Brett and Yount is becoming a thing of the past, because free agency will make it inevitable that players will move on to a higher bidder at some point in their careers. This is particularly true of players from the smaller markets represented by Brett and Yount. As if to underscore the point, this past winter saw Paul Molitor, a 15-year veteran of the Brewers, move on to bigger bucks with the Blue Jays.

But is this perception really true? Or is it just sentimental hogwash put forth by major league owners and old-woman sportswriters who want to return to a past that never really existed? (Our apologies to all the old women out there who take offense at being compared to sportswriters.) Let's use our historical database to try and find the answers.

What we'll do is go back, by five-year intervals, from 1992, and count the number of active players who had been with the same club for 15 consecutive years. Military time is counted, so that Ted Williams' 15th year would be 1953; but of course, if a guy was off fighting a war for an entire season, he wouldn't be considered part of his team's roster for that particular year. In some cases we'll find players who didn't actually start their careers with the club, like Hal McRae with the Royals in 1987 . . . but those cases are rare, and anyway, 15 straight seasons with the same club connotes one-club identity in most people's eyes. Here are the total number of active 15-year players in each of the seasons; we'll stop at 1917, because we wanted to restrict the study to the modern era, which began 16 years prior to that, in 1901:

Players With the Same Club for 15 Years (By 5-Year Periods)

Year	Players	Year	Players	Year	Players	Year	Players
1992	6	1972	6	1952	3	1932	4
1987	6	1967	7	1947	6	1927	3
1982	5	1962	4	1942	6	1922	5
1977	5	1957	7	1937	6	1917	3

As you can see, there's been no dramatic changes over the course of baseball history — and in particular, no dramatic changes since the free agent era began in 1977. You can argue that there ought to be more one-club players nowadays, since there are more clubs than there were prior to expansion. But there were twice as many 15-year veterans in 1992 than there were in 1952, 1927, or 1917, and there aren't twice as many clubs.

Are these years unusual? Not at all; they're typical of the course of baseball history. The highest total of 15-year veterans was 12 in 1946, when a lot of old-timers came back from World War II. But that was a highly unusual season; the next year, 1947, there were only six. What's the second-highest total of 15-year vets? It was nine, and it came in 1979, when the free-agent era was well under way.

Interestingly, there was a period during baseball's past, back when all the rules were stacked against voluntary player movement, when the number of 15-year vets was consistently low, between two and four a year for seven straight seasons. The period was from 1930 to 1936, when a lot of clubs were strapped for cash — just as a lot of teams claim they are now. What happened back then was that some of the high-salaried vets (at least by the standards of the times) were sold or traded to clubs which could better afford them. Major league players, it seems, aren't the only ones with their eye on the bottom line.

You could argue that this is what's about to happen in baseball now, that high-salaried veterans will wind up with the rich teams, as Molitor did this year. But you can't argue that it's happened already, and that free agency has made the one-club player a dinosaur. That simply hasn't happened, except perhaps to a minor extent.

Consider that in 1992, when the sky was supposedly about to fall, there were six 15-year one-clubbers: Brett, Yount, Alan Trammell, Lou Whitaker, Jim Gantner and Molitor. The first four re-signed with their old clubs; the fifth, Gantner, wasn't wanted by the Brewers. Only Molitor moved on because of financial considerations. And consider that two veterans with strong one-club identities, Cal Ripken and Kirby Puckett, opted to stay where they were. There are still players who **want** to stay with their old clubs, it seems.

The sky hasn't fallen yet.

	TEAM	YEARS
George Brett	Royals	20
Robin Yount	Brewers	19
Jim Gantner	Brewers	17
Alan Trammell	Tigers	16
Lou Whitaker	Tigers	16
Paul Molitor	Brewers	15

MILWAUKEE BREWERS: DOES THE RUNNING GAME ALSO DISTRACT THE HITTER?

When Phil Garner took over the Brewers last season, he vowed to bring in an aggressive running game, the kind he'd first learned while playing under Chuck Tanner with the 1976 Athletics. Did he ever! The Brewers stole 256 bases, the best performance by an American League club in years. The aggressive style was given a lot of credit for Milwaukee's 92-win season.

Throughout the season people commented constantly on how Milwaukee's running game distracted the opposition. There's no question that a runner on the bases can disrupt a pitcher's concentration, but what does it do to the hitter? Isn't it possible that a runner taking off for second also disrupts the hitter from what he's trying to do?

To study this, let's look at all major league plate appearances last year when there was a runner on first, and second base open — a potential stolen base opportunity. First, we'll look at the results of the at-bat if no stolen base was attempted; then, the results if the runner took off (whether he was safe or not); and finally, for purposes of comparison, the results of all the other at-bats during the season. Here are the results:

Major League Batting in Stolen Base Situations — 1992

	All Batters	LH Batters	RH Batters
No stolen base attempted	.271	.280	.265
Stolen base was attempted	.235	.227	.240
All other at-bats	.252	.255	.250

As you can see, the hitters are most effective when a stolen base is **not** attempted. There are good reasons for this: the pitcher's attention is indeed distracted, and the first baseman has to hold the runner on the bag, which gives the hitter (particularly a lefty hitter, as you can see) a gap in the infield to hit through. Once the steal attempt is made, the first baseman can play normally, and the hitter's had his concentration disrupted by the runner going and the catcher throwing down to second. And he's suddenly batting in a new situation: either with a runner on second, or with the bases empty. There's another factor as well — the hitter has often fallen behind on the count, or even swung and missed deliberately, in order to give the runner a chance to steal.

How did this affect the Brewers last year? Did their team average decline as a result of all the stolen base attempts? Here's a team-by-team breakdown:

Batting in Stolen Base Situations — 1992

Team	SB Situation, No Attempt		After SB Attempt		All Other	
	AB	Avg	AB	Avg	AB	Avg
Baltimore Orioles	1,280	.259	96	.198	4,109	.261
Boston Red Sox	1,224	.270	52	.173	4,185	.240
California Angels	1,019	.264	161	.205	4,184	.240
Chicago White Sox	1,191	.302	133	.293	4,174	.248
Cleveland Indians	1,223	.273	140	.243	4,257	.265
Detroit Tigers	1,281	.264	66	.227	4,168	.254
Kansas City Royals	1,154	.272	129	.202	4,218	.254
Milwaukee Brewers	1,073	.295	217	.258	4,214	.262
Minnesota Twins	1,213	.293	129	.233	4,240	.273
New York Yankees	1,284	.285	69	.188	4,240	.255
Oakland Athletics	1,210	.280	102	.137	4,075	.254
Seattle Mariners	1,191	.267	93	.323	4,280	.261
Texas Rangers	1,198	.270	73	.151	4,266	.247
Toronto Blue Jays	1,208	.262	90	.278	4,238	.263
Atlanta Braves	1,067	.262	120	.308	4,293	.250
Chicago Cubs	1,279	.260	73	.219	4,238	.253
Cincinnati Reds	1,175	.271	120	.167	4,165	.259
Houston Astros	1,107	.271	114	.281	4,259	.239
Los Angeles Dodgers	1,138	.262	123	.179	4,107	.247
Montreal Expos	1,064	.257	160	.269	4,253	.250
New York Mets	1,041	.286	94	.202	4,205	.223
Philadelphia Phillies	1,200	.267	99	.283	4,201	.249
Pittsburgh Pirates	1,096	.264	90	.311	4,341	.252
St. Louis Cardinals	992	.281	203	.207	4,399	.260
San Diego Padres	1,107	.253	75	.213	4,294	.256
San Francisco Giants	1,078	.260	117	.274	4,261	.239
MLB Average	30,093	.271	2,938	.235	109,864	.252

The Brewers, as you can see, handled this situation about as well as any club did. They batted .295 when no steal was attempted — a sign, perhaps, of how much their hitters distracted the opposition pitcher. They also hit a very respectable .258 after the steal was attempted, far less of a dropoff than most teams.

But Brewer lefty hitters did much better when the runner stayed on first (.317) than they did when the runner took off (.214). Are we saying that they would have been better off not running? Of course not; but we **are** saying that there's a hidden cost involved. It's not just the opponents whom the running game disrupts.

MINNESOTA TWINS: WOULD THE TWINS LOVE REALIGNMENT?

If some major league owners could have their way, the Twins might be entering 1993 as two-time defending World Champions. No, this is not some sort of hopeless bias on the part of major league baseball toward Minnesota . . . it has to do with one of the latest buzzwords in baseball circles, "realignment." In their latest scheme to bring home a few extra nickels, a substantial number of owners are promoting the idea of splitting each league into three divisions, thereby producing three division champions and an NFL-style "wildcard" — with an extra round of playoffs to sell to television.

How do the Twins figure in this? Only indirectly. If the American League had been split into three divisions last year, a logical split would have been:

East: Baltimore, Boston, Cleveland, New York, Toronto
Central: Chicago, Detroit, Milwaukee, Minnesota, Kansas City
West: California, Oakland, Seattle, Texas

On that basis, the three division champions would have been Toronto, Milwaukee and Oakland. The wildcard? There would have been a furious last-week struggle between Minnesota (90-72) and Baltimore (89-73); Chicago (86-76) would have probably also figured in the fight. Depending on what sort of tie-breaker was used (doesn't this excite you already? — another playoff scheme too complicated to understand!), the Twins would have met either Oakland or Toronto in the first round of the playoffs.

How you feel about this undoubtedly depends on how you feel about 100-plus years of major league baseball tradition. Truthfully, though, our feelings don't matter much; if they think they can make money with this scheme, they'll go for it. So let's go ahead and see how it might have worked in the recent past. What we'll do is to go back to 1977, when the American League expanded to 14 teams, and assume they split into three divisions back then, aligned as stated above. We'll also assume that the schedule remained the same; it almost certainly would have been a little different, but probably not a lot. The final assumption will be that if two teams finish with the same record, the first tie-breaker would be head-to-head records between the teams. Oh, and one more thing: for the 1981 strike season, we'll use full-season records, instead of that split-season thing. That particular gimmick was designed mostly to do nothing more than produce what we have here, four teams from each league in the playoffs.

Okay, then, here's how the last 16 years of American League play would have gone. To get a feel for the pennant races, the won-lost records are followed by the number of games the team would have won its division or wild-card spot by:

If the American League Had Three Divisions

Yr.	East			Central			West			Wildcard		
77	NY	100-62	3	KC	102-60	12	Tex	94-68	20	Bos	97-64	a
78	NY	99-63	b	Mil	93-69	1	Tex	87-75	c	Bos	99-63	7
79	Bal	102-57	11	Mil	95-66	10	Cal	88-74	5	Bos	91-69	2
80	NY	103-59	3	KC	97-65	11	Oak	83-79	7	Bal	100-62	14
81	Bal	59-46	1	Mil	62-47	2	Oak	64-45	5	NY	59-48	d
82	Bal	94-68	5	Mil	95-67	5	Cal	93-69	17	KC	90-72	1
83	Bal	98-64	7	Chi	99-63	7	Tex	77-85	3	Det	92-70	1
84	Tor	89-73	2	Det	104-58	20	Cal	81-81	4	NY	87-75	1
85	Tor	99-62	2	KC	91-71	6	Cal	90-72	13	NY	97-64	125
86	Bos	95-66	5	Det	87-75	11	Cal	92-70	5	NY	90-72	3
87	Tor	96-66	7	Det	98-64	7	Oak	81-81	3	Mil	91-71	2
88	Bos	89-73	2	Min	91-71	3	Oak	104-58	29	Det	88-74	1
89	Tor	89-73	2	KC	92-70	11	Oak	99-63	8	Cal	91-71	4
90	Bos	88-74	2	Chi	94-68	15	Oak	103-59	20	Tor	86-76	3
91	Tor	91-71	7	Min	95-67	8	Tex	85-77	1	Chi	87-75	3
92	Tor	96-66	7	Mil	92-70	2	Oak	96-66	19	Min	90-72	1

a 1977 Orioles also 97-64; Boston won season series

b 1978 Red Sox also 99-63; New York won season series

c 1978 Angels also 87-75; Texas won season series

d 1981 Yankees one percentage point better than Det 60-49 (Bos 59-49)

There's some weird stuff right off. The four-team West almost always had one weak sister (Seattle) and usually more. Sometimes all four teams were pretty bad; just check that 1983 race, when mighty Texas led the division (by three games, yet) with a 77-85 record. Two other times, the West winner finished at .500. In recent times Oakland was often so much better than the other three that it won by as many as 29 games, meaning they could have clinched it by Labor Day. Putting Kansas City there would have helped, but only a little; in '83, for example, the Royals would have won the division with a record of 79-83.

Another problem is that a lot of these "close divisional races" lose their starch when you remember that the second-place club will often make the playoffs anyway. In 1978, to use the most obvious example, there would have been no dramatic Red Sox-Yankee struggle down the stretch; the runner-up would have been the wildcard. Other classic races like Milwaukee-Baltimore in 1982 and Detroit-Toronto in 1987 would never have happened because the clubs were in different divisions.

The counter-argument is that new races would be created, particularly for the wildcard spot. It's true; nine times in 16 years, the wildcard winner would have made it by two games or less, and you can't get much better than that. The idea is that it would create more September interest in the game, building up gradually toward the World Series. While we purists blanch at the thought, it would probably hold the casual fan's interest better than the current system. At least, it seems to work that way with the NBA and NFL.

And what of the Twins? Yes, they would have had a chance to defend their title last year. But forget about their glorious 1987 championship — Minnesota would have finished a distant third in the Central Division behind Detroit and Milwaukee, and six games behind the Brewers for the wildcard spot.

Someone will probably use that as an argument to get even **more** teams into the playoffs.

NEW YORK YANKEES: WILL DANNY GET HURT AGAIN THIS YEAR?

Just because you're paying a guy a lot of money, it doesn't mean he's going to stay healthy. The Yankees signed Danny Tartabull last season, then watched him spend two stints on the disabled list while getting into only 123 contests. It was a pretty darn good 123 games — there's nothing wrong with 25 homers and 85 RBI, especially in only 421 at-bats — but a lot of people in New York felt ripped off anyway. What did they expect, Cal Ripken? Tartabull hasn't appeared in 140 games in a season since 1988; he's topped the 150 mark only once in his career, back in 1987.

So as a sort of "Consumer Guide to the Yankees," we thought we'd do a Q&A-within-a-Q&A about injuries, and when and where to expect them:

Is Tartabull the most-frequently injured player in the majors? No, not even close. People don't talk about Bob Walk much . . . but what's there to say about someone who goes out twice within six weeks with a "strained right groin"? Bob's motto is sort of, "Speak softly, and carry a big stretcher"; he's been on the DL six times over the last three years. Danny T's been on the list four times, ranking behind Walk and several others, most of whose names are familiar to New Yorkers:

Most DL Stints — 1990-92

Player	Times on DL
Bob Walk	6
Larry Andersen	5
Eric Davis	5
Danny Jackson	5
Lenny Dykstra	5
Vince Coleman	5
Keith Miller	5

Just looking at this list makes your right groin ache, doesn't it? Lenny Dykstra volunteered to be the ambulance driver.

Are the Yankees a team which gets injured a lot? Despite Danny, they're not . . . at least judging by 1992. The Yanks used the DL 13 times in 1992, which was exactly the major league average. In the course of winning the American League West, the Oakland A's used it 22 times:

Most DL Stints By Team

Team	Times on DL
Oakland Athletics	22
Philadelphia Phillies	21
St. Louis Cardinals	19
San Francisco Giants	19
Texas Rangers	19

Who used the DL least often? The Orioles (must be Cal's example), White Sox and Twins, with only seven each.

Do older players get injured more? You'd better believe it. Look at this chart of DL stints for each 100 regular position players and pitchers in 1992:

1992 DL Stints by Age
Per 100 Regulars

Age	Position Players	Pitchers
25 or Younger	29.4	14.3
26 to 29	42.6	34.6
30 or Older	53.1	39.2

This makes it seem like pitchers are much less likely to get injured than position players, but that's not quite right; remember that it's per 100 **regulars**, based on 1991 and '92 usage; a lot of frequently-injured pitchers don't qualify. The point is that injuries go up with age, and especially past the age of 30. And what age did Danny Tartabull just reach last October 30? You guessed it; imagine what he can accomplish, now that he's in his "injury-prone" years.

Are guys who play certain positions more likely to get injured than others? Yes, no surprise that it's pitchers, with 136 trips to the DL last year. Among position players, it's left fielders (a traditional old-guy position) and catchers (the dangers speak for themselves). The complete list:

DL Stints By Position — 1992

Position	Times on DL
Pitcher	136
Catcher	35
First Base	16
Second Base	23
Third Base	16
Shortstop	26
Left Field	36
Center Field	15
Right Field	33
Designated Hitter	8

The Yankees, the epitome of a smart organization, kept Tartabull off the pitching mound last year, weren't even **tempted** to let him catch, and cannily avoided the Bermuda Triangle of left field by only using him there for one game. And yet Tartabull still got hurt. Isn't it time to give him a nice, safe job as a full-time designated hitter?

OAKLAND ATHLETICS: HOW COSTLY IS A BLOWN SAVE?

The Athletics, led by Dennis Eckersley, had only 11 blown saves in all of 1992. That was the second-lowest total in the majors, to Toronto's 10, but Oakland had everyone beat when it came to converting save opportunities:

Best Team Save Percentages — 1992

Team	Sv	SvOpp	Pct
Athletics	58	69	.841
Blue Jays	49	59	.831
Orioles	48	64	.750
Angels	42	56	.750
Twins	50	68	.735

Impressive stuff, but what does it all mean? Aren't a lot of save opportunities blown in the sixth inning? And doesn't the club come back to win the game frequently, anyway?

It's true that some saves are blown in the sixth, but not very many — only 78 last year in over 2,000 major league games. Basically, as the game gets later, the more saves are blown, and the harder it is for the team to come back to win.) Here is the composite won-lost record for all major league clubs, by inning, after they blew a save opportunity last year:

1992 Blown Saves — Major League Baseball

Inning of Blown Save	W	L	Pct
6	32	46	.410
7	45	70	.391
8	59	88	.401
9	34	97	.260
10+	2	8	.200
TOTAL	172	309	.358

diff home/visitor?

You can see that a blown save is hard to come back from; teams won only a little over 35 percent of the games in which they blew a save opportunity last year. Blowing a save in the ninth or later wasn't quite fatal, but it put most teams on the critical list: the winning percentage was only .255.

The A's actually fared better than most clubs when they blew a save last year. They came back to win five of their 11 blown opportunities:

1992 Blown Saves — Oakland Athletics

Inning of Blown Save	W	L	Pct
6	1	1	.500
7	1	2	.333

8	2	2	.500
9	1	1	.500
10+	0	0	.000
TOTAL	5	6	.455

You'll note that the A's had only two blown saves in the ninth inning or later all year, one of which they won. Is this the mark of a superior bullpen? It sure is:

Fewest Blown Saves —
9th Inning or Later — 1992

Team	Total	Won	Lost
Athletics	2	1	1
Royals	3	2	1
Blue Jays	3	1	2
Phillies	3	1	2
Yankees	3	0	3

Clubs with superior closers: Eckersley, Jeff Montgomery, Mitch Williams, Steve Farr . . . well, all except Williams, we'd say. But which club blew the **most** saves in the ninth or later last year? The two clubs which had Jeff Reardon: the Braves and Red Sox each had nine blown saves in the ninth or later last year. To be fair to Reardon, who had enough bad numbers last year to fill this book, most of the Braves' blown saves came during a traumatic early-season period when Alejandro Pena couldn't get anyone out. Those of us who watch TBS will never forget it.

The most bizarre blown save record belonged to the Pirates — they blew 20, and wound up winning 13 of them:

1992 Blown Saves — Pittsburgh Pirates

Inning of Blown Save	W	L	Pct
6	5	0	1.000
7	2	2	.500
8	4	3	.571
9	2	2	.500
10+	0	0	.000
TOTAL	13	7	.650

Every Pirate fan must be thinking the same thing: If only that last playoff game had been in Pittsburgh, we could have come from behind to win after the blown save!

A complete listing for this category can be found on page 250.

SEATTLE MARINERS: WHO WILL KEN GRIFFEY BE WHEN HE GROWS UP?

Last season, at the age of 22, Ken Griffey Jr. had another routinely great season: he batted .308 while reaching career highs with 27 homers and 103 RBI. We say "routinely great" because people are getting used to this kind of performance from Griffey, and expecting even more. There have even been grumblings about Griffey's supposed lack of motivation and leadership abilities . . . the same sort of criticism, veteran fans will recall, that was leveled against the young Joe DiMaggio and Mickey Mantle, among others.

We'll leave other people to analyze that stuff; we just want to talk about Griffey, the ballplayer. Bill James made this point years ago, but it bears repeating: when a player this young is this good, it's a sign of extraordinary talent. Look at the best seasons by a 22 year old since 1901, in terms of James' runs created; age here is as of July 1 of the season in question:

Best Runs Created Seasons by a 22-Year Old

Batter	Year	RC	AB	R	H	HR	RBI	SB	BB	Avg
Ted Williams	1941	202	456	135	185	37	120	2	145	.406
Joe Jackson	1911	175	571	126	233	7	83	41	56	.408
Joe DiMaggio	1937	173	621	151	215	46	167	3	64	.346
Ty Cobb	1909	159	573	116	216	9	107	76	48	.377
Jimmie Foxx	1930	154	562	127	188	37	156	7	93	.335
Stan Musial	1943	147	617	108	220	13	81	9	72	.357
Jimmy Sheckard	1901	138	554	116	196	11	104	35	47	.354
Arky Vaughan	1934	135	558	115	186	12	94	10	94	.333
Dick Allen	1964	135	632	125	201	29	91	3	67	.318
Eddie Collins	1909	134	572	104	198	3	56	67	62	.346

Not a bad list; all but three — Jackson, Sheckard and Allen — are in the Hall of Fame, and Jackson would certainly be there if not for the Black Sox scandal. Williams, Jackson, DiMaggio, Cobb, Foxx, Musial and Collins would be on anyone's list of the greatest players ever.

Griffey, with 104 runs created last year, was a ways away from making **that** list, but he's already put up some imposing career numbers. Here are the lifetime leaders in home runs through age 22:

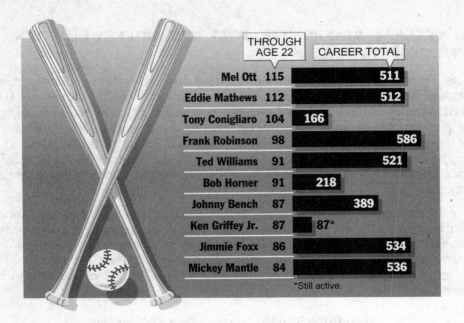

	THROUGH AGE 22	CAREER TOTAL
Mel Ott	115	511
Eddie Mathews	112	512
Tony Conigliaro	104	166
Frank Robinson	98	586
Ted Williams	91	521
Bob Horner	91	218
Johnny Bench	87	389
Ken Griffey Jr.	87	87*
Jimmie Foxx	86	534
Mickey Mantle	84	536

*Still active.

Griffey's in some august company here, with six players who topped 500 home runs — all of them, of course, are in the Hall of Fame. His chances of reaching that total will be minimal unless he steps up the pace, however; he'd need to duplicate last year's career high of 27 homers for 16 more seasons in order to reach 500.

Griffey also has 344 lifetime RBI, a total which ranks eighth on the career list through age 22. The top 10: Ott 485, Cobb 383, Williams 378, Foxx 377, Al Kaline 365, George Davis 363, Mantle 346, Griffey 344, Bench 326, Buddy Lewis 314. Again, he's in some very impressive company, with all except Davis and Lewis in the Hall of Fame.

How about hits? Once again, Griffey's among the career leaders:

Base Hits	Through Age 22	Career Total
Ty Cobb	765	4,190
Buddy Lewis	753	1,563
Robin Yount	717	*3,025
Mel Ott	715	2,876
Al Kaline	710	3,007
Freddy Lindstrom	689	1,747
Ken Griffey Jr.	652	*652
George Davis	643	2,660

Base Hits	Through Age 22	Career Total
Cesar Cedeno	618	2,087
Sherry Magee	605	2,169

* Still Active

Will Griffey wind up like Cesar Cedeno, who never lived up to his youthful promise? It's possible, and there are those who could cite some parallels. But thus far, it looks like he's headed for an extraordinary career.

A complete listing for this category can be found on page 251.

TEXAS RANGERS: ARE THEY BEING KILLED BY THEIR FAILURE TO MAKE CONTACT?

After leading the major leagues in runs scored in 1991, the Rangers did not have a very good offense last year. They ranked ninth in the American League in runs scored with 682, and they were 12th in team batting with a .250 average. Texas had a few bright spots like Juan Gonzalez' awesome display of power, but basically it was a very disappointing season.

In searching for an explanation, one thing that jumped out at us was what a Jekyll-and-Hyde team the Rangers were. When they swung at the first pitch and got it in play, they were the best-hitting club in baseball:

Team Batting on First Pitch — 1992

Team	AB	H	HR	RBI	Avg	Slg
Rangers	645	220	30	103	.341	.552
Twins	903	299	21	131	.331	.468
Brewers	824	270	21	130	.328	.476
Blue Jays	763	248	26	123	.325	.514
Padres	877	277	26	109	.316	.483

Everybody hits well on the first pitch — the major league average with the first pitch in play last year was .302 — but the Rangers' figures were exceptional. How's this for a season's work: 645 at-bats, 220 hits, 30 home runs, 103 RBI, a .341 average with .552 slugging? We're talking Cooperstown here. Some of the Ranger hitters were simply awesome when they put the first pitch in play. Three examples: rookie David Hulse was 8-for-15, .533; catcher Pudge Rodriguez was 27-for-64, .422; and most overwhelming of all was Juan Gonzalez, who was 23-for-51, .451, with eight homers and a .941 slugging average. Those sound like figures from a slow-pitch softball league.

But most plate appearances don't end with the first pitch, and that's where the Rangers' problems began. The deeper they got into the count, the worse off they were. When the count reached two strikes, they were the worst-hitting club in the American League, and the second-worst in baseball, next to the New York Mets. The Mets, at least, had the excuse that their pitchers were at the plate some of the time:

Lowest Team Averages With Two Strikes — 1992

Team	AB	H	HR	RBI	Avg	OBP	Slg
Mets	2,379	400	29	176	.168	.247	.241
Rangers	2,596	445	49	230	.171	.244	.267
Angels	2,331	414	19	161	.178	.242	.233

Giants	2,562	455	29	174	.178	.238	.247
Expos	2,472	442	23	185	.179	.241	.249

Most clubs hit poorly with two strikes — the major league average was .187 — but the Rangers were especially inept. As good as their hitters looked on the first pitch, that's about how bad they looked with two strikes. Brian Downing, who would retire after the season, batted .262 with two strikes, but the next-best mark belonged to Rafael Palmeiro, at .216. Gonzalez batted .163 with two strikes (though ever-dangerous, he hit 12 two-strike homers). Dean Palmer was even worse at .126. Monty (Let's Make a Deal) Fariss found out that behind door number three was another strike: he was 8-for-83, .096, with 51 strikeouts after the count reached strike two.

Why were the Rangers so good on the first pitch, and so bad with two strikes? One explanation is that they're a notorious fastball-hitting team; pitchers will usually throw the fastball on the first pitch, but when they get to two strikes and have the advantage, they're more likely to feed the hitters breaking stuff. That's not what the Rangers feed on.

But there was another explanation: the Rangers' failure to make contact. In many ways, that first-pitch average is very deceptive. It's the average **when the first pitch is in play**; it doesn't include the times when the hitter fouled the pitch off, or swung and missed. And the Rangers swung and missed more than any club in the American League last year, and more often than anyone else in baseball except for the National League Giants and Expos, who had the pitcher-hitting disadvantage. While the Rangers boasted that gaudy .341 first-pitch average, they put the first offering in play only 645 times, fewer than any club in baseball. And their failure to make contact led them to have more two-strike at-bats (2,596) than any other club in baseball. It's hard to hit when you're consistently in a hole.

It's obvious that hitters like Palmer (154 strikeouts last year) and Gonzalez (143 times) are always going to swing and miss a lot. But a little improvement on their part — and improvement on the part of some of their non-slugging teammates — might result in some better numbers for the Texas offense.

A complete listing for this category can be found on page 252.

TORONTO BLUE JAYS: DO THE HITTERS PREFER THE SKY OR THE DOME?

Toronto's SkyDome: there's no place like it in all of baseball, so why should it be easy to figure out? Ever since the Blue Jays opened it in June of 1989, the place with the retractable roof has played differently depending on whether the dome is open or closed. But is it better for the hitters with the roof open, or with it closed? That depends on whom, and when, you ask. Let's study the park year by year:

1989: SkyDome opened to great fanfare on June 5, 1989, and the early word was: it's a pitcher's park. The Jays and their opponents averaged less than eight runs a game for their 55 games in the dome, very low for the AL. As for whether the park was better for hitters with the dome open or closed, the answer wasn't definite, as only 10 games were played with the dome closed. But the numbers were all much better when it was open.

Year	Dome	G	R/G	HR/G	Avg
1989	Closed	10	5.40	1.10	.232
1989	Open	45	7.93	1.62	.251

1990: Pitcher's park? Better with the dome open? All those theories went through the roof in 1990, when the hitters seemed to go crazy every time the lid was shut. In 45 games with the dome closed, SkyDome yielded an average of 2.5 home runs a game, numbers which dwarfed every other park in baseball. The numbers weren't bad with the roof open, either, but nothing to compare with what happened with the dome closed. Everyone agreed: with the roof closed, this park is home run heaven.

Year	Dome	G	R/G	HR/G	Avg
1990	Closed	45	9.56	2.58	.269
1990	Open	36	8.22	1.64	.259

1991: Oh, yeah? SkyDome had more surprises in store during 1991. While the Jays were wrapping up another division title, the park reversed its characteristics again. In '91 all the levels of offense rose whenever the roof was opened; they dropped whenever it was closed. In 1990 the Jays and their opponents had batted .269 with the roof closed; in 1991 they batted .241. The home run rate dropped by over one a game with the roof closed, but increased by 22 percent with the roof open. But those 1990 figures were so overwhelming that most people still thought it was better for the hitters with the roof closed.

Year	Dome	G	R/G	HR/G	Avg
1991	Closed	29	7.72	1.48	.241
1991	Open	52	9.21	2.00	.267

1992: The Jays finally won it all in 1992, and maybe we began to figure out this bewildering ballpark. For the third time in four years, both scoring and batting average were higher with the dome open; it begins to seem that those big dome-closed figures of 1990 were a one-year aberration. The home run rate was a little higher with the dome open, but the levels were hardly sensational: our park factors system labeled SkyDome a neutral park based on the 1992 figures, on balance favoring neither the hitter nor the pitcher. Dome open or closed, it continues to be a good park for a right-handed power hitter, helping Joe Carter and Dave Winfield last year. But it's very tough on lefties like John Olerud.

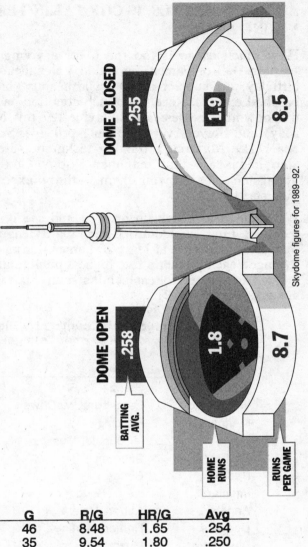

Skydome figures for 1989–92.

DOME CLOSED
.255 1.9 8.5

DOME OPEN
.258 1.8 8.7

BATTING AVG.

HOME RUNS

RUNS PER GAME

Year	Dome	G	R/G	HR/G	Avg
1992	Closed	46	8.48	1.65	.254
1992	Open	35	9.54	1.80	.250

The chart shows the four-year figures for the park with the roof open and closed. The 1990 blip still makes it look like a better home run park with the roof closed, but that number is very deceptive. The figures have changed so much from year to year that we hesitate to make a definitive conclusion, but if you were a hitter playing here, you'd probably prefer to see the sky — not the roof — when you looked up.

ATLANTA BRAVES: IS COX TAKING PROPER CARE OF HIS YOUNG ARMS?

How much usage is too much for a young pitcher's arm? Ever since "certain Hall-of-Famer" Fernando Valenzuela burned out before his 30th birthday, the subject of young arm abuse has been a hot topic among baseball experts. Recently, much attention has been given to the Braves' trio of young horses: Tom Glavine (27 this March), John Smoltz (26 in May) and Steve Avery (23 on April 14). Supposedly, Atlanta pitching coach Lee Mazzone's training techniques are fresh and innovative. It's also been said that manager Bobby Cox is very careful with his youngsters, not allowing them to throw excessive amounts of pitches in their starts.

We decided to check up on Cox and see if he deserves the credit he's received. First, we identified each major league pitcher who was no older than 26 and started at least 20 games during the 1992 season. Then, we averaged each pitcher's five highest pitch totals of the season. Finally, we created an average for each club's young starters. Here are the results (ages are as of July 1, 1992):

Average Pitch Counts, Five Highest Starts
Age 26 or Younger

Team	Pitchers	Avg Pitches
Yankees	Perez	134.4
White Sox	Fernandez, McDowell	132.7
Mariners	Fleming	132.4
Orioles	McDonald, Mussina	131.6
Phillies	Schilling	131.0
Padres	Benes	129.2
Indians	Nagy, Scudder	129.2
Angels	Abbott, Valera	128.2
Dodgers	Ramon Martinez	127.8
Blue Jays	Guzman	125.8
Braves	Avery, Glavine, Smoltz	125.0
Cubs	Castillo, Maddux	124.4
Twins	Erickson	123.4
Brewers	Bones, Navarro	119.1
Pirates	Tomlin	116.6
Royals	Appier, Pichardo	116.6
Mets	Schourek	115.8
Giants	Wilson	113.2

Astros	Harnisch, Henry, Kile	112.9
Expos	Hill, Nabholz	111.4
Cardinals	Cormier, Clark, Olivares, Osborne	111.2
Reds	Hammond	103.4

The Red Sox, A's, Tigers and Rangers were almost devoid of young starting pitchers last year and didn't make the list.

The clubs that worked their youngsters most heavily were basically teams for whom a young pitcher was the ace of the staff (Melido Perez, Jack McDowell, Dave Fleming, Mike Mussina, Curt Schilling). In some cases, the pitcher was 26, big and strong, and had good mechanics, like Jack McDowell; there was little reason to think he was being overworked. But in other cases, as with Baltimore's heavy use of Mussina (23 last year) and Ben McDonald (24), there was more risk involved. Apparently, the desire to get the most out of the manager's best pitchers outweighed concern about their longevity.

Which brings us to our Braves. Upon first examination, the Cox prodigies' 125.0-pitch average seems ordinary, ranking in the middle of the pack. However, these are all **good** pitchers, the kind a manager will be tempted to use to the max. Given other managers' temptation to stretch their talented young pitchers to the fullest, Cox's use of three aces seems very conservative. Further digging into the individual outings of each pitcher reveals clearly defined pitch limits for each of the three. Smoltz was not allowed past 135 pitches, and Glavine and Avery not past 130. Cox and Mazzone are indeed being careful with their talented young arms.

Surprisingly, Houston's Art Howe, who ran up big reliever inning-totals in 1992 (see Houston essay, p. 53), was possibly the most cautious manager with his young starters. In fact, the highest pitch count for any Astro starter all year was a mere 122 pitches by Butch Henry in a complete game shutout of the Cubs. It will be interesting to see how Howe uses workhorses Doug Drabek and Greg Swindell this season . . . they're older, and there's less reason to be cautious. In any case, it's doubtful we'll see Pete Harnisch struggling to retire Mexican League hitters when he's 32, like Valenzuela was in 1992.

A complete listing for this category can be found on page 253.

CHICAGO CUBS: WILL THEY GROUNDBALL THEIR WAY TO SUCCESS?

The Cubs did not have a very successful season in 1992 — what else is new? — but they had to be pleased with the progress made by their pitching staff. After tying the San Francisco Giants for last place in the National League in team ERA in 1991 (4.03), the Cubs led the NL in ERA for much of last year before finishing with the fifth-best mark in the circuit (3.39). That's an impressive performance for a club which plays its home games in cozy Wrigley Field.

What's even more amazing is that the Cub pitchers had a much better ERA at Wrigley (2.92) than they did on the road (3.92). In the Wrigley Field essay (p. 88), we discuss the importance of the unusually cold Chicago weather last summer in making Wrigley much less of a hitters' park than it usually is. But we also point out another reason: the Cubs' groundball pitching staff, which had the highest groundball-to-flyball ratio in the National League last year (1.63).

Why is a groundball staff important to the Cubs? Well, a minor reason is that groundball pitchers, on average, tend to be a little more effective than flyball pitchers. Here are the ERAs for all pitchers over the last three years, separated by their ability to induce groundballs:

All Pitchers — 1990-92

	IP	ERA
Groundball Pitchers	31,745.2	3.78
Neutral Pitchers	57,903.1	3.82
Flyball Pitchers	23,513.2	3.96

And the Cubs, of course, had **good** groundball pitchers, led by Mike Morgan and Cy Young Award winner Greg Maddux. But groundball pitchers are doubly important in a park like Wrigley Field, where the home run balls fly.

Let's look at how groundball and flyball pitchers have fared in the each of the 26 parks over the last few seasons. In general, we'll use data based on three seasons, but in cases where a club moved into a new park (the White Sox in 1991, the Orioles last year) or the club changed its park configuration to a significant degree (like Cleveland last year) we'll use one or two-year data, depending on what's appropriate. The best way to judge park effects is to look at how all players — **both the home club's and its opponents** — fare at the home field, then compare those results with how the team and its opponents fare in the club's road games. Here's a ranking of each of the 26 parks for flyball pitchers, based on subtracting the ERA at home from the ERA on the road:

Parks by Effect on Flyball Pitchers

		ERA		
Park	Year	Home Games	Road Games	Diff
Houston	1992	3.16	4.52	1.36
Oakland	90-92	3.52	4.35	0.83
California	90-92	3.53	4.34	0.81
New York Mets	90-92	3.22	3.93	0.71
Texas	90-92	3.98	4.55	0.57
Los Angeles	90-92	3.30	3.73	0.43
Pittsburgh	90-92	3.90	4.33	0.43
Milwaukee	90-92	3.78	4.09	0.31
San Francisco	90-92	3.57	3.87	0.30
Toronto	90-92	4.02	4.16	0.14
St. Louis	1992	3.63	3.72	0.09
Montreal	91-92	3.45	3.37	−0.08
Cincinnati	90-92	3.74	3.66	−0.08
Philadelphia	90-92	3.79	3.68	−0.11
New York Yankees	90-92	4.58	4.30	−0.28
Detroit	90-92	5.01	4.70	−0.31
Kansas City	90-92	4.38	4.04	−0.34
Seattle	1992	4.68	4.27	−0.41
San Diego	90-92	3.84	3.25	−0.59
Chicago White Sox	91-92	4.96	4.34	−0.62
Atlanta	90-92	4.21	3.47	−0.74
Baltimore	1992	4.14	3.39	−0.75
Chicago Cubs	90-92	4.42	3.67	−0.75
Boston	90-92	4.47	3.65	−0.82
Cleveland	1992	4.35	3.46	−0.89
Minnesota	90-92	4.85	3.90	−0.95

The best parks for a flyball pitcher are the Houston Astrodome and the Oakland Coliseum — no surprise, since they're big, spacious yards where it's hard to hit a home run. The worst parks for a flyballer are Minnesota (not great for home runs, but good for extra-base hits in general), Cleveland (a hitter-friendly park in its new configuration) and Boston (where The Wall makes even a routine flyball a hit). Wrigley Field, not surprisingly, is the worst park in the National League for a flyball pitcher.

Flyball pitchers for the Cubs and their opponents had a 4.42 ERA at Wrigley, 3.67 in Cub road games.

Now let's look at the parks by their effect on groundball pitchers:

Parks by Effect on Groundball Pitchers
ERA

Park	Year	Home Games	Road Games	Diff
Baltimore	1992	2.51	4.26	1.75
Chicago White Sox	91-92	3.49	4.24	0.75
Kansas City	90-92	3.84	4.36	0.52
San Francisco	90-92	3.55	3.93	0.38
Oakland	90-92	3.98	4.30	0.32
New York Mets	90-92	3.65	3.93	0.28
Texas	90-92	4.06	4.25	0.19
Los Angeles	90-92	3.49	3.64	0.15
Toronto	90-92	4.02	4.13	0.11
Pittsburgh	90-92	3.53	3.63	0.10
San Diego	90-92	3.35	3.44	0.09
Detroit	90-92	4.22	4.30	0.08
Boston	90-92	4.05	4.12	0.07
Montreal	91-92	3.04	3.09	0.05
Houston	1992	3.56	3.60	0.04
St. Louis	1992	3.31	3.21	−0.10
California	90-92	3.75	3.63	−0.12
Chicago Cubs	90-92	3.69	3.45	−0.24
Seattle	1992	4.95	4.70	−0.25
Cleveland	1992	3.86	3.49	−0.37
Philadelphia	90-92	4.14	3.71	−0.43
Atlanta	90-92	4.47	4.04	−0.43
New York Yankees	90-92	4.29	3.83	−0.46
Cincinnati	90-92	3.74	3.16	−0.58
Minnesota	90-92	3.93	3.25	−0.68
Milwaukee	90-92	5.01	4.13	−0.88

The best parks for a groundballer, to our surprise, were the new fields in Baltimore (Camden Yard) and Chicago (Comiskey II). Some sort of "new grass" effect, maybe? Your guess is as good as ours. The data for these two parks is limited; we may see some changes here in the future.

Wrigley's ranking — ninth-worst — might make it seem like there is no advantage to pitching groundballers there, that in fact it's a disadvantage. But that's the wrong conclusion for several reasons:

1. The park data is based on three years, and waters down the boost the Cubs got by signing super-groundballer Mike Morgan last season. Morgan, who ranked third in the National League in groundball ratio, was 9-2 with a 1.38 ERA at Wrigley last year (7-6, 3.94 on the road).

2. Wrigley is a tough place to pitch, period; it's not going to look like a "pitchers park" in almost any kind of longterm study. A 3.69 ERA — the mark posted there by groundball pitchers over the last three years — is quite good, considering the park's overall effect on offense.

3. Groundball pitchers are **much** more effective here than flyball pitchers. Pitching at Wrigley cost groundball pitchers 0.24 runs per game, but it cost flyballers by 0.75 — a full half a run a game. Starting a groundballer does the **least** damage.

The Cubs seem to be aware of all this; they signed Morgan before last season, and made a deal for Greg Hibbard, who had the highest groundball ratio in the American League last year, for 1993. However, they've lost Maddux, who is not only a great pitcher, but a great **groundball** pitcher. That makes the loss even more devastating. Maddux is probably the one player the Cubs could least have afforded to lose.

A complete listing for this category can be found on page 254.

CINCINNATI REDS: IS THE DUAL-CLOSER SYSTEM DEAD?

What with dogs running loose on the field, managers wrestling with pitchers in the clubhouse and owners dispensing "wisdom" in the boardroom, the 1992 Reds were a very unique club. They were unique in another way, and this one actually had to do with the play of the team. With Norm Charlton recording 26 saves and Rob Dibble posting 25, the Reds were the first team to have two pitchers with 25 saves.

BEST LEFTY-RIGHTY CLOSER DUOS

YEAR	TEAM	LEFTY	TOTAL	RIGHTY	TOTAL
1992	Reds	Norm Charlton	26	Rob Dibble	25
1970	Twins	Ron Perranoski	34	Stan Williams	15
1984	Mets	Jesse Orosco	31	Doug Sisk	15
1986	Mets	Jesse Orosco	21	Roger McDowell	22
1983	Giants	Gary Lavelle	20	Greg Minton	22
1988	Mets	Randy Myers	26	Roger McDowell	16

Minimum 15 saves by both a right- and left-handed pitcher in the same season.

What's interesting about this combination is that Charlton's a lefty and Dibble's a righty. It's only the third time in history that a lefty and righty have both recorded 20 saves for the same team: Gary Lavelle and Greg Minton did it for the 1983 Giants, and Jesse Orosco and Roger McDowell accomplished the feat for the 1986 Mets.

A lefty-righty closer tandem used to be fairly common, going back to Don Mossi and Ray Narleski with the Indians in 1954, but the system seems to be going out of style. Dibble and Charlton, for instance, didn't really share the closer's role, with one coming in to face lefties and the other to face righties. Lefthander Charlton, in fact, faced a righty as his first hitter more often than he did a lefty, almost twice as much in fact. Here's the first batter breakdown for each pitcher last year:

1992 Save Opportunities by Charlton & Dibble

	Dibble (r)	Charlton (l)
First batter was a lefty	13	14
First batter was a righty	21	27

The fact that each accumulated such high save totals was more or less accidental. Either one was pitching well, and the other wasn't; or one was hurt and the other wasn't. One guy or the other was usually the top man, and got the save opportunities no matter who the hitter was.

Why is that? In this age of specialization, where you have pitchers like John Candelaria making a career out of just pitching to lefthanders, why don't managers use dual closers to gain a platoon advantage? It might be helpful to look at the list of successful "dual-closer" bullpens (one lefty, one righty) to see who the pitchers were and what their clubs were like. There have been only 17 tandems where both a lefty and righty each got 15 saves for the same club in a season. It didn't happen until 1961, and it happened in Cincinnati:

Lefty-Righty Combinations, 15+ Saves in a Season

Year	Team	Lefty	Saves	Righty	Saves
1961	Reds	Bill Henry	16	Jim Brosnan	16
1970	Twins	Ron Perranoski	34	Stan Williams	15
1971	Royals	Tom Burgmeier	17	Ted Abernathy	23
1973	White Sox	Terry Forster	16	Cy Acosta	18
1975	Reds	Will McEnaney	15	Rawly Eastwick	22
1976	Indians	Dave LaRoche	21	Jim Kern	15
1982	Padres	Gary Lucas	16	Luis DeLeon	15
1983	Giants	Gary Lavelle	20	Greg Minton	22
1984	Mets	Jesse Orosco	31	Doug Sisk	15
1985	Mets	Jesse Orosco	17	Roger McDowell	17
1986	Mets	Jesse Orosco	21	Roger McDowell	22
1987	Mets	Jesse Orosco	16	Roger McDowell	25
1988	Mets	Randy Myers	26	Roger McDowell	16
1989	Giants	Craig Lefferts	20	Steve Bedrosian	17
1991	Cubs	Paul Assenmacher	15	Dave Smith	17
1991	Giants	Dave Righetti	24	Jeff Brantley	15
1992	White Sox	Scott Radinsky	15	Bobby Thigpen	22
1992	Mets	John Franco	15	Anthony Young	15
1992	Reds	Norm Charlton	26	Rob Dibble	25

Looking at this list, you can see pretty quickly that only a few good clubs had tandem closers like this. The Reds had two sets with Bill Henry and Jim Brosnan in 1961, and Will McEnaney and Rawly Eastwick in 1975. But the only other clubs to win a pennant were the 1986 Mets, with Jesse Orosco and Roger McDowell, and the 1989 Giants, with Craig Lefferts and Steve Bedrosian. Two more, the 1970 Twins (Ron Perranoski/Stan Williams) and the 1988 Mets (Randy Myers, Roger McDowell) won division crowns. But the rest were also-rans like the 1976 Indians or the 1982 Padres.

Then there are the pitchers — some stars, yes, but mostly guys like Tom Burgmeier and Cy Acosta. A lot of these clubs used the dual-closer system simply because there was no one pitcher good enough to handle the role by himself. Often the pairings were accidental, due to injuries or ineffectiveness, as with the 1992 Reds, Mets and White Sox.

Oddly enough, in this era of increased specialization, the closer's role seems to be one of the few that's still best handled by one pitcher. Thus far managers have found it difficult to keep two closers sharp and effective; it's happened, but not very often. When the Reds traded Charlton, the lefty half of their "bullpen tandem," no one thought the move questionable at all. Charlton and Dibble won't be emulating Brosnan and Henry in 1993.

A complete listing for this category can be found on page 256.

COLORADO ROCKIES: WILL THE HITTERS HAVE A MILE-HIGH SEASON?

The Rockies enter the National League this year, and for a while, they're going to be playing at Mile High Stadium, which was the long-time home of the Denver American Association team (as well as the home of the NFL Broncos). Thanks to the altitude, which helps the home run balls fly, Mile High has long been known as a great park for hitters. And the expectation is that National League hitters are going to enjoy their trips to Denver this year — possibly as much as American League hitters loved L.A.'s tiny Wrigley Field, the sight of "Home Run Derby," when the league moved into Los Angeles in 1961.

Is Denver's reputation justified, and **will** the hitters go wild at Mile High? Fortunately for us, we have quite a bit of data to work with. Since the mid-1970s, the Denver franchise has been the farm club of the Expos, the Rangers, the White Sox, the Reds and finally the Brewers. So a nice mix of hitters has passed through town. And most of them enjoyed their stay. Here is how the Denver team, as a whole, has batted over the last 12 seasons:

Year	Affiliation	Avg	HR	Year	Affiliation	Avg	HR
1981	Expos	.287*	103	1987	Brewers	.299*	192*
1982	Rangers	.281	158	1988	Brewers	.273	108*
1983	White Sox	.289*	158*	1989	Brewers	.261*	97*
1984	White Sox	.274	119	1990	Brewers	.271	118*
1985	Reds	.272*	134*	1991	Brewers	.271*	99
1986	Reds	.278*	114	1992	Brewers	.286*	114

* Led league

While the home run totals have not been as overwhelming as you might have thought (except in 1987, when even minor league hitters went wild), it's obviously a nice place to hit, no matter who's been providing the prospects. Denver led the American Association in batting eight of the last 12 years, and in home runs six of the 12. Andres Galarraga is probably getting excited already.

How about some of the individual performances? Here are some Denver hitters' numbers; you'll recognize most, but not all, of the names:

Passing Through Denver:
Minor League Numbers — 1976-92

Player	Year	AB	H	HR	RBI	Avg
Andre Dawson	1976	240	84	20	46	.350
Tim Wallach	1980	512	144	36	124	.281
Tim Raines	1980	429	152	6	64	.354
Dave Hostetler	1981	440	140	27	103	.318
Pete O'Brien	1982	477	148	25	102	.310
Tim Hulett	1983	477	130	21	88	.273
Daryl Boston	1984	471	147	15	82	.312
Eric Davis	1985	206	57	15	38	.277
Lloyd McClendon	1986	433	112	24	88	.277
Barry Larkin	1986	413	136	10	51	.329
Kal Daniels	1986	132	49	8	32	.371
Steve Stanicek	1987	474	167	25	106	.352
Steve Kiefer	1987	361	119	31	95	.330
Joey Meyer	1987	296	92	29	92	.311
Gary Sheffield	1988	212	73	9	54	.344
Greg Vaughn	1989	387	107	26	92	.276
John Jaha	1992	274	88	18	69	.321

Does Don Baylor have Joey Meyer's phone number? Heck, Baylor will be tempted to come out of retirement. This has been a **nice** park for right-handed power hitters.

We'll give you one more sample of the "Denver effect." We looked at all the Brewer farmhands who played at Denver over the last five years, and then went on to get at least 250 plate appearances for Milwaukee. Here is how their figures compared:

Brewer Farmhands — 1988-92

	Avg	OBP	Slg
At Denver	.289	.364	.420
At Milwaukee	.264	.323	.363

While numbers will normally decline as a player moves from the minors to the majors, this is a pretty big drop-off, especially in slugging percentage. The players looked like high-average hitters with good power at Denver; they turned out to be nothing special at Milwaukee.

We suspect that a bit of a reverse will take place with the Rockies: some players who had previously been nothing special will look like high-average hitters with good power. National League hitters, especially righty sluggers, are probably going to love this place.

FLORIDA MARLINS: WHAT WILL THE NEXT FEW YEARS BE LIKE FOR THE MARLINS?

Some questions and answers about the 1993 expansion teams, based on the expansions of the past:

How many games will the Marlins win in 1993?

Judging by the records of the 10 previous expansion teams, they'll go 59-103. If they're good, they'll challenge the record of 70 wins set by the best expansion team, the 1961 Angels. If they're bad, they'll challenge the record of 120 losses set by the 1962 Mets. Every expansion team has lost at least 90 games; five of the 10 have lost more than 100.

Will the year of careful planning given the Marlins and Rockies help them win more games this year?

There's no reason to think so. The Toronto Blue Jays had about as much time to prepare their franchise as the Marlins and Rockies did, and went 54-107 their first year. On the other hand, the Los Angeles Angels had exactly eight days between the time they were awarded their franchise and the first expansion draft; they went 70-91. What happens is that when you give the new clubs a lot of time to plan for expansion, you also give the other clubs time to prepare; they figure out who they want to protect. The short time the Angels had in 1960 actually worked to their advantage, because some of the other clubs did a haphazard job of preparing their protected lists.

Did any of the teams end up with useful players from their expansion draft?

Yes, very much so. The Angels got Dean Chance, who would win a Cy Young Award; Jim Fregosi, who was a several-time All-Star; Ken McBride and Fred Newman, who were among their best pitchers for several years; and Albie Pearson, who was one of their first stars. The 1962 Houston Colt .45s got Turk Farrell, who was the ace of their staff for several years, Ken Johnson, another useful pitcher, and Bob Aspromonte, who would play over 1,000 games for them. The Royals got Bob Oliver, Dick Drago and Jim Rooker, all of whom had decent careers, along with Roger Nelson and Joe Foy, who were the bait they used to obtain Hal McRae from the Reds and Amos Otis from the Mets. The Montreal Expos got Bill Stoneman, who would pitch two no-hitters for them. The Padres got Nate Colbert and Clay Kirby, who were their best players in their early years. The Seattle Pilots got Lou Piniella, though they quickly traded him to the Royals. The Seattle Mariners got Ruppert Jones, Dave Collins and Julio Cruz, and the Blue Jays got Jim Clancy, Ernie Whitt and Pete Vuckovich. There were others.

Who did the best job of drafting? The worst?

The '61 Angels, obviously, were the best. The '62 Mets, whose first two picks were Hobie Landrith and Elio Chacon, were easily the worst. Next-best were the Royals, who won 69 games and finished fourth their first year; next-worst were probably the '69 Expos; they seemed to pick either young guys who couldn't play (Gary Sutherland, Mike Wegener) or old guys who were ready to retire (Maury Wills, Larry Jackson).

How important was the expansion draft in building the franchise?

It helped, but it wasn't all-important. The draft helped the Angels win 86 games their second year, but that was their high-water mark for a long time; they didn't win a division title until their 19th season. The Royals won 85 games their third season, slid back, and then became perennial contenders, but the draft was not a big factor in their success. The other clubs all took eight seasons or more before they got that first winning record; by then, the expansion draft was more or less irrelevant. The Mets, who drafted worse than anyone, were the quickest to win a world championship (eight seasons).

Are the Marlins and Rockies smarter than the early expansion clubs — picking young minor league prospects instead of veterans who can help right away?

Well, they're smarter than the 1961 Washington Senators, whose first three picks were Bobby Shantz (age 35), Dave Sisler (29) and Johnny Klippstein (33). But most of the expansion teams have concentrated on trying to get good young players, without a lot of success. For instance, 20 of the San Diego Padres' 30 picks were age 24 or younger; most of them turned out to be pretty bad players. The thing is, the other clubs aren't stupid; if the guy was a really hot prospect, he would have been protected.

What was the crucial factor for the expansion clubs which eventually reached success?

Smart, stable ownership, more than anything. The Royals had Ewing Kauffman; the Mets had Joan Payson; the Blue Jays had all those anonymous Labatt's guys who kept out of Pat Gillick's way. On the other hand, the franchises which struggled (like the Senators, the Pilots and the Mariners) all had underfunded, unstable ownership groups which simply couldn't weather the tough years every expansion franchise has to endure. Time will tell whether the Marlins and Rockies have the type of ownership the Royals, Mets and Jays had; that's going to be the crucial factor, not the expansion draft.

HOUSTON ASTROS: DID THEY BLOW OUT THEIR BULLPEN LAST YEAR?

As you'll see in another essay, the big reason the Astros went out and signed Doug Drabek and Greg Swindell was that their starting staff was the worst in the National League last year. Along with quality, Drabek and Swindell offer durability to (a starting staff which averaged only 5.7 innings an outing last year.) Drabek has worked at least 230 innings in each of the last four seasons; Swindell has logged at least 210 IP during each of the last three campaigns.

That kind of durability is important if Houston wants to preserve its bullpen, which was the best in the league in 1992. Manager Art Howe used his relief corps so much that three of his relievers — Doug Jones, Joe Boever and Xavier Hernandez — all worked more than 75 games and 110 innings in relief last year. That's very heavy usage in this day and age; in fact, the three Astros are the only pitchers to log 110 relief innings since 1990.

The evidence also suggests that it's a dangerous amount of usage, and that Jones, Boever and Hernandez will pay a price, perhaps as soon as this year. In the years from 1987 through 1991, there were a total of 16 seasons turned in by relievers in which they worked at least 110 relief innings. Here's the roll call:

Pitchers With 110+ Relief Innings, 1987-91

Pitcher	Year	IP	ERA
Mark Eichhorn	1987	127.2	3.17
Duane Ward	1990	127.2	3.45
Jim Acker	1989	126.0	2.43
Jeff D. Robinson	1988	124.2	3.03
Jeff D. Robinson	1987	123.1	2.85
Lance McCullers	1987	123.1	3.72
Danny Darwin	1989	122.0	2.36
Andy McGaffigan	1987	120.1	2.39
Chuck Crim	1989	117.2	2.83
Greg W. Harris	1990	117.1	2.30
Mark Grant	1989	116.1	3.33
Duane Ward	1989	114.2	3.77
DeWayne Buice	1987	114.0	3.39
Mark Williamson	1987	113.1	3.73
Dennis Lamp	1989	112.1	2.32
Duane Ward	1988	111.2	3.30

(innings totals and ERAs are for relief appearances only)

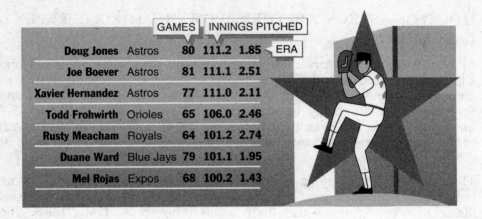

		GAMES	INNINGS PITCHED	ERA
Doug Jones	Astros	80	111.2	1.85
Joe Boever	Astros	81	111.1	2.51
Xavier Hernandez	Astros	77	111.0	2.11
Todd Frohwirth	Orioles	65	106.0	2.46
Rusty Meacham	Royals	64	101.2	2.74
Duane Ward	Blue Jays	79	101.1	1.95
Mel Rojas	Expos	68	100.2	1.43

Only one of the pitchers on the list, Duane Ward, has remained consistently effective in the years following such usage. But look at the others:

Eichhorn — his ERA rose to 4.18 in 1988 and 4.35 in 1989. He went back down to the minors before finally regaining his effectiveness with the Angels in 1990.

Acker — since working 126 relief innings in 1989, his ERAs have been 3.83, 5.20 and 5.28.

Robinson — he had two consecutive good years with heavy usage, 1987 and 1988. That's a rarity. But in 1989 his ERA was 4.58, and since then he's been with three different clubs and had to work his way back up from the minors while battling arm problems.

McCullers — he had another good year with lighter usage in 1988 (2.49 ERA in 97.2 IP), but in '89 his ERA was 4.57, and in 1990 he went on the disabled list with a sore arm. Still only 29, he's yet to recover.

Williamson — his ERA rose to 4.90 in 1988. He rebounded to post a 2.93 ERA in 107.1 innings in 1989, but in 1990 he had arm problems; in 1991 his ERA was 4.48, and he missed almost all of '92 with arm trouble.

Darwin — he had a very good year in 1990, winning the NL ERA title with a 2.21 mark while both starting and relieving. In '91 he signed with the Red Sox and has had ERAs of 5.16 and 3.96 while suffering from arm trouble.

McGaffigan — he had an ERA of 2.76 in 1988, but spent time on the DL. In 1989 he was hurt again, and his ERA was 4.68. In 1990 he was in the minors.

Crim — In the three years since his big workhorse season of 1989, his ERAs have been 3.47, 4.63 and 5.17.

Harris — shifted to a starter's role in 1991, he's been on the DL in '91 and '92, missing almost half of each season.

Grant — his ERA rose to 4.73 in 1990, and he's had continual arm problems since then.

Buice — he spent time on the DL in 1988, when his ERA rose to 5.88, and he quickly disappeared.

Lamp — his ERA rose to 4.68 in 1990, and 4.70 in 1991.

This is an almost uncanny pattern. The relievers have seldom followed a season of heavy usage with another good year. And except for Ward, they've all run into arm problems or had alarming increases in ERA within two years — usually both. As for Ward, his innings totals have declined, and it may not be a coincidence that both his innings totals (101.1) and ERA (1.95) in 1992 were career lows.

So what can we expect from Jones, Boever and Hernandez in 1993? It would be a shock if all three had good years again. One or two of them is likely to have a bad year, or hurt his arm. Drabek and Swindell may have arrived too late to save them.

LOS ANGELES DODGERS: HOW COSTLY WERE ALL THOSE ERRORS?

Once baseball's glamour franchise, the Dodgers have lately become famous — or perhaps we should say infamous — for their erratic defense. Last year Los Angeles committed 174 errors, 20 more than any other major league club, and 43 more than the Philadelphia Phillies, who had the second-highest total in the National League. By contrast, the Milwaukee Brewers committed only 89 miscues, about half the Dodgers' total. While Dodger Stadium is a notorious rock-pile which can contribute to the error total, that wasn't the club's problem last year. L.A. committed 74 infield errors at home last year, 75 on the road.

We know the Dodgers had trouble getting a grip on things, like a baseball; the question is how costly those errors really were. We'll begin by looking at the major leagues as a whole. Everyone's entitled to make an error now and then, but when major league clubs committed even one miscue in a game last year, their won-lost percentage was only .451; if they played errorless ball, their winning percentage was .580. As the number of errors increases, the winning percentage goes down even more. Here's how the clubs fared according to the number of errors they committed last year:

Won-Lost Record by Number of Errors — MLB — 1992

0 errors			1 error			2 errors			3+ errors		
W	L	Pct	W	L	Pct	W	L	Pct	W	L	Pct
1,224	887	.580	628	763	.451	207	318	.394	47	138	.254

A sobering thought: when a club made two or more errors in a game last year, their winning percentage was .358 (254-456); if they did that in every game, their record would be 58-104.

Fortunately, the Dodgers didn't commit **that** many errors, but they had nothing to brag about. Here's how they fared according to the number of errors they committed in a game last year:

Zero Errors: The average major league club played errorless ball in 81 games last year, or half its schedule. The Blue Jays had 101 errorless games last year (two less than their 1990 major league record), the Cardinals 100. The Dodgers, though, had only 62 errorless games in 1992; only the Texas Rangers, with 60, had fewer. The Dodgers were only 27-35 (.435) in those errorless games, indicating that this was only one of many problems for them. But that .435 percentage was still a lot higher than their .389 overall winning percentage.

One Error: The average club committed one error in a game 54 times last year, one-third of the time. The Dodgers, surprisingly, met the norm, going

23-31 (.426) when they committed one miscue last year. But they shouldn't be encouraged by this news. The problem was that they committed **more** than one error so many times . . . as you're about to see.

Two Errors: The average major league team committed two errors in a game 20 times last year, with a winning percentage of .394. The Astros committed two errors in a game only 11 times all year. The Dodgers, though, did it **32 times**, about one game in every five. That was the highest total of two-error games in the majors; the Angels and Rangers each had 31 two-error contests, but no one except the Dodgers in the National League had more than 25. So they were in a class by themselves, not that they were proud of it. The Dodgers were 9-23 (.281) in those two-error contests. A few clubs had worse percentages, but Tommy Lasorda would probably tell you that .281 is low enough.

Three or More Errors: Another Dodger specialty. The average club committed this many errors only seven times over the course of the year; the sure-handed Brewers did it only twice. The Dodgers did it 14 times, once again the highest total in the majors. They were 4-10 (.286) when they committed that many errors, which was about average for the National League (.270).

How many wins did the errors wind up costing the Dodgers? If they'd had just an average distribution of zero-error, one-error, etc. games, and their same winning percentage in those games (.435 in zero-error games, and so on), it would have meant three more victories — not enough to turn their season around, but an improvement:

Dodgers' 1992 Won-Lost by Number of Errors (Actual and Projected)

	0 errors			1 error			2 errors			3+ errors		
	W	L	Pct	W	L	Pct	W	L	Pct	W	L	Pct
Actual	27	35	.435	23	31	.426	9	23	.281	4	10	.286
With average distribution	35	46	.432	23	31	.426	6	14	.300	2	5	.286

Above-average work would have meant even more wins. Any way you look at it, this was a bad club. But the errors were a contributing factor.

A complete listing for this category can be found on page 257.

MONTREAL EXPOS: WILL THEY KEEP WINNING FOR FELIPE?

Last May the Expos were going nowhere when they decided to replace manager Tom Runnells with veteran coach Felipe Alou. The switch worked, as Montreal moved into contention under the popular Alou — even reaching first place briefly — before settling for second place. The final figures show that the Expos played .459 ball under Runnells (17-20), .560 under Alou (70-55), an impressive improvement of 101 percentage points.

Last year we wrote about midseason managerial changes, focusing on the skippers who had induced the biggest improvements in their teams. That's part one of the story; part two is how those managers fared the following season. Often when a club plays great ball under a new manager, it's a result of a shift in personalities — usually a change from a stern taskmaster to a more easy-going type, or vice versa. But are such changes only temporary? Does the club go back to its previous level once the novelty of the managerial change wears off?

Let's use our historical database to try to find the answer. The following 15 clubs had the highest winning percentages after shifting to a new manager in midseason. The final columns show how the club fared in the season following the change:

The Year Following a Successful Managerial Change

Year	Team	Manager	Rec.	Pct	Start	Fin	Next Year W	L	
1978	Yankees	Bob Lemon	48-20	.706	4	1	34	31	4th*
1932	Cubs	Charlie Grimm	37-18	.673	2	1	86	68	3rd
1950	Red Sox	Steve O'Neill	63-32	.663	4	3	87	67	3rd
1938	Tigers	Del Baker	37-19	.661	5	4	81	73	5th
1919	Indians	Tris Speaker	40-21	.656	3	2	98	56	1st
1952	Phillies	Steve O'Neill	59-32	.648	6	4	83	71	3rd
1977	Rangers	Billy Hunter	60-33	.645	5	2	86	75	2nd
1940	Cardinals	Billy Southworth	69-40	.633	7	3	97	56	2nd
1956	Braves	Fred Haney	68-40	.630	5	2	95	59	1st
1985	Yankees	Billy Martin	91-54	.628	7	2	Replaced		
1982	Brewers	Harvey Kuenn	72-43	.626	5	1	87	75	3rd
1905	Cubs	Frank Chance	55-33	.625	4	3	116	36	1st
1975	Royals	Whitey Herzog	41-25	.621	2	2	90	72	1st
1938	Cubs	Gabby Hartnett	44-27	.620	3	1	84	70	4th
1989	Blue Jays	Cito Gaston	77-49	.611	6	1	86	76	2nd

* Replaced by Billy Martin in midseason

Felipe Alou is probably thankful he doesn't work for George Steinbrenner; less than halfway through the season following the most successful managerial shift in history, the Yankees replaced Bob Lemon with Billy Martin, the man whose place Lemon had taken. As you can see, most of the clubs in question slipped back the following season, though not by much. But Alou can take heart from this history lesson:

- In 1905, the Chicago Cubs replaced Frank Selee, an outstanding manager who was ill with tuberculosis, with first sacker Frank Chance. The Cubs played well under Chance in '05, and won the National League pennant the next three years.

- In 1919, the Cleveland Indians replaced Lee Fohl, a pretty good skipper in his own right, with center fielder/superstar Tris Speaker. The Indians played much better under Speaker that year, and won one of their two world championships the next season.

- In 1925, the St. Louis Cardinals replaced manager Branch Rickey, one of the smartest baseball men ever, with second baseman/superstar Rogers Hornsby. The Cardinals won their first world championship the next year.

- In 1933, the Cardinals replaced Gabby Street, who had won two pennants for them, with veteran second baseman Frankie Frisch. The Cards won the world championship in 1934.

- In 1956, the Milwaukee Braves replaced skipper Charlie Grimm with coach Fred Haney. The Braves nearly won the National League pennant under Haney that year, won the world title in 1957, and took another pennant in 1958.

- In 1968, the Baltimore Orioles replaced manager Hank Bauer, who had led them to a world title in 1966, with coach Earl Weaver. The O's won the AL pennant the next year, the first of three straight.

- In 1975, the Kansas City Royals replaced manager Jack McKeon with Whitey Herzog, who had had a brief stint as manager of the Rangers. Herzog would produce three straight AL West titles starting in 1976.

- In 1989, the Toronto Blue Jays replaced manager Jimy Williams with veteran coach Cito Gaston. Gaston brought the Jays home in first that year, won another division crown in 1991, and finally brought Toronto its first world championship in 1992.

In most of these cases, the replacement manager was a "father figure" who had been around the club for awhile, and someone who had the complete confidence of his players. Doesn't that sound like Felipe Alou?

NEW YORK METS: DO THEY UNDERESTIMATE THE IMPORTANCE OF DURABLE STARTERS?

The New York Mets have had some, shall we say, puzzling ways of operating their franchise in recent years. We could focus on a number of areas of their operation, but let's examine just one: their starting pitching.

Five years ago, in 1988, the Mets won 100 games with the most enviable starting rotation in baseball: Dwight Gooden, David Cone, Ron Darling, Bobby Ojeda and Sid Fernandez. They were not only good, they were durable: all five worked at least 187 innings, and Cone, Gooden and Darling each worked more than 230. A year later, Gooden came down with a sore arm, so the Mets moved quickly and made a trade for Frank Viola.

Let's think about those six pitchers: Gooden, Cone, Darling, Ojeda, Fernandez, Viola. We'll add one more, Bret Saberhagen, whom the Mets dealt for before the 1992 season began. Managers are always stressing the importance of "innings-eaters": the guys who can regularly work 200 innings a season, pitch effectively, and not break down. There aren't too many pitchers like that in baseball, and they're usually considered prized possessions. Let's look at the short list of pitchers who have had at least five consecutive 200-inning seasons:

Consecutive 200-inning Seasons (current)

Pitcher	Seasons
Frank Viola	10
Tom Candiotti	7
Roger Clemens	7
Mark Langston	7
Bruce Hurst	6
David Cone	5
Doug Drabek	5
Greg Maddux	5
Dennis Martinez	5

Aren't these some of the most desirable pitchers in baseball? Sure, and the Mets had two of them in Viola and Cone. They let both get away — a decision based in good part on economics, but then the Mets haven't been shy about spending free agent dollars. For whatever reasons, they preferred to spend their money on other players.

The Mets also had Ron Darling, who has worked 200 innings seven times in the last nine seasons. Darling is part of a secondary group of the most durable pitchers, all of whom have had at least five 200-innings in the last seven years:

200+ Innings — At Least 5 of Last 7 Years	
Pitcher	200+ seasons
Jack Morris	10 of last 11
Mike Moore	8 of last 9
Dave Stewart	5 of last 6
Bob Welch	6 of last 7
Ron Darling	7 of last 9
Walt Terrell	7 of last 9
Mike Boddicker	7 of last 9
Tom Browning	6 of last 8
Jimmy Key	6 of last 8
Orel Hershiser	6 of last 8
Kevin Gross	6 of last 8

This group is not quite as impressive; Boddicker and Terrell are basically washed up, and some of the others have shown some signs of wear. But it's a good group of pitchers. The great Oakland staff of the last five years relied heavily on three of them (Moore, Stewart and Welch), and then brought in Darling in 1991. Last year's Toronto staff had Morris and Key, along with Cone for the stretch run. The Jays never expected to keep Cone, who served his purpose, and have replaced Key this year with Stewart.

Now consider the Mets' decisions. Of those seven pitchers, they let Viola, Cone and Darling leave, either by trade or free agency; they also dealt away Ojeda, whom Cleveland signed this year specifically to "give us some innings." They've kept Gooden, whose arm still has to be considered questionable; Saberhagen, who is notorious for breaking down every other year; and Fernandez, who has weight problems, bad knees, and pitched all of 44 innings in 1991.

As we say, we're not naive, and we know economics play a big part in today's decisions. But if durable pitchers are important — and everyone says they are — doesn't it seem curious that a club would let the most durable ones get away, and hold onto the ones who seem most likely to break down? Especially considering that Gooden, Saberhagen and Fernandez are not exactly low-salaried themselves.

It just seems like a lot of other New York Met decisions in recent years: not well thought-out.

PHILADELPHIA PHILLIES: WERE THEY TOO CONSERVATIVE ON THE BASE PATHS?

One of the few bright spots in a long 1992 season for the Phillies was their excellent work on the base paths. The Phils stole 127 bases in 158 attempts, giving them a stolen base percentage of .804. They were the only major league team to succeed on more than 80 percent of their steal attempts. Lenny Dykstra was 30 for 35, Mariano Duncan 23 for 26, Darren Daulton 11 for 13. Stan Javier was 17 for 18 after coming over to Philadelphia from the Dodgers.

But while the Phils were very successful, they were also very conservative. They attempted only 158 steals, the third-lowest total in the steal-conscious National League. Were they **too** conservative, or were they just smart? One way to look at this question is to examine the way major league teams divide up their stolen base attempts. We considered any runner who succeeded over 70 percent of the time (with at least five attempted steals) last year to be a "high percentage" stealer; all others were considered low percentage, since stealing under 70 percent adds little or nothing to a club's offense. If a club is smart, they won't give an excessive number of attempts to low-percentage stealers.

Here are the figures for the 1992 American League:

Team	All SBA			Low Pct			High Pct		
	SBA	SB	Pct	SBA	SB	Pct	SBA	SB	Pct
Baltimore	129	87	.674	60	34	.567	69	53	.768
Boston	78	38	.487	71	33	.465	7	5	.714
California	241	151	.627	108	57	.528	133	94	.707
Chicago	197	149	.756	15	8	.533	182	141	.775
Cleveland	192	140	.729	81	47	.580	111	93	.838
Detroit	92	55	.598	75	42	.560	17	13	.765
Kansas City	188	127	.676	103	62	.602	85	65	.765
Milwaukee	355	248	.699	127	73	.575	228	175	.768
Minnesota	183	118	.645	96	55	.573	87	63	.724
New York	96	66	.688	54	31	.574	42	35	.833
Oakland	189	135	.714	57	31	.544	132	104	.788
Seattle	136	90	.662	82	44	.537	54	46	.852
Texas	105	71	.676	37	19	.514	68	52	.765
Toronto	152	120	.789	19	9	.474	133	111	.835
AL Totals	2333	1595	.684	985	545	.553	1348	1050	.779

Excludes players with less than 5 stolen base attempts

The most active basestealing club in the AL — **in fact in all the majors** — was the Milwaukee Brewers. The Brewers had 371 steal attempts, the most of any club in either league. But in the process, they sent their marginal runners 127 times. Scott Fletcher was only 17 for 27, Kevin Seitzer 13 for 24, Greg Vaughn 15 for 30. Continually sending low-percentage runners like that reduced Milwaukee's overall success rate to only .690 — right around the break-even point.

By contrast, the Toronto Blue Jays gave only 19 attempts to their low-percentage stealers, the Chicago White Sox only 15. As a result, the Jays had an overall success rate of .768, the Sox .737. Though the Brewers got all the publicity, Toronto and Chicago actually had more effective running games than Milwaukee did.

Here are the National League figures:

	All SBA			Low Pct			High Pct		
Team	SBA	SB	Pct	SBA	SB	Pct	SBA	SB	Pct
Atlanta	165	117	.709	75	48	.640	90	69	.767
Chicago	104	66	.635	66	37	.561	38	29	.763
Cincinnati	174	118	.678	89	53	.596	85	65	.765
Houston	175	127	.726	39	22	.564	136	105	.772
Los Angeles	197	133	.675	134	82	.612	63	51	.810
Montreal	226	179	.792	32	21	.656	194	158	.814
New York	157	115	.732	46	28	.609	111	87	.784
Philadelphia	147	117	.796	39	23	.590	108	94	.870
Pittsburgh	135	96	.711	51	29	.569	84	67	.798
St. Louis	318	205	.645	174	94	.540	144	111	.771
San Diego	108	58	.537	86	40	.465	22	18	.818
San Francisco	163	105	.644	86	45	.523	77	60	.779
NL Totals	2069	1436	.694	917	522	.569	1152	914	.793

Excludes players with less than 5 stolen base attempts

National League clubs were generally more active on the base paths than their American League counterparts . . . but not necessarily smarter. Clubs like the Cardinals and Dodgers ran indiscriminately, sending runners whether they had good success rates or not. It wasn't smart baserunning, and it cost their clubs runs.

By contrast, clubs like the Expos and Astros used the running game intelligently, shutting down the runners who had poor percentages. As for the Phils, you could argue that they overdid it, not sending their high-percentage runners enough. But we think they handled the running game a lot more intelligently than many of their counterparts. For them, basestealing paid off where it counted; the Phils were second in the league in runs scored.

A complete listing for this category can be found on page 258.

PITTSBURGH PIRATES: ARE THEY STILL BUNTING IN THE FIRST?

They called it the "Pittsburgh strategy" — it was that unique. The Pirates would get their leadoff man on in the first, move him over with a sacrifice by expert bunter Jay Bell, and have a runner in scoring position for the big boppers: Andy Van Slyke, Bobby Bonilla and Barry Bonds. Often Pittsburgh would cash in a run, take the lead and go on to another victory. What could be simpler?

It **was** simple, but it wasn't necessarily smart. We studied Pittsburgh's "bunt-in-the-first" strategy a year ago, and concluded that it wound up costing Pittsburgh runs. While it did often produce a run for the Pirates, the benefits usually stopped there, with one run. The Pirates, with the National League's best offense in '91, had one of the lowest totals of runs scored in the first. Without that conservative, little-ball strategy, Pittsburgh would have undoubtedly scored more runs and won more games.

Or so we concluded. But did the Pirates agree? The chart shows the number of first-inning sacrifices laid down by each team, the number of first-inning runs, and the total number of runs scored by each club over the course of the season. Some conclusions:

1. The Pirates haven't completely abandoned bunting in the first. They laid down 10 first-inning sacrifices, tying the Los Angeles Dodgers for the most in the majors. However, that was a sharp decline from 1991, when they recorded 16 first-inning sacrifices. The average major league club had only 3.5 sacrifices in the first inning last year.

2. Bunting less, the Pirates scored more. In 1991, the Bucs scored only 75 first-inning runs, 9.8 percent of their season's total of 768. In 1992, they scored 88 first-inning runs, 12.7 percent of their season total of 693.

3. Even so, that wasn't a very impressive performance. The Bucs led the National League in runs scored with 693; however, their 88 first-inning runs were only the fifth-highest total in the league.

4. The Pirates, despite their drop in first-inning bunts last year, were still on the cutting edge as far as the strategy was concerned. Seven of the 26 clubs had only one first-inning sacrifice last year. The San Diego Padres had zero sacrifices for the second year in a row.

One can get carried away with criticizing the Pirates and what they were doing last year. The Detroit Tigers, who led the majors in runs scored with 791, also led both leagues in first-inning runs with 119. The Tigers also had only one first-inning sacrifice. But before you can say "Aha!" we have to add that the Kansas City Royals also laid down only one first-inning

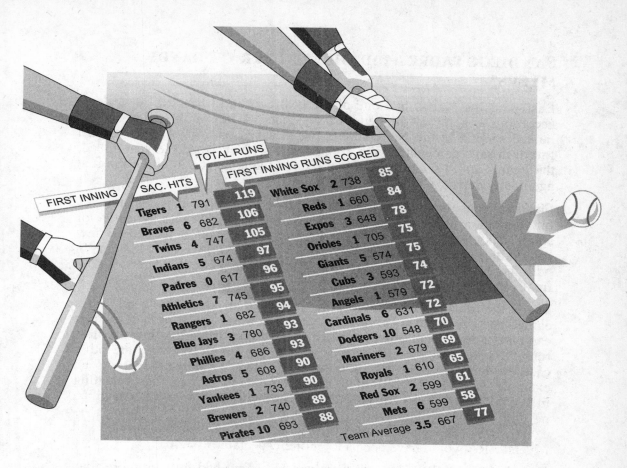

TOTAL RUNS						
FIRST INNING	SAC. HITS	FIRST INNING RUNS SCORED				
Tigers	1	791	119	White Sox	2 738	85
Braves	6	682	106	Reds	1 660	84
Twins	4	747	105	Expos	3 648	78
Indians	5	674	97	Orioles	1 705	75
Padres	0	617	96	Giants	5 574	75
Athletics	7	745	95	Cubs	3 593	74
Rangers	1	682	94	Angels	1 579	72
Blue Jays	3	780	93	Cardinals	6 631	72
Phillies	4	686	93	Dodgers	10 548	70
Astros	5	608	90	Mariners	2 679	69
Yankees	1	733	90	Royals	1 610	65
Brewers	2	740	89	Red Sox	2 599	61
Pirates	10	693	88	Mets	6 599	58
				Team Average	3.5 667	77

sacrifice last year. The Royals scored only 65 runs in the first, 10.7 percent of their overall total of 610 runs.

But the Pirates nonetheless seemed to be handling their offense more intelligently last year. While they lost Bonilla to free agency before the 1992 season began, they didn't miss him all that much. Van Slyke and Bonds, the Pirates' No. 3 and 4 hitters, both had outstanding seasons last year, and did a lot to make up for the loss of Bonilla by themselves. With Bonilla gone, manager Jim Leyland felt it necessary to make Bell, a pretty good hitter in his own right, a bigger part of the Pirate offense.

We think that was the smart thing to do. (Former Oriole manager Earl Weaver always said that the most precious commodity a manager had was his 27 outs; Weaver thought it was foolish to give up one of those outs, unless there was a very good reason.) Bunting in the first is giving up an out before the necessity to do so has even been established. Though Bell is a brilliant bunter, he's also a good hitter. Letting him swing away in the first, when a club has a chance to do a lot of damage, only makes sense.

SAN DIEGO PADRES: DID THEY UNDERRATE RANDY MYERS?

Last year, the Padres had one of the best closers in baseball — at least according to some of the better-known stats — in Randy Myers. Myers ranked second in the National League in saves with 38, and he ranked fourth in save percentage with a mark of .826. Yet, when the year ended, the Padres didn't seem to have any second thoughts about letting the free agent lefty depart to the Chicago Cubs.

Financial considerations were undoubtedly a big part of that decision . . . but the Padres also seem to think that Myers' 4.29 ERA was indicative of some shaky work last year. Were they right? Did Myers just have a few bad outings which spoiled his ERA, or was he the sort who would come in with the bases empty and a 4-1 lead, and give up a couple of runs before finally nailing down the save?

That's the issue we want to consider here. We all know that a reliever's earned run average can be very deceptive. In the simplest case, a reliever can enter a game with the bases loaded, give up a triple to allow all three runs to score, and yet suffer no damage to his ERA. But there are other cases which can cloud the issue even further. We'll use Myers as an example. Last year he permitted 38 earned runs in 79.2 innings, resulting in that 4.29 ERA. Let's say he had three horrendous outings, ones in which he didn't have a thing, permitting eight earned runs in 1.2 innings — exactly what happened to him, in fact. Remove those three outings and Myers' ERA would have been a lot more respectable at 3.46.

So was Myers' ERA deceptive, ruined by a few bad outings more than most other closers' were? Let's be generous and give the 1992 relief aces (those with 25 saves) three "mulligans" — we won't count their three worst outings. We'll show you their new ERAs; then we'll also show how many games in which they got a save, but allowed at least one run in the process. Here are the figures:

1992 Relief Aces Without Their Three Worst Outings

	All Outings		Without Three Worst		Svs Allow-ing	
Pitcher, Team	IP	ERA	IP	ERA	Sv	Runs
Randy Myers, SD	79.2	4.29	78.0	3.46	38	9
Doug Henry, Mil	65.0	4.02	63.2	2.54	29	3
Mitch Williams, Phi	81.0	3.78	78.2	2.52	29	2
Jeff Reardon, Bos-Atl	58.0	3.41	56.2	2.38	30	3
Lee Smith, StL	75.0	3.12	72.2	2.35	43	2
Rob Dibble, Cin	70.1	3.07	68.1	2.11	25	4

1992 Relief Aces Without Their Three Worst Outings

Pitcher, Team	All Outings		Without Three Worst		Svs Allow -ing	
	IP	ERA	IP	ERA	Sv	Runs
Norm Charlton, Cin	81.1	2.99	76.2	2.11	26	3
John Wetteland, Mon	83.1	2.92	81.2	1.87	37	5
Rick Aguilera, Min	66.2	2.84	64.1	1.26	41	4
Steve Olin, Cle	88.1	2.34	83.0	1.30	29	3
Tom Henke, Tor	55.2	2.26	53.1	1.35	34	6
Jeff Montgomery, KC	82.2	2.18	80.2	1.45	39	2
Gregg Olson, Bal	61.1	2.05	59.1	1.21	36	1
Dennis Eckersley, Oak	80.0	1.91	77.0	1.17	51	8
Doug Jones, Hou	111.2	1.85	107.0	1.18	36	5
Jeff Russell, Tex-Oak	66.1	1.63	64.0	1.13	30	2
Steve Farr, Yanks	52.0	1.56	50.0	0.72	30	2
Average	74.0	2.72	71.1	1.79	34	4

(Minimum 25 saves)

As you can see, the sort of thing which happened to Myers wasn't unusual at all; it was typical of most relief aces. Rick Aguilera of the Twins had an overall ERA of 2.84, but without his three worst outings, the figure would have been 1.26. Doug Henry of the Brewers would have dropped from 4.02 all the way down to 2.54.

As for Myers, this exercise doesn't make him look better; it makes him look even worse. Sure, without his three worst outings, his ERA would have been 3.46. But every other 25-save man would have dropped to 2.54 or less. Jeff Russell's figure would have been 1.13. The White Sox' Bobby Thigpen, who is not listed here because he had only 22 saves, would have seen his ERA drop from 4.75 to 2.87 — nearly two runs — without his three worst outings.

Myers also permitted runs in nine of his 38 saves. The only pitcher who was close to that was Oakland's Dennis Eckersley, who allowed runs in eight of his saves . . . but, of course, Eckersley had 13 more saves than Myers did. You could probably conclude that the 4.29 ERA was as indicative of Myers' pitching last year as his 38 saves were. That seems to be the conclusion the Padres reached.

That's a good reason why Myers will be wearing a Cub uniform this year instead of the Padre colors.

A complete listing for this category can be found on page 259.

ST. LOUIS CARDINALS: HOW IMPORTANT IS TEWKSBURY'S PINPOINT CONTROL?

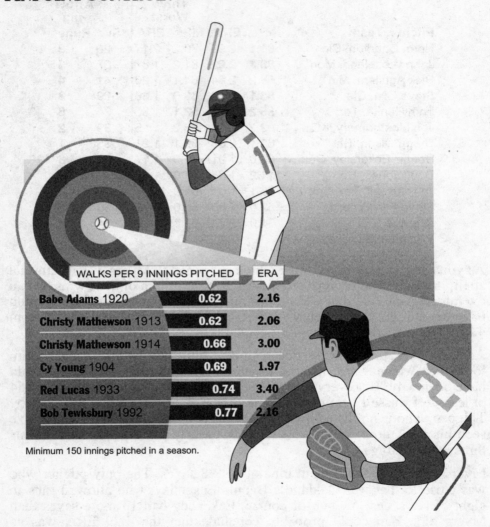

WALKS PER 9 INNINGS PITCHED	ERA
Babe Adams 1920 — 0.62	2.16
Christy Mathewson 1913 — 0.62	2.06
Christy Mathewson 1914 — 0.66	3.00
Cy Young 1904 — 0.69	1.97
Red Lucas 1933 — 0.74	3.40
Bob Tewksbury 1992 — 0.77	2.16

Minimum 150 innings pitched in a season.

There's a wonderful scene in the classic Western, **The Magnificent Seven**. One of the banditos is riding away, and he appears to be about a half mile down the road when James Coburn raises his gun, calmly takes aim, and shoots the guy right off his horse. Horst Bucholtz, the excitable young kid who's watching this, says, "That's . . . that's the greatest shot I've even seen!" Coburn shakes his head disgustedly and says, "The worst. I was aiming for the horse."

In 1992, the Cardinals' Bob Tewksbury **was** James Coburn . . . and he wasn't aiming for the horse, either. Taking a page from Dennis Eckersley's book, Tewksbury issued only 20 walks all season while working 233 innings. That was such an amazing display of control that it it put Tewksbury in the company of pitchers like Cy Young and Christy Mathewson; among pitchers who had worked 150 innings in a season since 1901, his walk rate was the sixth lowest. Here's the top 10:

Fewest Walks per Nine Innings, Season, Since 1901

Pitcher, Team	Year	IP	BB	BB/9	ERA
Babe Adams, Pirates	1920	263.0	18	0.62	2.16
Christy Mathewson, Giants	1913	306.0	21	0.62	2.06
Christy Mathewson, Giants	1914	312.0	23	0.66	3.00
Cy Young, Red Sox	1904	380.0	29	0.69	1.97
Red Lucas, Reds	1933	220.0	18	0.74	3.40
Bob Tewksbury, Cardinals	1992	233.0	20	0.77	2.16
Cy Young, Red Sox	1906	287.2	25	0.78	3.19
Babe Adams, Pirates	1919	263.0	23	0.79	1.98
Slim Sallee, Reds	1919	228.0	20	0.79	2.05
Babe Adams, Pirates	1922	171.0	15	0.79	3.58

(Minimum 150 innings pitched)

You might not have heard of Babe Adams, who pitched for 19 seasons, the last 18 of them with the Pirates, while winning 194 games from 1906 to 1926. If there had been rotisserie leagues back then, Adams would have been a very popular pick: he led the National League in hits-plus-walks ratio four times.

What's so remarkable about Tewksbury's presence on the list is that he's the first new name since 1933. Most of the others are from the pre-1920 era in which the strike zone was larger and the ball deader, so that pitchers could be pretty fearless about laying the ball down the middle. If you compare Tewksbury with more modern pitchers, say since World War II, you find that he's one of only two to permit less than one walk per nine innings:

Fewest Walks per Nine Innings, Season, Since 1946

Pitcher, Team	Year	IP	BB	BB/9	ERA
Bob Tewksbury, Cardinals	1992	233.0	20	0.77	2.16
LaMarr Hoyt, Padres	1985	210.1	20	0.86	3.47
Dennis Eckersley, Cubs	1985	169.1	19	1.01	3.08
Gary Nolan, Reds	1976	239.0	27	1.02	3.46

Fewest Walks per Nine Innings, Season, Since 1946

Pitcher, Team	Year	IP	BB	BB/9	ERA
Ferguson Jenkins, Cubs	1971	325.0	37	1.02	2.77
Juan Marichal, Giants	1966	307.0	36	1.06	2.23
LaMarr Hoyt, White Sox	1983	260.2	31	1.07	3.66
Lew Burdette, Braves	1961	272.0	33	1.09	4.00
Don Newcombe, Reds	1959	222.0	27	1.09	3.16
Jimmy Key, Blue Jays	1989	216.0	27	1.13	3.88

Tewksbury not only has the best control; he has the lowest ERA as well. While there were two overpowering pitchers on the list — Hall of Famers Ferguson Jenkins and Juan Marichal — most of the others were guys like LaMarr Hoyt: they **needed** good control, because they weren't going to blow too many hitters away.

So has Tewksbury found the key to success, that as long as he throws strikes, he'll win? We'd like to say yes, but we have to keep in mind that he entered 1992 as a 31-year old journeyman with a 32-34 lifetime record and a 3.67 career ERA. And the radar control is nothing new for him, either. Tewksbury had equally good control in 1990, but no one noticed because he only worked 145.1 innings. He had much less success with this style in '90:

	IP	H	UBB*	UBB/9	W	L	ERA
Tewksbury, 1990	145.1	151	12	0.74	10	9	3.47
Tewksbury, 1992	233.0	217	20	0.77	16	5	2.16

* unintentional walks

A 2.16 ERA is **very** unusual for a pitcher who only had 91 strikeouts, as Tewksbury did last year. Control alone didn't do it for him in 1990, and he'll need more than that to succeed in 1993.

A complete listing for this category can be found on page 260.

SAN FRANCISCO GIANTS: SHOULD THEY HAVE EXPECTED THE MATT WILLIAMS SLUMP?

In 1991, Giant third baseman Matt Williams was one of the top young power hitters in baseball. He belted 34 homers, his second straight 30-home run season; drove in 98 runs, his second straight season with 95 or more RBI; and batted a respectable, if not overwhelming .268. He would be 26 in 1992, headed into his prime years.

But in '92, everything went wrong for Williams. Though he batted over 500 times, he only hit 20 home runs, drove in only 66 runs, and batted .227. It was a shocking drop in most people's eyes, but the question we want to examine is this: should we have expected it? Williams has always been a wild swinger who seldom walks and strikes out a high number of times. Even in his excellent 1990 and 1991 seasons, his strikeout-to-walk ratio was horrible. In 1990, he fanned 138 times while drawing only 33 walks, nine of those intentional; in '91, he fanned 128 times with another 33 walks, six intentional. Not exactly Wade Boggs.

A hitter like this, one would assume, would soon teach pitchers that they didn't need to throw him strikes. He'd swing at everything, and when the pitches got bad enough, the hitter would go into a big slump. Sound reasonable? It did to us, so we decided to set up a model. Let's divide all active hitters with more than 2,000 career at-bats into three groups.

Group One, the Wild Swingers, would be the players with terrible strikeout/walk ratios — more than three-to-one. Players in this group would include Shawon Dunston, Andres Galarraga, Pete Incaviglia, Cory Snyder . . . and Matt Williams. Your basic brutes.

Group Two, the Regular Guys, would be the players with mid-range strikeout/walk ratios — between 3.00 and 1.25. This is a much bigger group than Group One, and includes hitters as diverse as Joe Carter, Will Clark, Cecil Fielder and Kirby Puckett.

Group Three, the Disciplinarians, are the players with very low strikeout/walk ratios. This is also a fairly diverse group. Some, like Wade Boggs and Rickey Henderson, walk a lot and strike out infrequently. Others, like Gregg Jefferies and Jody Reed, don't do either very much. But as a group, they handle a bat very well and don't strike out very often.

Now let's compare the three groups. We'll look at all their seasons with at least 250 at-bats, and compare consecutive 250-AB seasons; in the vast majority of cases these were back-to-back chronologically, but occasionally there was a gap due to injury or a season in the minors. At any rate, we looked for drastic change: how often did the player's average rise or fall by 40 or more points? Our theory was that the Wild Swingers would show the greatest change, the Disciplinarians the least. Here are the results:

Group	Seasons with 40 or more pt. change	Seasons with less than 40-pt. change	Pct of Big change
Wild Swingers	11	53	17.2
Regular Guys	143	602	19.2
Disciplinarians	98	354	21.7
TOTAL	252	1,009	20.0

The results were the opposite of what we thought we'd see. The Wild Swingers had the least fluctuation; the Disciplinarians had the most. How can this be? Well, think about it a minute:

1. Your typical Wild Swinger is a guy like Greg Gagne. In a bad year, he'll hit .236; in a great year, he'll hit .272. That's a big fluctuation for him, and defines whether people see him as "good" or "bad" hitter, but it's a fluctuation of only 36 points.

2. There is no typical Disciplinarian, but one member of the group is George Brett. In 1979, he hit .329, in 1980 .390, in 1981 .314 — three excellent years, but two 40-plus point changes. He could drop by 40 points, and still be a strong performer, because his top end is so much higher than Gagne's is.

So the sort of fluctuation that Williams underwent last year — a 41-point drop in batting average — is not to be expected. But what is expected of a hitter like Williams? Much less than is expected of a hitter in Brett's group. Williams' lifetime average is .241, and he's hit over .270 only once. His limitations are sharply defined, while a truly disciplined hitter has no real limits.

A complete listing for this category can be found on page 261.

II. GENERAL BASEBALL
QUESTIONS

HOW MUCH DIFFERENCE DOES THE UMPIRE MAKE?

You're sitting at home with your feet propped up watching Game 7 of one of the greatest National League Championship Series ever. Pittsburgh has a 2-0 lead over Atlanta in the bottom of the ninth inning, but the bases are loaded. Jim Leyland decides to put the fate of the season on somewhat-wild fireballer Stan (Opie) Belinda.

Soon after, Francisco Cabrera is anointed Saint Francisco and Belinda is sent packing to Mayberry. Home plate umpire John McSherry isn't even an afterthought to the drama. But if you consider his effect on that contest, and in particular the ninth inning, he's anything but insignificant. To discount McSherry or any home plate umpire's spin on a game outcome is to prove you haven't been reading your **Baseball Scoreboard** carefully enough.

As loyal readers know, STATS has been studying umpires yearly and proving that there is great variance between individual umpire strike zones. Over a three year period, our studies show that there are a group of umps who clearly call more (or fewer) strikes than their counterparts.

Some umps (also known as Cy Young's Disciples) believe on giving a pitcher an extra half-inch or so on that inside corner or just below the knee.

Highest Called Strike Percentage by Umpire

NL 1992		NL 1990-92		AL 1992		AL 1990-92	
Umpire	Pct	Umpire	Pct	Umpire	Pct	Umpire	Pct
Gerry Layne	16.7	Bob Davidson	16.2	Larry McCoy	17.2	Larry McCoy	16.8
Paul Runge	16.2	Paul Runge	15.9	Ted Hendry	17.0	Ted Hendry	16.7
Bob Davidson	16.2	H. Wendelstedt	15.8	D. Merrill	16.9	Greg Kosc	16.6
Ed Rapuano	16.2						
NL Average	15.5	NL Average	15.1	AL Average	15.8	AL Average	15.5

(Minimum 24 games behind home plate for 1992, 72 games for 1990-92)

American league umps called more strikes last year and over the last three years than their National League counterparts — though this was supposed to be a thing of the past, maybe they still give that high strike to pitchers a little more often!

Larry McCoy has perennially had the most liberal strike zone in the junior circuit; if you have a plane to catch, this is the man you want behind the plate. Over in the National League, Harry Wendelstedt and Bob Davidson are the two guys that will bring a smile to the lips of any moundsman forced to do battle in Riverfront Stadium or Wrigley Field — and a downright smirk at Chavez Ravine.

But there is also a group of umpires that are certain to bring those cries of "He's pinching him!" and "Where was it?" from pitcher lovers and hometown announcers around the globe.

Lowest Called Strike Percentage by Umpire

NL 1992		NL 1990-92		AL 1992		AL 1990-92	
Umpire	Pct	Umpire	Pct	Umpire	Pct	Umpire	Pct
B. Froemming	14.4	J. McSherry	14.0	D. Phillips	14.6	D. Cousins	14.3
G. Davis	14.5	B. Froemming	14.1	R. Roe	14.7	R. Roe	14.5
J. McSherry	14.5	R. Marsh	14.1	D. Ford	14.9	D. Phillips	14.8
NL Average	15.5	NL Average	15.1	AL Average	15.8	AL Average	15.5

This notorious group makes 'em earn each passage into the precious strike zone. Cousins called the most walks per game in 1991, with Roe close behind, while Froemming led the NL. But the stingiest of all?

Little did poor Jim Leyland, Stan Belinda and Pirate fans know that in those dire straits, with the sacks jammed and no one out and a somewhat jittery 26-year-old reliever heading into the game, that behind the plate was the one umpire in all of baseball who had called the fewest strikes of any umpire over the last three years — the proverbial King of the Pinchers, John McSherry.

To his credit, McSherry called Belinda's four key at-bats as consistently as he had all year. Belinda had seven pitches called balls and none called strikes. There is some speculation that McSherry was going to call Belinda's fourth pitch (after he fell behind 2-0) to Cabrera a strike had he not whacked it for the game winner. If only Leyland could have called for an umpire change . . . maybe Larry McCoy was available.

If only.

A complete listing for this category can be found on page 262.

WHO ARE THE BIGGEST DRAWS?

As recently as the 1950s, before baseball attendance took off, a club's bottom line depended on pulling in fans for the "big draws." Sunday doubleheaders. Night games (if you're old enough to remember when they were a Tuesday and Friday novelty). Ted Williams. Bob Feller. And most of all, the New York Yankees. The big games would draw 40,000, the others 7,000.

The game isn't like that any more, not with midweek games routinely drawing 30,000. But some clubs still pull in the fans more than others, and some players can still "put fannies in seats." Which clubs have the best impact on attendance? The simplest way to do it would be on the basis of average road attendance, and on that basis the answer would be the Boston Red Sox, who drew an average of 30,250 fans to their 1992 road games.

That's the simplest answer, but not the best one. Using that system, the Red Sox are credited with "drawing" 50,000 to SkyDome, where there's a sellout every night, while the Jays could fill every seat in Fenway and still pull in only 33,000 fans. So the fairest way, using Boston as an example, would be to compute each opponent's average attendance in their non-Red Sox games, see how many the Sox drew when they played there, and then compute the difference. On that basis, the following clubs had the biggest positive impact on attendance last year:

Team	Weighted Avg	Avg for Other Tms	Difference
Atlanta	27,216	24,207	3,009
Los Angeles	27,272	24,784	2,488
Toronto	29,071	26,704	2,367
Chicago Cubs	27,636	25,288	2,348
Boston	30,311	28,094	2,217

Ah, the power of television. The self-proclaimed "America's Team" had the biggest positive impact on attendance, while their cable rivals, the Cubs, were fourth. The presence of the Dodgers and Red Sox isn't a big shock, despite their last-place finishes last year; both are glamour franchises, and were perennial contenders until last season. The presence of the Blue Jays, though, is something of a pleasant surprise. It used to be that this "foreign" franchise had trouble getting fans to come out, but no more. They've been excellent for too long.

But those former big draws, the Yankees and Mets, have been lousy too long. They ranked a very mediocre 10th and 11th in affect on attendance last year. Shame on them.

Which clubs made the fans stay away last year? There are a couple of surprises on this list as well:

Team	Weighted Avg	Avg for Other Tms	Difference
Philadelphia	22,497	25,458	−2,961
Montreal	22,995	25,737	−2,742
California	26,304	28,568	−2,264
Seattle	26,985	28,961	−1,976
Houston	24,465	26,345	−1,880

Houston, Seattle, and that cure for insomnia, the Angels, are no great surprise. The Expos aren't a good enough Canadian team, we guess, to pull in the fans. But the Phillies, the worst? Maybe the other clubs will have to stage "John Kruk Doughnut Night" or something.

Can we use the same system to identify the pitchers who were the best draws? Yes, but it's a somewhat inexact science. Decisions about when to attend a game are usually made before the pitching opponent is known, and a pitcher who starts on an opponent's Opening Day or Fireworks Night gets an artificial boost. Nonetheless this list is pretty good:

Pitcher, Team	Games	Actual Avg	Opp Team Weighted Average	Difference
Nolan Ryan, Tex	27	33,664	27,646	6,018
Scott Erickson, Min	32	33,400	29,168	4,232
Joe Hesketh, Bos	25	33,380	30,062	3,318
Roger Clemens, Bos	32	31,903	28,771	3,132
Jack Morris, Tor	34	40,884	37,863	3,021
Tom Candiotti, LA	30	29,513	26,646	2,867
Tom Glavine, Atl	33	34,932	32,139	2,793
Jose Rijo, Cin	33	28,673	26,060	2,613
Greg Maddux, Cubs	35	28,244	25,820	2,424
David Cone, Mets-Tor	34	30,823	28,402	2,419

Nolan on top, as you'd expect. And most of the others are pretty classy names. But we wonder how many fans call up the women of their dreams and say, "Hey, babe . . . busy tonight? Joe Hesketh's in town." As we said, it's an inexact science.

A complete listing for this category can be found on page 263.

DO THEY HAVE TO THROW TO FIRST MORE THAN ONCE?

Chicagoans that we are, we can tell you all about Rick Sutcliffe. Not about Rick's fine pitching, or his wonderful leadership ability . . . heck, you know all about that. No, we're here to bury Sutcliffe, not to praise him. We want to talk about the way, every time there's a runner on first, he makes at least 300 pickoff tosses, and sometimes more, to "hold the runner close." Then, the runner steals second anyway — not that we'd notice, being sound asleep by that point.

Okay, we exaggerate a little. But Rick Sutcliffe **does** like to throw to first, and more than just once, which is what really annoys us. Our own data has shown time and again that pickoff throws do work: the runner stays a little closer to the bag, and as a result the stolen base percentage goes down. But isn't throwing over multiple times just a complete waste of time? Hasn't the runner gotten the point by then?

So we decided to check Rick's record for 1992. Here's how he "held" baserunners in cases where he made no throw to first, one throw, and then two or more:

	No Throws		One Throw		Two or More	
	SB	CS	SB	CS	SB	CS
Rick Sutcliffe	6	2	7	0	8	1

What a waste of time. Sutcliffe doesn't even get the usual advantage a pitcher gains out of making a throw to first. When he made no pickoff tosses, they were 6-for-8 against him; when he threw over, they were 15-for-16. As for tossing over more than once, forget it; 8-for-9 vs. 7-for-7 might seem like an improvement to Rick, but it seems like a big waste of time to us.

But just when we thought this closed the book on the subject, we noticed the stolen base record of another veteran pitcher, Montreal's Dennis Martinez:

	No Throws		One Throw		Two or More	
	SB	CS	SB	CS	SB	CS
Dennis Martinez	9	1	7	2	4	14

Martinez' record indicated that, in his case, multiple tosses to first were anything but a waste. One throw reduced basestealers' effectiveness a little, but two or more were deadly, shutting down the running game completely. There was obviously something worth investigating about this subject.

So we went back over our database for the last four seasons, and recorded stealers' success rates as the number of pickoff throws went up. Here are the results:

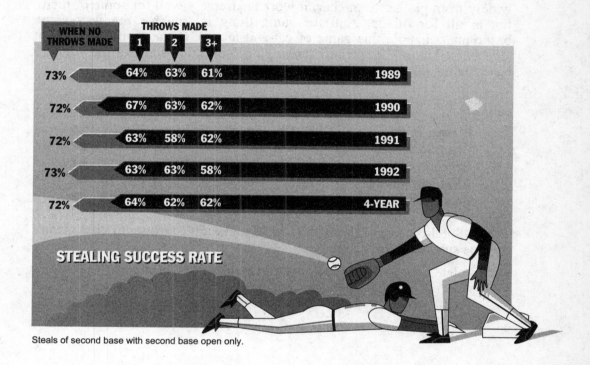

Steals of second base with second base open only.

Here's additional detail:

Stolen Base Percentages By Number of Pickoff Throws

Year	No Throws Made Att	Pct	1 Throw Made Att	Pct	2 Throws Made Att	Pct	3+ Throws Made Att	Pct
1989	1,926	73	857	64	533	63	477	61
1990	1,983	72	960	67	555	63	532	62
1991	1,996	72	976	63	583	58	482	62
1992	2,064	73	1,077	63	604	63	464	58
Total	7,969	72	3,870	64	2,275	62	1,955	61

As fans who prefer a fast-paced game, we wish this **wasn't** the data, but it is: the more frequently pitchers throw to first, the more they reduce the chance for a successful steal. Three pickoff tosses reduce the success rate by over 10 percent, though the first throw over to first base has the biggest impact. The exercise is anything but a waste of time.

As the Sutcliffe/Martinez comparison shows, however, the results vary widely from pitcher to pitcher; it works extremely well for some of them, not at all for others. And the same thing is true for the way some baserunners handle this game of cat-and-mouse. Some aren't affected at all; but look how the "pickoff throw game" muzzled some of the younger basestealing threats in 1992:

Player, Team	No Throws Made			1 Throw Made			2+ Throws Made		
	SB	CS	Pct	SB	CS	Pct	SB	CS	Pct
Chad Curtis, Cal	14	4	78	13	4	76	10	7	59
Delino DeShields, Mon	18	4	82	11	2	85	11	7	61
Ray Lankford, StL	15	1	94	12	7	63	10	14	42
Kenny Lofton, Cle	19	2	90	18	0	100	22	8	73

When Sutcliffe hears about this, he'll make **500** throws to first. Don't anyone show him this article!

A complete listing for this category can be found on page 264.

WHAT'S THE LATEST IN PARK FACTORS?

In one of our other books this year, **STATS 1993 Major League Handbook**, we published up-to-date park factors on all 26 major league teams. We also included diagrams of each park; this is handy as an instant reference to see how the outfield walls and foul territory come into play. Because we didn't have room in that book to analyze the data (or the time given it's November 1 publication date), we'll do it here. We'll also give you a synopsis of the data in the appendix.

Let's go around the horn:

Atlanta-Fulton County Stadium: The best hitter's park in baseball. A "tomahawk chop" swing might not be a bad idea for some hitters, as infield errors are far more frequent here than elsewhere in the NL.

Oriole Park at Camden Yards: The first season there indicates a neutral park, except that home runs are 50% easier for left-handed batters. Not surprising, given the 318-foot right-field foul line.

Fenway Park: Once an extreme hitter's park, it's now just a very good one. But not because of easy home runs over The Wall; changes in the wind currents due to the building of a new stadium club have made it a lot less friendly to righty sluggers than in the past (though still a little above average). Batting average is up 8%, doubles up 23% and infield errors up 21% compared to other American League parks.

Anaheim Stadium: Probably the most average park in baseball. Doubles and triples are slightly below other AL parks, but everything else is neutral.

Wrigley Field: A major hitter's park. Last season's Chicago weather almost brought it down to a neutral park for the season, but not quite. That was probably an aberration; see essay on page 42.

New Comiskey Park: Scoring is slightly down here due to a below-average rate for doubles and triples. Home runs are 5% above other AL parks based on two years of data; however, the same cold, windy weather that hurt hitters at Wrigley last year bothered them at Comiskey as well. We should learn more this year.

Riverfront Stadium: The most prolific home run park in baseball, most benefitting right-handed hitters. Righties hit 54% more home runs here than they do on the road. Kevin Mitchell, traded to the Reds in the off-season, thinks he's died and gone to heaven. Nevertheless, scoring is up only 7% in Cincinnati, significantly short of Atlanta's +13%.

Cleveland Stadium: They brought in the fences last year and the difference from 1991 was like night and day, especially home run-wise.

Home runs went from −51% in 1991 to +16% in 1992. Albert Belle says "Thank you very much!" Cleveland was the best AL hitter's park in 1992.

Tiger Stadium: A hitter's park primarily due to its short fences, especially in right field. Better for lefty power hitters than righties, but it helps Cecil a little.

Astrodome: They shortened the dimensions and now home runs are "only" 27% harder to hit rather than 45%. Still the best NL pitcher's park.

Royals Stadium: This is the most difficult AL park in which to hit home runs. Nevertheless, it's neutral offensively because of the dramatic increase in other extra-base hits. Great park for triples, especially (69% higher than normal).

Dodger Stadium: A pitcher's park overall, but only by 6%; the runs scored index is 94%. Extra-base hits are down in LA. The compensating factor is infield errors, due to the notoriously rocky infield — and it's not just the Dodger infield that makes errors. Opponents made 50% more errors in Dodger home games than they did in Dodger road games in 1992!

County Stadium: A pitcher's park across the board. Almost every offensive statistic is cut 5 to 10% in this park. Aaron and Mathews really earned all those home runs.

Hubert H. Humphrey Metrodome: The Homerdome? Not by a longshot. It should be called the Tripledome; they're up 80% here (highest in the majors) while home runs are actually down 4%. Overall the park is neutral.

Olympic Stadium: They made renovations in 1991. They moved home plate 40 feet closer to center field and cut down on the foul territory dramatically. Once a pitcher's park, it's now fairly neutral.

Shea Stadium: A pitcher's park somewhat. Scoring is down 3%. Otherwise, fairly boring with nearly every statistical category around an index of 100.

Yankee Stadium: The short right-field fence is a boon to lefty swingers. Home runs for LHB are up 39% here; tougher than normal for righty sluggers, but the reduction of "Death Valley" has helped them. Triples are down 34% overall. On balance, a neutral park.

Oakland-Alameda County Coliseum: The best pitcher's park in the American League. Home runs are tough to hit overall, but primarily for lefties (see essay on page 136).

Veterans Stadium: Very neutral, except that for some reason, lefties hit more home runs there (up 34% from the average NL park). Nobody notices, though, because the Phils never have any lefty sluggers.

Three Rivers Stadium: A pitcher's park with home runs down 18% while other extra-base hits are up.

San Diego/Jack Murphy Stadium: A very good home run park (23% higher than other NL parks) with scoring up 6% overall.

Candlestick Park: Run scoring is somewhat tougher here (down 6%) but most other statistical factors are neutral. The triples index, at 88, is the main explanation for fewer runs (and maybe the "depression index" on cold, damp nights).

Kingdome: They moved the fences back for the second year in a row in 1992. As a result, the park no longer favors home runs. Last season home runs were only up 1% compared to other AL parks while doubles were up 36%. Still a slight hitter's park, especially for lefties. Ken Griffey Jr. is happy about that.

Busch Stadium: The shorter (height-wise) fences in 1992 made home runs neutral after being 18% tougher to hit in previous years. It's now a neutral park overall, too.

Arlington Stadium: This season (1993) will be the last year for this park. It's basically a neutral park that slightly favors home runs for lefty swingers.

SkyDome: See essay on page 38. The super 1990 numbers make it look better for home runs than it probably is; basically, it helps righty sluggers but hurts lefties. Right-handed hitters enjoy a 37% advantage in Toronto while lefties suffer with a 13% deficit. Scoring is up 5% overall.

A complete listing for this category can be found on page 265.

DO EMOTIONAL WINS FIRE UP A TEAM?

An "emotional win" is the kind of game that makes everyone run out to home plate to greet the guy who scored the winning run. The kind where fists are pounded in the air and hysterical high fives are exchanged. The kind where the breathless announcer says, "What a comeback! That's exactly what this club needed."

One would think that an emotional win — victory snatched from the jaws of defeat, in most cases — would fire up a team, and cause it to play better for the next few games. But in order to study it, we'll first have to define exactly what kind of games we're looking for. We came up with four kinds of emotional wins:

Type 1: Team is trailing by three or more runs in the ninth inning, but comes back to win. On July 29 at Detroit, the White Sox went into the ninth inning trailing the Tigers, 6-2; they staged a monumental rally to win, 8-6.

Type 2: Team is trailing by five or more runs at some point during the game, but comes back to win it. On May 22 at New York, the Brewers trailed the Yankees, 9-3 in the top of the seventh. They came back to score one in the seventh, five in the eighth, and then one more in the 14th for a thrilling 10-9 win.

Type 3: Home team only — opponents score in extra innings to take the lead, but the home club comes back to win. On September 6 at Cleveland, the Mariners and Indians battled into the 12th inning. In the top half of the 12th, the Ms scored two runs to take a 9-7 lead. However, the Tribe battled back to win it in the bottom half, getting a run on a double by Carlos Baerga and then four more on a grand slam home run by Carlos Martinez for a 12-9 victory.

Type 4: A no-hitter. There was only one of these in the majors last year — by Kevin Gross of the Dodgers against San Francisco on August 17.

You might think of a couple more categories, and even by these criteria, some wins are probably more emotional than others. But if you've ever been at the park for a game like the ones described above, you know the special rush of excitement that runs through the stadium if the home club is the winner. By their actions and comments, the players seem to feel the same way.

But does it inspire them to play better ball over the next few games? We have to admit we've had our doubts about the notion ever since August of '91. On August 11, Wilson Alvarez of the White Sox pitched a no-hitter against the Orioles. For the Sox, this was an "emotional win" and then some. It was Alvarez' first start for the White Sox, and the second of his major league career. It was the club's seventh straight victory, and it put the club only a game out of first. So what happened? The Sox lost their next three games, and 15 of their next 17. They even got no-hit themselves — by Kansas City's Bret Saberhagen — along the way. So don't tell a Chicagoan about the boost you can get from an emotional win.

With that background, let's look at the data. We found a total of 52 emotional victories over the course of the 1992 season, an average of two per team. Since this sort of win doesn't happen every day, we looked for a carry-over effect, a boost in a club's winning percentage over the next few games. If there was an effect, it should be noticeable very soon, and it probably wouldn't last very long. So we looked at how clubs performed in their next three games, and also in their next six. Here are the results:

After an Emotional Win — 1992

	W	L	Pct.
Next Three Games	87	67	.565
Next Six Games	158	135	.539

If you're wondering why the totals don't add up to 52 times three or six, it's because one of the wins happened on the next-to-last day of the season (Kansas City rallied from a 5-0 deficit to beat the Twins, 7-6; they lost the next day), and because there was an overlap of **two** emotional wins in a six-game period in a few cases. There was no double boost from this, that we could see.

Was there a boost at all? Clubs had an average winning percentage of .565 over their next three games after an emotional win, and a .539 mark over the next six. But you'd expect them to be over .500, since clubs with winning records are more likely to post an emotional victory (or any kind of victory). Indeed, teams with winning marks accounted for 30 of the 52 wins, clubs with losing records only 19; the Houston Astros, who finished at .500, had three. The Athletics, Twins and White Sox, three of the better clubs in baseball, accounted for 12 emotional victories (four each), or 23 percent of the total.

So the boost is only a small one, if any: emotional wins don't seem to have a major carryover effect. Wilson Alvarez would probably tell you the same thing.

DO PLAYERS SUCCUMB TO FATIGUE?

To hear some people tell it, today's players are **to put it mildly** "wimps." They go on the disabled list with a hangnail. They want out of the lineup when a tough pitcher is going for the other team. Cal Ripken is the only real man left any more. And blah blah blah.

This is one debate we'll happily stay out of. The question we want to address here is a simple one: how does fatigue affect ballplayers? The 162-game player like Ripken is a rarity, but is that necessarily bad? Do players wear down after too many consecutive games in the lineup?

We decided to look at what happens to players after they've been in the starting lineup for 30 consecutive games — a pretty long stretch of playing without a break. If fatigue was getting to them, we'd notice a decline in their performance. So we compared their performance during their first 30-game stretch without a break with their performance in the following two weeks (whether the streak continued or not). For purposes of comparison, we'll adjust the "after streak" figures to the same number of plate appearances as the "before streak" numbers. There were 132 players who had a 30-game playing streak; here's how they performed during the streak, and afterward:

1992 Players — Before and After a 30-Game Playing Streak

	Before Streak Completed					Two Weeks After Streak				
	AB	HR	Avg	OBA	Slg	AB	HR	Avg	OBA	Slg
Average (132 Players)	89	2	.274	.344	.416	89	2	.262	.331	.390

As you can see, there was a definite drop in performance. Batting average declined by 12 points, on-base percentage by 13 points, slugging percentage by 26. This clearly suggests that the players were wearing down.

Of course, in a group this large, you're bound to find some players whose performance actually improved after the 30-game streak. There were a half-dozen players who hit at least 100 points higher in the two weeks after the streak:

100 or More Point Improvement After a 30-Game Playing Streak

	Before Streak Completed					Two Weeks After Streak				
Player, Team	AB	HR	Avg	OBA	Slg	AB	HR	Avg	OBA	Slg
Eric Anthony, Hou	90	3	.256	.320	.411	95	5	.389	.420	.821
Delino DeShields, Mon	87	1	.287	.364	.402	88	3	.409	.469	.580
Kelly Gruber, Tor	94	3	.223	.260	.394	100	0	.400	.400	.400

Dave Hollins, Phi	80	2	.225	.374	.350	85	4	.388	.460	.682
David Justice, Atl	84	3	.226	.330	.369	79	0	.392	.520	.506
Robin Yount, Mil	89	2	.247	.320	.393	90	3	.367	.430	.522

That seems to suggest that it's all a matter of luck — players have hot and cold streaks all the time, right? True enough. But it's stretching things to say that a 12-point drop over a sample of 132 players is simply coincidental. And while a half-dozen players improved by 100 points following a 30-game playing steak, three times that number suffered a 100-point decline:

100 or More Point Swing After a 30-Game Playing Streak

	Number of Players
100 or More Point Increase	6
100 or More Point Decline	18

Here's just a sampling of the players who suffered a massive drop in performance:

100 or More Point Decline After a 30-Game Playing Streak

Player, Team	Before Streak Completed					Two Weeks After Streak				
	AB	HR	Avg	OBA	Slg	AB	HR	Avg	OBA	Slg
Milt Cuyler, Det	94	1	.266	.296	.340	91	0	.121	.184	.143
Glenn Davis, Bal	89	4	.292	.360	.483	93	0	.161	.198	.247
Travis Fryman, Det	91	4	.319	.380	.484	94	2	.191	.220	.277
Charlie Hayes, Yanks	96	2	.313	.330	.406	90	2	.133	.192	.222
Felix Jose, StL	89	3	.337	.406	.528	92	2	.185	.250	.293
Chuck Knoblauch, Min	84	0	.333	.414	.381	72	0	.125	.337	.181
Pat Listach, Mil	89	0	.315	.378	.360	93	0	.151	.177	.151
Harold Reynolds, Sea	89	1	.270	.337	.371	76	0	.145	.295	.171
Mickey Tettleton, Det	83	6	.277	.390	.554	88	2	.114	.220	.205
Dave Winfield, Tor	88	5	.364	.420	.591	82	2	.220	.360	.366

Some of these players went from the .300s to the .100s. Just a coincidence? In a few cases, sure; over so many players, doubtful. We admire Ripken as much as anyone, and it may be manly to stay in the lineup day after day after day. But the evidence suggests that it's counter-productive. Everyone needs a day off now and then.

A complete listing for this category can be found on page 266.

WAS AN ILL WIND BLOWING AT WRIGLEY LAST SUMMER?

It was a strange summer at Wrigley Field. We don't mean the Cubs' losing ways; that happens almost every year. We mean the low level of scoring at what is traditionally one of the best hitter's parks in baseball. Even a flurry of higher scores late in the year could only make it look like a neutral park by year's end. The final 1992 offensive figures showed that the Cubs and their opponents scored only seven more runs at Wrigley Field than in Cub road games (612 to 605), and hit only five more home runs (108 to 103).

This is very unlike Wrigley, as anyone who's studied similar comparisons over the years can attest. What happened? A big part of it, no doubt, was the Cubs' groundball pitching staff (see Cubs essay, page 42), which kept the ball out of the air and took advantage of the stadium's long grass. Last year, Cub pitchers were actually more effective at Wrigley than they were on the road — a most unusual occurrence. As you look at this chart, it's clear that both the Cub hitters **and** pitchers preferred playing at Wrigley last season:

Cubs and Their Opponents — 1992

	At Wrigley		On the Road	
	Cubs	Opp	Cubs	Opp
Batting average	.257	.237	.251	.255
Runs Scored	315	297	278	327
Home Runs	59	49	45	58

So the groundball staff was a very important factor. But there was more going on than that. Those of you who read our book last year will remember that we presented a chart showing how the level of offense at the Friendly Confines was affected by the direction in which the wind was blowing. In brief, what we discovered was that Wrigley was a terrific hitter's park when the wind blew out, a good hitter's park when the wind blew across, and a neutral park when the wind blew in.

The graphic updates that study, this time comparing Wrigley between 1991 and 1992. The differences are immediately obvious. One is that the wind blew in much more often: in 1991 it blew in 35 percent of the time, out 37 percent; in 1992 it blew in 52 percent of the time, out only 22 percent. (The wind blew across about the same amount of time both years.) The other major difference is that, even when the wind blew out, the park was still a lot less friendly to the hitters. The scoring rate with the wind blowing out dropped by over three runs a game from 1991, the home run rate by nearly one a game.

The groundball staff does a lot to explain that dropoff, and so does the shift in the wind. The third factor at work was the low temperature. It was

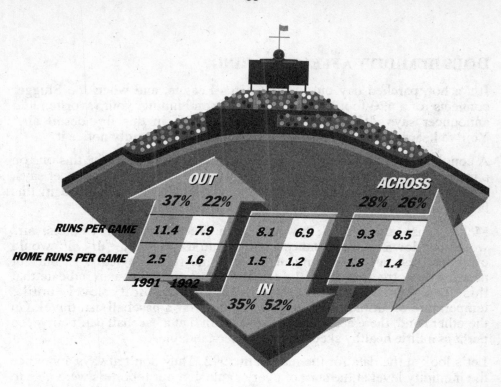

	OUT				ACROSS	
	37%	22%			28%	26%
RUNS PER GAME	11.4	7.9	8.1	6.9	9.3	8.5
HOME RUNS PER GAME	2.5	1.6	1.5	1.2	1.8	1.4
	1991	1992				
	IN					
	35%	52%				

an unusually cool summer in Chicago; heck, any summer in which the wind blows in at Wrigley more than half the time is positively **Antarctic**. Our studies have shown again and again that when temperature drops, so does scoring. Here are the figures at Wrigley Field for 1991 and 1992:

Temperature and Scoring at Wrigley

	1991			1992		
Temperature	G	R/G	HR/G	G	R/G	HR/G
80 and up	22	11.82	2.23	8	9.25	1.25
70 to 79	34	8.82	1.91	25	7.68	1.68
69 and below	27	8.22	2.00	48	7.21	1.16

It was an amazingly cool summer at Wrigley in '92, with only eight games in which the temperature was over 80, and 48 contests in which it was either in the sixties or worse. And that, too, worked against the hitters. In brief, the combination of the three factors — a groundball pitching staff, the wind blowing in, and much lower temperatures than usual — resulted in much less offense. The Friendly Confines weren't nearly so friendly.

We still think Wrigley is a heck of a hitter's park . . . but just to make sure, we'll be checking with the weather man this year.

A complete listing for this category can be found on page 269.

DOES HUMIDITY AFFECT SCORING?

It's a hot, parched day out in the Cactus League, and when Joe Slugger connects for a 420-foot home run in the second inning, your favorite radio announcer says, "Boy, the ball really took off in this dry desert air." You've heard this sort of statement so often that you hardly notice it.

A couple of months later, you're listening to another broadcast, this one on a muggy night with a strong possibility of rain. The same announcer says, "One thing for sure. The ball's not gonna leave the yard much in this heavy air." Once again, you don't think to question it.

Makes sense, doesn't it? It would seem pretty logical that "moist air" would cut down on the distance a ball would travel, while "dry air" would offer less resistance, resulting in more home runs. Logical . . . but not necessarily correct. Most of the scientific studies we've seen indicate that this theory is completely wrong, that the humidity level, unlike temperature or altitude has **no** affect on how far a baseball can travel. On the other hand, there are scientists who claim that a baseball can't curve, so perhaps a little healthy skepticism is understandable.

Let's look at the data for the majors in 1992. They don't always announce the humidity level at the start of every game, but our reporters were able to get the information for 90 percent of the contests last year. We'll compare the humidity level to the average number of runs scored and the home run rate. Here are the results for each level (there were no games with the humidity below 10 percent):

Humidity and Scoring — 1992

Humidity	G	R/G	HR/G
10 - 20	440	8.19	1.40
21 - 40	207	8.00	1.36
41 - 50	304	8.18	1.43
51 - 60	305	8.52	1.46
61 - 70	311	8.03	1.51
71 - 80	241	7.96	1.36
81 - 100	196	8.00	1.34
10 - 100	2,004	8.15	1.42
Unknown	102	9.94	1.97
All Games	2,106	8.23	1.44

If there's a relationship between humidity and scoring, it's not immediately evident. At the lowest level — between 10 and 20 percent — the scoring (8.19) and home run (1.40) rates were about the same as for all major league games last year (8.23 and 1.44) . . . a little lower, in fact. There's no evidence at all that the "ball really takes off in dry air."

As for the upper levels, there was, in fact, a small drop in the scoring and home run rates when the humidity was above 70 percent. However, those rates were also low when the humidity was between 21 and 40 percent, so that is likely to be just a random occurrence.

The point we're trying to make is that there appears to be no neat, direct, relationship between humidity and scoring, the way there is between temperature and scoring. Here's a similar chart to the one above, but based on temperature:

Temperature and Scoring — 1992

Temperature	G	R/G	HR/G
80 - above	407	8.49	1.61
70 - 79	1,082	8.20	1.42
60 - 69	398	8.28	1.46
59 - below	219	7.84	1.23

As you can see, there's a fairly consistent relationship between offense and temperature: as the weather gets hotter, so do the bats. The reason the ball takes off in the desert air is not because the humidity is low; it's because the temperature is high.

This is an important point, because some people think that the new Miami park will favor pitchers, simply because the Marlins will be playing in humid weather. Joe Robbie Stadium may well favor pitchers because of its dimensions, the wind currents, or even low altitude. But there's no reason to think that the humidity, by itself, will cut down on the home run rate.

WHICH TEAMS MOVE THE FASTEST?

Ask someone which major league team played at the fastest pace last year, and he'll probably say the Chicago Cubs. The average nine-inning Cub contest took a snappy 2:37. The slowest? That would seem to be two American League clubs, the Oakland A's and the Detroit Tigers, whose contests averaged an even three hours.

But game times depend, to a good extent, on the number of pitches thrown. Some pitchers miss the strike zone consistently; some hitters (and some teams) draw a lot of walks. So when we ask, "Who moves the fastest?" we ought to look at more than just game times.

What we'll do is rate the teams in terms of time per pitch thrown. To use an example, the Minnesota Twins played 148 nine-inning games last year, and there was a total of 39,865 pitches thrown in those games, by both the Twins and their opponents. (We ought to know; we counted them all.) The average time of a Minnesota game was 2:49, and a little simple arithmetic tells us that Twins games took an average of 37.6 seconds a pitch.

That might seem like a long time, but 37.6 seconds per pitch was exactly the American League average last year. Of course, it's not like the pitcher is holding the ball for 35 seconds between every pitch before delivering it . . . it just **seems** that way. Remember that there are two-minute-plus breaks every half inning, pitching changes, Sparky's "strategy sessions" and . . . By the time you add it all up, 37 seconds a pitch begins to seem pretty fast. (Well, not really).

Anyway, partly to help you get a new slant on things, and partly for reasons of whimsy, here are the average times per pitch thrown for the American League last year:

Time Per Pitch — 1992 American League

Team	Pitches Per Game	Avg Time	Seconds Per Pitch
Seattle Mariners	277.7	2:49	36.51
Kansas City Royals	263.5	2:42	36.89
Cleveland Indians	271.5	2:49	37.35
Texas Rangers	282.3	2:56	37.40
Chicago White Sox	276.5	2:53	37.53
Minnesota Twins	269.4	2:49	37.64
Detroit Tigers	286.7	3:00	37.67
Oakland Athletics	285.9	3:00	37.77
New York Yankees	276.6	2:55	37.96
Toronto Blue Jays	281.2	2:58	37.97
California Angels	263.5	2:47	38.02
Boston Red Sox	275.9	2:56	38.27

Baltimore Orioles	279.9	2:59	38.36
Milwaukee Brewers	267.6	2:52	38.57
AL TOTALS	275.6	2:53	37.65

The results surprised even us. Those "pokey" Athletics and Tigers, who averaged three hours a game, were actually about average in terms of time per pitch. A big reason their games take so long, one we never considered, is that their hitters take so many pitches (they ranked first and second in the league in walks drawn). They took less time per pitch than the Angels, whose low game time was basically due to their impatient hitters (last in walks).

Here's the National League data:

Time Per Pitch — 1992 National League

Team	Pitches Per Game	Avg Time	Seconds Per Pitch
Chicago Cubs	259.5	2:37	36.30
Philadelphia Phillies	274.0	2:46	36.35
Pittsburgh Pirates	264.5	2:43	36.97
Cincinnati Reds	264.1	2:43	37.02
San Francisco Giants	262.5	2:44	37.48
San Diego Padres	256.7	2:41	37.63
St. Louis Cardinals	258.0	2:42	37.67
Houston Astros	267.3	2:48	37.70
Atlanta Braves	263.9	2:46	37.73
Montreal Expos	267.0	2:48	37.75
Los Angeles Dodgers	265.5	2:49	38.18
New York Mets	269.5	2:52	38.29
NL TOTALS	264.5	2:45	37.43

The NL data is similarly instructive. Cubs games, the league's swiftest, were nine minutes faster than those of the Phillies. But the real reason for the difference is that their hitters drew only 417 walks, fewest in the league; Phillies hitters drew 509. In terms of time per pitch, the clubs were nearly identical.

We did this same study for individual pitchers, and found out that Zane Smith of the Pirates was the fastest workman in the majors last year at 35.01 pitches per second. There were surprises here, as well. Seattle's Randy Johnson, whose games averaged 2:55 last year, turned out to be one of the faster workers in time per pitch. The next time you sit through one of Randy's three-walk innings, you'll no doubt find some comfort in that.

HOW DOES A PLAYER DO WHEN HE COMES OFF THE DISABLED LIST?

Fantasy players will love this one: how does a player perform immediately after coming off the disabled list? The way clubs nurture their high-priced talent these days, what with rehabilitation stints, expensive workout equipment and highly skilled doctors and trainers, you might think a player would be ready to hit the ground running. On the other hand, the player hasn't faced major league competition in at least a couple of weeks. Does he need some sort of break-in period before he finally hits his stride?

Let's restrict this study to hitters and look at their immediate results after coming off the DL: the first 10 plate appearances, and then the first 15. This is somewhere between two and four games, enough — since we're studying a lot of players — to get a good idea of whether players show any rust in their first few games back.

Here are the players' batting average, on-base average and slugging averages after coming off the disabled list, then their 1992 averages for the rest of the season for purpose of comparison:

1992 Players After Returning From the Disabled List			
	Avg	OBP	Slg
First 10 PA	.223	.310	.315
First 15 PA	.221	.306	.316
Rest of Season	.243	.306	.358

The "Rest of Season" figures are so low for one simple reason. All players' season stats (including bench players) who were coming off the DL were scaled down to 100 plate appearances and weighted equally so we could fairly compare them with the 10- and 15-plate appearance totals (which were scaled up to 100 PA). All players dumb enough to get hurt **aren't** .243 hitters. It just seems that way.

At any rate, the interesting numbers are the first two lines in the chart, and how badly the players did when they came off the DL. They batted 20 points lower than they did over the rest of the season, and their slugging averages were more than 40 points lower. On-base percentage was about the same; since the batting average dropped, that indicated that the players were drawing a few more walks. Were they in such great pain that they simply couldn't swing the bat?

This probably doesn't mean much to a major league general manager — if a guy needs two or three games to get his batting eye back, the club is just going to have to suffer with him. But it **does** mean a lot to fantasy league players. A lot of people will routinely activate their players as soon as they're ready to return to the lineup. As this study shows, that may not be a good idea. Unlike major league GMs, fantasy leaguers have the luxury of being able to wait a couple of games and see how their guys are recovering.

While the general trend is for players to struggle, there were several spectacular comebacks from the DL over the course of the 1992 season. Probably the most dramatic was by the Cubs' Sammy Sosa, who returned from the injury list on July 27 after missing several weeks with a broken hand. His first series back was against the first-place Pirates at Wrigley Field, and the Cubs desperately needed a series sweep to get back into the race. Facing Pirate ace Doug Drabek, Sosa hit the first pitch he saw for a home run over the left field fence to tie the game at 1-1. The Pirates took a 2-1 lead, but in the fifth Sosa came through again, singling in Derrick May with the tying run. Then in the eighth, with the contest still tied, Sosa singled again and then came around to score the winning run. He was nearly as spectacular the next day, going 3-for-5 in an 11-1 Cub romp. He had only one hit in the series finale, but he made it count: it was a two-run homer in the 11th to give the Cubs a 6-4 victory. What a return. But it had to end sometime. The next week Sosa fractured his ankle and missed the rest of the year. That's baseball on the North Side of Chicago.

Ozzie Smith of the Cardinals also had a spectacular return from the DL last year. Smith took a lot of kidding when he missed several weeks with the chicken pox, but as usual, Ozzie had the last laugh. He returned on July 1 and got at least one hit in each of his first four games back, going 7 for 16.

The Sosa and Smith stories, however, are the exception. As a general rule, players struggle for their first few games. That's a useful thing to remember for this season.

WASN'T BIP A PIP IN SEPTEMBER?

On his way to hitting a career-high .323 last year, Bip Roberts had a remarkable month of September. While the Reds were basically playing out the string, Roberts was batting .464 (39 for 84), including a National League record-tying 10 straight hits at one point. How good a month was it? Over the last four seasons, only one hitter has had a better monthly average (minimum 75 plate appearances). Back in September of 1989, Paul Molitor batted .476. Obviously, the Bipper was boppin'.

But while Roberts deserves a lot of praise, another major leaguer probably had an even better all-around September. Look at Barry Bonds' figures, which were unmatched last year in terms of across-the-board brilliance:

	AB	R	H	2B	3B	HR	RBI	SB	CS	BB	K	BA	OBP	SLG
Bonds in Sep.	92	28	37	10	1	9	25	9	0	33	14	.402	.556	.826

Is this what used to be known as a "salary drive"? If so, it worked.

The chart shows the best monthly batting and earned run averages of 1992. There were some truly outstanding performances, like Brett Butler's .442 average in July — except for Roberts, the best mark since Molitor in '89.

1992

	HITTERS	HR	RBI	AVG.	ML Avg.	PITCHERS	W	L	ERA	ML Avg.
APRIL	John Kruk	0	16	.407	.249	Bill Krueger	4	0	0.84	3.74
MAY	Andy Van Slyke	1	17	.415	.255	Kevin Gross	3	1	1.65	3.96
JUNE	Mark Grace	0	9	.404	.259	John Smiley	4	0	1.34	3.82
JULY	Brett Butler	1	12	.442	.255	John Smoltz	3	1	0.94	3.48
AUG.	Edgar Martinez	3	19	.395	.258	Cal Eldred	4	0	0.61	3.82
SEP.	Bip Roberts	2	11	.464	.259	Nolan Ryan	0	1	0.99	3.73

Hitters: Minimum 75 plate appearances. Pitchers: Minimum 25 innings pitched.

But as with Bonds, some great months got left off the list. They include:

Batting Average Darren Daulton, May, .412; Spike Owen, August, .394; Bernard Gilkey, September, .392; Fred McGriff, May, .392.

Home Runs Juan Gonzalez, August, 12; Juan Gonzalez, June, 11; Mark McGwire, April, 10; Gary Sheffield, August, 10; Ryne Sandberg, September, 10.

RBI Cecil Fielder, June, 32; Tom Brunansky, July, 32; Dave Winfield, August, 32.

Is Juan Gonzalez a streak hitter? Yes, but last year the streak lasted half the season. In June, July and August, Gonzalez batted 295 times, with 31 homers and 70 RBI. Wait 'til he grows up.

The list of best pitching months always seems to turn up some odd names. And sure enough, there's Bill Krueger, who did his best last April to make Twins fans forget the loss of Jack Morris. Come August, it was time to forget Krueger. After going 1-4 with a 9.69 ERA for the month, the Twins dealt him to Montreal.

While he made the list only for his August performance, we ought to recognize Milwaukee's Cal Eldred for his follow-up month. The rookie was 6-0 with a 1.17 ERA in September, and played a huge part in keeping the Brewers in the pennant race. After winning 10 straight decisions, Eldred finally lost a game on the last day of the season (October 4), suggesting that he may be human after all.

Who had the **worst** months of 1992? Here they are:

	Player, Team	HR	RBI	BA	Pitcher, Team	W	L	ERA
April	Ruben Amaro, Phi	3	7	.138	Terry Mulholland, Phi	0	3	7.28
May	Greg Vaughn, Mil	5	15	.157	Rheal Courmier, StL	0	2	7.80
June	Robby Thompson, SF	1	5	.136	Bob Milacki, Bal	1	2	6.90
July	Charlie Hayes, Yanks	2	10	.155	Kirk McCaskill, WSox	1	2	7.63
Aug	Billy Doran, Cin	1	8	.154	David Wells, Tor	1	4	13.14
Sept	Andujar Cedeno, Hou	0	5	.152	Rick Sutcliffe, Bal	2	4	8.31

There always seem to be some famous names on this dubious list, which goes to show you what a streaky game baseball is. Rick Sutcliffe might have been a great guy to have around the Oriole clubhouse, but he couldn't teach the young O's hurlers very much about consistency. Sutcliffe's monthly ERAs were 2.65, 6.33, 3.21, 5.85, 1.60 and 8.31. In July, he was 0-5; in August, 4-0. Maybe they should make him a non-playing pitching coach every other month.

Then there's Nolan Ryan. In July, he was 4-0 with a 1.96 ERA; in August, 0-5, 7.16; in September he was 0-1, but his ERA was 0.99, the lowest in baseball for the month. Ryan also had a 10.80 ERA in April, when he probably made his manager want to reach for a couple Advils. One wonders whether he and Sutcliffe, who worked 237.1 innings in '92, weren't being asked to deliver more than their bodies could handle last year.

A complete listing for this category can be found on page 270.

III. QUESTIONS ON OFFENSE

ARE THERE REALLY RIGHTIES WHO CAN HIT RIGHTHANDERS BETTER?

If you've been reading this book over the years, you're well aware that platoon differentials aren't the figment of someone's imagination: as a rule, left-handed hitters have trouble with southpaws, and right-handed hitters suffer against righties. Hitters will always say, "Of course I can hit righties (or lefties)!" But then they'll go out and prove our point.

Yet every year there are exceptions to the rule. Does this mean that there are some hitters who really have "reverse" differentials — righties who hit righties better and lefties who clean up on lefties? Or are these just statistical flukes? Let's look at one aspect of the question, the righty swingers who hit righthanders better in 1992.

We found a total of 33 players who met these three standards: they had at least 1,000 at-bats in their careers, they had at least 250 at-bats last year, and they had higher batting averages against righties than they did lefties last year. In some cases the advantage was minuscule — for example, Lance Parrish hit .233 vs. righties last year, .232 vs. lefties. But it was an advantage.

Was this advantage part of the players' history? Looking at the group as a whole, the answer is no. Out of a total of 99 seasons with 250-plus at bats for the group from 1987 through 1991, the players had hit righties better only 33 times — only one third of the time. So there was no strong history of batting better against righties.

How about the players with a **big** righty-vs.-righty advantage in 1992 — was **that** a career pattern? There were a total of 12 right-handed hitters who hit righties better than lefties in 1992. Their 1992 "reverse platoon advantage" appeared to be a fluke in almost every case:

RHBs at Least 20 Points Better Against Righties — 1992

Player, Team	1992		1987-1991	
	LHP	RHP	LHP	RHP
Tom Brunansky, Min	.227	.282	.252	.241
Glenn Davis, Bal	.252	.285	.251	.262
Greg Gagne, Min	.181	.266	.286	.242
Brian Harper, Min	.275	.316	.308	.306
Charlie Hayes, Yanks	.213	.276	.271	.233
Rickey Henderson, Oak	.267	.289	.315	.284
Darrin Jackson, SD	.202	.271	.276	.236
Shane Mack, Min	.297	.320	.319	.273
Keith Miller, KC	.267	.291	.268	.260

Cal Ripken, Bal	.230	.258	.278	.266
Luis Rivera, Bos	.179	.229	.241	.239
Don Slaught, Pit	.322	.395	.274	.265

Of the 12, only one, Glenn Davis, had hit righties better than lefties over the previous five seasons. In some cases the players had had relatively even platoon stats — like Brian Harper, who had hit .308 vs. lefties, .306 vs. righties. That's no small accomplishment, but except for Davis, there was no previous history of hitting righties better, much less significantly better. So the 1992 numbers can't really be trusted in predicting future performance.

But Davis is something of an intriguing case. Is there anyone else like him — players who hit righties better in 1992, whatever the size of the advantage, and also did over the 1987-91 period? Out of the group of 33, there were only four:

Better Against Righthanders — 1992 and 1987-91

	1992		1987-1991	
Player, Team	LHP	RHP	LHP	RHP
Craig Biggio, Hou	.275	.278	.253	.282
Jay Buhner, Sea	.230	.248	.237	.253
Glenn Davis, Bal	.252	.285	.251	.262
Tom Pagnozzi, StL	.244	.252	.251	.263

If there are any righty swingers who really do hit righthanders better, these are the ones. Buhner has had three major league seasons with at least 250 at-bats, and he's hit righties better than lefties in all three of them. Pagnozzi has accomplished that trick twice in two 250 at-bat seasons, Biggio three times out of four, Davis three times out of five.

So there is something of a career pattern with these players; none of them hits righties better to a large degree, but they've all done so overall. They're the only ones, however, and none of them have done it six seasons in a row, or anything close to it. You can hardly take it to the bank that even these players will do so again in 1993.

A complete listing for this category can be found on page 271.

HOW IMPORTANT IS A GOOD "HEART OF THE ORDER"?

The "heart of the order" consists of the glamour spots, numbers three, four and five, where the big boppers reside. Just thinking about Ruth-Gehrig-Meusel, DiMaggio-Gehrig-Dickey, Snider-Hodges-Campanella, F. Robinson-B. Robinson-Powell, and Morgan-Bench-Perez summons up memories of some of the most fearsome offenses in baseball history. Have some punch in the 3-4-5 spots, one would think, and you're well on the road to success.

Or are you? The chart below lists the best "hearts of the order" for 1992 in terms of home runs, RBI and slugging percentage. Each category is important, and the lists aren't identical. So let's rank the best hearts of the order for 1992. Five teams stood out:

1. Toronto. Blue Jays manager Cito Gaston doesn't like to complicate things, and his lineup selection was simplicity itself. All season long Joe Carter hit third and Dave Winfield fourth; Gaston basically split the number five spot between John Olerud (vs. righties) and Kelly Gruber (vs. lefties). Although Gruber's lack of production was a problem, you'd have to say the system worked. The heart of the Jays' order ranked first in slugging, second in RBI, and second in home runs, the best overall record of any team. The Jays also ranked second in baseball in runs scored, and first where it really counted — in the World Series.

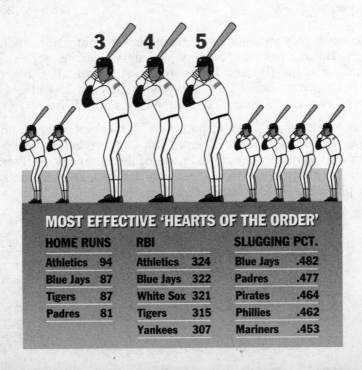

MOST EFFECTIVE 'HEARTS OF THE ORDER'

HOME RUNS		RBI		SLUGGING PCT.	
Athletics	94	Athletics	324	Blue Jays	.482
Blue Jays	87	Blue Jays	322	Padres	.477
Tigers	87	White Sox	321	Pirates	.464
Padres	81	Tigers	315	Phillies	.462
		Yankees	307	Mariners	.453

2. Oakland. The A's ranked sixth in slugging percentage, but were first in both home runs and RBI. Unlike the Jays, Oakland moved different players in and out of their heart of the order spots, even replacing Jose Canseco with Ruben Sierra late in the year. But for the most part, it was Canseco/Sierra, Mark McGwire and the combination of Harold Baines (vs. righties) and Terry Steinbach (vs. lefties). Some weaknesses in the rest of the lineup reduced the Athletics to fourth in the American League in runs scored, but the heart of the order remained productive all year, despite the changing cast.

3. Detroit Tigers. Sparky Anderson's team led the majors in runs scored, and they had great success bludgeoning people to death with the trio of Travis Fryman, Cecil Fielder and Mickey Tettleton. Detroit didn't go very far in the standings, but you could hardly blame that threesome, or the rest of the Tiger offense.

4. Chicago White Sox. Here you can begin to see the limitations of too much reliance on the heart of the order. The White Sox got great productivity (third in RBI) from the trio of Frank Thomas, George Bell and Robin Ventura, but the rest of the lineup came up short. The Sox were only sixth in the league in runs scored, as they paid the price for an underpowered outfield. The Sox had a good heart to their order, but not much else.

5. San Diego Padres. The Padres had the National League's best heart of the order, thanks to the duo of number-three hitter Gary Sheffield and cleanup man Fred McGriff. But the third part of the trio — usually Darrin Jackson or Benito Santiago — wasn't all that great, and the rest of the lineup, except for Tony Gwynn, was downright bad. The Padres ranked seventh in the National League in runs scored, despite an effective heart of the order, and despite the fact that they played in a good hitters park.

So how important is the heart of the order? Well, Cito Gaston would probably tell you it was pretty important . . . but on the other hand, his Blue Jay bosses let Winfield walk via free agency. Teams like the White Sox and Padres found that an effective threesome (in San Diego's case, it was really a twosome) wasn't enough to make up for weaknesses in the other spots in the order. Even Ruth, Gehrig and Meusel, you'll recall, had some hard-hitting teammates.

Who had the worst hearts of the order in 1992? It's easy to pinpoint the Royals (only 35 homers and 207 RBI) and the Angels (36 homers, 215 RBI). Considering their terrible won-lost records, you'd have a hard time convincing **them** that the heart of the lineup isn't important. (But then, they didn't have a whole lot else, either.)

A complete listing for this category can be found on page 272.

WHY DON'T MORE CLUBS PLATOON?

Every year, we like to take a look at the best platoon combinations in the major leagues over the previous season. And every year, we're astonished to discover how few clubs even bother to platoon anymore. It's hard to understand why. Lots of clubs have one or more weak positions, and available lefties and righties who could rotate in those spots. The Earl Weaver argument still makes perfect sense: platooning can make a weak position strong, and keep the bench players strong by giving them frequent action.

Yet the idea has pretty much gone out of fashion. Even managers like Bobby Cox and Jim Leyland, who used to have successful platoons at several positions, don't do it as much as they used to. So as we go through our annual list of "best platoons of 1992," we find the pickings pretty slim; there were only five reasonably effective ones. The figures quoted here are the players' overall 1992 numbers when playing that particular position only:

Atlanta Braves - 1B	AB	H	HR	RBI	Avg
Sid Bream	360	93	10	58	.258
Brian Hunter	202	52	12	35	.257

This platoon has been in effect for two seasons, and you can't knock the results: 22 homers and 93 RBI last year, 20 and 88 the year before. It's a perfect combination, a veteran and a younger player. The youngster, Hunter, obviously would like to play full-time, but he hit only .181 against righties last year. So expect this combination to be in place this year, unless first-base prospect Ryan Klesko is deemed ready, or unless Bream can no longer waddle around the bases in his unique fashion.

Pittsburgh Pirates - C	AB	H	HR	RBI	Avg
Mike LaValliere	292	75	2	29	.257
Don Slaught	241	84	4	36	.349

As we've often noted, when clubs platoon these days, it's usually behind the plate, where two players routinely share the work anyway. This combination has worked for three years, and it's been perfect for Slaught, who has batted .300, .295 and .345 in his three seasons with the Bucs. The platoon helps both. LaValliere, a good defensive player, has hit only .240 against lefties the last five years; Slaught can hit righties (.289 over the last five campaigns), but at 34, he'd have trouble handling full-time work, and his glove can't compare with LaValliere's.

New York Yankees - C	AB	H	HR	RBI	Avg
Matt Nokes	371	82	21	57	.221
Mike Stanley	150	39	7	25	.260

Does Mike Stanley want to be Don Slaught when he grows up? Each one played for awhile with the Rangers, then went to the Yankees. Each can hit, but has defensive shortcomings (though Slaught is considered superior to Stanley). So a platoon role became a natural way to get their bats into the lineup on a part-time basis. Platooning Stanley with Nokes worked out pretty well for the Yanks last year; Nokes is a very dangerous hitter, and 28 homers and 82 RBI from your catchers is a nice total. This one may be used again in '93, if the Yankees can put up with their defense.

Cleveland Indians - 1B	AB	H	HR	RBI	Avg
Paul Sorrento	405	110	14	54	.272
Carlos Martinez	115	32	1	10	.278

Sorrento, who came to Cleveland from the Twins last year, had a fine first season, but he batted only .156 in 45 at-bats vs. lefties. Hence the need to platoon, and Martinez was the man when he was healthy last year. The Tribe also has another promising young first baseman in Reggie Jefferson, who's a switch hitter. It seems likely that Sorrento will platoon with someone this year; we just don't know who it will be yet.

Houston Astros - LF	AB	H	HR	RBI	Avg
Luis Gonzalez	370	89	9	48	.241
Pete Incaviglia	170	43	6	25	.253

Another veteran/youngster combination, this one was satisfactory for the Astros last year, at least from Incaviglia's viewpoint: he batted .282 last year vs. lefties. However, the lefty-swinging Gonzalez hit .350 in 80 at-bats vs. lefties (though with only one homer), so the Astros would like to try him as a full-time player. Incaviglia has moved on to the Phillies where he'll probably get some platoon work again.

WILL OAKLAND'S PATH TO VICTORY GO THROUGH TROY?

For the second consecutive year, we present a set of "long shot" hitting prospects to keep an eye on for the coming season. Most folks know about Bret Boone and J.T. Snow and Mike Piazza. We'd prefer to tell you about players who are not under the spotlight as much. Last year we hit on one of four (Chad Curtis), a pretty good percentage for the kind of players we're looking at. This time, two of our picks are hardly youngsters; however, that kind of player often surprises people. The "MLE," which stands for "major league equivalency," is a Bill James translation of how the player would have performed in the majors, based on his minor league numbers.

Troy Neel, 27, Oakland, DH-OF

	AB	R	H	2B	3B	HR	BI	BB	SO	SB	Avg	OBP	Slg
92 AAA Tacoma	396	61	139	36	3	17	74	60	84	2	.351	.439	.586
MLE	370	47	113	29	1	11	57	46	89	1	.305	.382	.478
Avg Min Lg Year	339	52	101	22	1	14	65	51	75	2	.298	.390	.493
92 Winter League	142	30	49	10	0	12	49	27	33	1	.345	.453	.669

This former Indian looks like he's ready to stick in the majors at the ripe old age of 27. And "stick" certainly seems the word to fit Neel's talents. A poor fielder, he led the Pacific Coast League in hitting, was second only to phenom Tim Salmon in on-base percentage, and was third only to Salmon and Mike "The Godson" Piazza in slugging. Unlike Salmon and Piazza, who had friendly parks to work in, Neel played at Tacoma, possibly the worst hitters' park in the PCL.

The A's seem intent on giving Neel a full chance, as they dealt away designated hitter Harold Baines, the main obstacle standing in his way. Neel should get lots of playing time as Oakland's DH this year; he's also a left field possibility if Rickey Henderson continues to be bothered by injuries.

Frank Bolick, 27, Montreal, 3B

	AB	R	H	2B	3B	HR	BI	BB	SO	SB	Avg	OBP	Slg
92 AA/AAA Jacksnvl/Calgary	498	67	139	27	6	27	96	81	90	5	.279	.380	.520
MLE	476	50	117	23	4	21	71	57	99	2	.246	.326	.443
Avg Min Lg Year	376	67	107	24	3	16	67	74	79	7	.285	.402	.492
92 Winter League	79	6	24	6	0	1	10	13	7	4	.304	.404	.418

While most people are talking about Sean Berry, we'll focus on Montreal's other third-base candidate, Frank Bolick. Bolick was a hot Mariner prospect after a super 1990 season at two single-A stops (.324, 18 homers). However while Edgar Martinez emerged in 1991, Bolick had a slightly disappointing year at AA Jacksonville (.254, 16 HR). Bolick was subsequently shipped to the Expos for a player to be named later.

Bolick and Berry (the older of the two) are both unproven. But two factors definitely favor Bolick: his plate discipline and his ability to switch-hit.

Matt Mieske, 25, Milwaukee, OF

	AB	R	H	2B	3B	HR	BI	BB	SO	SB	Avg	OBP	Slg
92 AAA Denver	524	80	140	29	11	19	77	39	90	13	.267	.319	.473
MLE	499	59	115	24	6	13	56	28	94	9	.230	.271	.381
Avg Min Lg Year	436	82	136	28	6	15	86	59	72	26	.312	.394	.507
92 Winter League						Did	Not	Play					

Some day Mieske might make the Padres sorry they gave him up to obtain Gary Sheffield. Well, not quite. (The scary thing is that Sheffield is younger than Mieske.) Anyway, what's so exciting about a guy who hits only .267 at Denver, where everyone hits .320? Well, there are two factors to consider. First, Mieske made a two-step jump from single-A in 1992. Second, as of May 17, he was limping along with a .188 average, but hit .286 with 18 home runs in 423 at-bats afterwards.

Once Mieske got adjusted, he looked more like the player whose previous career-low batting average was .340. If there are concerns, they are in the fact that his walk total fell from 94 at High Desert in 1991 to 39 last year; his stolen bases also dropped from 39 to 13. But there are few teams that can't use a .300 hitter with power.

Jesse Levis, 25, Cleveland, C

	AB	R	H	2B	3B	HR	BI	BB	SO	SB	Avg	OBP	Slg
92 AAA Colo Spr	253	39	92	20	1	6	44	37	25	1	.364	.444	.522
MLE	237	25	76	16	0	4	28	24	26	0	.321	.383	.439
Avg Min Lg Year	300	39	91	16	2	6	45	41	31	2	.303	.387	.430
92 Winter League	86	9	26	5	0	1	10	7	11	1	.302	.355	.395

While expansion draft followers were shocked that Boston catcher Eric Wedge was still available in the third round, they were also surprised that neither new club took a chance on Cleveland's Jesse Levis. Though not the hitter Wedge is, Levis is a fine batsman and good enough defensively to catch in the majors.

With Sandy Alomar in possession of the starting Indian backstop job for the foreseeable future, don't look for Levis to become a regular. However, defensive specialist Joel Skinner is out for at least the first half of 1993, and Alomar is injury-prone. The lefty-swinging Levis could see lots of playing time.

WHO TAKES 'EM, WHO SWINGS AT 'EM, WHO FOULS 'EM OFF?

Have you ever wondered why American League games take longer than National League contests? Most explanations talk about higher scoring and dawdling ballplayers. We have a simpler reason: American League hitters take more pitches, both for balls and called strikes. If American League games seem more passive — and in some opinions, a little more boring — that's the reason. The chart tells the story:

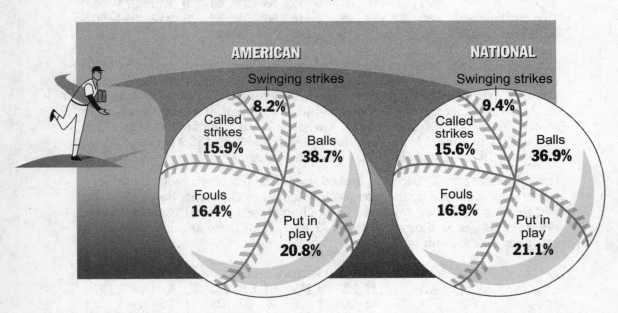

At STATS we know these things because we keep track of every pitch as well as every play. What follows are some slices of that information, to hopefully tell you more about the confrontation between hitters and pitchers than you knew before. For instance, which hitters take the most pitches for balls, and which pitchers miss the strike zone most often? Here they are:

Batters	Ball%	Pitchers	Ball%
Rickey Henderson, Oak	47.1	Greg Cadaret, Yanks	44.8
Frank Thomas, WSox	46.5	Tim Leary, Yanks-Sea	44.2
Lance Blankenship, Oak	45.6	Scott Scudder, Cle	43.4
Mickey Tettleton, Det	45.5	Bobby Witt, Tex-Oak	42.3
Randy Milligan, Bal	45.4	Wilson Alvarez, WSox	41.9

We're **told** they don't swing the bat much in the American League, and here's more proof: the top five hitters and top five pitchers in this category were all in the AL last year. You have to dip down to No. 6 among batters (Barry Bonds, 45.3) and No. 8 among pitchers (Bobby Ojeda, 41.3) to find your first National Leaguer. Thomas and Henderson were first and second in this category a year ago, in the reverse order. Is it time for the AL to adopt a shot clock?

How about the hitters who take the most pitches for strikes?

Batters	Called Strike%	Pitchers	Called Strike%
Mike Bordick, Oak	23.8	Bert Blyleven, Cal	22.2
Lance Blankenship, Oak	23.7	Frank Tanana, Det	19.9
Jody Reed, Bos	22.7	Mark Gardner, Mon	19.7
Wade Boggs, Bos	22.6	Doug Jones, Hou	19.4
Craig Biggio, Hou	22.4	Scott Sanderson, Yanks	19.4

Once again, American League players dominate. The pitchers are finesse types who can cross up a hitter — Tanana has ranked first or second in this category each of the last three years; the hitters are contact-types who aren't afraid to lay off a pitch they don't like. Reed and Boggs have made the top five three straight years. Considering their declining fortunes, maybe they should try swinging the bat a little more.

The opposite group are the hitters who swing and miss most consistently, and the pitchers who dodge the most bats:

Batters	Swinging Strike%	Pitchers	Swinging Strike%
Cory Snyder, SF	17.1	Mel Rojas, Mon	15.6
Cecil Fielder, Det	15.4	David Cone, Mets-Tor	14.3
Gary Gaetti, Cal	15.2	Xavier Hernandez, Hou	13.4
Rob Deer, Det	15.0	Juan Guzman, Tor	13.0
Pedro Munoz, Min	15.0	Duane Ward, Tor	12.9

Repeaters from 1991: Fielder, Gaetti, Deer, Cone, Ward. Most of the hitters are the big-swingers you'd expect, but Gary Gaetti? He neither strikes out much (79 times in 456 at-bats last year) nor hits many homers (12); we guess he swings and misses until he gets to strike two, then shortens his stroke and hits a nice, sensible popup. Rojas' No. 1 among the pitchers marks him as a potential star.

Souvenir kings — these hitters and pitchers produce the most foul balls:

Batters	Fouls%	Pitchers	Fouls%
Joe Carter, Tor	24.1	Sid Fernandez, Mets	22.9
Ivan Rodriguez, Tex	23.9	Pete Harnisch, Hou	21.4
Joe Oliver, Cin	22.3	Mike Mussina, Bal	20.7
Luis Polonia, Cal	22.2	Danny Darwin, Bos	20.6
Andre Dawson, Cubs	21.7	Curt Schilling, Phi	20.3

Joe Carter, idol of a million fans in the stands — numero uno in foul balls in both 1991 and '92, number two in 1990. The theory that fouling 'em off is a veteran's trait is torpedoed by Pudge Rodriguez, 20 years old in 1992. The pitchers on this list are all pretty good (except maybe Darwin), but we confess that we're mystified why Pete Harnisch has made this list three years in a row. The souvenir-hunter's ideal matchup, Carter vs. Harnisch, has been prevented by the fact that they're in separate leagues. (What a great argument on behalf of interleague play.)

Sportswriter's dream — these players and pitchers put the ball in play without messing around, and get you home (or to the bar) fast:

Batters	In Play%	Pitchers	In Play%
Lance Johnson, WSox	29.0	Bob Tewksbury, StL	28.0
Tony Gwynn, SD	28.1	Bill Gullickson, Det	26.7
Gary DiSarcina, Cal	27.5	Zane Smith, Pit	25.8
Don Mattingly, Yanks	26.9	John Doherty, Det	25.7
Joe Orsulak, Bal	26.7	Mark Clark, StL	25.3

You can keep Joe Carter vs. Pete Harnisch; we want Lance Johnson and Co. to take the field against Bob Tewksbury. The hour and a half game returns! Johnson nobly succeeded his fallen teammate, Ozzie Guillen, as the king of "swing the bat and get it over with." A close-knit bunch, those White Sox.

All kidding aside, what's interesting about these lists is how consistent they've been from year to year. Rickey Henderson is always going to take 'em, Cecil Fielder is always going to swing at 'em, Joe Carter is always going to foul 'em off. It's sort of comforting, isn't it?

A complete listing for this category can be found on page 273.

IF HE SOARED TO THE SKIES IN 1992, WILL HE STAY UP THERE IN '93?

At STATS, we feel we can do more than just talk about what happened in the past; we feel we can also make some intelligent speculations about what will happen in the future. In one of our books, the **STATS Major League Handbook**, Bill James and John Dewan put together a list of player projections for the next season. It might sound like pure guesswork, but in fact the system works very well. As Bill discovered years ago, players (hitters, anyway) usually have an established level of performance, and they won't deviate from it very much.

But there are bound to be exceptions. Every year some players improve their averages dramatically from the previous season, while others experience a serious dropoff. Let's see if we can learn anything by looking at the players who had the biggest variations in 1992. First, the biggest gainers:

Batting Average Improved Most

Player, Team	1991	1992	Change
Bernard Gilkey, StL	.216	.302	+ 86
Darren Daulton, Phi	.196	.270	+ 74
Scott Fletcher, Mil	.206	.275	+ 69
Rob Deer, Det	.179	.247	+ 68
Mark McGwire, Oak	.201	.268	+ 67
Omar Vizquel, Sea	.230	.294	+ 64
Mike Bordick, Oak	.238	.300	+ 62
Jerry Browne, Oak	.228	.287	+ 59
Andy Van Slyke, Pit	.265	.324	+ 59
Sammy Sosa, Cubs	.203	.260	+ 57

(Minimum 250 plate appearances each year)

Some of these changes were fairly easy to understand. Bernard Gilkey and Sammy Sosa are highly regarded young players; they matured quickly in 1992, as talented youngsters often do. Scott Fletcher and Jerry Browne had been successful hitters in the past, and a change of scenery helped them return to their former levels. Mark McGwire had struggled for several years, but he's a hard-working player and still fairly young; it was no great shock that he made a strong comeback. Can these players stay at this level in 1993? Chances are that they'll regress somewhat, but it's very unlikely that they'll slip all the way down to their 1991 levels, which were unusually low.

But then there are the others. Andy Van Slyke had never hit higher than .293 in nine previous seasons until 1992; he's 32, and you can almost bet the house that he won't hit close to .324 this year. Omar Vizquel and Mike Bordick had never hit .290 before last year, even in the minors. Yeah, we know all about how they "changed their hitting philosophy," but when a guy who's been around awhile has an unusually good year, it's highly probable that there was some luck involved . . . and very **un**likely that the luck will continue. As for Darren Daulton, he's hit .201, .268, .196 and .270 the last four years; if you want to wager any money on how Daulton will do in 1993, you're probably a graduate of the Pete Rose Investment School. Daulton is one of the few players who never established any reliable level of performance.

The following players had the biggest dropoffs in performance in 1992:

Batting Average Declined Most

Player, Team	1991	1992	Change
Willie Randolph, Mets	.327	.252	−75
Wade Boggs, Bos	.332	.259	−73
Cal Ripken, Bal	.323	.251	−72
Steve Sax, WSox	.304	.236	−68
Bill Pecota, Mets	.286	.227	−59
Chris Sabo, Cin	.301	.244	−57
Rafael Palmeiro, Tex	.322	.268	−54
Bobby Bonilla, Mets	.302	.249	−53
Danny Tartabull, Yanks	.316	.266	−50
Luis Salazar, Cubs	.258	.208	−50

Again, many of these falloffs were fairly predictable. From 1988 to 1991, Danny Tartabull batted .274, .268, .268 and .316; he merely returned to his normal level (.266) last year. Similarly, Cal Ripken had batted .252, .264, .257 and .250 before jumping to .323 in 1991; his return to the .250 level was no great surprise. There was no reason to think aged Willie Randolph would hit anywhere near .327 again, or that Bill Pecota was really a .286 hitter. Chris Sabo's drop to .244 was due in good part to injuries, but his .301 average in 1991 was unusually high for him.

But oh, the others. Wade Boggs down to .259? Almost unthinkable; it's reasonable to expect a big improvement in 1993, even though he'll be 35 this year. Steve Sax, .236? Again, his age (33) is a concern, but Sax should also do much better this year; his track record is too impressive. Rafael Palmeiro, .268? A 40- or 50-point improvement this year wouldn't be unreasonable. As for Bobby Bonilla, we expect improvement, but so does everyone else. It all depends on how he handles New York after a year to adjust.

A complete listing for this category can be found on page 274.

WERE TERRY PENDLETON'S 105 RBI LAST YEAR BETTER THAN CECIL FIELDER'S 124?

Last year Cecil Fielder tied a unique record when he joined Babe Ruth as the only players to lead both leagues in RBI for three straight seasons. Fielder had a total of 124 RBI; meanwhile Terry Pendleton was the National League's runner-up in ribbies with 105. Yet last year, in our estimation, Pendleton was the superior man when it came to bringing home runners. How can that be?

Minimum 200 runners on base in 1992.

THE BEST	RUNNERS ON BASE	DRIVEN IN	PCT.
Kevin Mitchell	277	58	20.9%
Terry Pendleton	415	84	20.2%
Dave Winfield	415	82	19.8%
Carlos Baerga	437	85	19.5%
Andy Van Slyke	386	75	19.4%
THE WORST			
Mark Lemke	298	20	6.7%
Omar Vizquel	266	21	7.9%
Phil Plantier	280	23	8.2%
Walt Weiss	252	21	8.3%
Casey Candaele	204	17	8.3%
ML Average			13.4

Those of you who are familiar with this book already know the answer . . . so don't even bother raising your hands. As for the rest of you, we submit this notion: the RBI is not an equal-opportunity stat. Playing on a team with Tony Phillips and Lou Whitaker at the top of its lineup, Fielder came up with a total of 499 men on base, one of the highest totals in baseball. He drove home 89 of them, or 17.8 percent; that plus his 35 homers, gave him the 124 ribbies. Though he played on a solid Braves team, Pendleton batted with a total of only 415 men on base; he plated 84, or 20.2 percent. Add in his 21 homers, and you get his 105 RBI.

To play one of our favorite games, try reversing the roles. Give Cecil the 415 opportunities Pendleton had, and at his rate of production (17.8 percent), he would had driven home 74 teammates; with the 35 homers, he'd have had 109 RBI. Now give Pendleton Cecil's 499 men on base. Terry's rate of production (20.2 percent) would yield 101 teammates driven home, plus the 21 homers, for 122 RBI.

We perform this exercise not to denigrate Cecil Fielder, who is a tremendous run producer in anyone's book, including this one. Along with everything else, his great home run power gives him an edge, as he drives himself home with a four-bagger more than almost any player in baseball. But Fielder's reign as the RBI king is a credit to the Detroit teammates who get on base for him, as well as to Cecil. Take him off the Tigers, and put him on a team which doesn't put many men on base, and he'd have trouble holding onto his crown. Put Pendleton or Dave Winfield or Ken Griffey Jr. in the middle of the 1990-92 Tiger attack, and they'd probably produce 120-plus RBI, also.

The chart lists the leaders and trailers in teammates driven in per opportunity, and there are a few surprises on it. Kevin Mitchell was considered a miserable failure in Seattle last year, getting into only 99 games and hitting just nine homers. (When you go on the disabled list with strained ribcage muscles produced while vomiting, as Kevin did last year, you've had a few problems.) Yet the record shows that when Mitchell played last year, he was an outstanding run producer. No wonder Cincinnati wanted him.

While Mitchell's appearance on the list is a surprise to some, others are surprises because they're nowhere near the top of the category. As we say, the RBI is dependent on opportunity as well as skill. If you look at the top five players in RBI opportunities for 1992, you'll find two players (Travis Fryman and George Bell) who needed all the opportunities they got. On a per-opportunity basis, their production was less than sensational:

1992 Leaders, RBI Opportunities

Player, Team	TBI	Opp	Pct.	HR	Total RBI
George Bell, WSox	87	557	15.6	25	112
Travis Fryman, Det	76	536	14.2	20	96
Frank Thomas, WSox	91	521	17.5	24	115
Cecil Fielder, Det	89	499	17.8	35	124
Kirby Puckett, Min	91	495	18.4	19	110

(TBI = Teammates Batted In)

A flop with the Cubs in 1991, when he drove home a disappointing 86 runs, Bell was considered a star for the White Sox in '92, when he drove in 112. The truth is that he was basically the same player; the extra RBI were the result of moving from a mediocre offense to one which put a lot of guys on base for him — 168 more, to be exact:

Player, Team	TBI	Opp	Pct.	HR	Total RBI
George Bell, 1991 Cubs	61	389	15.7	25	86
George Bell, 1992 WSox	87	557	15.6	25	112

The trailers list in this category consists mainly of middle infield types, like Mark Lemke and Omar Vizquel. But among the supposed power hitters who had very low RBI rates last year were Phil Plantier (8.2 percent), Chris Hoiles (8.8), Reggie Sanders (9.3), Rob Deer (10.4), Kelly Gruber (10.6), Randy Milligan (11.7), Jack Clark (11.8), Kent Hrbek (11.9), Candy Maldonado (12.0), Glenn Davis (12.0) and Eric Davis (12.0). Some of them were on the trading block over the winter; now you know why.

A complete listing for this category can be found on page 275.

WHATEVER HAPPENED TO THE CLASS OF '87?

It seemed, even then, like a season out of the 1930s. A total of 27 players hit 30 or more homers, 19 of them in the American League. A rookie, Mark McGwire, blasted 49; so did a veteran, Andre Dawson, a guy who'd hit over 30 only once in 10 previous seasons. George Bell hit 47 homers and drove in 134 runs; Eric Davis hit 37 homers, drove in 100, scored 120, and stole 50 bases in 56 attempts. Wade Boggs batted .363 with 24 homers. Wade Boggs, 24 homers? Tim Raines batted .330 with 18 homers. Tim Raines, 18 homers? Larry Sheets hit 31 homers, drove in 94 runs, and batted .316. Larry Sheets?

The year, as you have surely guessed by now, was 1987. The American League averaged 2.3 home runs per game that season, a record, the best year ever for home runs in one league. The National League, the "pitchers' league," averaged 1.9 dingers per contest, its best home run season in 26 years. Everyone claimed the ball wasn't livelier, and maybe it wasn't, but **something** was going on in '87 that didn't happen before, and hasn't happened since.

We bring this up because we want to talk about perceptions: perceptions of players and their careers. Most of us try to look at things in context, but it isn't easy. The 1920s and 1930s produced high batting averages and lots of slugging, and the tendency is to look on players from that era with awe; just scan the Hall of Fame roster. And a few of the players who went crazy in 1987 were able to live off that year for long afterward, creating expectations that could never be fulfilled. Here are a few of them:

Wally Joyner. Wally Joyner is a good first baseman, and a fine fellow. But he is not what he was in 1987 when he had 34 homers, drove in 117 runs, and scored 100 for the Angels. He's had only one really solid year since then, 1991, and even that (21 homers, 96 RBI) couldn't compare with '87. Yet last year the Royals signed Joyner as a free agent, and eagerly gave him a long-term contract in the middle of a nine homer, 66-RBI campaign. They didn't even bother to protect Jeff Conine, a fine first base prospect, in the expansion draft. People remember what Joyner did in '87 the way they remember Eddie Fisher was once married to Liz Taylor. It's almost like he never has to do anything else with his career, apart from being a nice guy.

Matt Nokes. In 1987 Matt Nokes, a rookie, hit 32 homers and drove in 87 runs for the Tigers. He had that nice left-handed pull stroke, and people expected that he'd have a great career. They've probably stopped expecting it now. Nokes has since moved on to the Yankees, and he's taken advantage of the Stadium enough to hit 24 and 22 homers the last two years. But his average was down to .224 last year, and he's considered a terrible defensive catcher. On the other hand, he hit 32 homers once . . .

Mike Pagliarulo. Mike Pagliarulo has only had two good seasons in his career. The best by far was 1987, when he, too, hit 32 homers with 87 RBI for the Yankees. Since then he's totalled 35 homers in five years, and his lifetime average is only .235. Yet he's still around, or at least he was last year. He can't run, he doesn't draw walks, he's a low-average hitter, and he's not a good fielder. But his '87 magic has lived on.

Cory Snyder. A few years ago, the White Sox traded for Cory Snyder, and at the winter banquet Jeff Torborg, who was then the Sox manager, said "We're really excited about getting Cory. You know, he hit 33 homers a few years ago." I (Don) was the one who got up and shouted, "But that was in 1987, you idiot!" Snyder does have some power, with other seasons of 24 and 26 homers, but since '87 his totals have been 26-18-14-3-14. Last year revived his career, but let's face it, he has fewer dingers in the last three seasons (31) than he did in that big '87 campaign. Yet he's still getting mileage out of it, even at the age of 30.

Dale Sveum. In 1987, his first full year, Dale Sveum hit 25 homers and drove in 95 runs for the Brewers. The next year, in September, he broke his leg, and missed the entire 1989 campaign. Since then Sveum has drifted around, and people still say, "Too bad he broke his leg. He would have had a hell of a career." What they forget is that in '88, he had only nine homers and 51 RBI in 467 at-bats **before** the fracture. There's every reason to think the 1987 numbers were a fluke, but Sveum carries them around, and they still look good on his resume. Chances are he'll interest somebody this year, somebody who hopes he can regain a little of "his past form." Right.

There are others we could mention. Brook Jacoby milked his 32-homer campaign in '87 for the next five years (44 homers total); maybe he can hit 32 again, now that he's in the Japanese League. People still remember Kal Daniels' 1987 (26 homers in 368 at-bats, .617 slugging), and it helps them forget a lot of other things. Others think the "real Juan Samuel" is the guy who hit 28 homers with 100 RBI in '87. It's not that these guys didn't have other good years, but they never had anything quite like '87, either. Somehow, a lot of people still think that was the true measure of their ability.

ARE THERE TOO MANY AVERAGE GUYS IN YOUR LINEUP?

Who's an average major league performer these days? Well, if you're an American League catcher, Mr. Average is none other than the World Series MVP, Pat Borders. If you're a National League first baseman, your average guy is the man who scored the winning run in the playoffs, Sid Bream. If you're an AL center fielder, the average performer is the 3,000-hit man and future Hall of Famer, Robin Yount.

And for those of you who read this book regularly and were getting worried, yes, Kevin McReynolds was still the nice, modest, unassuming, average left fielder for the fourth year in a row in 1992 — this time carrying the colors of the American League. You can sleep a little easier now.

As you can probably begin to understand from those examples, the "average performer" is often a surprisingly big name. Here are the average levels of performance at each major league position in 1992, along with the players whose totals came closest to matching the norm. You'll see that some well-known players were just average performers last year:

Average Performance
1992 American League (per 600 PA)

Pos	Avg	OBP	Slg	HR	RBI	Most Typical Performer
C	.244	.310	.369	14	60	Pat Borders
1B	.262	.344	.417	17	75	Tino Martinez
2B	.264	.336	.361	7	54	Scott Fletcher
3B	.263	.328	.385	11	66	Carney Lansford
SS	.254	.313	.335	5	49	Mark Lewis
LF	.269	.340	.401	13	62	Kevin McReynolds
CF	.265	.321	.395	12	65	Robin Yount
RF	.257	.328	.400	15	66	Tom Brunansky
DH	.258	.334	.405	17	73	Harold Baines

Average Performance
1992 National League (per 600 PA)

Pos	Avg	OBP	Slg	HR	RBI	Most Typical Performer
C	.245	.307	.357	10	58	Tom Pagnozzi
1B	.272	.343	.422	14	73	Sid Bream
2B	.259	.326	.361	8	49	Mickey Morandini
3B	.265	.329	.397	14	67	Steve Buechele
SS	.251	.315	.340	6	42	Jay Bell

LF	.257	.320	.400	13	64	Ron Gant
CF	.276	.341	.398	9	51	Sammy Sosa
RF	.261	.324	.399	15	68	Paul O'Neill

Tom Brunansky? Harold Baines? Tom Pagnozzi? Jay Bell? It seems a little strange to think of them as average. In many cases, the performances by the players mentioned was a little above the norm; it's just that no one else came as close. But let's face it, none of them set the world on fire in 1992. Which is not to say they're bad ballplayers. That's the whole point; they're not **bad**, they're average.

What can we learn from this exercise? Well, a few things:

1. The average performance at each position is usually in the .260 range, with moderate power numbers. There's nothing horrible about a right fielder hitting .257 with 15 homers and 66 RBI, which are basically Tom Brunansky numbers (he was, in fact, a little better than that). A lot of clubs don't get that kind of performance, and suffer as a result.

2. Most clubs, though, want a little more than that, and a lot more if they can get it. You won't see many everyday performers with these kind of totals, because clubs will juggle a few players, hoping to get something better if they don't already have it.

3. The players who can stay in the lineup with these kind of figures are usually veterans who have done better than this in the past. In a way, they're still living off their reputations; people don't think of Robin Yount as a .260 hitter, even though that's what he is. In other cases, the players offer potential (Lewis, Martinez), or good defense (Bream, Pagnozzi).

4. For some reason, there are a lot more of these "average performers" — guys who hit .269 with 13 homers — playing full-time in the American League than there are in the National. In the NL, there was no player who really fit the mold of "average center fielder," for instance; Sosa was the best we could find. It's probable that because of the DH rule, American League clubs keep more of these veteran, average-type players around.

So if you have a guy like this in your lineup, you're probably not going to be hurt. But if have too many of them — or if your team makes a big trade to add somebody like Kevin McReynolds to its lineup — you're going to end up with a bad ballclub. Clubs don't need average performers, they need stars.

A complete listing for this category can be found on page 277.

WHO ARE THE "HUMAN AIR CONDITIONERS"?

The Tigers' Cecil Fielder has led both leagues in RBI three straight times, matching a hallowed record held by Babe Ruth. Fielder's probably a little less proud, though hardly apologetic, about another category in which he's led the majors three straight times. In 1990, Fielder swung and missed at 465 pitches, more than any player in baseball. In 1991, he fanned the breeze 438 times, once again setting the pace. In 1992, Cecil seemed to be turning into a veritable contact hitter, as he swung and missed only 400 times. But as the chart shows, that was still 49 more than the No. 2 man, Seattle's Jay Buhner.

Long ago, swinging-and-missing had a stigma to it, as hitters were expected to make contact and hit .300. Ruth started to change that in the 1920s . . . his mighty strikeouts are remembered fondly along with his towering home runs. But everything is relative; Ruth never struck out more than 93 times in a season, and his lifetime batting average was .342. It wasn't until the late 1940s, with Ralph Kiner, that people started accepting the notion that a player could concentrate on hitting home runs, and the heck with hitting .300. Kiner paved the way for hitters like Harmon Killebrew, who batted .243 with 142 strikeouts in 1962 — numbers which were forgotten because of Killebrew's 48 homers and 126 RBI.

So Fielder's swings and misses don't bother people; they're seen as part of the cost of producing his power numbers. On the other hand, Devon White's failure to make contact was considered unacceptable, since White was a leadoff man who was expected to get on base.

One reason Fielder leads in swings-and-misses year after year is that he swings so often: 1,295 times last year, more than anyone in baseball. When we rate hitters on the basis of percentage of swings that missed, we find that Cecil wasn't even in the top five last year:

Highest % of Swings that Missed — 1992

Batter	Swung	Missed	Percent
Archi Cianfrocco, Mon	515	173	33.6
Pete Incaviglia, Hou	753	245	32.5
Jay Buhner, Sea	1,090	351	32.2
Rob Deer, Det	883	284	32.2
Andujar Cedeno, Hou	486	153	31.5
Cecil Fielder, Det	1,295	400	30.9
Brian Jordan, StL	410	124	30.2
Dean Palmer, Tex	1,144	345	30.2
Danny Tartabull, Yanks	915	274	29.9
Cory Snyder, SF	854	253	29.6

(Minimum 400 pitches swung at)

Once again, no one minds the guys like Fielder or Danny Tartabull, who

swing and miss, __and__ produce. But Archi Cianfrocco, Andujar Cedeno and Brian Jordan aren't in that category; they're expected to listen when hitting coaches tell them, "Cut down on your swing!" Of course, sometimes they never do, and their careers stagnate. Remember when people thought that Pete Incaviglia and Cory Snyder would develop into superstars?

There's another group of players which is far different from this last one. We're talking about the guys who drink their milk, help old ladies across the street, get eight hours of sleep . . . and hit almost everything they swing at. Wade Boggs and Tony Gwynn at the top of this list is no surprise.

Lowest % of Swings that Missed — 1992

Batter	Swung	Missed	Percent
Wade Boggs, Bos	820	34	4.1
Tony Gwynn, SD	812	53	6.5
Lance Johnson, WSox	922	66	7.2
Doug Dascenzo, Cubs	619	45	7.3
Jody Reed, Bos	807	61	7.6
Omar Vizquel, Sea	941	74	7.9
Harold Reynolds, Sea	747	60	8.0
Gregg Jefferies, KC	933	75	8.0
Tim Raines, WSox	944	81	8.6
Brett Butler, LA	1,072	95	8.9

(Minimum 400 pitches swung at)

Singles-hitters galore; about the only exception would be Gregg Jefferies, who has a little power, with 49 extra-base hits last year. Boggs is remarkably consistent, swinging and missing only about five percent of the time year after year. With his average down to .259 last year, do you think Wade might swing from the heels a little more in 1993? Somehow we doubt it.

A complete listing for this category can be found on page 278.

WHO GETS THOSE CRUCIAL GO-AHEAD RBI?

The RBI is one of baseball's glamour stats, but some RBI are simply more important than others. That's why we keep track of the "go-ahead RBI" — a run driven in which gives a player's club the lead. That's obviously a crucial step toward victory, because it forces the other team to come from behind if they're going to win.

Here are the 1992 leaders in go-ahead RBI:

1992 Go-Ahead RBI Leaders

Player, Team	Go Ahead RBI
Carlos Baerga, Cle	42
Frank Thomas, WSox	39
Terry Pendleton, Atl	35
Juan Gonzalez, Tex	33
Andy Van Slyke, Pit	33
Gary Sheffield, SD	32
Albert Belle, Cle	31
Larry Walker, Mon	30
Ryne Sandberg, Cubs	29
Jeff Bagwell, Hou	28
Ray Lankford, StL	28
Paul Molitor, Mil	28
Kirby Puckett, Min	28

Only 24 years old, Carlos Baerga of the Indians is one of baseball's rising young stars, and this stat underscores his ability to hit in the clutch. His total of 42 go-ahead RBI is quite impressive; in the four years we've been keeping this stat, only one player has come close to it — Pedro Guerrero of the 1989 Cardinals, with 40. It was just one more impressive clutch-hitting number for Baerga, who hit .308 with runners in scoring position last year, and .317 in the late innings of close games.

The rest of the leaders list has a lot of familiar names, but you might be wondering about a couple of names that are missing. Three-time major league RBI leader Cecil Fielder just missed the top 10, with 27, and he's always done pretty well in this category. But National League MVP Barry Bonds was well off the pace last year, with only 19 go-ahead RBI. In the four years we've kept track of this stat, Bonds has never been anywhere near the top 10: his go-ahead RBI totals have been 8, 18, 23 and 19, all very mediocre. Bonds is obviously a tremendous player, but his consistent inability to come through with the important RBI is right there in the figures. Couple that with his consistent post-season failures, and throw in his mediocre .263 average in the late innings of close games over the last five years, and you don't exactly get a picture of "Mr. Clutch."

A purer way of looking at this stat is to put it on a percentage basis, which helps eliminate the bias created by the fact that some players have more RBI opportunities than others. Since you can get only one go-ahead RBI per plate appearance even if you hit a grand-slam home run, we compare the player's appearances in which he had a go-ahead RBI with his total plate appearances in which he drove in one or more runs. Here are the 1992 leaders (minimum 50 or more total RBI):

1992 Leaders — Go-Ahead RBI Percentage

Player, Team	Go Ahead RBI	PA with 1+ RBI	Percent
Carlos Baerga, Cle	42	87	48.3
Gary Sheffield, SD	32	69	46.4
Cory Snyder, SF	20	45	44.4
Ryne Sandberg, Cubs	29	66	43.9
Terry Pendleton, Atl	35	82	42.7
Ray Lankford, StL	28	66	42.4
John Kruk, Phi	25	60	41.7
Eddie Murray, Mets	26	63	41.3
Andy Van Slyke, Pit	33	80	41.3
Frank Thomas, WSox	39	97	40.2

Baerga leads again, but some new names appear: Cory Snyder, John Kruk, Eddie Murray. Bonds, at 25.7 percent, was once again far down the list.

Some players hardly ever drove in the lead run last year. Here are the trailers in go-ahead RBI percentage:

1992 Trailers — Go-Ahead RBI Percentage

Player, Team	Go Ahead RBI	PA with 1+ RBI	Percent
Darryl Hamilton, Mil	5	52	9.6
Tim Wallach, Mon	7	51	13.7
Candy Maldonado, Tor	8	54	14.8
Dean Palmer, Tex	8	53	15.1
Lou Whitaker, Det	8	53	15.1

Hamilton, who hits at the top of the order, can probably be excused, but Tim Wallach and Candy Maldonado? No wonder they'll be modeling new uniforms in 1993.

A complete listing for this category can be found on page 280.

WHO GETS RUNG UP?

One night last summer in the Comiskey Park pressbox, Bill Brown, the Detroit Tigers' traveling secretary, had a question for the STATS man: Which players get called out on strikes most often? We looked it up, and were happy to inform Bill that the major league leader was none other than The Lord of Looking, Mickey Tettleton, of his very own Tigers. You could see Bill's chest swell with pride.

Tettleton would go on to claim the called strikeout trophy — perhaps we should call it "The Mickey" — but it wasn't easy, not with guys like Jose Canseco, Mark McGwire and Jose Offerman on the lookout. There must have been a lot of bats on shoulders during those furious final days, but at the wire it was Mickey by two lengths:

Most Called Strikeouts — 1992

Player, Team	Called K's
Mickey Tettleton, Det	42
Jose Canseco, Oak-Tex	40
Mark McGwire, Oak	40
Jose Offerman, LA	40
Pat Listach, Mil	39
Jack Clark, Bos	38
Albert Belle, Cle	37
Fred McGriff, SD	37
Paul O'Neill, Cin	37
Tom Brunansky, Bos	35
Mark Whiten, Cle	35
Frank Thomas, WSox	35

What kind of players get called out on strikes a lot? Not surprisingly, there are lots of guys like Tettleton, Clark and Thomas who take a lot of borderline pitches and get numerous walks along with the called K's. However, not everyone fits that profile — Offerman drew only 57 walks last year, Listach 55, Belle 52. These are young players without good strike zone judgement; one would expect their called strikeout totals to go down and their walk totals (hopefully) to go up as they mature.

****

Another way to determine the called strikeout kings is on a percentage basis. Let's look at the players who fanned 50 or more times last year. Which ones have the greatest percentage of called (to total) strikeouts?

Highest % of Strikeouts Looking — 50 or more Total K's

Player, Team	Total K's	Called K's	Pct
Lance Blankenship, Oak	57	34	59.6
Kenny Lofton, Cle	54	30	55.6
Scott Leius, Min	61	33	54.1
Alex Cole, Cle-Pit	67	33	49.3
Chris Hoiles, Bal	60	27	45.0
Cal Ripken, Bal	50	22	44.0
Jack Clark, Bos	87	38	43.7
Paul O'Neill, Cin	85	37	43.5
Rickey Henderson, Oak	56	24	42.9
Kal Daniels, LA-Cubs	54	23	42.6

Blankenship, who's an extraordinarily patient hitter, had only 23 swinging strikeouts last year, but 34 called ones. That's an extraordinary ratio (59.6%), more than twice as high as the major league average of 26.8 percent. The only prolific strikeout man on the list is Jack Clark; the others offer a range of talents, from leadoff men (Lofton, Cole, Henderson) to middle-of-the-order types (Ripken, Hoiles, O'Neill). Tettleton was way down the list at 30.7 percent, but he's still the champ in our book.

On the other hand, there's the Joe Carter School of Hitting — if I've got two strikes, I'm swinging! Carter fanned 109 times last year, only six of them called. No one else had a ratio close to that:

Lowest % of Strikeouts Looking — 50 or more Total K's

Player, Team	Total K's	Called K's	Pct
Joe Carter, Tor	109	6	5.5
Mark Carreon, Det	57	5	8.8
Chris Sabo, Cin	54	5	9.3
Phil Plantier, Bos	83	8	9.6
Archi Cianfrocco, Mon	66	7	10.6

Question for Bill Brown: What do Mickey Tettleton and Mark Carreon talk about when they discuss hitting?

A complete listing for this category can be found on page 281.

IS FRANK THOMAS UNDERRATED?

THE RUN MAKERS

AMERICAN	RUNS CREATED
Frank Thomas	142
Brady Anderson	118
Paul Molitor	116

NATIONAL	
Barry Bonds	148
Andy Van Slyke	122
Gary Sheffield	118

Runs Created is a number invented by Bill James to estimate each player's contribution to his club's offense. The formula is complex, but it takes into account hits, extra-base hits, walks, stolen bases, caught stealings — virtually everything a player does offensively, both good and bad. The number works out much like runs scored and RBI; the best players will create more than 100 runs in a season. Sometimes many more: according to **Total Baseball**, Babe Ruth created 238 runs in 1921, the top season of all time.

No 1992 player reached such Ruthian levels, but Barry Bonds and Frank Thomas had nothing to be ashamed of. Bonds and Thomas led their respective leagues in runs created; each created more than 140, and each was well ahead of the competition in his league:

1992 Leaders — Runs Created

Player, Team	Runs Created
Barry Bonds, Pit	148
Frank Thomas, WSox	142
Andy Van Slyke, Pit	122
Gary Sheffield, SD	118
Brady Anderson, Bal	118
Ryne Sandberg, Cubs	117
Paul Molitor, Mil	116
Fred McGriff, SD	116
Edgar Martinez, Sea	116
Shane Mack, Min	114
Kirby Puckett, Min	114

For Bonds, it was his third straight runs created crown; for Thomas, his second. How do Bonds and Thomas create so many runs? Each can hit for both power and average; each draws well over 100 walks a year; and Bonds has a bonus, the ability to steal a lot of bases. No other players can match their breadth of offensive skills — Gary Sheffield, who's close, doesn't draw enough walks to match their ability to get on base.

Frank Thomas knows all this, and that's why he's turning into something of a grump. Over the past three years, Bonds has finished first, second and first in the National League Most Valuable Player voting. Thomas, though, hasn't won such recognition. In 1991, his first full season, he finished third behind Cal Ripken and Cecil Fielder in the voting, but last year he slipped all the way to eighth. "Seven other players didn't have a better year than me," says Thomas, and we have to agree (even though we've watched him play first base). One of Thomas' major skills — that extraordinary ability to get on base via the walk — continues to be underrated (some fools even consider it a negative). The runs created formula gives Thomas the full credit he deserves.

A variation on runs created is the "offensive winning percentage." This is a James estimate of what kind of winning percentage a team of Barry Bondses (or whoever) would have compiled against a team of average opponents. In 1992, the Bonds team would have had an extraordinary winning percentage of .896:

1992 Leaders
Offensive Winning Percentage

Player, Team	Win %
Barry Bonds, Pit	.896
Frank Thomas, WSox	.815
Darren Daulton, Phi	.806
Gary Sheffield, SD	.804
Fred McGriff, SD	.801
John Kruk, Phi	.793
Andy Van Slyke, Pit	.792
Edgar Martinez, Sea	.791
Mark McGwire, Oak	.781
Rickey Henderson, Oak	.781

(Minimum 250 Plate Appearances)

In the four years we've been keeping track of this number, Bonds' .896 winning percentage has been the highest, by far; Rickey Henderson had an .869 percentage in 1990 for the next-best figure. We're not saying Barry's worth all that money, but if he isn't, no one is.

Frightening thought: how would a team of Barry Bondses fare against a team of Rafael Belliards? The Braves' shortstop may have a nifty glove, but his .196 winning percentage marks him as the weakest offensive player of 1992:

1992 Trailers
Offensive Winning Percentage

Player, Team	Win %
Rafael Belliard, Atl	.196
Luis Salazar, Cubs	.216
Hubie Brooks, Cal	.230
Walt Weiss, Oak	.251
Luis Rivera, Bos	.257

Belliard and Weiss, at least, can handle a glove. What was Hubie Brooks' excuse last year?

A complete listing for this category can be found on page 283.

SHOULD THEY BE LEAVING THOSE "FLYBALL HITTERS" ALONE?

Back when we were growing up in the fifties, there was a Wheaties commercial that featured Hall of Famer Bill Dickey and a wide-eyed Little Leaguer. Dickey offered two bits of advice to his young protege:

1. Eat at least six boxes of Wheaties per day (well, maybe it was two bowlfuls).

2. Swing level. Or, as Dickey put it in his Louisiana twang, "Sweeeng leah-vull."

We're sure that, as children, Mark McGwire and Willie McGee had nourishing breakfasts every morning. But when it came to developing their hitting strokes, these two had their own ideas . . . and they were as far from "swinging level" as they could get. As veteran readers of this book well know, McGee and McGwire represent the polar extremes when it comes to hitting styles. Singles hitter McGee chops down on the ball and hits so many grounders that, in his home town of San Francisco, the worm might become an endangered species. Across the bay in Oakland, slugger McGwire has stuck with his extreme uppercut swing, one which produces a groundball about as often as McGee hits a home run. (Well maybe a **little** more often.)

Here are two of our favorite leader boards. One, the "groundball hitters" list, is dominated by singles hitters with good batting averages. The other, the "flyball hitters" list, is dominated by players who can hit the long ball. The lists are led, appropriately enough, by the two Macs:

Groundball Hitters: Highest Groundball/Flyball Ratio — 1992

Player, Team	GB	FB	Ratio	HR	Avg
Willie McGee, SF	242	67	3.61	1	.297
Otis Nixon, Atl	215	72	2.99	2	.294
Steve Sax, WSox	312	118	2.64	4	.236
Luis Polonia, Cal	261	104	2.51	0	.286
Ozzie Smith, StL	273	109	2.50	0	.295
John Kruk, Phi	224	92	2.43	10	.323
Brett Butler, LA	230	98	2.35	3	.309
Bip Roberts, Cin	254	110	2.31	4	.323
Lance Johnson, WSox	293	128	2.29	3	.279
Shane Mack, Min	272	119	2.29	16	.315

Flyball Hitters: Lowest Groundball/Flyball Ratio — 1992

Player, Team	GB	FB	Ratio	HR	Avg
Mark McGwire, Oak	84	214	0.39	42	.268
Joe Carter, Tor	146	266	0.55	34	.264
Leo Gomez, Bal	116	188	0.58	17	.265
Mickey Tettleton, Bal	128	184	0.70	32	.238
Dean Palmer, Tex	127	173	0.73	26	.229
Barry Bonds, Pit	139	189	0.74	34	.311
George Bell, WSox	177	249	0.74	25	.255
Greg Vaughn, Mil	127	172	0.74	23	.228
Lou Whitaker, Det	130	174	0.75	19	.278
Darren Daulton, Phi	132	172	0.77	27	.270

For McGee, 1992 represented the norm: a .298 lifetime hitter, he batted .297. But for McGwire, 1992 offered redemption. We were not the only ones who thought that McGwire's uppercut stroke might be partially to blame for his decline after his 49-homer rookie season in 1987. As we pointed out a year ago, he was hitting more and more flyballs, but finding less and less success. But though he tinkered with his stance last year, McGwire didn't change his basic stroke at all — his groundball ratio was lower than ever. Yet his batting average and home runs both jumped:

Mark McGwire	Avg	HR	G/F
1987	.289	49	0.67
1988	.260	32	0.60
1989	.231	33	0.65
1990	.235	39	0.54
1991	.201	22	0.55
1992	.268	42	0.39

McGwire's best season, 1987, was the year in which his groundball ratio was highest; but his next-best year, 1992, was the one in which his ratio was lowest. McGwire's 1989-91 problems were apparently not the result of hitting "too many flyballs."

Another interesting name on the flyball list is two-time National League MVP Barry Bonds. Blessed with outstanding speed, Bonds must have been told to "level out" his swing at points during his career, in order to enable him to beat out more groundball hits. If that's the advice he got, it did anything but help him. The best seasons of Bonds' career have been the ones in which he hit the **fewest** groundballs; when his groundball ratio was up, his batting average went down:

Barry Bonds	Avg	HR	G/F
1987	.261	25	1.13
1988	.283	24	0.83
1989	.248	19	1.03
1990	.301	33	0.83
1991	.292	25	0.87
1992	.311	34	0.74

McGwire and Bonds, of course, have had great seasons in their careers. And nobody's going to question the hitting styles of Joe Carter, George Bell, and Lou Whitaker — they've got the numbers in their corner. But some of the others, particularly Dean Palmer and Greg Vaughn, haven't found consistent success yet. Last year both hit in the .220s, and their home run totals weren't quite high enough to deflect the criticism. Would they hit for a higher average — and still maintain decent home run totals — if they abandoned those uppercut swings? It's tempting to say yes. But hitting is complicated; as the leaders list shows, there are a lot of very successful hitters with exactly the same sort of strokes. (Palmer and Vaughn could always try eating more Wheaties.)

How about the other type of hitters, the groundballers? We often hear that so-and-so stubbornly "refuses to hit the ball on the ground to take advantage of his speed"; this axiom is repeated about almost every fast guy with a low batting average, including players like Gary Pettis, who already **are** groundball hitters. The usual example cited is Matty Alou: he learned to hit the ball on the ground, people say, and became a batting champion.

But is this really true? As Bill James pointed out, Alou had some pretty good years in the majors before he supposedly learned how to hit. Other examples of these "success stories" are just as hard to pin down. The latest is Otis Nixon, who's finally found success in Atlanta after years as a .220 hitter.

Did Nixon raise his average simply by "becoming a groundball hitter"? Not really. Nixon had a pretty high groundball-to-flyball ratio even in 1988: his ratio that year was 1.85, his batting average .244. You could argue that Nixon found success the last two years by becoming **more** of groundball hitter, pushing his ratio over two. Of course, there were other factors involved in his success, not the least of which is that he finally got a chance to play regularly. But even if you credit Nixon's success to hitting more groundballs, you have to note that he had the basics of a groundball hitter all along. It's a lot easier to improve a hitter like that, than to re-make a flyball hitter with speed (Gary Redus, maybe?) into a totally different type of hitter.

A complete listing for this category can be found on page 284.

CAN YOU LEARN TO HIT LEFTIES?

Our colleague Rob Neyer has contributed several of the ideas in this book, and he suggested this one. We'll let Rob speak for himself: "During the ESPN game on August 23, Bob McClure came in to pitch, and he struck out Deion Sanders on four pitches, Sanders looking terrible in the process. In defense of Sanders, Joe Morgan said that if a left-handed hitter doesn't face lefties very often, it's that much harder, because the more you face them, the easier it gets." Rob rather colorfully expressed his own doubts about Morgan's theory, but the idea intrigued us as much as it did him.

So let's look at some left-handed hitters. What we wanted to do was measure progress: how did the hitter do in his first 200 plate appearances against left-handed pitchers, and then how did he perform (in a minimum of 200 appearances) afterwards? As it turned out, it was pretty difficult to find lefty hitters who met the minimum qualifications, which were 400 career plate appearances vs. lefties who began their careers in the last six years. Most hitters are righties to begin with, and most of the lefties in the majors seldom get to play against lefthanders. Even the ones who play full-time need more than two seasons to get 400 appearances against lefthanders.

So the lefties we did find, going back to 1987, are a group of pretty good hitters. Nonetheless, here is how this group of 11 performed in their first 200 plate appearances against lefties, and then thereafter, with the figures scaled down to 200 appearances so that we can compare them:

Lefties vs. Lefties — 1987-92

Player	1st 200 Plate Appearences						Thereafter per 200 PA					
	AB	H	HR	Avg	OBA	Slg	AB	H	HR	Avg	OBA	Slg
Brady Anderson	168	29	1	.173	.282	.250	159	32	3	.201	.325	.314
Delino DeShields	173	48	2	.277	.367	.393	170	44	2	.259	.355	.324
Steve Finley	182	34	2	.187	.224	.253	179	49	1	.274	.320	.346
Mark Grace	174	47	4	.270	.360	.414	179	51	2	.285	.343	.380
Ken Griffey Jr.	186	49	6	.263	.310	.419	178	57	7	.320	.385	.500
Lance Johnson	183	47	0	.257	.299	.317	187	51	0	.273	.312	.310
David Justice	181	61	11	.337	.395	.569	177	49	7	.277	.347	.458
Ray Lankford	183	46	0	.251	.303	.344	175	44	2	.251	.333	.383
B.J. Surhoff	182	41	4	.225	.268	.324	176	51	2	.290	.333	.381
Robin Ventura	170	39	0	.229	.325	.253	168	43	3	.256	.355	.357
Larry Walker	182	40	8	.220	.283	.401	185	58	7	.314	.358	.481
Average	179	44	3	.246	.310	.358	176	48	3	.273	.343	.375

The figures indicate that some hitters, indeed, can learn to hit lefties. The group as a whole increased its average by 27 points, and eight of the 11 players raised their averages after their first 200 appearances; one, Ray Lankford, stayed the same. That's impressive.

But the figures are a little less than what they seem. In the first place, this is an elite group of hitters; you'd expect Robin Ventura and Larry Walker to show some improvement once they'd learned their way around the league, and they did. But then there's the nature of the improvement.

The home run rate for these players against lefties stayed the same, even with more experience. Their rate of extra-base hits, expressed in terms of "isolated power" — slugging average minus on-base average — was actually slightly worse (112 points before, 102 points after). The increase in on-base percentage was primarily due to the rise in batting average. So basically, the improvement was due to hitting more singles: a useful gain, to be sure, but it's not like they suddenly learned to terrorize southpaws with the longball.

Look at one of the hitters in the study, David Justice of the Braves. All throughout the playoffs and World Series, Sean McDonough and Tim McCarver told us about 300 times that Justice "hits lefties better than he hits righties." It was like they had just discovered nuclear fission or something. It's true that Justice hits lefties better — if batting average is the only figure you're considering. But look at Justice's entire 1992 batting line:

David Justice, 1992	AB	H	2B	3B	HR	RBI	BB	SO	Avg	OBP	Slg
Vs. Lefties	159	45	9	1	5	17	16	28	.283	.352	.447
Vs. Righties	325	79	10	4	16	55	63	57	.243	.362	.446

Yes, he hit .283 vs. lefties, .243 vs. righties. But despite the 40-point head-start, his on-base and slugging averages were virtually identical. And in a little more than twice as many at-bats against righties, he had more than three times as many homers and RBI, and four times as many walks. If you still think he "hits better against lefties," close this book immediately. We can't help you.

So when you ask, "Can you learn to hit lefties?", the answer is yes. But, for the most part, you're learning to hit more singles.

A complete listing for this category can be found on page 286.

WHO GETS THE "SLIDIN' BILLY" TROPHY FOR LEADOFF MEN?

Last year, after careful consideration, we chose Paul Molitor as the best leadoff hitter in baseball for 1991 — the first winner of our "Slidin' Billy Hamilton Trophy." The Milwaukee Brewers were so impressed by the award that they moved Molitor out of the leadoff spot before the season was two months old. And went on to challenge for the pennant. But, hey, what do **they** know?

Now it's awards time once again. We traditionally rank leadoff hitters according to their on-base percentage when batting first, although other factors are obviously important. Here are the top 10 for 1992:

Player, Team	OBP	AB	R	H	BB	SB
Rickey Henderson, Oak	.426	392	77	111	94	47
Brian Downing, Tex	.414	202	41	59	37	0
Bip Roberts, Cin	.396	505	85	164	60	44
Paul Molitor, Mil	.383	133	18	42	17	9
Craig Biggio, Hou	.378	602	94	166	93	37
Chuck Knoblauch, Min	.377	264	42	79	34	12
Tony Phillips, Det	.377	550	103	152	92	10
Gregg Jefferies, KC	.377	145	17	45	15	6
Lenny Dykstra, Phi	.375	345	53	104	40	30
Ray Lankford, StL	.375	236	36	68	30	19

(Minimum 150 plate appearances while batting leadoff)

And now, the candidates for the Hamilton trophy, which is named for the legendary 19th-century great who had more runs scored than games played during his career:

Rickey Henderson — the leadoff man's leadoff man. Led in leadoff on-base percentage (.426) and showed his powerful bat by also leading in slugging (.459). Despite playing in only 117 games, he was second in walks (94), fourth in stolen bases (47) and third in home runs (15). A runaway pick, if he hadn't missed so much time.

Bip Roberts — strong in almost every category. Led in batting average (.325), was third in OBP (.396). With 34 doubles, five triples and 44 stolen bases, he put himself in scoring position more often than anyone else except Brady Anderson. A strong candidate.

Tony Phillips — led in runs scored (103), was fourth in walks (92) and strong in almost every category except one: stolen bases (10). That hurts his chances, but he has to be considered.

Brady Anderson — just missed the top 10 in OBP (.374), but was among the leaders in every important category. He has unusual power for the role, leading with 21 homers and 80 RBI, a total which was among the most ever amassed by a leadoff man. But he still did his primary job, ranking first in walks (98) and second in both runs scored (100) and stolen bases (53). He was on base 267 times via hits and walks, more than anyone else.

Time for the envelope. The choice comes down to Henderson and Anderson. It's a weird parallel to last year, with Henderson dominating on a per-game basis, but losing strength because of all the missed time. While Anderson ranked 11th in OBP, he was only nine points out of fourth. With his broad range of strengths and season-long health, he gets the nod. The winner of the second annual Slidin' Billy Hamilton Trophy is Brady Anderson. (Well, we **had** a trophy, but someone stole it. Probably not Tony Phillips.)

So much for the best. Who were the worst leadoff men in 1992? Here they are:

Player, Team	OBP	AB	R	H	BB	SB
Jose Vizcaino, Cubs	.233	166	12	34	6	1
Billy Hatcher, Cin-Bos	.250	207	24	43	10	3
Doug Dascenzo, Cubs	.285	179	21	47	6	2
Gary Redus, Pit	.287	157	17	38	10	9
Darren Lewis, SF	.287	255	28	56	25	21
Steve Sax, WSox	.289	234	34	58	14	13
Jody Reed, Bos	.294	191	27	45	17	3
Devon White, Tor	.304	640	98	159	47	37
Harold Reynolds, Sea	.307	136	16	31	16	6
Stan Javier, LA-Phi	.314	167	25	38	21	9

Isn't it strange how, even in this sophisticated age, some clubs still don't seem to realize that a leadoff hitter has to get on base? The Cubs went into last season with Shawon Dunston and Sammy Sosa, two legendary free swingers, as their leadoff choices. When both got injured, they were left with the likes of Jose Vizcaino and Doug Dascenzo. As a result, their leadoff men scored just 79 runs; only the Red Sox, with 78, were worse.

Using his great speed and baserunning ability, Devon White scored 98 runs last year despite his low on-base percentage. The Blue Jays weren't satisfied, however; they went out and signed Molitor. Will the former Slidin' Billy winner return to his old No. 1 spot this year? That's what we would do (not that anyone listens to our advice).

A complete listing for this category can be found on page 287.

WILL JOSE LIGHT UP THE ARLINGTON SKY?

During all the years that Jose Canseco played for Oakland (where it was always win, win, win), he continually complained about the Coliseum's deep home run alleys. He was being robbed of numerous home runs, he'd say; put him in a good home run yard, and he might just hit 50 or more. Now Canseco's moved on to Texas, and the expectations are that he'll hit a lot more homers. But will he? Let's examine the evidence:

1. Jose at Oakland. There's no question, that in his days with the Athletics, Canseco hit more home runs on the road (127) than he did in the Coliseum (104). However, those numbers look a lot more compelling than they really were. In all but two of his Athletic seasons, Canseco's home runs were fairly evenly split between home and road:

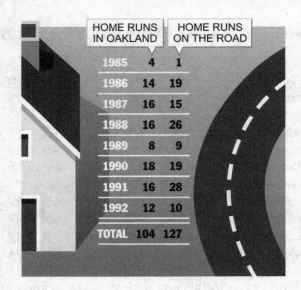

	HOME RUNS IN OAKLAND	HOME RUNS ON THE ROAD
1985	4	1
1986	14	19
1987	16	15
1988	16	26
1989	8	9
1990	18	19
1991	16	28
1992	12	10
TOTAL	104	127

Except for 1988 and 1991, he hit 72 home runs in the Coliseum, 73 on the road. What happened in those other two years was that he went crazy on the road; his home performance stayed about the same. We won't try to figure that out; we'll just point out that the numbers don't show him being heavily penalized by the home park, year after year. For his career, Canseco averaged a home run every 16.3 at-bats when he was playing in the Coliseum, a very good rate.

2. Jose at Arlington. Canseco has now had 202 career at-bats in his new park, Arlington Stadium: not a lot, but enough to give us a sample as to how he'll perform there. In those 202 at-bats, he's hit 14 home runs, or one every 14.4 at-bats. That's a better rate than he had at Oakland, but not that much better. If he gets 275 at bats in Arlington this year (an optimistic projection, considering his frequent injuries), he'd hit 19 homers. His Oakland rate for 275 at-bats would be 17 homers. So, judging by past performance, we don't appear to be in for an all-out assault on Roger Maris' record.

3. Comparing the park factors. We keep a park index for every major league stadium (see essay on page 81), and there's no doubt that Oakland is a tougher home run park than Texas is. The index compares performance by the club and its opponents in the home park vs. how they did in the club's road games. An index of 100 indicates a neutral park; below 100 means it penalizes the hitter, above 100 means it helps the hitter. According to that system, the Coliseum has had a park index of 92 for home runs over the last three seasons, meaning that a hitter playing there would be expected to hit about eight percent fewer homers than normal. The Arlington index for 1990-92 was 101, meaning that a Texas hitter got about a one percent benefit.

However, that's for **all** hitters. We like to break down the park factors so that it shows how it affects right- and left-handed batters. It turns out that Oakland penalizes lefty hitters, Arlington helps them. When it comes to righty swingers like Canseco, Arlington is actually a little tougher than the Coliseum is:

Comparing Oakland and Arlington, 1990-92

	Home Games	Road Games	Park Index
Oakland Coliseum for RHB	310 HR	330 HR	98
Arlington Stadium for RHB	254 HR	270 HR	94

Is Canseco the kind of righty slugger who goes to the opposite field frequently, and thus can take advantage of Arlington's friendly right field breezes? Not really. Since 1988, Canseco has homered to right field only 13 percent of the time, just slightly more than the average hitter (10 percent).

So will Jose light up the Arlington sky? Maybe he will; maybe he'll be healthy, motivated, and have himself a stellar year. But if he's going to do it, he'll have to do it all on his own; his new park offers him no real benefit.

A complete listing for this category can be found on page 288.

CAN YOU HIT SACRIFICE FLIES ON PURPOSE?

An excerpt from "Cactus," the opening article of Bill James' **The Baseball Book 1990**: "Stepping into the cage, McGwire says aloud 'Runner on third, one out,' then drives the first pitch to deep right-center, nodding in satisfaction as the imaginary runner trots home. (In the ninth inning of the game that very day, McGwire came to the plate with the A's one run behind, runners on first and third and one out. He drove the first pitch on the exact trajectory that he had hit the pitch in practice, not as far but far enough to send the game into extra innings.)"

That sounds so ideal; you practice hitting a sacrifice fly, and then you do it. But is it really so easy? Can a hitter really hit a flyball when the situation demands, any more than he would otherwise?

We took a look at the sacrifice fly leaders from last season, as well as all hitters in baseball for the last five years, to find out how easy it really is to hit a medium-to-long flyball when the situation demands. We deemed a "sacrifice fly situation" to be one in which there is a runner at third (regardless of other baserunners), less than two outs, and the batter's team ahead or behind by no more than two runs. There are other situations in which he might be trying for a sac fly, and he might not always be trying to do so under these circumstances. But for the most part, this is the time when he'd be trying to bring the runner home with a fly.

Okay, then. First we'll determine the number of opportunities by adding up the hitter's at-bats under sac fly situations to his number of actual sacrifice flies in those situations; that's the number of times he would be trying to hit a sacrifice fly. Then we'll count how many times he hit a flyball or liner more than 290 feet, which is far enough to guarantee bringing the runner home in almost every case. Then we'll compare his percentage when he was trying to hit a sac fly to his percentage of 290-plus foot flyballs or liners in all other situations, when they wouldn't be the result of design. Here's how the major league leaders in sacrifice flies fared under those circumstances:

Batter, Team	Sac Fly Situations			All Other Situations		
	AB + SF	F/L > 290	Pct	AB + SF	F/L > 290	Pct
Joe Carter, Tor	32	10	31.3	603	126	20.9
Jeff Bagwell, Hou	41	11	26.8	558	144	25.8
Robin Yount, Mil	25	7	28.0	544	115	21.1
Chuck Knoblauch, Min	21	2	9.5	591	92	15.6
Paul Molitor, Mil	39	9	23.1	581	115	19.8
Will Clark, SF	27	4	14.8	497	124	24.9

Frank Thomas, WSox	37	8	21.6	547	143	26.1
Brian Harper, Min	27	8	29.6	485	86	17.7
Ruben Sierra, Tex-Oak	18	6	33.3	593	130	21.9
B.J. Surhoff, Mil	22	6	27.3	468	95	20.3
Total	289	71	24.6	5,467	1,170	21.4

Upon examination, it seems anything but easy to hit a 300-foot flyball just because you want to. Even the player with the highest success rate, Ruben Sierra, could only do it one-third of the time. Some players **seem** more adept at this than others: Carter, Yount, Harper, Sierra and Surhoff all produced the medium-to-long fly at least five percent more often when they were trying to do so than when it didn't matter. But with the others the difference was either negligible, or they hit more flyballs when they **weren't** trying. Overall, the hitters produced flies when they needed to only three percent of the time more often than when they didn't — a difference too small to be considered the result of skill. And these are the best sac fly producers, the cream of the crop.

Now let's look at all hitters, under the same ground rules, over the past five years:

Sac Fly Situations			All Other Situations		
AB+SF	F/L>290	Pct	AB+SF	F/L>290	Pct
26,857	4,725	17.6	693,472	122,783	17.7

As you can see, players don't hit a medium-to-long fly when they're trying to do so any more often than when they're not. The rate of medium-to-long flies is lower than that of the top sacrifice fly man, however. The main advantage for the sac fly leaders is not that they can hit more 300-foot flies when they want to; it's that they hit more 300-foot flies, period.

And how did that future sacrifice-fly-hitting coach, Mark McGwire, fare? Last year McGwire hit only five long flies in 19 sac fly situations (26.3 percent) and had one extra SF which wasn't hit that far. In other situations, he hit long flies 28.2 percent of the time. So it appears conclusive that hitters cannot hit sacrifice flies on purpose — even if they practice in the batting cage.

WHICH TEAMS GET THROWN OUT NEEDLESSLY ADVANCING ON A THROW?

We've all seen this happen a million times . . . or at least, too many times. The home team has a runner on second, and the batter lines a single to the outfield. It looks like the runner can beat the throw easily, but just to make sure, the batter rounds first and heads for second. The defensive team cuts the ball off, fires to second and gets an easy out. Sure the run scored, but your team may have just cost itself the chance for a big inning. Dumb, isn't it?

Well, yes, it's dumb, but how often does this really happen? Do some teams send the man to second needlessly, and wind up with a lot of extra outs? Or is the man actually safe at second more often than we think? Are there teams which stay away from the strategy completely?

Let's look at some data. What we did was isolate the situation described above: runner on second, batter singles to the outfield, batter continues on to second to draw a throw. Who does this most, and who does it best? Here are the American League figures:

AL Team	Outfield Single with Man on 2nd	Out at 2nd While Runner Scores	Safe at 2nd While Runner Scores
Baltimore	158	8	8
Boston	146	6	4
California	140	7	17
Chicago	161	2	8
Cleveland	147	12	15
Detroit	165	5	5
Kansas City	148	9	23
Milwaukee	191	4	14
Minnesota	197	7	15
New York	148	1	5
Oakland	157	5	9
Seattle	151	7	5
Texas	153	8	5
Toronto	170	7	11
Total	2,232	88	144

This situation doesn't happen all that often — the batter takes off for second on a little more than 10 percent of all outfield singles — and there's a lot of variance in the results. Rob Neyer, who suggested the study, thought the Royals sent the batter to second a lot, and he was right: they did it 32 times, more than anyone. The Yankees, though, did it only six times; maybe the hitter was injury-prone Danny Tartabull, and they were afraid he might break in half between first and second. Rob thought the Royals ran into a lot of foolish outs, and their batters were retired at second nine times, more than anyone except the Indians. But the Royals' batters were **safe** 23 times, more than anyone, and to us that looks like good strategy. In many ways, it's just like a stolen base attempt: you risk an out to gain an extra base, so for the move to pay off, you need to succeed two-thirds of the time. Maybe a little less than that, in this case, since the move guarantees the run will score from second. But there seems little doubt that the Royals were good at this, while the Cleveland Indians — tossed out 12 times on 27 advances to second — were a little reckless.

Here are the National League figures:

NL Team	Outfield Single with Man on 2nd	Out at 2nd While Runner Scores	Safe at 2nd While Runner Scores
Atlanta	158	6	16
Chicago	153	6	11
Cincinnati	143	5	7
Houston	148	5	10
Los Angeles	130	4	12
Montreal	158	3	13
New York	123	8	14
Philadelphia	150	1	12
Pittsburgh	179	4	14
St. Louis	173	1	19
San Diego	134	6	8
San Francisco	140	6	10
Total	1,789	55	146

National League clubs were noticeably more successful with this strategy than the AL clubs were. The batter was safe at second 73 percent of the time vs. 62 percent in the American League. Some of this was probably due to more turf fields: the Cardinals (19 for 20), Phillies (12 for 13) and Pirates (14 for 18) were all very successful with this move, and all are turf clubs (as are the Royals). So is this a dumb strategy with teams continually running into outs? Not at all; it looks pretty smart, especially on turf fields.

WHO BEATS OUT THOSE INFIELD HITS?

The infield hit seems like a lucky break: a player hits the ball on the ground, often a slow roller, and motors down the line before the fielder can pick up the ball and throw him out. But for the true infield-hit artist, luck has little to do with it. A lot of players realize their legs are their livelihood; they deliberately try to hit the ball on the ground, coolly figuring that those "lucky toppers" are going to add a lot of points to their batting averages.

We thought you might be interested in the players who logged the most infield hits last year. We hope to answer some of the following questions:

1. Do hitters who play on turf fields have an advantage . . . or is it just the opposite, that grass fields slow down the ball and give the hitter a better chance to beat it out?

2. Are the guys who get a lot of infield hits strictly punch-and-judy hitters, the Otis Nixon types . . . or do power hitters, who force the infielders to play back, make the list as well?

3. Do right-handed hitters, who are more likely to hit the ball to the third baseman and shortstop, and thus force a longer throw, have any advantage?

4. Just how many infield hits do the best hitters really get, anyway?

Keeping all that in mind, here are the players who recorded the most infield hits last year — **not** counting bunt hits, which are covered in another essay. Since clubs' definitions of what constitutes an infield hit will vary, our list might be a little different from some of theirs.

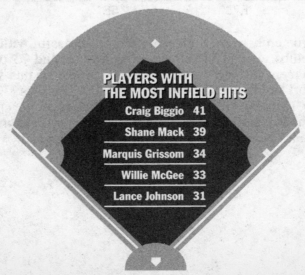

PLAYERS WITH THE MOST INFIELD HITS

Craig Biggio	41
Shane Mack	39
Marquis Grissom	34
Willie McGee	33
Lance Johnson	31

Since we have no trailers, let's also list #6 through #15:

1992 Most Infield Hits — #6-#15

Player, Team	Hits
Ryne Sandberg, Cubs	30
Brett Butler, LA	29
Kirby Puckett, Min	28
Mariano Duncan, Phi	26
Paul Molitor, Mil	25
Ozzie Smith, StL	24
Tony Phillips, Det	23
Luis Polonia, Cal	23
Pat Listach, Mil	23
Otis Nixon, Atl	22
Bip Roberts, Cin	22
Felix Jose, StL	22
Carlos Baerga, Cle	22
Dave Hollins, Phi	22

One question is answered right away. The runner-up, Shane Mack, is no powder-puff hitter — not with 16 homers last year. Marquis Grissom, Ryne Sandberg, Kirby Puckett, Paul Molitor, Felix Jose, Carlos Baerga, and Dave Hollins can also hit the ball a long way, and so can a few of the others.

As for the grass vs. turf controversy, there's a pretty good mix. Craig Biggio, Mack and Grissom play on turf, but the next four all play on grass. No real edge there.

There doesn't seem to be an advantage to batting right-handed. Most of the players here bat righty, but that's true of hitters in general. There are plenty of switch-hitters and lefty swingers on the list.

As for the total number of hits, the best guys get 30 to 40 infield hits or so. Everybody's going to get a few over the course of a year. **Harold Baines,** for God's sake, **had 11** so the advantage to Biggio and company is probably around 20 or 25 extra hits a year. Take away 25 infield hits from Biggio last year, and he would have batted .237 instead of .277. That's a huge difference; Biggio must bless the day the Astros preserved his future speed by moving him out from behind the plate.

A complete listing for this category can be found on page 289.

WHO ARE THE MOST PRODUCTIVE BASERUNNERS?

On-base percentage is probably the most useful offensive statistic there is, and correlates higher with winning than almost any other number. But reaching first is only half the battle for a player; once he gets there, his job is to come around and score. Obviously, he depends heavily on his teammates to bring him around. But a guy can do a lot on his own, especially with speed and baserunning ability.

Let's ask a simple question: which players score most often per time reached base? There are a couple of ways to examine the question. The way we do it in our STATS On-Line service is to count the number of runs scored, and divide that by the number of times reached via hits, walks and hit by pitches. By that measure, the 1992 leaders in runs scored per time reached base were Devon White, Joe Carter and Otis Nixon, all of whom came around to score 46 percent of the time.

But that method gives players credit for scoring on a home run, and it doesn't consider the extra times reached on fielder's choices, errors, interference, etc. In this exercise, what we want to do is measure baserunning skill. So we'll eliminate the home runs, and count all the times reaching base by **any** other method.

Okay, then, for the first time here on our stage — the 1992 leaders in runs scored per time reached base (minimum 150 times on base):

1992 Leaders
Runs Scored Per Time Reached Base

Player, Team	Runs Scored	Reached Base	Pct
Otis Nixon, Atl	77	203	.379
Tim Raines, WSox	95	264	.360
Pat Listach, Mil	92	258	.357
Bip Roberts, Cin	88	251	.351
Tony Phillips, Det	104	297	.350
Luis Polonia, Cal	83	238	.349
Devon White, Tor	81	233	.348
Delino DeShields, Mon	75	216	.347
Chuck Knoblauch, Min	102	294	.347
Kenny Lofton, Cle	91	267	.341

This is mostly a list of players with great baserunning skill. All of them except for Phillips are outstanding basestealers; he's excellent at running the sacks, but he also benefitted greatly from being the leadoff man for the best offense in the majors.

Otis Nixon, a fast guy at the top of a good offense, was the top man last year, scoring nearly 38 percent of the time he got on. Nixon's teammate Deion Sanders was even better, scoring 39 percent of the time he reached base, but Sanders didn't meet our 150-times on base minimum.

Sometimes a player can do well in this category even though he doesn't have a lot of speed. Relatively slow players like Edgar Martinez (.333), Jay Bell (.331), Terry Pendleton (.321) and Don Mattingly (.321) all made up for lack of speed with baserunning smarts.

The trailers in this category, though, had too much lack of speed to make up for:

1992 Trailers
Runs Scored Per Time Reached Base

Player, Team	Runs Scored	Reached Base	Pct
Sid Bream, Atl	20	150	.133
Tom Pagnozzi, StL	26	162	.161
Tom Brunansky, Bos	32	196	.163
Joe Oliver, Cin	32	178	.180
Fred McGriff, SD	44	242	.182
Mark Lemke, Atl	32	175	.183
Andre Dawson, Cubs	38	200	.190
Kevin McReynolds, KC	32	164	.195
Dave Magadan, Mets	30	153	.196
Steve Buechele, Pit-Cubs	43	216	.199

What a sentimental leader: Sid Bream, the man who lumbered (and we mean **lumbered**) around the bases with the run which brought the Braves the National League pennant. But what was Bobby Cox thinking of, anyway? Bream nearly got thrown out on a play on which Otis Nixon might have scored from first (well, almost).

The rest of the trailers are your typical group of catchers and other assorted lead-foots. It's a shock to see Andre Dawson, once a marvelous basestealer, and Kevin McReynolds, who was a perfect 21-for-21 on the sacks (still a major league record) only five years ago, on the list of trailers. This makes **us** feel old!

A complete listing for this category can be found on page 290.

WHY IS BARRY BONDS SECOND(ARY) TO NONE?

As most people know, a player's batting average often doesn't convey his full offensive value. That axiom can apply even to someone who batted .311, which was Barry Bonds' average in 1992. For in addition to hitting for a fine average, Bonds drew 127 walks, the most in the majors, had 75 extra-base hits with a .624 slugging average, the best in either league, and stole 39 bases in 47 attempts. He was great at just about everything, in other words.

In order to quantify those extra skills — the ones that batting average hides — Bill James came up with the idea of "secondary average." Secondary average measures the contributions made by stealing bases, drawing walks and hitting for extra bases, putting it on a percentage basis, just like batting average. The formula is:

Secondary Average = (2B + 3Bx2 + HRx3 + BB + SB - CS)/ AB

A normal secondary average looks like a batting average, only a bit lower: the major league secondary average last year was .229. The difference is that the range between the best and worst is much greater than with batting average. The top players in secondary average will have figures over .500; the worst will be below .100.

Here are the 1992 leaders in secondary average (minimum 250 plate appearances):

1992 Leaders — Secondary Average

Player, Team	Secondary Average
Barry Bonds, Pit	.647
Rickey Henderson, Oak	.508
Mark McGwire, Oak	.507
Danny Tartabull, Yanks	.468
Darren Daulton, Phi	.454
Fred McGriff, SD	.454
Mickey Tettleton, Det	.451
Rob Deer, Det	.435
Frank Thomas, WSox	.431
Chris Hoiles, Bal	.403

What a great all-around year Bonds had: he was 139 points ahead of the next-best hitter in this category. He even put himself to shame; Bonds was the leader in secondary average in 1991 as well, but his average in '91 was much lower (.490).

The best players in secondary average sometimes do it all, as Bonds and Rickey Henderson do. But more often they have two of the three skills: **power and drawing walks** while falling short in stolen bases. That's true of everyone on the 1992 list except for Barry and Rickey. As you can see, secondary average gives low-average hitters, like Mickey Tettleton (.238) and Rob Deer (.247), full recognition for their other contributions. But of course, batting averages have value also, so secondary average needs to be examined alongside batting average, not used as a replacement for it.

That last comment ought to be kept in mind when we look at the trailers in secondary average for 1992:

1992 Trailers — Secondary Average

Player, Team	Secondary Average
Junior Ortiz, Cle	.070
Rafael Belliard, Atl	.074
Joe Girardi, Cubs	.093
Jose Lind, Pit	.094
Gary DiSarcina, Cal	.097
Sandy Alomar Jr, Cle	.117
Milt Cuyler, Det	.120
Doug Dascenzo, Cubs	.122
Billy Hatcher, Cin-Bos	.122
Tony Pena, Bos	.124

Joe Girardi, who played for the Cubs last year and who will be with the Rockies in 1993, batted a respectable .270. That obviously did the Cubs some good, but a decent average was basically all Girardi provided. In 270 at-bats, he had only five extra-base hits with just 19 walks, and he didn't steal a base all year. Girardi's low secondary average (.093) puts that .270 average in better context. Other players in the same category last year were Brian Harper (.307 batting average, .153 secondary average), Ricky Jordan (.304, .141) and Willie McGee (.297, .137). We're not saying they were useless; we **are** saying that the batting average, by itself, greatly magnifies their value.

A complete listing for this category can be found on page 292.

WHY DIDN'T CECIL "GO TO THE MOON" IN 1992?

Was Big Cecil feeling all right last year? Pardon us if we worry a bit about Cecil Fielder's health. You see, we seem to have detected a little loss of strength in the big fellow. It isn't just that his home run total has been dropping: 51 in 1990, 44 in 1991, a measly 35 in 1992. No, the news is a lot more alarming than that.

One of the tasks performed by our reporters is to record the direction and distance of every ball in play. That includes home runs, so we have a pretty accurate measurement of how far each four-bagger traveled. It's not perfect, of course, but it's pretty darned accurate.

And that's where Fielder comes in. In 1990, Cecil clouted a mighty 510-foot home run, the longest of the year in our estimation. In 1991, he took Harry Caray's advice and had "one more biscuit for breakfast" — possibly more than one, judging by the way he looked. It paid off, as this time he hit one 520 feet.

But in 1992, Cecil suffered a power outage, even though he appeared to be on the same diet. There were no 500-foot home runs from Fielder in 1992. Or 490-footers, or 480. The longest Fielder clout of 1992 was 440 feet; even guys with names like "Candy" (Maldonado) were hitting home runs farther than that.

The "Tiger tradition," at least, was upheld by Fielder's teammate, Rob Deer. As the chart shows, Deer's 480-foot clout, which came off Baltimore's Ben McDonald at Tiger Stadium on June 11, was the longest

450 FEET
Fred McGriff(2)
Albert Belle
Eric Davis
Juan Gonzalez
Candy Maldonado
Ron Karkovice
Darryl Strawberry
Mo Vaughn

460 FEET
Albert Belle
Felix Jose
Gary Sheffield
Danny Tartabull
Frank Thomas

470 FEET
Jack Clark

480 FEET
Rob Deer

THE LONGEST HOMERS

one we measured last year. It was an appropriate matchup, as the Orioles seem to be developing a little tradition of their own, though not the kind they relish. Three Baltimore pitchers (McDonald, Bob Milacki and Mike Mussina) gave up 450-foot (or greater) homers last year; Rick Sutcliffe, the man credited with teaching those youngsters everything they know about pitching, permitted a 440-footer. The O's survived last year's loss of the gopher-balling Jeffs (Ballard and Robinson) without missing a beat.

Without Cecil to lead the way, no one could manage a 500-footer in 1992. That's the first time this has happened since 1989. Jack Clark, who had belted a 530-footer in '91, couldn't reach that level last year, but he still has to be regarded as the king of the tape measure home run. Despite his miserable 1992 season, Clark's 470-footer (off Kansas City's Mike Magnante, on May 10) was the second-longest of the year. And he's the only player to make the elite chart (450-plus feet in 1989, 460-plus since then) during each of the last four seasons.

Giving Clark a battle has been Cleveland's Albert Belle, who's clouted one 460 feet or longer during three of the last four seasons. (Although actually, it was "Joey" Belle who clouted that 460-footer back in 1989.) The only year Belle missed, 1991, was the one he spent in the minors. Bo Jackson had made the elite list in 1989, 1990 and 1991, and had a golden excuse for missing it last year: he didn't play a major league game.

****

Is there a relationship between the number of long home runs hit and the total number of four-baggers hit in a particular season? If there was, you could surmise that the ball might have been livelier that year. However, our data shows no such relationship. The number of long home runs (450 feet or more) hit over the last six years has remained pretty steady, ranging between 16 and 32 each year. Even in the home run happy 1987 season, there was no significant upward surge in tape-measure dingers.

Year	Total HR	450-ft. HRs
1987	4,490	32
1988	3,180	32
1989	3,083	19
1990	3,317	32
1991	3,383	19
1992	3,038	16

A complete listing for this category can be found on page 293.

WHO'S THE BEST BUNTER?

Brett Butler must have taken offense to our conclusion last year that the Astros' Steve Finley was the best bunter in baseball. We don't know whether Brett spent the winter of 1991-92 in the bunting cage, working on his technique. We do know that when it came to overall value, both bunting for a sacrifice and bunting for a hit, Butler was The Man in 1992.

Let's take a look, first, at the art of sacrifice bunting. One would think it easy to lay down a sacrifice, but major league hitters don't find it so. Last year they laid down over 2,000 bunts in sacrifice situations, an average of about one per game. But they succeeded in moving the runner over only 81 percent of the time, meaning that they failed almost once every five tries. Sure, many of them are National League pitchers, but it seems that they ought to have a better success rate than that.

We'll rate bunters here in terms of their success rates, with a minimum of 10 successful sacrifices last year. Here is the top 10:

Top Sacrifice Bunters — 1992

Bunter, Team	Sac	Att	Pct
Jay Bell, Pit	19	19	100
Rafael Belliard, Atl	13	13	100
Ozzie Smith, StL	12	12	100
Jeff Frye, Tex	11	11	100
Walt Weiss, Oak	11	11	100
Dick Schofield, Cal-Mets	10	10	100
Dennis Martinez, Mon	10	10	100
John Smoltz, Atl	10	10	100
Craig Grebeck, WSox	10	10	100
Steve Finley, Hou	16	17	94

When it comes to laying down a sacrifice, Jay Bell of the Pirates is the established master. His sacrifice total has been declining — from 39 in 1990 to 30 in '91 to 19 last year — but only because Pirate manager Jim Leyland no longer has Bell bunt every time the leadoff man reaches base. Bell was a perfect 19-for-19 in sacrifice attempts last year, a remarkable record. Several others were perfect, but none of them came close to Bell's number of attempts.

Where was Butler? He didn't make the top 10 because he failed on two sacrifice attempts last year. But Butler led both leagues in sacrifices with 24, and his success rate of 92 percent just missed the top 10. He was one of the very best, without question.

But what makes Butler so good is that he has both bunting skills: he can lay down a sacrifice, and he's also superb at bunting for a hit. Last year might have been his best ever; he beat out 42 bunt hits, exactly twice his excellent 1991 total of 21. Cleveland's Kenny Lofton, who ranked second, had 10 fewer bunt hits. Butler also had an excellent success rate of 60 percent; that's outstanding, considering that he never had the element of surprise working for him, as less-frequent bunters do (the major league success rate on bunt hit attempts last year was 53 percent). Here is the top 10, based on number of bunt hits:

Top Base-Hit Bunters — 1992

Bunter, Team	Hits	Att	Pct
Brett Butler, LA	42	70	60
Kenny Lofton, Cle	32	64	50
Tim Raines, WSox	19	32	59
Otis Nixon, Atl	17	38	45
Kirby Puckett, Min	13	17	76
Brian McRae, KC	13	32	41
Pat Listach, Mil	11	28	39
Milt Cuyler, Det	11	20	55
Roberto Alomar, Tor	10	12	83
Steve Finley, Hou	10	23	43

We've mentioned in the past that it surprises us that players don't bunt for a hit more often, given that it's a pretty high-percentage play for players with good speed and reasonable bunting skills. Butler and Lofton seem to be showing the way for some of the others; both had many more bunt hits last year than the 1991 leader, Otis Nixon (23).

Is it any wonder why we think Brett is the best?

A complete listing for this category can be found on page 294.

WHO'LL BE THE NEXT TO REACH 3,000?

We comment in the Royals essay about how special it was for baseball fans when Robin Yount and George Brett reached the 3,000 hit mark last September. No sport values its past like baseball, and none so honors the players who reach the magic milestones: 3,000 hits, 500 home runs, and 300 victories.

Your guess is as good as ours as to which active pitchers, if any, will reach the 300 victory level. Pitchers have such ups and downs over their careers that it's difficult to project how they'll do **this** season, much less five or 10 years into the future. But hitters are a different story.

A number of years ago, Bill James came up with a tool called "The Favorite Toy" which projects the chances a hitter has to reach the major career milestones. The Favorite Toy starts with established levels of performance, factors in a player's age, and then estimates his chance to reach the goal. We carried the formula in this book a couple of years ago, and that edition is still available from us if you're curious enough about the subject. It's a reasonable mathematical projection, but as the name indicates, it's also a toy, something to have fun with.

Based on "The Favorite Toy," the following players have the best chances to reach 3,000 hits in their career:

Player	Chances for 3,000 Hits			
	Opening Day Age	Current Total	Projected Total	Chance
Dave Winfield	41.5	2,866	3,099	95.5
Kirby Puckett	32.1	1,812	2,751	29.0
Ken Griffey Jr	23.4	652	2,412	25.0
Roberto Alomar	25.2	862	2,456	24.6
Eddie Murray	37.1	2,646	2,910	24.6
Ruben Sierra	27.5	1,160	2,506	23.2
Cal Ripken	32.6	1,922	2,696	21.8
Ryne Sandberg	33.6	1,939	2,639	16.0

As you can see, the estimates are conservative: Dave Winfield, who will reach 3,000 this year if his performance even approaches what he did last season, is given only a 96 percent chance; that's because he could become injured or suffer a sudden decline in performance. We like his chances. The other players, who are younger and farther away from the goal, are given less chance, but the odds are that one of them, at least, will make it. We still like Kirby Puckett, as we did last year.

Does anyone have a chance to reach 4,000 hits? Yes, a chance, but a mighty slim one. Naturally, it's the young players, Griffey (2.6%) and Alomar (0.8%). Those are what you call long shots.

We also project players chances to reach 500 homers, and that's probably the most fun category. No one has reached this milestone since Mike Schmidt in 1987, and nobody's close to it now: Winfield (432) and Eddie Murray (414) are the only guys over 400, and they're probably too old to get the remaining homers they need. So the players given a chance (see chart) are all younger, and our estimates fluctuate from year to year, depending on how they've fared recently. For instance, a year ago, we gave Darryl Strawberry a 34 percent chance to reach 500. But after an injury-riddled campaign in which he managed only five homers, he's disappeared from the projection list. He could be back, with a strong comeback season in 1993.

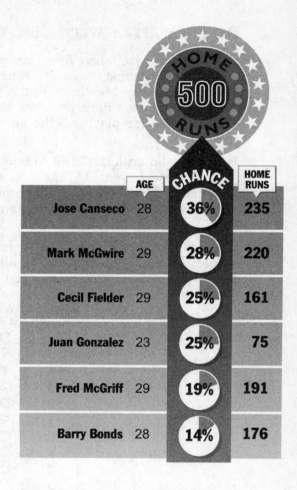

	AGE	CHANCE	HOME RUNS
Jose Canseco	28	36%	235
Mark McGwire	29	28%	220
Cecil Fielder	29	25%	161
Juan Gonzalez	23	25%	75
Fred McGriff	29	19%	191
Barry Bonds	28	14%	176

Most of the other names on the chart are more familiar. Jose Canseco, Mark McGwire, Cecil Fielder and Fred McGriff were given at least a 13 percent chance to reach 500 homers a year ago. The big gainer in that group from 1992 was McGwire; his 42-homer season increased his chances of hitting 500 from 13 percent to 28 percent.

Juan Gonzalez enters the list of players with a chance at 500 homers this year. Canseco (13%), Gonzalez (11%), Fielder (8%), McGwire (8%) and McGriff (2%) all have a slight chance at 600 homers, according to the formula. Only 23, Gonzalez is the only player on the chart with even a miniscule chance at 700 homers. At one percent, it's pretty slim.

DO THEY STEAL WITH A BIG LEAD THESE DAYS?

A few years ago, when Jose Canseco was becoming the first player to amass both 40 home runs and 40 steals in a season, one of the stars of the 1950s — Mickey Mantle or Willie Mays, or maybe both — commented that he could have done that, too, but the game was different back then. "When we were playing," the superstar said, "we didn't steal with a five-run lead."

Is this a valid criticism? Did Marquis Grissom really amass 78 steals last year because he got 35 of them when they had no influence on the outcome of the game? Seems doubtful, but how does the score of the game affect whether or not a club is going to be running? Let's look at some data.

The first thing we'll do is look at steal attempts for the major leagues as a whole. Here's a breakdown of all 1992 steals, with the stolen base percentage, according to the score of the game:

Stealing by Score — 1992
All SB Attempts

Lead	SB	CS	Pct
–5 or more	73	5	94
–4	62	6	91
–3	132	32	80
–2	235	73	76
–1	388	179	68
0	1,105	564	66
1	453	302	60
2	329	188	64
3	240	135	64
4	161	77	68
5 or more	86	40	68

As you can see, the bulk of steal attempts take place when you'd expect: either the score is tied, or the club is up or down by a run. The numbers decline sharply when the lead is greater than three runs — considered a fairly safe lead — or the deficit is more than two. As for stealing when the club is up or down by five runs, forget it. There were over 4,800 stolen base attempts in the major leagues last year; only 204 of them came when the club was leading or trailing by at least five runs.

Mantle and/or Mays are right in one sense, though: the game **has** changed from the 1950s. Back then, the success rate was lower (around 60 percent, and often less); it didn't make a lot of sense to steal when the chance of being thrown out was so high. Clubs especially wouldn't steal when they were down by two or three runs. Now they will, at least on occasion, because the chance of success (over 75 percent, when the deficit is two or more runs) makes the gamble worthwhile.

There's also been a slight change in that curious thing known as "baseball etiquette." It used to be completely taboo to steal with a lead of three or more runs, because it was considered "showing up the opposition." Okay, but if the opponents are still trying to win the game, does it make sense to worry about their feelings? Whitey Herzog had the perfect philosophy about stealing with a lead: "I'll agree not to steal any more bases, if you agree not to get any more hits." Nobody ever took him up on this.

Those running fools, the 1992 Milwaukee Brewers, never worried about what the opposition thought of them. Phil Garner's club was one of the few which would steal even when leading by four or five:

Stealing by Score — 1992
Milwaukee Brewers

Lead	SB	CS	Pct
−5 or more	8	1	89
−4	4	0	100
−3	9	1	90
−2	13	7	65
−1	30	6	83
0	68	38	64
1	40	26	61
2	33	14	70
3	15	8	65
4	22	6	79
5 or more	14	8	64

This, however, is still not typical of most teams or players. They **don't** steal with a big lead, as a rule. And Marquis Grissom? He had exactly one steal when his club was up by five or more last year, one more when the deficit was at least five. When the score ranged from a three-run lead to a three-run deficit — game up for grabs, in anyone's book — Grissom logged 72 of his 78 steals. Hey, maybe he steals so many bases because he's a great base stealer!

A complete listing for this category can be found on page 295.

HOW WILL WINFIELD DO IN '93?

It was, by almost every standard, the best season ever by a player in his forties. Dave Winfield, who turned 41 the day before the 1992 season ended, drove in 108 runs, the first 100-RBI season for a player over 40 years old. He also hit 26 home runs — only Darrell Evans and Ted Williams had hit so many at such an advanced age — and batted .290. Fifteen years previously, when Winfield was 25, his figures were 25 homers, 92 RBI and .275. Imagine what he'll be able to accomplish when he gets the hang of this game.

Now the amazing Winfield moves from the Blue Jays to his native area, Minnesota, and we have to wonder what he'll be able to accomplish this year. Will he play power forward for the Timberwolves, catch a few passes for the Vikings, take his turn on the power play for the North Stars . . . and star for the Twins in his spare time? After last year, it's really impossible to put any limits on what he can accomplish this season, when he'll be 41. But it might be useful to look at the best numbers put up by players at that age. The following players were 41 in the season in question (age as of July 1 of that year):

The Best Seasons — Age 41

Batter	Year	AB	R	H	HR	RBI	Avg
Stan Musial	1962	433	57	143	19	82	.330
Ted Williams	1960	310	56	98	29	72	.316
Ty Cobb	1928	353	54	114	1	40	.323
Luke Appling	1948	497	63	156	0	47	.314
Sam Rice	1931	413	81	128	0	42	.310
Carlton Fisk	1989	375	47	110	13	68	.293
Brian Downing	1992	320	53	89	10	39	.278
Honus Wagner	1915	566	68	155	6	78	.274
Pete Rose	1982	634	80	172	3	54	.271
Darrell Evans	1988	437	48	91	22	64	.208

There are plenty of good seasons here, led by the masters, Ted Williams and Stan Musial. Winfield probably won't hit .330 — he hasn't hit that high since 1984, when he batted .340 — or even belt 29 homers, a figure he hasn't reached since he belted 32 in 1983. But Musial's record of 82 RBI by a 41 year old seems within reach; Winfield could fall off considerably from his 1991 figures and still be able to reach that total.

As remarkable an athlete as Winfield is, **some** sort of decline seems inevitable. Lots of veteran players have had outstanding seasons at the age of 40; almost all of them saw their figures decline at 41, though many continued to be very good performers. Here are some comparisons:

Batter	Year	Age	AB	R	H	HR	RBI	Avg
Ty Cobb	1927	40	490	104	175	5	93	.357
	1928	41	353	54	114	1	40	.323
Sam Rice	1930	40	593	121	207	1	73	.349
	1931	41	413	81	128	0	42	.310
Pete Rose	1981	40	431	73	140	0	33	.325
	1982	41	634	80	172	3	54	.271
Luke Appling	1947	40	503	67	154	8	49	.306
	1948	41	497	63	156	0	47	.314
Brian Downing	1991	40	407	76	113	17	49	.278
	1992	41	320	53	89	10	39	.278
Carlton Fisk	1988	40	253	37	70	19	50	.277
	1989	41	375	47	110	13	68	.293
Honus Wagner	1914	40	552	60	139	1	50	.252
	1915	41	566	68	155	6	78	.274
Willie Mays	1971	40	417	82	113	18	61	.271
	1972	41	244	35	61	8	22	.250
Henry Aaron	1974	40	340	47	91	20	69	.268
	1975	41	465	45	109	12	60	.234
Darrell Evans	1987	40	499	90	128	34	99	.257
	1988	41	437	48	91	22	64	.208
Dave Winfield	1992	40	583	92	169	26	108	.290
(projected)	1993	41	544	69	137	18	78	.252

The general trend, not surprisingly, is for players' figures to drop off from age 40 to age 41; some declined dramatically, among them Willie Mays and Henry Aaron. But that's certainly not true of everyone; some actually got better, including Williams and Musial, who bounced back from sub-par years at 40 to have great seasons at age 41. Based on our projection (shown in the chart), Winfield seems a good bet to have one of the better years for a player his age. Again.

A complete listing for this category can be found on page 297.

IV. QUESTIONS ON
PITCHING

DID THE PADRES AND BREWERS TAKE THEIR MIDDLE RELIEF CORPS FOR GRANTED?

Middle relief is one of the most thankless jobs in baseball. Not only do middle men not get the saves and the big money that goes along with them, they often don't get proper appreciation even from their own clubs.

To realize this, all you have a do is look at the graphic, which shows the best and worst middle relief team ERAs last year (we define "middle relief" as all bullpen appearances from the first through the eighth innings). The top team in 1992 was the San Diego Padres, with a 2.53 ERA; number two was the Milwaukee

THE BEST	
Padres	2.53
Brewers	2.76
Expos	3.04
Astros	3.05
Cardinals	3.10
Reds	3.10

THE WORST	
Rangers	5.36
Mariners	4.78
Yankees	4.48
Phillies	4.40
Angels	4.13
ML AVG.	3.69

Brewers, with a 2.76 mark. Yet over the winter, the Padres let middle reliever Larry Andersen depart via free agency, and traded away Jose Melendez and Mike Maddux. The Brewers, meanwhile, let one of their best middle men, Darren Holmes, go unprotected in the expansion draft; the Colorado Rockies snapped up Holmes in the first round. The attitude seemed to be, "No big deal . . . these guys aren't hard to replace."

Oh, yeah? Milwaukee and San Diego might want to check with the Seattle Mariners. In 1991, Seattle had the second-best middle relief ERA in the majors (3.10). Figuring they could sacrifice some of their bullpen and still come out okay, the M's packaged Bill Swift, Mike Jackson and Dave Burba, middlemen all, in order to obtain Kevin Mitchell from the Giants.

What happened in '92? The Mariners' middle relief corps went from second-best to second-worst (4.78) — a key factor in Seattle's terrible season.

Here's the complete middle relief list for 1992, from the Padres down to those terrible Texas Rangers:

1992 Relief ERA — 1st through 8th Innings		
San Diego Padres	309.2	2.53
Milwaukee Brewers	250.2	2.76
Houston Astros	377.2	3.04
Montreal Expos	310.2	3.05
St. Louis Cardinals	301.2	3.10
Cincinnati Reds	295.2	3.10
Baltimore Orioles	280.1	3.40
Los Angeles Dodgers	278.2	3.42
San Francisco Giants	381.1	3.42
Minnesota Twins	297.1	3.42
Kansas City Royals	410.1	3.44
Cleveland Indians	351.2	3.51
Chicago White Sox	256.2	3.61
Pittsburgh Pirates	304.0	3.67
Atlanta Braves	257.1	3.81
Oakland Athletics	343.1	3.85
Chicago Cubs	287.0	3.86
Toronto Blue Jays	274.1	3.87
Boston Red Sox	282.0	3.93
New York Mets	279.2	4.05
Detroit Tigers	403.0	4.11
California Angels	268.0	4.13
Philadelphia Phillies	313.0	4.40
New York Yankees	275.0	4.48
Seattle Mariners	335.1	4.78
Texas Rangers	277.0	5.36
MLB Average	307.2	3.69

If you've read the essay called "Which Starting Staffs Star, and Which Relief Staffs Reek?" (p. 167) you'll probably notice many similarities between the middle and overall relief numbers. True enough, but there are a number of exceptions. Let's divide the Padres bullpen into middle and late (ninth inning or later) relief ERAs:

Club	Middle	Late
Padres	2.53	4.07

With Randy Myers often having problems last year, the Padres probably needed good middle relief more than most clubs. After looking at these figures, we can more easily understand letting Myers depart than trading both Maddux (2.37 ERA) and Melendez (2.92).

Several other clubs had the opposite problem — good late relief, bad middle:

Club	Middle	Late
Athletics	3.85	2.36
Blue Jays	3.87	2.59
Yankees	4.48	3.16
Rangers	5.36	3.03

The Blue Jays and Athletics proved that a good closer can overcome less-than-stellar middle relief; after all, they were the American League division champions last year. But Oakland's middle relief problems undoubtedly put greater strain on Dennis Eckersley last season, and very likely were a contributing factor in his poor postseason performance.

ARE HIGH-PITCH OUTINGS DANGEROUS?

Since our play-by-play reporters keep track of every pitch, we're probably a little more conscious of pitch counts than most people in the baseball business. We're also aware that studies by STATS' Craig Wright and others have shown that there's a danger in overworking young pitchers, those under 25 years old. Two years ago, in an essay in this book called "What's Lasorda Doing With Ramon Martinez?" we mentioned the numerous high-pitch outings Dodger manager Tommy Lasorda had given his young ace, and commented that such usage was dangerous. The Dodgers and others scoffed, but by 1992 Martinez was looking like just another struggling pitcher with arm problems. His record last year was 8-11 with a 4.00 ERA.

Though nobody is thanking us for the warning, it appears that some people in baseball are getting more cautious with their younger arms. The list of 1992 high-pitch outings includes only one effort by a young hurler — Milwaukee's Cal Eldred, who was 24 when he tossed 146 pitches against the Orioles on Sept. 13. Here's the top 11:

Most Pitches in a Game — 1992

Pitcher, Team	Date	Opp	Fin	W/L	IP	H	ER	BB	K	Pit
David Cone, Mets	Jul 17	SF	1-0	W	9.0	6	0	4	13	166
Randy Johnson, Sea	Sep 27	Tex	2-3	-	8.0	6	2	4	18	160
Randy Johnson, Sea	Aug 15	Min	3-2	W	9.0	4	2	7	13	159
Roger Clemens, Bos	Jun 21	Tex	2-3	L	6.2	5	3	6	4	151
Frank Viola, Bos	Aug 26	Oak	2-1	W	10.0	6	1	3	4	151
Scott Sanderson, Yanks	Jun 4	Det	2-6	L	7.1	8	6	6	7	148
Charlie Hough, WSox	Jul 8	Bal	3-5	L	7.2	8	4	6	5	148
Mark Langston, Cal	Oct 2	Tex	6-3	W	9.0	6	0	1	13	147
Randy Johnson, Sea	Jul 9	NYA	6-7	L	7.0	5	1	9	3	146
Tim Wakefield, Pit	Jul 31	StL	3-2	W	9.0	6	0	5	10	146
Cal Eldred, Mil	Sep 13	Bal	3-1	W	9.0	4	1	1	12	146

Managers do seem to be using more discretion with their younger starters, but do they need to worry about the veterans, whose arms are fully developed? That question got a pretty good airing last July, after Mets manager Jeff Torborg let David Cone throw 166 pitches against the Giants. Though Cone and the Mets said he was fine, he struggled for over a month, posting a 5.13 ERA in his next nine starts. It wasn't until September that Cone was pitching effectively again.

Was that just a coincidence? The evidence suggests that while it's great to be a "manly man," leaving a starter in to throw 150 pitches or more is probably not a good idea — except, maybe, if the pitcher is 6 foot 10 and weighs 225 pounds. Seattle's Randy Johnson, who's that size, had 160 and

159-pitch efforts last year, and seven contests in which he threw 140 or more. If the workload was bothering him, it didn't show in his pitching. Johnson followed his 159-pitch game with seven shutout innings against the Red Sox, and his famous 160-pitch, 18-strikeout game against the Rangers with a fine effort against the White Sox (seven innings, two runs).

The more normal-sized people, however, showed some strain from their high-pitch outings. The Yankees' Scott Sanderson was raked for seven hits and six runs in an inning and two-thirds in the game after his 148-pitch start against the Tigers. The Red Sox' Frank Viola was also chased in the second inning (after allowing seven earned runs) in his first time out after his 151-pitch game against Oakland. Even the Sox' Roger Clemens, who's built like a horse, had a few problems after throwing 151 pitches at Texas on June 21. Clemens' next outing was fine (eight innings, one earned run), but he was roughed up for five runs in each of his two subsequent starts. The evidence indicates that its probably counter-productive to tempt the 150-pitch mark with all but the most durable pitchers.

Well, how about the 80-pitch mark? Minnesota's John Smiley tossed that many in a complete game against Kansas City last October 2, and he was still smiling when he left the mound; so were a lot of people in the press box, after that two-hour, eight-minute contest. Smiley's effort made him the winner of our annual "Red Barrett Trophy," named for the pitcher who once threw only 58 pitches in a complete game. Here's Smiley's competition for the lowest-pitch outings of the year:

Fewest Pitches in a 9-Inning Complete Game — 1992

Pitcher, Team	Date	Opp	Fin	W/L	IP	H	ER	BB	K	Pit
John Smiley, Min	Oct 2	KC	5-1	W	9.0	4	1	0	4	80
Bill Gullickson, Det	May 26	KC	8-1	W	9.0	6	1	0	0	84
Tom Glavine, Atl	Jun 23	SF	7-0	W	9.0	5	0	0	4	84
Bill Krueger, Min	Apr 17	ChA	7-0	W	9.0	5	0	0	5	85
Jaime Navarro, Mil	Jul 27	Cle	4-0	W	9.0	3	0	0	5	85
Bob Tewksbury, StL	May 30	SD	5-1	W	9.0	4	1	0	2	86
Scott Sanderson, Yanks	Jun 30	KC	6-0	W	9.0	4	0	0	4	86
Dennis Martinez, Mon	Sep 12	NYN	4-1	W	9.0	5	1	1	4	88
Chris Bosio, Mil	Sep 24	Cal	4-0	W	9.0	5	0	0	9	88
Dwight Gooden, Mets	Oct 3	Pit	2-1	W	9.0	4	1	1	3	88

Only one of these games took longer than 2:23 to play: Tom Glavine's June 23 shutout against the Giants took an amazing two hours, 56 minutes. The uncooperative Giant hurlers threw exactly 99 more pitches (183) than Glavine did that night. (Ted Turner probably needed the extra commercials.)

A complete listing for this category can be found on page 298.

WHICH RELIEVERS TIRE EASILY?

In the increasingly-specialized world of modern baseball, every pitcher has his role. The starters are no longer expected to go nine innings; seven innings are enough, but they'll settle for six. Then the middle men come in, ready to go two innings if needed, sometimes a little more if the starter gets knocked out early. Finally, they bring in the closer; if he's asked to work more than one inning, his agent will probably make a nasty phone call to the manager the next morning.

We've been studying this trend toward increased specialization for awhile, and while we agree that it sometimes can get out of hand, it often makes perfect sense: pitchers thrive when given the right kind of usage, fail when asked to do too much.

That's especially true of the ultimate specialists, relief pitchers. For whatever reason, some pitchers are far more effective in short stints than they are when they have to work longer. Here's a list of 1992 pitchers who had one thing in common — they were great when worked for about an inning (15 pitches or less), not nearly so good in their longer outings:

| | One-Inning Specialists | | | | | |
| | Pitches 1-15 | | Pitches 16-30 | | Pitches 31+ | |
Pitcher, Team	AB	Avg	AB	Avg	AB	Avg
Mike Gardiner, Bos	84	.131	86	.291	328	.274
Rod Beck, SF	206	.150	100	.250	21	.286
Kent Mercker, Atl	148	.155	66	.273	32	.313
James Austin, Mil	127	.157	54	.259	18	.222
Mark Leiter, Det	95	.158	87	.287	237	.321
Mike Perez, StL	229	.188	87	.264	17	.235
Bryan Hickerson, SF	195	.195	88	.295	31	.323
Wilson Alvarez, WSox	96	.198	80	.338	203	.281
Dennis Powell, Sea	116	.198	56	.339	34	.206
Jack Armstrong, Cle	103	.214	116	.267	435	.283

Interestingly, not all of these pitchers were relievers. Mike Gardiner, Mark Leiter, Wilson Alvarez and Jack Armstrong all started for much of the year, and they didn't exactly set the world on fire. While one year's worth of data doesn't tell us everything, the 1992 figures suggest that these pitchers might be more effective working out of the pen for short stints.

Some of them already **are** relievers, though, and the data suggests that it might be a good idea to get them out of the game more quickly. Guys like Rod Beck, Kent Mercker, James Austin and Mike Perez were outstanding

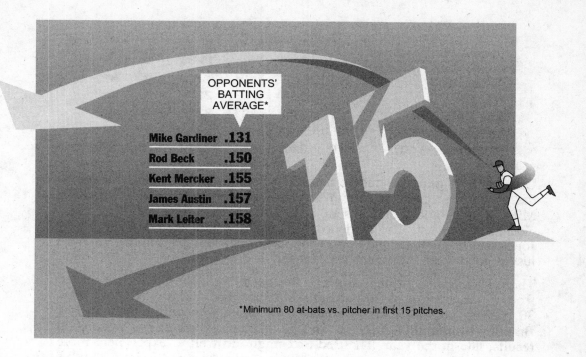

OPPONENTS'
BATTING
AVERAGE*

Mike Gardiner	.131
Rod Beck	.150
Kent Mercker	.155
James Austin	.157
Mark Leiter	.158

*Minimum 80 at-bats vs. pitcher in first 15 pitches.

for their first 15 pitches, but very hittable thereafter. Getting them in and out of a game quickly might make optimum use of their abilities.

Other relievers don't require such careful handling. They're good when they first come into the game (first 15 pitches); they're just as good, often better, for their next 15, and sometimes longer:

Good for Two or More

Pitcher, Team	Pitches 1-15 AB	Pitches 1-15 Avg	Pitches 16-30 AB	Pitches 16-30 Avg	Pitches 31+ AB	Pitches 31+ Avg
Duane Ward, Tor	237	.232	106	.170	24	.125
Xavier Hernandez, Hou	263	.213	112	.179	29	.172
Jeff Montgomery, KC	200	.215	86	.186	11	.182
Cris Carpenter, StL	215	.242	84	.190	14	.071
Mike Maddux, SD	186	.253	83	.193	32	.250
Doug Jones, Hou	258	.256	121	.198	30	.200
Jeff Parrett, Oak	197	.223	118	.203	43	.302
Matt Young, Bos	75	.213	73	.205	121	.314
John Wetteland, Mon	180	.222	101	.208	20	.150
Mel Rojas, Mon	213	.183	108	.213	36	.250
Jeff Brantley, SF	148	.209	93	.215	82	.195

Good for Two or More

Pitcher, Team	Pitches 1-15		Pitches 16-30		Pitches 31+	
	AB	Avg	AB	Avg	AB	Avg
Joe Grahe, Cal	131	.221	83	.217	132	.288
Roger Mason, Pit	191	.215	93	.226	41	.439
Rich Rodriguez, SD	195	.226	84	.226	57	.246
Rusty Meacham, KC	210	.224	113	.230	55	.273

Usually these guys are middle men already, and the list includes some of the best in the game: Duane Ward, Xavier Hernandez, Cris Carpenter, Mike Maddux and Mel Rojas are among them. But you'll also find a few closers on the list. The evidence suggests that Jeff Montgomery, Doug Jones and John Wetteland don't need to be one-inning specialists: they're just as good when they have to go longer.

There are a few part-time starters on this list as well. Joe Grahe was shifted from a starter's role to the pen early last year, and that proved ideal: after 30 pitches, he was about finished. The Giants were intrigued with Jeff Brantley's durability in relief and gave him several starts, with good results, late in the year. The Red Sox might do well to experiment more with Matt Young as a one- or two-inning reliever. Lord knows, they've tried everything else.

A complete listing for this category can be found on page 299.

WHICH STARTING STAFFS STAR, AND WHICH RELIEF STAFFS REEK?

How important is good starting pitching? Well . . . that depends on when you're asking. Looking at the 1991 figures, the answer seemed crystal clear. In '91 the American League's best starting staffs belonged to the two division champions, the Blue Jays and Twins; the best National League staffs belonged to the Dodgers (who missed a division title by one game), Pirates (East champs) and Braves (West champs). What could be clearer than that?

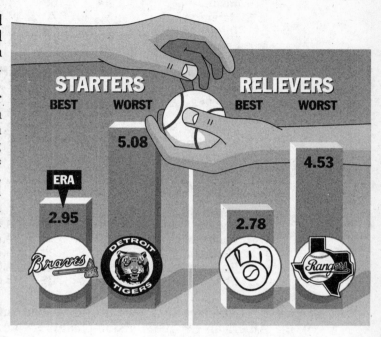

But then we come to 1992. The best corps of starters in the American League belonged to Boston, with the tandem of Roger Clemens and Frank Viola. The only trouble was, Boston finished last. The number two staff belonged to the contending Brewers, but then came the California Angels, who were 72-90. The division-winning A's and Jays? They ranked fifth (Oakland, 3.88) and eighth (Toronto, 4.09).

Okay, so then Toronto and Oakland made up for that with their super bullpens, right? Wrong. In relief ERA the A's ranked seventh (3.42), the Jay's eighth (3.46). Here are the somewhat bewildering figures:

AL Starters	Won	Lost	ERA	IP
Red Sox	51	63	3.65	1028.2
Brewers	68	52	3.67	1071.2
Angels	47	68	3.80	1057.1
Twins	65	51	3.86	1020.0
Athletics	67	52	3.88	962.2
Rangers	59	61	3.92	1031.2
White Sox	60	54	4.03	1057.1
Blue Jays	75	54	4.09	1037.2
Orioles	66	59	4.11	1034.0

	Won	Lost	ERA	IP
Royals	47	59	4.15	896.1
Yankees	54	66	4.30	1032.1
Indians	44	65	4.55	955.1
Mariners	50	70	4.58	975.2
Tigers	52	63	5.08	901.2
League Avg.	57	59	4.11	1004.0

AL Relievers	Won	Lost	ERA	IP
Brewers	24	18	2.78	385.1
Orioles	23	14	3.03	430.0
Royals	25	31	3.27	551.0
Indians	32	21	3.31	514.2
White Sox	26	22	3.34	404.1
Twins	25	21	3.37	433.0
Athletics	29	14	3.42	484.1
Blue Jays	21	12	3.46	403.0
Red Sox	22	26	3.60	420.0
Tigers	23	24	3.83	534.0
Angels	25	22	3.96	388.2
Yankees	22	20	4.03	420.1
Mariners	14	28	4.47	469.1
Rangers	18	24	4.53	428.2
League Avg.	23	21	3.60	447.0

Despite the old adage that "pitching is 75 percent of baseball" (or 80, or 90), the American League division champions ranked seventh and eighth in team ERA. While both clubs had extremely reliable late relievers, they also relied very heavily on their offenses. Toronto was second in the league in runs scored, Oakland fourth, and you don't need the best pitching staffs when you hit like that.

The National League figures are more what we're accustomed to seeing. The Braves had the league's best starting staff; the Pirates were fourth, but only .04 out of second. Neither club had a superior bullpen, but with their excellent starting staffs and good offenses, that wasn't a major loss.

Here are the National League figures:

NL Starters	Won	Lost	ERA	IP
Braves	72	42	2.95	1066.0
Cubs	59	56	3.21	1028.0
Expos	65	55	3.23	998.2
Pirates	59	47	3.25	1010.0
Dodgers	48	70	3.35	1036.1
Mets	49	59	3.52	1031.2
Reds	63	54	3.55	1008.1
Cardinals	50	51	3.58	1007.1
Padres	57	58	3.83	994.2

	Won	Lost	ERA	IP
Giants	46	63	3.91	925.0
Phillies	45	64	4.10	1005.2
Astros	42	60	4.23	924.1
League Avg.	**54**	**56**	**3.54**	**1003.0**

NL Relievers	Won	Lost	ERA	IP
Astros	39	21	2.89	535.0
Cardinals	33	28	2.95	472.2
Padres	25	22	3.05	466.2
Giants	26	27	3.09	536.0
Reds	27	18	3.26	441.1
Expos	22	20	3.30	469.1
Dodgers	15	29	3.56	401.2
Pirates	37	19	3.56	469.2
Braves	26	22	3.68	394.0
Cubs	19	28	3.82	441.0
Mets	23	31	4.06	415.0
Phillies	25	28	4.20	422.1
League Avg.	**26**	**24**	**3.42**	**455.0**

The most interesting club here was Houston, with the league's worst starters, but best bullpen. No wonder they spent all that money to sign Doug Drabek and Greg Swindell. The Cubs were also hurt badly by a shaky bullpen, and so were the Mets, who dropped from second in relief ERA in 1991 to 11th in 1992.

In the American League, where the DH rule allows pitchers to remain in the game as long as they're still effective, you'd think that the starting pitchers would work more innings. Yet last year the average AL club got 1004 innings out of its starters; the average NL club got 1003.

But one difference between the leagues is that in the American League, the relievers consistently post ERAs much lower than the starters, usually around half a run. In the NL, the ERA difference has been smaller:

	1989	(Diff)	1990	(Diff)	1991	(Diff)	1992	(Diff)
AL Starters	4.05		4.06		4.26		4.11	
AL Relievers	3.54	(0.51)	3.62	(0.44)	3.75	(0.51)	3.60	(0.51)
NL Starters	3.61		3.88		3.73		3.54	
NL Relievers	3.26	(0.35)	3.61	(0.27)	3.59	(0.14)	3.42	(0.12)

Does this mean the American League has lousier starters than the National League? Don't ask us; ask Sparky Anderson.

A complete listing for this category can be found on page 300.

WHICH PITCHERS ARE HOT WHEN IT'S COLD?

Imagine it's a typical April evening in Chicago, and you're a young White Sox hitter just trying to stay warm as the temperature dips into the 40s. The wind is coming in off the lake, and a few snow flurries are falling. You're wondering if it's okay to hit with mittens on. Naturally, the opposing pitcher is that nice, polite friend of hitters everywhere, Roger Clemens. You can barely hold the bat, and he keeps coming inside on you all night long, sawing that piece of lumber out of your hands. What a great guy. Three hours later, he walks off the mound, smiling, with another easy victory under his belt. Three weeks later, your fingers are still numb.

Hitting in cold weather is no picnic; hitting against a good pitcher on a cold day is twice as difficult. We record the temperature at the start of every game, and we wondered which pitchers were most effective when it's a frigid day for baseball — say, 50 degrees or less. There aren't a lot of days like that, so we'll go back over the last four years to gather our data. Here are the best cold-weather pitchers (minimum 35 innings pitched):

Best ERAs When It's 50 Degrees or Less — 1989-92

Pitcher	G	W	L	IP	ER	ERA	Other Games
Dave Stewart	5	4	1	37.2	5	1.19	3.61
Dave Stieb	9	7	0	69.1	13	1.69	3.51
Roger Clemens	14	10	3	114.1	22	1.73	2.71
Charles Nagy	5	4	0	38.2	9	2.10	3.85
John Smiley	8	5	3	56.0	14	2.25	3.38
John Candelaria	6	3	1	38.1	10	2.35	3.90
Greg Maddux	13	8	4	103.0	29	2.53	3.05
Danny Jackson	6	1	1	38.1	11	2.58	4.03
Jack McDowell	8	5	1	61.0	18	2.66	3.60
Bill Wegman	7	3	2	44.0	13	2.66	3.73

It figures that Dave Stewart would be the best; heck, he comes from Oakland, where it's been 50 degrees his entire life. So, it's something of a mystery why Stewart signed with the Blue Jays, who play indoors when it gets too cold. If he's Toronto's Opening Day starter, and they decide to keep the roof open and "let the fresh air in," we'll know who requested it.

A far better career move, in our estimation, was the one made by Dave Stieb, who fled SkyDome for the great outdoors of Chicago. The Sox will be set for those April series with the combination of Stieb (7-0, 1.69) and Black Jack McDowell (5-1, 2.66). What a combination: Stieb and

McDowell, and pass the hot towel. Not to mention Alex Fernandez, who's 3-0 with a 1.44 ERA in four sub-50 degree starts.

While Stewart and Stieb lead the ERA parade, the real master of "winter league" play is probably Clemens. This Rocket runs on anti-freeze: Clemens has pitched more innings (114.1) and won more games in sub-50 degree weather than any pitcher in baseball over the last four years. Doesn't the man have enough advantages?

Other pitchers you might want to start those playoff night games would be Greg Maddux (8-4, 2.53) and Chris Bosio (9-5, 3.38 in a manly 16 sub-50 degree starts). They must have Dave Stewart's agent, however: Maddux opted to play in balmy Atlanta this year, while Bosio went all the way to Seattle just to come in out of the cold. When they both prove to be free-agent duds, you'll know the reason why.

How about the wimps who shiver out on the mound for a couple of innings, serving up lollipops until the manager takes them out? We hesitate to question the fortitude of pitchers like Frank Tanana and Jack Morris, but look how they let a little cold bother them:

Worst ERAs When It's 50 Degrees or Less — 1989-92

Pitcher	G	W	L	IP	ER	ERA	Other Games
Frank Tanana	8	1	5	44.1	32	6.50	4.08
Todd Stottlemyre	11	1	4	37.2	27	6.45	4.21
Jaime Navarro	6	3	1	35.2	22	5.55	3.62
Jack Morris	10	4	5	63.1	38	5.40	4.04
Scott Sanderson	7	2	3	43.0	25	5.23	4.10

Another cagey free agent move: Frank Tanana will be working in Shea Stadium this year, where it's always cozy and warm. Todd Stottlemyre and Morris (Toronto), at least, are smart enough to come indoors.

A complete listing for this category can be found on page 170.

WHAT KIND OF PITCHER HAS TROUBLE IN THE FIRST?

Are good pitchers vulnerable in the first inning? If you listen to major league broadcasts or talk to managers, you might think there was no room for debate: "You've gotta get this guy early, before he settles down," is probably engraved on a plaque in every television booth, just so they won't forget to say it. But is the old adage really true?

From an overall perspective, it is. Major league starting pitchers do indeed have higher ERAs in the first inning than they do over the rest of the game. Here are the 1992 figures:

ERA in the first inning	4.23
ERA the rest of the game	3.78

When you think about, it makes a lot of sense that starters would have more trouble in the first inning than they would the rest of the game:

1. In the first, they're trying to learn which pitches are working best for them that day. When they find out, they'll concentrate on the ones which are working and stay away from the ones which aren't. Until then, they're a little more vulnerable than usual.

2. In the first, they have to face the opposing lineup in the order chosen by the opposing manager for optimum effect. It's the one time the leadoff man is guaranteed to bat first and the No. 3 hitter third; that, by itself, makes the opposition more dangerous.

But, of course, what the announcers are saying is always applied specifically to the best pitchers — get Clemens early, or it's all over. So let's look at the starters who had the worst ERAs in the first inning last year (minimum 25 innings), and see if we find any aces:

The Worst in the First

Pitcher, Team	First IP		Rest of Game	
	IP	ERA	IP	ERA
Jack Morris, Tor	34.0	6.88	206.2	3.57
Charlie Hough, WSox	26.2	6.75	149.2	3.43
Tim Belcher, Cin	33.2	6.15	194.0	3.53
Mark Gardner, Mon	30.0	6.00	149.2	4.03
Donovan Osborne, StL	29.0	5.90	150.0	3.36
Tom Candiotti, LA	29.2	5.76	174.0	2.53
Bill Gullickson, Det	33.0	5.73	188.2	4.10
Kevin Brown, Tex	35.0	5.66	230.2	2.97
Frank Tanana, Det	31.0	5.52	155.2	4.16
Tom Glavine, Atl	33.0	5.45	192.0	2.30
Ken Hill, Mon	33.0	5.45	185.0	2.19

There are a lot of good pitchers on this list, starting with 21-game winner Jack Morris; almost one-fourth of the earned runs Morris permitted last year (26 of 108) were tallied in the first. And look at some of the others, like Kevin Brown (5.66 ERA in the first, 2.97 thereafter) and the Braves' Tom Glavine, who is notorious for his first inning problems (5.45 ERA in the first, 2.30 from then on). Other aces who struggled in the first included Mark Langston (5.34), Bill Swift (5.32), Nolan Ryan (4.85) and Jack McDowell (4.76).

But how about the pitchers who were **best** in the first? Here's the leaders list:

The Best in the First

Pitcher, Team	First IP		Rest of Game	
	IP	ERA	IP	ERA
Mike Morgan, Cubs	34.0	0.53	206.0	2.88
Bud Black, SF	28.0	0.64	149.0	4.59
Dennis Martinez, Mon	32.0	1.13	194.1	2.69
David Cone, Mets-Tor	34.0	1.32	215.2	3.05
Frank Castillo, Cubs	33.0	1.36	172.1	3.86
Juan Guzman, Tor	28.0	1.61	152.2	2.83
Jose Rijo, Cin	33.0	1.64	178.0	2.73
Mike Mussina, Bal	32.0	1.69	209.0	2.67
Bill Wegman, Mil	35.0	1.80	226.2	3.41
Ben McDonald, Bal	35.0	1.80	192.0	4.69

There's some heavy-duty talent on this list also, including Morgan, Martinez, Cone, Guzman, Rijo, Mussina . . . just as many aces who did well in the first as on the other list. National League Cy Young Award winner Greg Maddux had a 2.06 ERA in the first, 2.20 thereafter. You'll notice that, as with the first list, there are many types of pitchers represented: power and finesse, fastball and breaking-ball.

So is it true that good pitchers are vulnerable in the first, and that if you don't get them then, it's all over? Not really; as a rule, the first inning is the toughest for **most** pitchers. As far as the staff aces are concerned, many of them are just as tough, or even tougher in the first than they are later. There are always guys like Glavine who seem to need an inning to settle down, but he's hardly typical.

A complete listing for this category can be found on page 302.

WHY CAN'T PITCHERS HIT ANYMORE?

PITCHERS WHO CAN HIT

	HR	AVG.
Don Robinson	13	.231
Tim Leary	1	.221
Rick Aguilera	3	.203
Dwight Gooden	5	.198

Active pitchers with a minimum of 150 plate appearances lifetime.

Looking at the way pitchers hit these days, George Uhle (.289 lifetime average) must be turning over in his grave. Not to mention Red Lucas (.281). Or Wes Ferrell (.280). Or Red Ruffing (.269). Even when you concede that these good-hitting pitchers of the past played in an era when batting averages were higher, you must admit that there's no one like them in baseball these days. And that's a shame; something has been lost from the game.

Scanning our annual list of the best-hitting pitchers in the game, we find that only three can even top the .200 mark. And those three are Don Robinson, who will be probably be out of baseball in 1993; Tim Leary, who has one foot out the door; and Rick Aguilera, the relief ace for an American League team. The active top 10 (minimum 150 lifetime plate appearances):

Best Hitting Pitchers — Active Career Leaders						
Pitcher	**Avg**	**AB**	**H**	**2B**	**3B**	**HR**	**RBI**
Don Robinson	.231	631	146	23	0	13	69
Tim Leary	.221	163	36	6	0	1	19
Rick Aguilera	.203	138	28	3	0	3	11
Dwight Gooden	.198	648	128	13	3	5	54
Sid Fernandez	.198	464	92	14	2	1	29
Orel Hershiser	.196	555	109	22	2	0	36
Dennis Rasmussen	.193	259	50	8	0	0	14
Tom Glavine	.185	356	66	5	2	0	27
Steve Avery	.184	185	34	3	2	0	6
Rick Sutcliffe	.184	539	99	21	1	4	54
Greg Maddux	.184	490	90	10	0	2	29

The tradition of good-hitting pitchers is still being carried on by Dwight Gooden (.264 last year), Tom Glavine (.247 in '92), Orel Hershiser (.221 last year) and others like Fernandez, Avery and Maddux. But these days .180 is a good batting average for a pitcher, and that's awfully low.

Why can't pitchers hit any more? As we've pointed out in past editions of this book, only a few clubs seem to realize that pitchers can help themselves win a few games with the bat: the Dodgers, the Mets and the Braves are about it. Those teams have the attitude that anyone can help himself with the bat, even if only a little. For example, last season Tom Candiotti signed with Los Angeles and found himself swinging a bat for the first time in his professional career. Candiotti batted only .107, but he made himself useful by laying down 12 sacrifice bunts, second only to Greg Maddux (13) among National League pitchers.

More pitchers could help themselves that way, but neither they nor their clubs seem to care. With the designated hitter rule in effect everywhere except the National League (including the minors), it becomes even more of an uphill struggle.

All of which makes the pitchers who really **can** handle a bat all the more valuable. Take Orel Hershiser, for example. He's not only a respectable hitter for average (.196 lifetime), but he also has 78 lifetime sacrifice hits, tops among pitchers, meaning that he can move up a runner with a bunt. And with five lifetime steals, he can't be taken for granted once he reaches base. Hershiser obviously thinks of himself as an athlete, not just a pitcher.

These guys don't have that same attitude — they have the lowest lifetime averages among active pitchers:

Worst Hitting Pitchers — Active Career Trailers

Pitcher	Avg	AB	H	2B	3B	HR	RBI
John Burkett	.052	174	9	2	0	0	6
Don Carman	.057	209	12	0	0	0	5
Mike Bielecki	.079	267	21	0	0	0	12
Bruce Ruffin	.080	263	21	3	0	0	6
Terry Mulholland	.082	294	24	3	0	0	6

Playing with the hitting-conscious Braves obviously helped Mike Bielecki last year. After entering the year with an .074 lifetime average, he hit .125. The Giants' John Burkett, though, seems to be following in the footsteps of the legendary San Francisco hurler Ron Herbel, who batted .029 lifetime. Last year Burkett had only one hit in 55 at-bats, a mighty .018 average. You can do better than that, John!

A complete listing for this category can be found on page 303.

WHAT HAPPENS TO ROOKIE PITCHERS THE SECOND TIME AROUND THE LEAGUE?

Back in 1981, when Fernando Valenzuela had his sensational rookie season with the Dodgers, he was simply unhittable for his first month or so. But then Valenzuela cooled off considerably, though he continued to pitch good ball. The smart baseball men nodded their heads wisely and said, "That's what happens the second time around the league."

This is part of baseball romance, of course. Supposedly there are hitters' and pitchers' grapevines, and when a hot new rookie comes around, the players on other teams studiously compare notes about the rookie's weaknesses. Then when they face the rookie again, they're able to exploit those weaknesses. Makes sense, doesn't it? — except, of course, when you consider that the rookies have been doing a little note-taking of their own.

Anyway let's give this theory a try. We'll begin by looking at last year's rookie starting pitchers. We found 22 who met the following standards: they were all rookies in 1992 (some had seen brief action prior to that); all of them started at least 10 games last year; and all of them faced at least two opponents a second time during the year. Most of them also faced clubs a third time or more, but that wasn't true of everybody.

Here's how the pitchers, as a group, fared when they faced a club the first time, the second time, and then in subsequent starts:

1992 Rookie Starters — the Second Time Around

First Time			Second Time			Subsequent		
GS	IP	ERA	GS	IP	ERA	GS	IP	ERA
227	1131.1	4.10	140	747.2	3.84	117	602.1	4.09

As you can see, the group, looked at as a whole, had no problems with the league their second time around; in fact, their ERAs improved. In subsequent starts their ERAs slipped back to their previous level.

However, there was enormous pitcher-to-pitcher variation. Some pitchers performed much better the second time they faced a club. Take the hottest rookie pitchers of 1992, Milwaukee's Cal Eldred and Pittsburgh's Tim Wakefield. Eldred had a 2.65 ERA the first time he faced a team. The second time, the acquired knowledge helped **him**, not the opponents: his ERA dropped to 1.60 in his second starts. Wakefield's results were similar: 2.51 ERA the first time he faced a club, 1.82 the second. Seattle's Dave Fleming, who cooled off after a sensational start, actually had a 5.06 ERA the first time he faced a club, a 2.60 mark the second time. If that seems puzzling, remember that there really is no "second time around the league" any more; the way the schedule is set up, a pitcher will usually face a club twice, in home-and-home series, over a short period of time.

There were other pitchers who had problems the second time they faced a club. The Cardinals' Donovan Osborne, who also started off pitching very well, had a 3.51 ERA the first time he faced a club, a 5.20 mark the second; Osborne then got his bearings and posted a 3.07 ERA in subsequent starts. The Padres' Frank Seminara, whose tricky crossfire motion takes some getting used to, had a 2.89 ERA the first time he faced a club, a 4.43 mark the second time, and a 4.68 ERA in subsequent starts. Dave Haas of the Tigers had a 3.32 ERA in his first outings, a 4.03 mark the second.

Looking over the entire group, we find that 13 pitchers had lower ERAs in their second starts against a club, while nine had higher ERAs. Not exactly overwhelming evidence. But the basic premise — that the league will do better against a rookie the second time they face him — simply isn't supported by the data.

How about the rookie relievers? There were 38 of them, and here are their figures:

1992 Rookie Relievers — the Second Time Around

First Time			Second Time			Subsequent		
G	IP	ERA	G	IP	ERA	G	IP	ERA
405	769.1	3.57	316	528.1	3.87	620	897.2	3.56

The hitters did have better luck the second time they faced a rookie reliever, as the pitchers' ERA rose from 3.57 to 3.87. However, the hitters apparently forgot what they learned almost immediately, as the ERAs went down to the original level in subsequent outings. Once again, you'd have trouble selling the notion that rookies get one free ride around the loop before the hitters catch on to their weaknesses. The pitchers are learning something, also; if they can really pitch, they'll have more going for them than just the element of surprise.

A complete listing for this category can be found on page 304.

WHO PITCHED BETTER IN 1992 — TOM GLAVINE OR MELIDO PEREZ?

Tom Glavine is the left-handed ace of the Atlanta Braves, and the Cy Young Award winner in 1991. There was no "Cy Young jinx" for Glavine last year; he followed up his 20-11 record and 2.56 ERA in '91 with similar figures in '92: 20-8, 2.76.

Melido Perez is the right-handed ace of the New York Yankees, and a guy who's never been near a Cy Young Award. Last year Perez went 13-16 for the Yanks, and yet, we submit, he was every bit as effective as Glavine. Look at their '92 figures in all the major categories except won-lost record:

	GS	CG	IP	H/9	BB/9	SO/9	ERA
Glavine	33	7	225.0	7.9	2.8	5.2	2.76
Perez	33	10	247.2	7.7	3.4	7.9	2.87

Each pitcher made 33 starts last year. Perez was the more durable, working more innings and completing more games. Despite pitching in the American League, where batting averages are higher, he permitted fewer hits per nine innings. He was the superior power pitcher, striking out over 50 percent more men per nine innings than Glavine did. Glavine gets the edge in walks and a slight edge in ERA, but remember that Perez was pitching in the heavier-hitting league. On the whole, there's little to choose between the two records; if anything, Perez had the superior numbers.

However, he was lacking in a number most people don't even know about: run support. As the chart shows, Glavine was blessed with 5.32 runs of

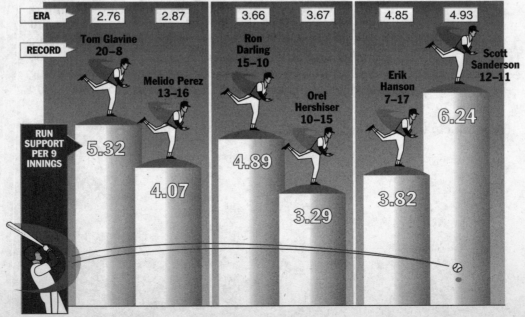

support for every nine innings he pitched last year. Perez, meanwhile, got only 4.07 runs on average from his Yankee teammates. Give Perez an extra 1.25 runs per game to work with over the course of his starts, and it's obvious that his won-lost record would have been a lot better than 13-16.

Or is it? The concept of run support, and its importance to a pitcher's record, has been around since Bill James brought it into prominence well over a decade ago. Yet even intelligent baseball people sometimes fall for the romance of the won-lost record.

Exhibit A in this regard last year was the Blue Jays' free-agent signee, Jack Morris. Throughout last year's regular season, Morris gave up a high number of runs — his ERA was a mediocre 4.04 — and yet he continued to pile up victories. We kept hearing how "Jack Morris just knows how to win" and that his ERA was irrelevant; we didn't hear much about the 5.98 runs per game the Blue Jays were scoring in his behalf. Morris (21-6) would even get considerable Cy Young support.

Then came the postseason, and the "Morris magic" was gone: in four starts Jack was 0-3 with a 7.43 ERA. The ERA suggests that he just pitched horribly and had no chance to win, but the facts say otherwise. In Game One of the playoffs, Morris gave up his usual four runs, but this time the Jays could score only three, and he was saddled with the loss. And in Game One of the World Series, he yielded three runs in six innings, but wound up a loser again when the Jays could score only one for him. Morris found it a lot tougher to win with only 2.7 runs per nine innings — his postseason level of support — than he did when the Jays were scoring six runs a game for him. So much for "knowing how to win."

The simple truth is that won-lost records, for the most part, depend on the pitcher's level of support as much they as they do on his ERA. Look at the other two comparisons in the graphic. The Yanks' Scott Sanderson had a higher ERA than the Mariners' Erik Hanson (4.93 to 4.85), yet he had the far superior record (12-11 to 7-17 for Hanson). The difference? Sanderson's mates scored an average of 6.24 runs per game for him (most in the majors), Hanson's only 3.82.

The other case is even more instructive. The Dodgers' Orel Hershiser and the A's Ron Darling worked almost the same number of innings (Hershiser 210.2, Darling 206.1) and had nearly identical ERAs (Hershiser 3.67, Darling 3.66). Yet Darling's record was 15-10, Hershiser's 10-15. Do you think the difference was the extra 1.6 runs per game Darling had to work with, or do you think that Orel Hershiser just doesn't "know how to win"? If anyone out there thinks so, why don't you try telling him that?

A complete listing for this category can be found on page 306.

IS THE AUTOMATIC CLOSER-IN-THE-NINTH STRATEGY THE RIGHT MOVE?

One inning ago, you watched your team's pitcher blow away the opposition on nine pitches — all swings and misses. Now, as you settle in to watch the closing moments of a sure victory, you notice a gate open in left center field and a goateed, burly figure, with a scowl that could make a mime start babbling, take the mound for the bottom of the ninth. It's The Closer. Nine pitches later, following a hit batter, line drive single, wild pitch, double, walk, and a three-run homer, you're dialing up the local all-sports radio station demanding the manager be fired and, while the general manager's at it, let's trade the closer.

These days, the automatic "bring-in-your-closer" strategy is the seed of much second-guessing . . . especially when it backfires. Is this strategy really that pervasive, or are we just overreacting every time we see a closer snatch defeat from the jaws of victory? It's definitely not just our imagination. Going back to 1987, we looked at all instances in which save situations were in force at the start of the ninth inning — a close game, in other words. We then broke down those situations into two simple categories: those in which a new pitcher started the ninth, and those in which the pitcher who completed the eighth (starter or reliever) remained in the game. The change has been dramatic, an upheaval in the way the game is played:

Save Situations Entering the Ninth

Year	Total Save Situations	New Pitcher Starts 9th	Pct
1987	1,079	208	19.3%
1988	1,130	272	24.1%
1989	1,120	359	32.1%
1990	1,117	424	38.0%
1991	1,152	511	44.4%
1992	1,169	563	48.2%

Why is there an ever-increasing tendency to switch to a new pitcher? A basic one is that managers are becoming increasingly reluctant to stay with a tiring starter, even if he's pitching effectively. Given the arm problems encountered by "nine inning pitchers" like Fernando Valenzuela, perhaps that's prudent. Dare we say that managers may even be watching pitch counts on occasion?

But a bigger one is the way relief pitchers are being used. These days, the accepted strategy is to have set-up men work the seventh and eighth innings, while the closer is reserved for the ninth. Even a few years ago, it was much more common for the closer to come into the game in the eighth inning than it is now. You can see that from the history of a pitcher who was his team's closer in both 1987 and 1992: Toronto's Tom Henke. In '87, Henke worked in 72 games, and pitched 94 innings — an average of nearly an inning and a third per appearance. But by 1992, Henke had become almost exclusively a one-inning pitcher: 57 games, 55.2 innings. Don't underestimate the effect of one man — Dennis Eckersley — on this new trend. Tony La Russa's unique method of using his closer has been copied by managers hopeful of recreating Oakland's success.

Is this new push-button strategy working, or is it merely being followed because everyone's copying LaRussa? Two factors indicate that it does indeed work. First, except for a dip from 1988 to 1989, closers starting off the ninth inning have been saving games at a gradually rising rate: from 84.6% in 1987 to 88.5% last season. That doesn't seem like much, but it can mean a gain of two to three wins a season for a club. Second, look at this ERA comparison between a new pitcher in the ninth, and that of a previous pitcher who remains in the game:

9th-Inning Team Earned Run Averages

Year	New Pitcher	Previous Pitcher Stays In	Difference
1987	3.58	3.55	+ .03
1988	3.01	3.07	− .06
1989	3.04	2.66	+ .38
1990	3.01	3.09	− .08
1991	2.96	3.40	− .44
1992	2.76	2.96	− .20

Except for a small difference in 1987 and a strange blip in 1989, the new pitcher has had a better ninth-inning ERA than one who remains in the game. In 1991 and 1992, as the game grew even more specialized, the ERA difference was substantial. Though it sometimes backfires, bringing in a fresh arm seems to be the proper strategy.

WAS MEL ROJAS BETTER THAN THE ECK LAST YEAR?

In other essays in this book, we talk about two of the tools we use to evaluate relief pitchers: saves (for closers) and holds (for middle relievers). While both numbers are very useful, they don't tell you how often the relief pitcher failed.

We already keep track of blown saves and we compute save percentages (saves per opportunity). The next step is perfectly logical. Since a "blown hold" is exactly the same as a blown save (and is recorded as such), it makes sense to create another percentage. What we do is add the saves and holds together, divide by the total number of opportunities (holds plus saves plus blown saves) and come up with a "hold-plus-save percentage."

This helps give us a better perspective on relievers, especially middle relievers. Let's use Mark Guthrie, the Twins' set-up man last year, as an example. Last year Guthrie had five saves, and two blown saves; his save percentage (71 percent) makes him look like nothing special. The hidden factor is that Guthrie had 19 holds in addition to the five saves. He actually converted 24 of the 26 opportunities he was given, a superior 92 percent. That was one of the best success rates in baseball last year. Here are the 1992 leaders in hold-plus-save percentage (minimum 20 opportunities):

1992 Leaders — Hold-Plus-Save Percentage

Pitcher, Team	Holds	Saves	H+S Opp	Hold+ Save Pct.
Mel Rojas, Mon	13	10	24	95.8
Jeff Parrett, Oak	19	0	20	95.0
Dennis Eckersley, Oak	0	51	54	94.4
Tom Henke, Tor	4	34	41	92.7
Mark Guthrie, Min	19	5	26	92.3
Roger Mason, Pit	11	8	21	90.5
Duane Ward, Tor	25	12	41	90.2
Mike Stanton, Atl	15	8	26	88.5
Doug Henry, Mil	1	29	34	88.2
Joe Grahe, Cal	1	21	25	88.0

The superior work of middle men like Mel Rojas, Jeff Parrett and Guthrie is apparent here, along with the outstanding work of closers like Dennis Eckersley and Tom Henke. As for the big question — was Rojas really better than Eckersley last year? — we can't really say yes; a hold isn't quite as good as a save. What we **will** say is that both Rojas and Eckersley were nearly perfect in completing their assigned tasks last year, whether it be to hold the fort or to nail down the save.

These pitchers, though, were quite **im**perfect last year; they had the lowest hold-plus-save percentages:

1992 Trailers — Hold-Plus-Save Percentage

Pitcher, Team	Holds	Saves	H+S Opp	Hold+ Save Pct.
Jeff Nelson, Sea	6	6	20	60.0
Roger McDowell, LA	5	14	27	70.4
Stan Belinda, Pit	0	18	24	75.0
Jeff Reardon, Bos-Atl	0	30	40	75.0
Mike Schooler, Sea	3	13	21	76.2
Anthony Young, Mets	2	15	22	77.3
Jeff Russell, Tex-Oak	1	30	40	77.5
Rod Beck, SF	4	17	27	77.8
Bobby Thigpen, WSox	3	22	32	78.1
Greg Harris, Bos	19	4	29	79.3
Scott Radinsky, WSox	16	15	39	79.5

Even when you factor in the holds they recorded last year, Jeff Nelson of the Mariners and Roger McDowell of the Dodgers still don't look like very good pitchers. As for closers Stan Belinda and Jeff Reardon, their nightmarish postseasons shouldn't have been a total shock; their shaky regular-season relief work is clearly identified here (and elsewhere in this book).

In case you're wondering, the average major league team converted 81 percent of its hold-plus-save opportunities last year. The A's, with Eckersley and Parrett, converted 92 percent for the highest total; the Phillies, who got only 18 holds from their relievers all year, converted only 69 percent for the lowest. The Phils were the only National League club with a conversion rate under 80 percent last year. You're not going to win many games with a bullpen like that, and the Phils didn't.

A complete listing for this category can be found on page 307.

DID BELINDA SQUANDER THE BUCS' INHERITANCE?

Game Seven of last year's National League Championship Series, bottom of the ninth; who can ever forget it? Let's go back to a pivotal moment, when Pirate manager Jim Leyland brought in his "ace" reliever, Stan Belinda, with the bases loaded, nobody out, and a 2-0 lead. Leyland stuck with Belinda the rest of the way, and Pirate fans watched in horror as all three runners came around to score. Bye-bye pennant.

Was it a total surprise that Belinda would let those runners come home? Not to anyone who knew about his "inherited runner" ratio. During the 1992 regular season, Belinda came in with a total of 28 Pirate runners on board. He permitted 18 of them to score, or 64.3 percent — the worst ratio in baseball last year (see chart). None of those runs were charged to Belinda, so his ERA of 3.15 was unaffected. But they scored just the same, and the statistic marked Belinda as a very risky guy to bring in with runners on base. Leyland chose to do so anyway, and paid a very heavy price.

Minimum 25 inherited runners.

BEST	Inherited runners	Inherited runners scored	PCT.	WORST			
Dennis Eckersley	31	2	6.5%	Stan Belinda	28	18	64.3%
Steve Frey	50	5	10.0%	Les Lancaster	38	24	63.2%
Wilson Alvarez	25	3	12.0%	Barry Jones	33	18	54.5%
Dennis Powell	50	6	12.0%	Jeff Reardon	30	15	50.0%
Scott Bankhead	28	4	14.3%	Marvin Freeman	42	20	47.6%
ML Average	6340	1955	30.8%				

Before we jump all over Leyland, however, consider how Tony La Russa must feel. Last year Tony had the best reliever in baseball in Dennis Eckersley, and not just the best in terms of saves. As the chart shows, Eckersley permitted only two of his 31 inherited runners to score last year (6.5 percent), the top figure in baseball. Yet in the Championship Series against Toronto, he permitted more inherited runners to score (3 out of 3) than he had all season long. La Russa, at least, had more reason to expect success than Leyland did.

Though it obviously can't tell you what'll take place in an individual situation, the inherited runner stat is one of the best when it comes to identifying hidden relief stars. That's especially true for middle relievers; in today's specialized age, it's the middle men who usually get the call when pitchers are changed with runners on base. The trend in recent years has been to have the closer come in at the start of the ninth, so closers get far fewer inherited runner situations than middle men do.

Take Steve Frey, for example. Last year the Angel lefty appeared in 51 games, and his 4-2 record, four saves and 3.57 ERA were nothing special. But he came in with 50 runners on base, and only five of them scored (10.0 percent) — a ratio second only to Eckersley's. Another example: Seattle's Dennis Powell looked out-and-out bad, with a 4.58 ERA over 49 appearances. But Powell's inherited runners figure (6 of 50 scoring, 12.0) shows that he did some good pitching.

This stat can identify some overrated pitchers, also. Belinda was one last year; another one was Jeff Reardon, a bad relief pitcher living off his reputation (as Bobby Cox would learn, the hard way). Baseball can be a merciless game, even to the all-time saves leader.

Here's how the teams performed in this category last year:

	American League		
Team	Runners Inherited	Runners Scored	Scored Percent
Athletics	305	78	25.6
Twins	261	70	26.8
Indians	328	93	28.4
Mariners	346	101	29.2
White Sox	226	67	29.6
Orioles	274	83	30.3
Brewers	280	86	30.7
Angels	231	71	30.7
Royals	208	68	32.7
Red Sox	332	110	33.1

Tigers	273	93	34.1
Blue Jays	132	45	34.1
Rangers	292	107	36.6
Yankees	203	75	36.9

National League

Team	Runners Inherited	Runners Scored	Scored Percent
Astros	259	60	23.2
Dodgers	260	66	25.4
Cardinals	211	54	25.6
Cubs	265	74	27.9
Expos	241	72	29.9
Reds	208	63	30.3
Giants	237	72	30.4
Braves	186	61	32.8
Pirates	210	71	33.8
Mets	188	64	34.0
Padres	221	78	35.3
Phillies	163	73	44.8

The A's, with Eckersley, and the Houston Astros, with a deep and effective bullpen, led the way. The surprise is the poor showing by the world champion Blue Jays. This was also a problem for the Jays in 1991. But you'll notice that Cito Gaston brought his relievers in with only 132 runners on base all season — fewer than any other team. If the Jays' relievers had problems coming in with runners on base, Gaston's straightforward solution was to not bring them in. You'd have to say it worked pretty well.

A complete listing for this category can be found on page 308.

WHY DON'T SOUTHPAWS WHO CAN HANDLE LEFTIES HAVE IT MADE?

Left-handed relievers . . . they're so misunderstood. It's not just that their left-handedness sets them apart in a predominantly right-handed world. It's something more fundamental: people don't completely understand the nature of their job.

When most people think about lefty relievers, they see them as specialists who come in to pitch to a left-handed hitter or two, then get out of there when the righties come to bat. That's the theory, but the reality is that even lefty specialists face more right-handed hitters than they do lefties. Most hitters are righties, and nearly 70 percent of all at-bats in the major leagues last year were recorded by right-handed hitters. When a lefty pitcher is brought in to pitch to a lefty, the opposing manager will quite often counter with a right-handed pinch hitter. Even when that doesn't happen, the southpaw will usually stay in the game, and the odds are overwhelming that most of the remaining hitters will be righties. Last year there were 68 pitchers who worked at least one game in relief, and pitched to at least 50 lefties and 50 righties, which isn't much. Know how many of them pitched to more lefties than righties? Exactly one — the ultimate specialist, John Candelaria, whose 50 appearances covered only 25.1 innings.

So when we look at the lefty relievers who were most effective against left-handed hitters last year, keep in mind that all of them faced more righties than lefties . . . usually many more. In many cases, it simply wasn't enough that they were effective against lefties:

Pitcher, Team	Vs. LHB				Vs. RHB			
	Avg	AB	H	HR	Avg	AB	H	HR
Bob MacDonald, Tor	.143	63	9	0	.336	122	41	4
Floyd Bannister, Tex	.174	46	8	2	.333	93	31	1
Scott Radinsky, WSox	.182	66	12	2	.269	156	42	1
Steve Frey, Cal	.189	53	10	5	.261	111	29	1
Mike Munoz, Det	.192	73	14	0	.283	106	30	3
Bob McClure, StL	.198	91	18	4	.315	108	34	2
Russ Swan, Sea	.198	81	16	0	.278	316	88	8
Derek Lilliquist, Cle	.200	90	18	1	.176	119	21	4
Vince Horsman, Oak	.203	74	15	1	.296	81	24	2
Mark Guthrie, Min	.205	88	18	0	.220	186	41	7

(Minimum 20 games in relief, 50 BFP vs. both lefties and righties)

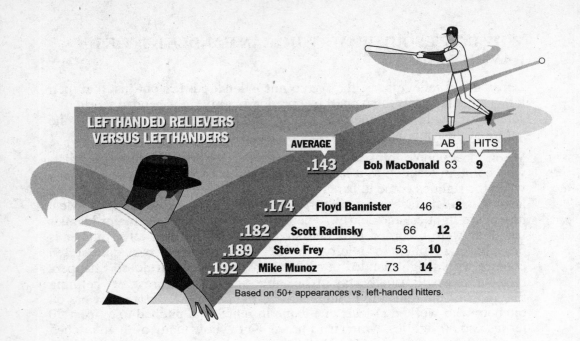

LEFTHANDED RELIEVERS VERSUS LEFTHANDERS

AVERAGE		AB	HITS
.143	Bob MacDonald	63	9
.174	Floyd Bannister	46	8
.182	Scott Radinsky	66	12
.189	Steve Frey	53	10
.192	Mike Munoz	73	14

Based on 50+ appearances vs. left-handed hitters.

If being effective against lefties were the only criterion for a southpaw reliever, Bob MacDonald would have been a vital part of the Blue Jays' championship drive last year. Instead he was a little-used reliever who didn't even make Toronto's post-season roster. The reason? Righties lit him up for a .336 average, and the Jays couldn't hide that weakness. Floyd Bannister was in the same situation with the Rangers. Brought back from Japan to be a lefty "specialist" for Texas, Bannister couldn't hold his job because he had too many problems against righties. The Rangers released him before the season was over. On the other hand, relievers like Derek Lilliquist and Mark Guthrie, who could retire both lefties **and** righties, found their jobs a lot more secure.

There are also, of course, lefty relievers who have the world backwards. These pitchers couldn't retire lefties at all; in most cases, they were worse against lefties than they were vs. righties. These were the 10 worst left-handed relievers against lefties in 1992 (same criteria):

Pitcher, Team	Vs. LHB				Vs. RHB			
	Avg	AB	H	HR	Avg	AB	H	HR
Mike Magnante, KC	.375	72	27	1	.312	282	88	4
Scott Bailes, Cal	.360	50	18	0	.347	118	41	7
Juan Agosto, StL-Sea	.349	63	22	0	.314	140	44	2
Paul Gibson, Mets	.338	71	24	3	.266	173	46	4

Pitcher, Team	Vs. LHB				Vs. RHB			
	Avg	AB	H	HR	Avg	AB	H	HR
Mark Davis, KC-Atl	.305	59	18	1	.299	154	46	8
Jim Pena, SF	.296	54	16	2	.275	120	33	2
Norm Charlton, Cin	.296	71	21	2	.251	231	58	5
David Wells, Tor	.293	92	27	3	.288	386	111	13
Kevin Wickander, Cle	.278	54	15	0	.250	96	24	1
Lee Guetterman, Yanks-Mets	.278	90	25	1	.362	185	67	9

This is not exactly an elite list, as you might imagine. Most of these guys will be scrambling for jobs in 1993; the exceptions would be Norm Charlton, who is a favorite of ex-Reds, and new Seattle, manager Lou Piniella, and David Wells, who redeemed himself last year with a good post-season. But as usual, all these pitchers faced many more righties than lefties; their problems with righties jeopardize their careers at least as much as their troubles with lefties do.

A complete listing for this category can be found on page 309.

WHERE WILL THE TREND TOWARD "SPECIALIST RELIEVERS" END?

Though he's now nearly 40 years old, John Candelaria is still blazing trails. Pitching for the Dodgers in 1992, Candelaria got into 50 games, which used to be considered a pretty heavy load for a pitcher. Yet in those 50 contests, he worked a grand total of 25.1 innings. Joe Oescher and Leon Cadore must have been turning over in their graves. Back in 1920, the Brave and Dodger hurlers worked more than that — 26 innings each — in **one afternoon**. What's baseball coming to?

What it's coming to is an era of massive specialization, more than could have been imagined even a few years ago. Lefty relief specialists have been around for awhile, but it wasn't until 1967 that a pitcher, Dan Schneider of the Astros, averaged less than one inning an outing in a 50-appearance season. Schneider's feat was so unusual that it wasn't duplicated until 1980: the Braves' Larry Bradford pitched 55.1 innings while working in 56 games. Throughout the 1980s, the feat was achieved by no more than one or two pitchers a year; in 1990 three pitchers did it, in 1991 four. Here's the complete list, through 1991; all the pitchers were lefties, and you'll notice how the number of outs per game gradually crept down as managers sought more and more specialization:

Pitchers with 50 or more games in a season averaging less than one inning an appearance

Year	Pitcher, Team	Games	IP	Outs/Gm
1967	Dan Schneider, Hou	54	52.2	2.93
1980	Larry Bradford, Atl	56	55.1	2.96
1982	Ed Vande Berg, Sea	78	76.0	2.92
1983	Ed Vande Berg, Sea	68	64.1	2.84
1984	Gary Lucas, Mon	55	53.0	2.89
	Jimmy Key, Tor	63	62.0	2.95
1985	Ed Vande Berg, Sea	76	67.2	2.67
1986	Joe Sambito, Bos	53	44.2	2.53
	Pat Clements, Pit	65	61.0	2.82
1987	Ray Searage, WSox	58	55.2	2.88
1988	Jesse Orosco, LA	55	53.0	2.89
1989	Kevin Hickey, Bal	51	49.1	2.90
1990	Keith Comstock, Sea	60	56.0	2.80
	Rob Murphy, Bos	68	57.0	2.51
	Scott Radinsky, WSox	62	52.1	2.53
1991	John Candelaria, LA	59	33.2	1.71
	Rob Murphy, Sea	57	48.0	2.53
	Tony Fossas, Bos	64	57.0	2.67
	Scott Ruskin, Mon	64	63.2	2.98

Just a little creeping specialization at work, right? Wrong. In '91, Tommy Lasorda used Candelaria differently than any reliever had ever been used before — 59 games, but only 33.2 innings, or less than two outs for each appearance. Candelaria was seen as fairly effective in that role, even though his ERA was 3.74, and the Dodgers came within an eyelash of winning a division title. People noticed, and in baseball everyone imitates success.

Then came 1992, and what happened was totally without precedent. Through 1991, there had been a total of 19 "specialist seasons" (50 or more games, average of less than one inning per outing) in 116 years of baseball history . . . all since 1967. But in 1992 alone, there were 22, more than in all the previous years combined. There were even some righty specialists for the first time:

Pitchers with 50 or more games in 1992 averaging less than one inning an appearance

Pitcher, Team	Games	IP	Outs/Gm
Tony Fossas, Bos	60	29.2	1.48
John Candelaria, LA	50	25.1	1.52
Jesse Orosco, Mil	59	39.0	1.98
Rick Honeycutt, Oak	54	39.0	2.17
Mike Munoz, Det	65	48.0	2.22
Vince Horsman, Oak	58	43.1	2.24
Bob McClure, StL	71	54.0	2.28
Scott Radinsky, WSox	68	59.1	2.62
Derek Lilliquist, Cle	71	61.2	2.61
Steve Frey, Cal	51	45.1	2.67
Al Osuna, Hou	66	61.2	2.80
Scott Ruskin, Cin	57	53.2	2.82
Rob Murphy, Hou	59	55.2	2.83
Doug Henry, Mil	68	65.0	2.87
Todd Worrell, StL	67	64.0	2.87
Pat Clements, SD-Bal	50	48.1	2.90
Jeff Reardon, Bos-Atl	60	58.0	2.90
Paul Assenmacher, Cubs	70	68.0	2.91
Kenny Rogers, Tex	81	78.2	2.91
Mike Schooler, Sea	53	51.2	2.92
Tom Henke, Tor	57	55.2	2.93
Mike Stanton, Atl	65	63.2	2.94

Worrell, Henry, Reardon, Schooler and Henke are all righties — the first ever to be used this way. Where will it end? Lord knows; this is getting like football, with "sack specialists" and the like. But as long as people perceive that it works — the truth is that a lot of the pitchers weren't terribly effective in the role — you can expect it to continue.

WHAT'S THE BEST PREDICTOR OF A PITCHER'S ERA?

Maybe you're a major league general manager, trying to strengthen your club for the upcoming season by adding another pitcher. Maybe you're a fantasy league player, trying to get a jump on the competition by acquiring a pitcher who you think will do well during the coming season. Or maybe you're just a serious fan, and want to have some sort of clue about which pitchers will succeed during the coming year. What are the best numbers to look at from the previous campaign?

Some of us thought the pitcher's earned run average during the first half of the previous season might be a good predictor. In the first half, his club will probably still be in the pennant race, and he (and his team) won't be merely playing out the string. If he has a slump in the second half, it might be due to fatigue; it's probable he would learn from that and be better able to deal with it the next season.

Others thought that the pitcher's second-half ERA would be more revealing. It's common for a pitcher to learn things during the course of a season: he'll work with the pitching coach, perhaps change his delivery, and things will finally fall into place over the second half of the year. Then, during the following season, he'll pick up where he left off.

Still others thought that you can't learn much by looking at a half-year's worth of numbers: the best predictor would be the full-season ERA. After all, numbers based on a few months of work are often extremely deceptive; a season is six months long, not three.

So, what is the best predictor of next-season success: first-half ERA, second-half ERA, or full-season ERA? We chose a sample of 177 pitchers, all of whom pitched at least 25 innings during each half of 1991, and all of whom pitched at least 50 innings in 1992. Which numbers correlated the best with the pitcher's 1992 ERA? Let's examine them one-by-one:

First-Half ERA: There were, indeed, a number of pitchers whose ERA during the first half in 1991 proved to be the best predictor of how they would fare in 1992. For example, Jack McDowell of the White Sox had a 3.20 ERA in the first half of 1991, weakened to a 3.63 mark in the second half of the year . . . but then posted a 3.18 ERA for the '92 season. McDowell's teammate Scott Radinsky proved to be a fooler: he had a 2.60 ERA in the first half of '91, a 1.47 mark in the second half . . . but then a 2.73 ERA for the full season of 1992. Eric King, then of the Indians, had a poor first half in '91 (5.49 ERA), a good second half (3.67), and then went out and proved that the second-half improvement was an illusion (5.22 ERA in 1992). However, there wasn't all that strong a correlation overall between first-half ERA and next-season performance. Adding up all 177 pitchers, the correlation to 1992 ERA was only 0.19, which is not very strong (1.00 would be perfect, 0 indicates no correlation).

Second-Half ERA: This proved to correlate more strongly with 1992 performance than the first-half ERA did. Randy Myers, who had a 2.42 ERA in the first half of 1991 and a 4.20 ERA in the second half, had a 4.29 ERA in 1992. The Dodgers' Ramon Martinez, whose ERA was 2.54 for the first half of 1991, 4.15 for the second, had a 4.00 ERA in 1992. Baltimore's Ben McDonald, who followed a 6.00 ERA first half of 1991 with a 4.20 second half, had a 4.24 ERA in 1992. Overall, the correlation between second-half ERA and 1992 performance was 0.38, twice as good as that for first-half ERA.

Full-Season ERA: This provided the best correlation of all, though only slightly better than second-half ERA did. The Angels' Jim Abbott sharply improved during the second half of 1992 (3.45 first half, 2.38 second), but it was his full-season figure (2.89) which best predicted his 1992 work (2.77). Charlie Leibrandt's up-and-down 1991 (3.16 first half, 3.85 second) worked out to a 3.49 ERA for the year; his ERA in '92 was 3.36. Cincinnati's Rob Dibble had a 1.29 ERA in the first half of '91, a 5.13 mark in the second half, but his overall '91 ERA of 3.17 almost perfectly matched the way he would pitch in '92 (3.07). Overall, the correlation between 1991 full season ERA and 1992 full season ERA was 0.40.

Pitchers, of course, are the most unpredictable of ballplayers, and an 0.40 correlation isn't sensational. But it's a reasonably good predictor. If you want to know what a pitcher's ERA will be this season, you should start by looking at what it was last season. What could be simpler?

Correlation to 1992 ERA	
Sample	**Correlation**
ERA, 1st Half 1991	0.19
ERA, 2nd Half 1991	0.38
ERA, Full Year 1991	0.40

A complete listing for this category can be found on page 310.

CAN A CLOSER RACK UP THOSE SAVES, WITHOUT A MAN TO HOLD THE FORT?

One of our inventions, the "hold," has earned increased respect in major league circles. We award a hold to a reliever when he enters a game in a save situation, preserves the lead, and (after recording at least one out) passes on the save situation to the next reliever. What the stat does is identify the superior middle relievers — the ones who hold the opposition, but don't get either a win or a save.

In 1989, the Athletics' Rick Honeycutt was the major league leader in holds, and was a key contributor to Dennis Eckersley's great season (33 saves, 1.56 ERA); in 1990 the hold leader was Barry Jones of the White Sox, who helped Bobby Thigpen to a record 57 saves; in 1991, the hold leader was Mark Eichhorn of the Angels, who was the set-up man for the major league save leader, Bryan Harvey (46). The relationship was becoming clear: any time a closer had a truly superior season, he had a major helper who recorded a lot of holds.

In 1992, Eckersley had another one of those awesome seasons, with 51 saves. For once, his set-up man didn't lead the major leagues in holds, but that was because he had **two** superior set-up men in Jeff Parrett (19 holds) and Honeycutt (18). Here are the hold leaders for '92:

HOLDING THE FORT

HOLDS

Duane Ward	25
Todd Worrell	25
Paul Assenmacher	20
Greg Harris	19
Mark Guthrie	19
Jeff Parrett	19
Rick Honeycutt	18
Scott Radinsky	16
Jeff Innis	16
Marvin Freeman	16
John Habyan	16
Kenny Rogers	16

One interesting thing about this list is that the co-leaders, Duane Ward and Todd Worrell, are slated for bigger things this year. The Blue Jays let Tom Henke depart via free agency to give Ward their closer's job, and the Dodgers signed Worrell to make him their late man. You might think that this would be a logical progression: a guy shows he can hold a lead, so you make him the closer. It does happen now and then — Rob Dibble and Norm Charlton are two recent examples — but the pitchers who record the holds tend to be guys like Paul Assenmacher and Greg Harris, who don't throw hard enough to handle a late relief job. They know their place, in other words . . . and an important place it is.

Here are the team hold totals for 1992:

American League		National League	
Team	Holds	Team	Holds
Athletics	68	Cardinals	60
Twins	52	Braves	47
Indians	47	Cubs	45
Tigers	46	Dodgers	44
Yankees	42	Reds	41
Red Sox	41	Mets	40
Blue Jays	38	Pirates	36
White Sox	38	Padres	35
Mariners	38	Expos	34
Orioles	35	Giants	33
Royals	34	Astros	32
Brewers	33	Phillies	18
Rangers	31		
Angels	25		

This is pretty neat and clean: the A's, who had Eckersley, led the American League in holds, and the Cardinals, who had Lee Smith, led the National League. It doesn't always work out this way, however. Team hold totals tend to be very manager-dependent. Tony LaRussa and Joe Torre, who like deep, specialized bullpens with one reliever neatly giving way to another, will naturally produce more holds than someone like Cito Gaston, who until this year depended heavily on Ward and Henke, but no one else. A low hold total doesn't mean a club has an ineffective bullpen — last year's Astros are a perfect example.

A complete listing for this category can be found on page 311.

DO SOME PITCHERS TURN IT ON WITH RUNNERS IN SCORING POSITION?

Some pitchers are tough to hit, period. Like Roger Clemens. But sometimes a pitcher will come along who has a reputation for giving up a lot of hits — except when it really counts. Hall of Famer Early Wynn was known as that kind of pitcher throughout his career. Pete Vuckovich of the Brewers had the same reputation in 1982 — he yielded numerous hits and walks, yet he bore down in the clutch enough to win the Cy Young Award.

We thought we'd look at the starting pitchers who had the lowest opponents' average with runners in scoring position over the last three years. Would they be the same guys who were tough to hit, period — the Clemenses? Or would we find a couple of Vuckovich-style surprises, pitchers who were a lot tougher when they needed to be? Here are the top 10 for 1990-92 in lowest opponents' average with runners in scoring position (minimum 350 innings); to look for Wynns and Vuckoviches, we'll also show you their overall opponents' average, and the difference between the two:

1990-1992 Leaders
Pitching with Runners in Scoring Position

Pitcher	Scor Pos	Overall	Diff
David Cone	.197	.227	−.030
Roger Clemens	.202	.224	−.022
Randy Johnson	.203	.212	−.009
Nolan Ryan	.203	.198	+.005
Bill Swift	.203	.247	−.044
Sid Fernandez	.203	.207	−.004
Greg W. Harris	.206	.235	−.029
Dennis Martinez	.209	.222	−.013
Jose Guzman	.210	.256	−.046
Doug Drabek	.214	.243	−.029

For the most part, the leaders are pitchers you'd expect: guys like David Cone, Roger Clemens, Randy Johnson, Nolan Ryan are difficult to hit in any situation, and this one is no exception. The interesting thing is how most of these guys gear it up even more with the pressure on than they do normally. Cone's opponents' average was 30 points lower with men in scoring position than it was otherwise, Clemens' 22. Nine of the 10 were tougher in this situation than overall, improving by anywhere from four to 46 points. That's impressive; over the same span, major league hitters batted two points **higher** with men in scoring position than they did overall (.258 to .256).

Are there any Wynns and Vuckoviches in the group? You could nominate Jose Guzman (.256 overall, .210 with men in scoring position) and Bill Swift (.247 vs. .203). You'd also have to include Boston's Joe Hesketh (.267 vs. .226). That's a tough way to pitch; frankly, we prefer the close-the-door-all-the-time strategy practiced by Nolan Ryan (.198 overall, .203 scoring position).

Then there are the guys who make the hitters' eyes light up when there are runners in scoring position:

1990-1992 Trailers
Pitching with Runners in Scoring Position

Pitcher	Scor Pos	Overall	Diff
Walt Terrell	.309	.298	+.011
Les Lancaster	.305	.274	+.031
Jack Armstrong	.303	.267	+.036
Bob Milacki	.299	.271	+.028
Zane Smith	.296	.258	+.038
Greg Hibbard	.292	.265	+.027
John Burkett	.290	.266	+.024
Terry Mulholland	.290	.258	+.032
Todd Stottlemyre	.285	.256	+.029
Tom Browning	.283	.274	+.009

A few of the pitchers on this list are strictly cases of "round up the usual suspects"; hitters **always** seem to be glad to face Walt Terrell, for instance. Everyone on this list had an overall opponents' average of at least .256, so we're not talking about Nolan Ryan here. What's surprising is how much **easier** these guys are to light up in this situation than they are overall. A few of them — Zane Smith, Terry Mulholland, Todd Stottlemyre, Tom Browning — have reputations as pretty good pitchers. By their deeds if not their words, the hitters disagree.

A couple of other pitchers should be mentioned here, not that they'd want us to. Trevor Wilson (.241) and John Smiley (.249) both had fine opponents' averages overall, but they were strictly chumps with men in scoring position (.277 Wilson, .279 Smiley). Should we say they're like "Early Loss"?

A complete listing for this category can be found on page 312.

WHICH PITCHERS CAN REST IN PEACE?

A tale of two lefties:

"Bill" is 34 years old, an even-tempered sort of guy (his major league record is 57-57), and as would befit a native of Waukegan IL, the home of Jack Benny, he knows the importance of thrift: if you trust something important to a friend, you expect them to take care of it for you.

"Bob" is 35 years old, has a world championship ring, and was born in L.A., that great big freeway, where all the stars who never were are parking cars and pumping gas. A few years ago, he nearly cut off one of his pitching fingers while trimming hedges, so you could hardly blame him if he takes nothing for granted: entrust something to somebody else, and you can't expect you'll ever get it back.

Welcome to baseball, that great big family, where everyone's performance depends (to an extent) on everyone else. In the modern game, that axiom particularly applies to pitchers. The average game will feature more than three pitchers working for each team, and as a result their lives — at least in terms of their ERAs — become interdependent. When a pitcher leaves a game with runners on base, he counts on his relievers to keep those runners from scoring; if the relievers can't do the job, those "bequeathed" runs will score, and he'll be stuck with the tab in terms of a higher ERA.

Which is where "Bill" and "Bob" enter the picture. "Bill" is Bill Krueger, the well-traveled lefty who pitched last year for the Twins and Expos. Over the course of the year, he left the game with a total of 28 runners on base. Given his background, Krueger might have expected his bullpen mates to take care of his bequest, but they didn't: of the 28 runners he entrusted to his relievers, 18 of them scored. That made him the most victimized pitcher in baseball in 1992 (20 or more runners left).

"Bob," on the other hand, is Bobby Ojeda, last year of the Dodgers and now a member of the Cleveland Indians. In 1992, Ojeda left the mound with a total of 22 runners on base. Given **his** background, one might have expected that Ojeda's relievers would have cut off his finger, in the figurative sense. Instead, his bullpen allowed only one of those runners to score all season, and that obviously worked to Ojeda's benefit.

How much benefit? You can see by performing one of our favorite annual exercises. Imagine that Krueger was the one with the miserly bullpen, and that Ojeda was stuck with the spendthrifts. (We're sure **they** can imagine the scenario.) In that case, Krueger would have allowed 17 fewer earned runs; instead of 4.53, his ERA would have been 3.68. The difference probably cost him more than a few bucks in the free agent contract he signed with the Tigers.

	'Bequeathed runners'	Later scored	PCT.
THEIR BULLPENS DESERTED THEM			
Bill Krueger	28	18	64.3%
Dave Righetti	24	14	58.3%
Mark Langston	21	12	57.1%
Jose Guzman	23	13	56.5%
Daryl Irvine	25	14	56.0%
THEIR BULLPENS RESCUED THEM			
Bobby Ojeda	22	1	4.5%
Jay Howell	22	1	4.5%
Dan Plesac	21	1	4.8%
Bill Sampen	23	2	8.7%
Rob Murphy	34	3	8.8%
ML Average	6340	1955	30.8%

Minimum 20 'bequeathed runners'.

Now apply this exercise to Ojeda. With Krueger-type bullpen support, he would have permitted 14 more earned runs over the course of the season. Instead of 3.63, his ERA would have been 4.38. Who knows? The Indians might not have even been interested.

Do the same with pitchers like Dave Righetti (14 of 24 bequeathed runners scored, 5.06 ERA), Mark Langston (12 of 21, 3.66 ERA), Jay Howell (1 of 22, 1.54 ERA) and Dan Plesac (1 of 21, 2.96 ERA) and you'll see just how much one pitcher's ERA depends on another pitcher. With better, or worse, help from their bullpens, the ERAs would have been very different.

As we pointed out last year, the pitchers who bequeath the most runners are usually left-handed relievers, the specialists who will pitch to a couple of hitters and then leave the game. A total of six pitchers left 40 or more runners to their relievers last year: Bob McClure (43), Jesse Orosco (42), Greg A. Harris (42), Tony Fossas (41), Mike Munoz (41) and Scott Radinsky (40). All but Harris was a lefty reliever. Since the runners these pitchers left were usually still on first base, they tended to benefit more than the average pitcher, whose relievers permitted 31 percent of their inherited runners to score.

A complete listing for this category can be found on page 313.

HOW IMPORTANT IS THE "QUALITY START"?

Wild-eyed radicals that we are, we're right up front in admitting that we have a lot of respect for that bane of announcers and ex-ballplayers, the "quality start." (Of course, we're also right up front in admitting that we have two heads. John's is the one on the right.) Imperfect though it may be, the quality start measures good, consistent pitching; if you can last six innings and give up three earned runs or less — the **minimum** qualifications, we keep pointing out — you're giving your club an excellent chance to win the game. Which is the whole idea.

But when you look at the list of leaders in highest percentage of quality starts for last year, think about a few of the names that are missing, as well as the ones which are present (minimum 20 starts):

1992 Leaders — Highest Percentage of Quality Starts

Pitcher, Team	GS	QS	Pct
Greg Maddux, Cubs	35	30	85.7
Curt Schilling, Phi	26	22	84.6
Bob Tewksbury, StL	32	27	84.4
Sid Fernandez, Mets	32	26	81.3
Mike Morgan, Cubs	34	27	79.4
Dennis Martinez, Mon	32	25	78.1
Bill Swift, SF	22	17	77.3
Kevin Appier, KC	30	23	76.7
Mike Mussina, Bal	32	24	75.0
Doug Drabek, Pit	34	25	73.5

You keen-eyed fans of pitching are probably wondering where Roger Clemens, Juan Guzman and David Cone, to name three, were. Not to worry, they were just out of the top 10, at 71.9, 71.4 and 70.6 percent. Still none of them were up to the level of the amazingly consistent Greg Maddux who was like money in the bank for the Cubs during the season (and money out of the bank for the Braves after it). But where are four other names — Kevin Brown, Jack McDowell, Jack Morris and Tom Glavine, the majors' other 20-game winners, along with Maddux? Farther down the list . . . in one case, much farther:

Pitcher, Team	GS	QS	Pct
Kevin Brown, Tex	35	23	65.7
Jack McDowell, WSox	34	22	64.7
Tom Glavine, Atl	33	21	63.6
Jack Morris, Tor	34	19	55.9

All four of these pitchers had one thing in common, along with winning 20 games: they were exceptionally well-supported by their teammates. Glavine had the best run support in the National League last year, McDowell and Morris were in the top six in the AL, and Brown just missed the top 10. When a pitcher has a big lead, it's natural for him to coast a little, pace himself, and maybe give up that fourth run which spoils the quality start. That's particularly true of McDowell, one of the few pitchers left who expects to work nine innings. Last year Black Jack had five victories in which he gave up four or more earned runs — not quality starts, just wins.

However, you can get carried away with this. As we point out in the essay on pitcher run support, Jack (He Just Knows How to Win) Morris' exceptional support hid a lot of shaky pitching last year. Morris had 10 starts in which he gave up at least **five** earned runs; thanks to the Blue Jay offense, his record in those games was 4-4. He also had starts in which he gave up six and seven earned runs, but wound up with a no-decision. That's not pacing yourself; that's just bad pitching.

Speaking of bad pitching, these hurlers had the lowest percentage of quality starts last year:

1992 Leaders — Lowest Percentage of Quality Starts

Pitcher, Team	GS	QS	Pct
Jack Armstrong, Cle	23	7	30.4
Tim Leary, Yanks-Sea	23	7	30.4
Kelly Downs, SF-Oak	20	7	35.0
Bob Milacki, Bal	20	7	35.0
Butch Henry, Hou	28	10	35.7
Dennis Cook, Cle	25	10	40.0
Greg W. Harris, SD	20	8	40.0
Ricky Bones, Mil	28	12	42.9
Scott Kamieniecki, Yanks	28	12	42.9
Jimmy Jones, Hou	23	10	43.5

What should we say — that they just know how to lose?

A complete listing for this category can be found on page 314.

Do Knuckleballers Prefer a Dome — or the Wind in Their Face?

Back in 1987, when the Minnesota Twins made a deal to acquire knuckleballer Joe Niekro, Twins officials commented that their studies had shown that knuckleballers generally performed well in domed stadiums. Niekro, of course had had a long and successful run working in the Houston Astrodome, with two 20-win seasons.

As it turned out, Niekro was a flop with the Twins, going 8-14 in 1987-88 before retiring. That doesn't prove the Twins were wrong; even knuckleballers, who have amazing longevity, seem to lose their effectiveness at some point in their 40s. But the Twins comment has always intrigued us, and two of our colleagues, Rob Neyer and Pat Quinn, asked us to study the subject. Both of them felt the Twins were dead wrong; indeed, the greatest knuckleballer of them all, Hoyt Wilhelm, always felt he pitched his best with a strong wind blowing out. The wind resistance, Wilhelm thought, gave the pitch more dance.

So let's look at the subject. Our stadium data goes back to 1987, and we have five knuckleballers we can study: Joe Niekro, his brother Phil, Charlie Hough, Tom Candiotti and Tim Wakefield. The Niekro brothers were both pretty washed up by '87 (it was Phil's last year, and he went 7-13), but they nonetheless might have pitched better indoors. Here is data for all five pitchers, comparing their work when they're working in and out of domed stadiums. The figures are for starting assignments only, and the "Opp-ERA" is the earned run average of their opponents in those games, for purposes of comparison:

Dome (Closed)

Pitcher	G	W	L	IP	ER	ERA	Opp ERA
Tom Candiotti	14	3	4	89.2	30	3.01	3.27
Charlie Hough	18	2	11	120.1	52	3.89	1.99
Tim Wakefield	1	0	0	7.0	0	0.00	0.64
Joe Niekro	9	4	5	50.2	36	6.40	4.62
Phil Niekro	2	1	1	13.2	4	2.63	4.50
Total	44	10	21	281.1	122	3.90	2.96

No Dome

Pitcher	G	W	L	IP	ER	ERA	Opp ERA
Tom Candiotti	173	69	71	1170.1	444	3.41	3.54
Charlie Hough	174	69	65	1187.2	510	3.86	4.04
Tim Wakefield	12	8	1	85.0	22	2.33	3.96
Joe Niekro	19	3	9	99.2	63	5.69	3.14
Phil Niekro	24	6	12	125.0	93	6.70	3.89
Total	402	155	158	2667.2	1132	3.82	3.77

As you can see, there's a lot of variance here. Of the three pitchers who had at least nine dome starts, Candiotti pitched a little better indoors, Joe Niekro a lot worse, and Charlie Hough about the same, in terms of ERA. The overall won-lost record in dome games was 10-21, but that was mostly because Hough (2-11) had no runs to work with in his dome games. Overall the pitchers had a 3.90 ERA in their dome games, a 3.82 ERA in their non-dome games. So you can't really say there's an effect one way or another — not based on this data, anyway.

But how about wind direction, and Hoyt Wilhelm's theory? In this case, our data is complete back to 1989, when we regularly started recording wind direction at the start of every game. We do have some data from 1987-88, however, and we include it here. Here are the results:

All 5 Pitchers 1987-92 — Starts Only Wind Direction

	G	W	L	IP	ER	ERA	Opp ERA
Blowing In	93	34	43	623.0	272	3.93	3.57
Blowing Out	80	25	32	528.0	234	3.99	3.88
Blowing Across	114	54	37	790.0	293	3.34	3.84
Not Recorded	115	42	46	726.2	333	4.12	3.79
All Games	446	165	179	2949.0	1254	3.83	3.68

This data surprised us. The pitchers performed about the same whether the wind was blowing in (3.93 ERA) or out (3.99); they were best with a crosswind (3.34). This crosswind difference was entirely due to Candiotti, who had a 2.57 ERA over 49 starts. Hough, the other knuckleballer we have a significant amount of wind data for, pitched about the same with a crosswind (3.95 ERA) as he did normally (3.87). Hough pitched well with the wind blowing out (3.47); Candiotti didn't (4.23). So no pattern (in, out, across, or no wind at all) seemed to offer any across-the-board advantage. As with any pitch, the knuckleball just seems to be working or not working on certain days, regardless of conditions.

WHOSE HEATER IS THE HOTTEST?

In baseball, there are few things as thrilling as a great fastball pitcher. I — this is Don speaking — am an avid collector of old baseball films, and usually the view they offer of the past is less than flattering: fat white guys waddling around the bases, soft-tossing pitchers lobbing the ball over the plate. The game seems to be moving at half speed, and that **isn't** an illusion created by the film.

But just the other day I saw something I'd never seen before: about 30 seconds of Walter Johnson pitching. All I could say was, "Wow." Johnson had this nice, easy sidearm motion, but he had tremendous arm acceleration; the ball simply exploded out of his hand, and it made me feel sorry for the unseen hitter. Just watching it gave me goosebumps — Walter Johnson, throwing the fastball.

If "The Big Train" were around today, how would they use him? Well, he might be Roger Clemens' main rival for starting supremacy, but there's a good chance that someone would look at the package — big guy, throws 100 MPH, intimidates righties with that motion — and say, "Let's make him a closer." For, as we've lamented several times in the past, these days the guys who can really bring it seem to wind up in the bullpen. Our annual survey of the pitchers who struck out the most batters per nine innings last year includes only three starters:

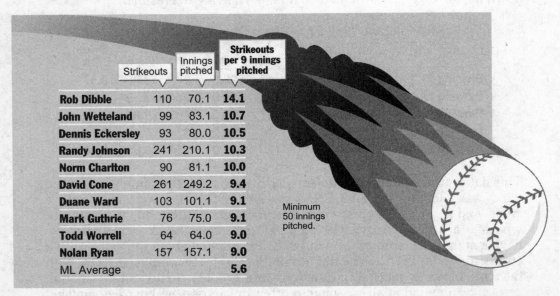

	Strikeouts	Innings pitched	Strikeouts per 9 innings pitched
Rob Dibble	110	70.1	**14.1**
John Wetteland	99	83.1	**10.7**
Dennis Eckersley	93	80.0	**10.5**
Randy Johnson	241	210.1	**10.3**
Norm Charlton	90	81.1	**10.0**
David Cone	261	249.2	**9.4**
Duane Ward	103	101.1	**9.1**
Mark Guthrie	76	75.0	**9.1**
Todd Worrell	64	64.0	**9.0**
Nolan Ryan	157	157.1	**9.0**
ML Average			**5.6**

Minimum 50 innings pitched.

This is probably blasphemous, but I'm not sure that any pitcher, even Walter Johnson, has ever thrown as hard as Rob Dibble. I grant you that he doesn't have to pace himself the way a starter does; grant, too, that he can be a world-class jerk. Forget all that and just look at his record: his strikeout rate is miles ahead of anyone else's. Last year, when he got a little "motivated" after the All-Star break, Dibble struck out 63 men in 34 innings of work — a strikeout rate of 16.7 per nine innings. Pretty unbelievable.

All in all, though, I think I'd rather have Walter Johnson on my pitching staff. (And he'd be a starter.)

Part two of our essay might be called, "Whose Slowball is the Slowest?" These were the pitchers who averaged the **fewest** strikeouts per nine innings last year:

Fewest Strikeouts Per Nine Innings — 1992

Pitcher, Team	IP	K	K/9 IP
Luis Aquino, KC	67.2	11	1.5
Jeff Johnson, Yanks	52.2	14	2.4
Brian Fisher, Sea	91.1	26	2.6
Bill Gullickson, Det	221.2	64	2.6
Curt Young, KC-Yanks	67.2	20	2.7
Terry Leach, WSox	73.2	22	2.7
Lee Guetterman, Yanks-Mets	66.0	20	2.7
Eric Hillman, Mets	52.1	16	2.8
John Doherty, Det	116.0	37	2.9
Tim Leary, Yanks-Sea	141.0	46	2.9

The Royals' Luis Aquino brought new shadings to the term "finesse pitcher" last year. In 67.2 innings, Luis walked only 20 batters, and that's pretty good control. But he still wound up with nearly twice as many walks as he had strikeouts (11). Did any of his pitches stop halfway to the plate, like in a Bugs Bunny cartoon? No, they all got there, and the grateful hitters whacked them for a .303 average.

Not to make the guys on this list nervous, but the top (or, I should say, bottom) five in this category from 1991 didn't exactly fare too well in '92. Four of them (Jeff Ballard, Roy Smith, John Barfield and John Cerutti) didn't pitch in the majors at all last year; the fifth, Dave (No Man is an) Eiland, got into seven games for the Padres, with a 5.67 ERA. So you might think that Bill Gullickson and Terry Leach are really clever fellows, and that they're going to keep fooling the hitters in 1993.

Don't count on it.

A complete listing for this category can be found on page 315.

IF THEY THROW GROUNDBALLS IN THE FIRST, WILL IT BE FLYBALLS IN THE SEVENTH?

One of our readers, a fine baseball analyst named John Rickert, had a theory about pitchers' groundball/flyball ratios. Rickert thought that pitchers, particularly groundball pitchers, might start out a game keeping the ball low and getting a lot of grounders; then, as they tired, they'd start pitching higher in the strike zone and give up more flyballs.

This seemed pretty logical. We decided to test the theory. It turned out that Rickert was absolutely right: groundball ratios do decline for starters as the game progresses. Here are the numbers for major league starters in 1992:

Groundball-to-Flyball Ratios for Starters — 1992

	Innings 1-3	Innings 4-6	Innings 7+
Groundball Ratio	1.32	1.25	1.20

That's something we'd never considered before. But does this relationship hold for most pitchers — all of whom induce at least **some** groundballs — or does it mostly affect the groundball specialists? Let's divide all 1992 starting pitchers into three groups — groundball, neutral, and flyball — and see how their groundball ratios changed over the course of the game:

Type of Pitcher	Innings 1-3	Innings 4-6	Innings 7+
Groundball	2.06	1.77	1.80
Neutral	1.23	1.20	1.12
Flyball	0.86	0.83	0.77

Everyone's ratio dropped by the fourth, but the primary falloff was by groundball pitchers. Their groundball rate actually rose again in the late innings, but the amount of increase was very small. They don't turn into flyball pitchers, but they don't get as many grounders as they did early on.

To study this effect in a little more depth, let's look at the starting pitchers who had the highest groundball ratios last year (minimum 162 innings):

Highest Groundball/Flyball Ratios in 1992

Pitcher, Team	Innings 1-3	Innings 4-6	Innings 7+
Bill Swift, SF	2.32	2.82	3.29
Greg Maddux, Cubs	3.33	2.30	2.19
Mike Morgan, Cubs	3.00	2.23	2.03
Greg Hibbard, WSox	3.29	1.95	2.71
Scott Erickson, Min	2.88	2.12	2.28

Charles Nagy, Cle	3.00	2.21	2.13
Kevin Brown, Tex	2.70	2.36	2.06
Erik Hanson, Sea	2.25	2.07	2.36
Jose Rijo, Cin	2.14	1.94	1.65
Roger Clemens, Bos	1.69	2.12	2.14

For the most part, the relationship holds: the top pitchers have a very high groundball/flyball ratio in the first three innings, but by the fourth it has dropped significantly. The ones with the biggest drop are the ones with the highest ratios at the start of the game: Maddux, Morgan, Hibbard, Nagy. Some pitchers' ratios continue to decline after the seventh; others seem to get a bit of a second wind.

The oddball cases on this list are Bill Swift and Roger Clemens; both of their ratios increased over the course of a game. Neither is a classic groundballer, and it's a shock to find Clemens among the groundball leaders at all. It's possible that Roger makes a conscious attempt to use a little more finesse as he begins to tire. National League ERA leader Swift throws a good, hard sinker — harder than most groundballers — and he was moved back into a starting role last year after a couple of seasons as a reliever. He may have consciously paced himself early in his game last year, then started throwing harder, and induced more grounders, as the game went on. That's just a theory, of course.

Now let's look at the pitchers who had the lowest groundball ratios:

Lowest Groundball/Flyball Ratios in 1992

Pitcher, Team	Innings 1-3	Innings 4-6	Innings 7+
Sid Fernandez, Mets	0.59	0.44	0.45
Dave Stewart, Oak	0.72	0.74	0.55
Pete Harnisch, Hou	1.03	0.79	0.58
Scott Sanderson, Yanks	0.90	0.87	0.52
Mike Mussina, Bal	0.96	0.86	0.73
Bill Gullickson, Det	0.85	0.85	0.95
Greg Swindell , Cin	0.98	0.84	0.81
Rick Sutcliffe, Bal	0.85	0.93	0.96
Alex Fernandez, WSox	0.91	0.93	0.89
Mark Gardner, Mon	0.97	0.89	0.69

In general, these pitchers also have their ratios drop by the fourth; most of them also decline in the late innings. (There are exceptions like Rick Sutcliffe.) The degree of change for the flyballers is smaller, which is what we'd expect; groundball pitchers are the ones who are prone to this effect.

A complete listing for this category can be found on page 317.

WHICH PITCHERS GET CHEAP STRIKEOUTS?

When you look at the list of pitchers who get the most strikeouts, you have to keep in mind that National League hurlers have one hidden advantage: they get to work against their fellow National League pitchers. And for some of them, it's money in the bank. Randy Johnson, Roger Clemens and Nolan Ryan will probably be contacting their agents when they find out that Sid Fernandez of the Mets got 35 of his 193 Ks last year in the cheapest way possible — he hit his fellow members of the pitcher's union for some extra dues. That made El Sid the leader in "cheap strikeouts" for 1992:

	STRIKEOUTS	CHEAP Ks
Sid Fernandez	193	35
Pete Harnisch	164	29
Jose Rijo	171	29
David Cone	214	28
John Smoltz	215	28

Most Strikeouts of Opposing Pitchers — #6-#10

Pitcher, Team	Total	vs. Pitchers
Dwight Gooden, Mets	145	27
Andy Benes, SD	169	27
Orel Hershiser, LA	130	24
Chris Nabholz, Mon	130	23
Mark Gardner, Mon	132	23

You might figure, from this, that Clemens and company should add 30 or 35 Ks to their strikeout totals in order to compare them fairly with their National League counterparts. But that overstates the National Leaguers' advantage a good deal. What with pinch-hitters and frequent sacrifice attempts, NL pitchers only get about two chances to swing away per game, on average. A National League starter will thus get about 70 opportunities, at most, to work against his opposing moundmates over the course of a season. If he can fan half of them, as Fernandez does, he's doing exceptionally well.

But of course, Clemens and any other fireballer will log a good number of strikeouts in 70 chances against the **non**-pitchers they face. Fifteen is probably a reasonable estimate, so the advantage Fernandez gets over Clemens would be about 20 strikeouts (35 minus 15). And Fernandez is exceptionally good at fanning opposing pitchers.

Most of Sid's NL moundmates don't do nearly so well. For example, Greg Maddux got only 14 of his 199 strikeouts against other pitchers last year: seven percent of his strikeout total, vs. Fernandez' 18 percent. Maddux' rate was on the low side — is he just a nice guy who feels sorry for the other pitchers? — but the normal NL strikeout pitcher will get only 20 or 25 strikeouts against opposition pitchers over the course of a campaign. So the "NL advantage" is more like 10 extra strikeouts a season — nice, but not all that big a deal.

It's also true that not all NL pitchers pad their strikeout totals by fanning opposition pitchers. The following group of Senior Circuit pitchers all fanned at least 50 batters last year . . . but in every case, no more than one of those strikeouts came at the expense of an opposing pitcher:

Least Strikeouts of Opposing Pitchers — 1992

Pitcher, Team	Total	vs. Pitchers
Rob Dibble, Cin	110	0
Doug Jones, Hou	93	0
Lee Smith, StL	60	0
Stan Belinda, Pit	57	0
Roger McDowell, LA	50	0
John Wetteland, Mon	99	1
Norm Charlton, Cin	90	1
Mike Hartley, Phi	53	1

The group, of course, consists of relief pitchers, most of them hard-throwing closers. They usually don't take the mound unless their club has the lead in the late innings. And in that case, the opponents are not going to send a pitcher up to hit against them. So don't start telling Rob Dibble about that "National League advantage"; if you do, his next pitch might be coming at you chin-high.

A complete listing for this category can be found on page 318.

WHO SHOULD (AND SHOULDN'T) BE A CLOSER?

Late relief isn't for the faint of heart. A club expects its closer to be able to come in when the pressure is on and shut the door on the opposition. Lots of pitchers would love the job — and the money and glory which go with it — but they don't have either the physical or mental makeup required.

Some do, however . . . or at least they show all the signs. We thought we'd go over the 1992 relief figures and try to identify 10 likely candidates for a closer's role, based on the way they pitched last year. All the pitchers we chose had to meet the following qualifications:

1. They had to have excellent ERAs in the late innings of close games last year (under 2.50), covering a respectable number of pressure-situation innings (at least 20).

2. They had to be tough to hit, with opponents' batting averages less than .240.

3. They had to be relatively tough to take out of the yard, permitting no more than three homers last year.

4. They didn't need to be strikeout-an-inning guys, but they had to have respectable strikeout ratios — at least six for every nine innings.

5. They had to be relatively untried as closers; Duane Ward and Todd Worrell, who would have qualified otherwise, weren't considered.

Here are the 10 candidates, and their figures for their 1992 "closer's audition" — numbers listed are for the late innings of close games only:

They Ought to Be Closers: 1992 Late and Close

Pitcher, Team	ERA	IP	Avg	HR	BB	K
Jose Melendez, SD	1.15	31.1	.215	0	10	29
Mike Fetters, Mil	1.20	30.0	.146	1	15	22
Mel Rojas, Mon	1.32	41.0	.238	0	18	30
Kent Mercker, Atl	1.63	27.2	.202	0	14	19
Darren Holmes, Mil	1.74	20.2	.237	0	10	19
Rusty Meacham, KC	1.93	51.1	.237	3	9	36
Derek Lilliquist, Cle	1.93	37.1	.231	3	11	29
Roberto Hernandez, WSox	2.12	46.2	.191	2	13	39
Xavier Hernandez, Hou	2.13	42.1	.207	1	17	34
Mark Guthrie, Min	2.33	27.0	.208	1	10	32

We think this is a fairly impressive list. The White Sox' Roberto Hernandez performed as a closer late last year, and could very well nail down the top job this year. The Rockies drafted Darren Holmes with the intention of making him their late man, and Fetters could get a look with the Brewers if Doug Henry has problems this year. Jose Melendez, who was traded to Boston over the winter, will be in the hunt for the Red Sox closer's job this spring.

As for the others, it seems to us that all they need is a chance. Rojas, Meacham, Xavier Hernandez and Guthrie have their paths blocked right now by incumbent closers John Wetteland, Jeff Montgomery, Doug Jones and Rick Aguilera; they may have to wait awhile. The most intriguing cases may be Cleveland's Derek Lilliquist, who struggled for years before finding himself in 1992, and Atlanta's Kent Mercker. The Braves' closer job is open, and Mercker has impressive numbers, but the Braves seem to doubt his mental makeup. He has the arm, as they say.

But how about this next group? They all pitched as closers last year, and for the most part their clubs were sorry they did:

They Shouldn't Be Closers: 1992 Late and Close

Pitcher, Team	ERA	IP	Avg	HR	BB	K
Dave Righetti, SF	3.42	26.1	.296	1	16	23
Jeff Reardon, Bos-Atl	3.59	42.2	.281	5	6	32
Anthony Young, Mets	3.74	33.2	.248	3	11	13
Randy Myers, SD	4.36	66.0	.275	6	28	55
Mike Schooler, Sea	5.40	26.2	.327	6	16	16

Jeff Reardon and Dave Righetti **used** to be good closers, but it's been awhile. Schooler's basically had his career destroyed by arm problems. The Mets' Anthony Young looked good for awhile, but then the roof caved in. We discuss Randy Myers' curious 1992 season in the San Diego essay.

A complete listing for this category can be found on page 319.

DO SAVES COME EASY FOR DENNIS ECKERSLEY?

Of all the studies we've done over the last few years, this one may have received the strongest response — our annual quest to learn which relievers get the easiest save opportunities. Nice guys that we are, we replaced our original label, "cheap," with "easy," but some people still aren't satisfied. Oakland manager Tony La Russa was especially irate on the subject last year. "There's no such thing as an easy save!" he proclaimed.

Give the man credit; he's right. There really is no such thing as an easy save, particularly if Dewan or Zminda is on the mound, but it's undeniable that some saves are easier than others. To placate Tony, we considered changing our three categories of saves to "Tough," "Really, Really Tough" and "Only a Real Man Can Convert This One," but we'll stick with our old labels for at least another year. The definitions, unchanged from the last edition, are:

Easy Save: first batter faced is not the tying run AND reliever pitches one inning or less. Example: Eckersley comes in with a 5-3 lead and no one on base to start the ninth. Under the current rules, this is a Save Opportunity. We call it an Easy Save Opportunity.

Tough Save: reliever comes in with the tying runs anywhere on base. Example: Eckersley comes in with a 5-3 lead, two outs and the bases loaded in the ninth. This is a Tough Save Opportunity.

Regular Save: All other saves fall in the "Regular" Category.

These are fairly straightforward definitions. We think that if a reliever can pitch one inning, give up a run (a 9.00 ERA for the day) and still come away with a save, he's got it a lot easier than someone who comes in with a runner on base and the potential lead run at bat. By their performance, the pitchers agree; last year they converted easy save opportunities at a 93 percent rate, regular opportunities at a 74 percent rate (very close to the overall save conversion rate of 70 percent), and tough opportunities at a 41 percent rate — well under half the time. Here are the '92 league figures:

	Easy			Regular			Tough			Total		
League	Sv	Op	%	Sv	Op	%	Sv	Op	%	Sv	Op	%
AL	214	231	93	313	407	77	92	232	40	619	870	71
NL	152	162	94	254	359	71	84	199	42	490	720	68
MLB Totals	366	393	93	567	766	74	176	431	41	1109	1590	70

As we commented last year, there is a real difference between the way the league's managers use their late relievers. Because their pitchers have to hit, National League managers tend to give their closers fewer easy save opportunities. The logic is simple: with the pitcher being pinch-hit for so many times, an NL manager goes through his roster more quickly, so he's more apt to hold the closer until a situation where he's really needed. You can see this by looking at how the average AL and NL team divided up their save opportunities last year:

Save Opportunities
Team Average by League

	Easy	Regular	Tough
1992 AL teams	16.5	29.1	16.6
1992 NL teams	13.5	29.9	16.6

The difference is primarily in the easy category, which is why American League closers tend to record higher save totals.

Here's how the American League save leaders converted their save opportunities in 1992 (Jeff Reardon pitched in both leagues last year, but mostly the American, so he's listed here):

Reliever, Team	Easy			Regular			Tough			Total		
	Sv	Op	%	Sv	Op	%	Sv	Op	%	Sv	Op	%
Dennis Eckersley, Oak	28	28	100	22	24	92	1	2	50	51	54	94
Rick Aguilera, Min	22	24	92	14	17	82	5	7	71	41	48	85
Jeff Montgomery, KC	16	16	100	21	24	88	2	6	33	39	46	85
Gregg Olson, Bal	18	18	100	14	20	70	4	6	67	36	44	82
Tom Henke, Tor	20	21	95	12	14	86	2	2	100	34	37	92
Steve Farr, Yanks	16	16	100	13	15	87	1	5	20	30	36	83
Jeff Russell, Tex-Oak	12	12	100	8	11	73	10	16	63	30	39	77
Jeff Reardon, Bos-Atl	19	21	90	10	15	67	1	4	25	30	40	75
Steve Olin, Cle	8	8	100	15	18	83	6	10	60	29	36	81
Doug Henry, Mil	10	11	91	15	17	88	4	5	80	29	33	88

Is La Russa a little sensitive about his Golden Boy, Dennis Eckersley? We're not criticizing the Eck when we point out that he received only two tough save opportunities in all of 1992, while Jeff Russell had 16. Without question, Eckersley deserved all his post-season awards, and you can't say he didn't pitch well when he came in with runners on base; after all, he allowed only two of 31 inherited runners to score. However, his total of 51 saves was boosted by those 28 easy opportunities (most in either league), and he only had to come in with the tying run on base two times all year. He usually had some leeway, in other words. When Bobby Thigpen got his record 57 saves in 1990, he had many more tough opportunities than

Eckersley in '92; he also had a few more easy ones, and blew several of them. We'll let you decide which is the superior season:

	Easy			Regular			Tough			Total		
	Sv	Op	%	Sv	Op	%	Sv	Op	%	Sv	Op	%
Thigpen, 1990	29	32	91	20	23	87	8	10	80	57	65	88
Eckersley, 1992	28	28	100	22	24	92	1	2	50	51	54	94

The low save percentages of Russell and the White Sox' Scott Radinksy (15 of 23, 65%) are more understandable when you look at all the tough chances they got. Russell was well above the league norm in the tough category; Radinsky (4 of 11, 36%) was only slightly below it. Each pitched a lot better than the overall percentage would indicate.

Here are the National League figures for 1992:

	Easy			Regular			Tough			Total		
Reliever, Team	Sv	Op	%	Sv	Op	%	Sv	Op	%	Sv	Op	%
Lee Smith, StL	21	21	100	19	25	76	3	5	60	43	51	84
Randy Myers, SD	13	15	87	19	22	86	6	9	67	38	46	83
John Wetteland, Mon	12	12	100	18	23	78	7	11	64	37	46	80
Doug Jones, Hou	8	8	100	26	31	84	2	3	67	36	42	86
Mitch Williams, Phi	11	11	100	17	23	74	1	2	50	29	36	81
Norm Charlton, Cin	6	6	100	16	20	80	4	8	50	26	34	76
Rob Dibble, Cin	13	14	93	8	12	67	4	4	100	25	30	83
Stan Belinda, Pit	4	4	100	8	12	67	6	8	75	18	24	75
Rod Beck, SF	1	1	100	13	16	81	3	6	50	17	23	74
John Franco, Mets	10	10	100	5	7	71	0	0	---	15	17	88
Alejandro Pena, Atl	7	7	100	5	7	71	3	4	75	15	18	83
Anthony Young, Mets	8	8	100	4	8	50	3	4	75	15	20	75

For the second year in a row, Lee Smith had more saves than any National League pitcher. And for the second year in a row, he also had more easy opportunities. Again, we're not trying to belittle Smith, who is a terrific relief pitcher. But no National League manager gives his closer more low-pressure opportunities to log a save than Joe Torre gives Smith. That's a big advantage. Looking at the breakdown, you could certainly argue that Montreal's John Wetteland, who was a superior 7 of 11 in tough save chances and slightly better than Smith in regular opportunities, was the better reliever last year. The difference was in the way he was used.

A complete listing for this category can be found on page 320.

V. QUESTIONS ON DEFENSE

ARE CATCHERS' THROWING STATS DECEPTIVE?

	STOLEN BASES	CAUGHT STEALING	PCT.
THE BEST			
Ivan Rodriguez	53	51	49.0%
Geno Petralli	22	19	46.3%
Kirt Manwaring	46	36	43.9%
Terry Steinbach	68	50	42.4%
Sandy Alomar Jr.	43	30	41.1%
THE WORST			
Chris Hoiles	87	16	15.5%
Lenny Webster	29	6	17.1%
Damon Berryhill	71	15	17.4%
Darrin Fletcher	70	15	17.6%
Matt Nokes	108	25	18.8%
ML average			28.8%

Minimum 300 innings caught.

The value that many people place on good-throwing catchers was demonstrated in the American League Gold Glove voting last year. While there were other, more highly-polished receivers around — Terry Steinbach and Ron Karkovice come to mind — the league's managers and coaches gave the award to young Ivan Rodriguez of the Rangers. They did this even though Rodriguez led the league in errors and demonstrated some mechanical problems behind the plate. Why did they pick him? The reason was Rodriguez' vaunted throwing arm, which is generally considered the best in the game.

There is no doubt that Rodriguez has exceptional throwing ability. Last year he threw out 49 percent of all opposing basestealers, the best success rate in the game. He also picked off five runners; no other catcher had more than two. Here is the 1992 leaders list — the other figures shown are the number of steals allowed per nine innings by each catcher, and the number of pitcher caught-stealings and pickoffs which occurred with each catcher behind the plate:

Leaders, Stolen Bases Off Catchers — 1992

Catcher, Team	SB	CS	%	PK	SB/9	CS	PK
Ivan Rodriguez, Tex	53	51	49.0	5	0.49	6	2
Geno Petralli, Tex	22	19	46.3	0	0.54	1	2
Kirt Manwaring, SF	46	36	43.9	1	0.47	11	0
Terry Steinbach, Oak	68	50	42.4	1	0.61	3	1
Sandy Alomar Jr, Cle	43	30	41.1	0	0.53	5	6
Charlie O'Brien, Mets	36	25	41.0	1	0.76	5	3
Ron Tingley, Cal	28	19	40.4	1	0.61	4	0
Chad Kreuter, Det	26	17	39.5	1	0.49	5	1
B.J. Surhoff, Mil	57	35	38.0	1	0.55	4	4
Joe Girardi, Cubs	46	28	37.8	0	0.64	4	2

(Minimum 300 Innings Caught)

Do these figures certify Rodriguez as numero uno when it comes to throwing out runners? You can't say so with complete certainty. As most people know, runners steal off the pitcher as well as the catcher, and a catcher can't do much to control the running game if his pitchers don't give him a chance. Take Karkovice and the 1992 National League Gold Glove winner, Tom Pagnozzi. Though both are considered to have excellent throwing arms, their throw-out rates dropped significantly last year (and Karkovice's has dropped two years in a row):

	1990	1991	1992
Pagnozzi	41.2	44.2	27.5
Karkovice	50.0	37.5	29.6

Is this a sign that Pagnozzi and Karkovice aren't throwing as well as they were a couple of years ago? Not by itself, it isn't. Karkovice's teammate Carlton Fisk has also seen his throw-out rate go down, which is a tipoff that the Sox pitchers aren't doing their part to control the running game. Pagnozzi's case is similar: his throw-out rate has always been much higher than teammate Rich Gedman's, and Gedman's rate (only 7.5% last year) has declined right along with Pagnozzi's. The St. Louis pitchers aren't giving their catchers much help.

Now let's look at the catchers with the poorest throw-out rates in 1992:

Trailers, Stolen Bases Off Catchers — 1992

Catcher, Team	Catcher					Pitcher	
	SB	CS	%	PK	SB/9	CS	PK
Chris Hoiles, Bal	87	16	15.5	0	0.96	6	3
Lenny Webster, Min	29	6	17.1	1	0.83	3	1
Damon Berryhill, Atl	71	15	17.4	0	0.97	5	6
Darrin Fletcher, Mon	70	15	17.6	0	1.22	9	4
Matt Nokes, Yanks	108	25	18.8	1	1.08	8	8
Mike Fitzgerald, Cal	41	10	19.6	0	0.79	8	4
Scott Servais, Hou	48	12	20.0	1	0.82	3	1
Todd Hundley, Mets	89	26	22.6	1	0.90	7	4
Brian Harper, Min	118	36	23.4	0	0.95	16	3
Lance Parrish, Cal-Sea	59	18	23.4	1	1.28	5	0

In general, the trailers list has more year-to-year consistency than the leaders list does — guys like Berryhill, Harper and Fitzgerald are perennials. Once again, comparisons with teammates can be very useful. For example, Chris Hoiles of the Orioles had a throw-out rate of 15.5%, worst in the majors, last year. But his teammate Jeff Tackett had a success rate more than twice as high as that (34.0%). Similarly, Scott Servais of the Astros had a much lower throw-out rate (20.0%) than his teammate Eddie Taubensee (33.0%), and the Angels' Fitzgerald (19.6) had a much lower rate than teammate Ron Tingley (40.4%). In these cases, the catchers deserved their low ratings.

So throw-out rate alone, while useful, gives only part of the picture. To get a more complete view, we should compare the catchers on the same team — when one has problems but another doesn't, that's a tipoff. It's also a good idea to study the catcher's figures over the course of several seasons. We'll be keeping an eye on Karkovice and Pagnozzi, among others, this year.

A complete listing for this category can be found on page 321.

WHICH CATCHERS ARE THE BEST HANDLERS OF PITCHERS?

Expected to be a Rookie of the Year candidate last year, the Mets' Todd Hundley had a difficult season. The young catcher struggled at bat, hitting only .209; even worse, his well-publicized throwing arm proved disappointing, as he tossed out only 27 percent of opposing basestealers. By year's end, a lot of New Yorkers were saying the Mets should go out and get another catcher.

Not so fast, Metsies. We have a tool called "Catcher's ERA," or CERA; it's simply the ERAs recorded by a pitching staff with each catcher behind the plate. Since catchers on a club with good pitching have an advantage over catchers with weak mound staffs, we like to compare each catcher's ERA with the other receivers on the club. The greater the difference, the better the catcher would seem to be at coaxing good work out of his pitchers. And who produced the best work out of his staff last year? None other than Todd Hundley. Here are the 1992 leaders:

Catcher, Team	Innings Caught	Own ERA	Others' ERA	Diff
Todd Hundley, Mets	892.1	3.31	4.27	- 0.96
Ivan Rodriguez, Tex	982.2	3.81	4.69	- 0.88
Mike LaValliere, Pit	767.0	2.97	3.76	- 0.79
B.J. Surhoff, Mil	926.0	3.16	3.92	- 0.76
Brent Mayne, KC	458.1	3.30	4.05	- 0.75
Terry Steinbach, Oak	998.2	3.50	4.24	- 0.74
Mike Scioscia, LA	864.2	3.14	3.81	- 0.67
Sandy Alomar Jr, Cle	729.2	3.81	4.41	- 0.60
Ron Tingley, Cal	412.2	3.42	4.01	- 0.59
Tony Pena, Bos	1,084.0	3.49	4.07	- 0.58

(Minimum 300 innings caught)

When Hundley was behind the plate last year, Mets pitchers had a 3.31 ERA; when they used their other catchers (including Charlie O'Brien, who has an excellent defensive reputation), the figure was nearly a run higher, at 4.27. No other catcher produced so great a difference. Another young receiver, Ivan Rodriguez of the Rangers, was second; Rodriguez' work at handling pitchers was greatly improved over 1991. There were some surprises on the list (Brent Mayne, Ron Tingley), along with some names you'd expect (Mike Scioscia, Terry Steinbach, Sandy Alomar, Tony Pena).

Of course, some catchers have the opposite effect — their staff ERAs go **up** when they go behind the plate:

Catcher, Team	Innings Caught	Own ERA	Others' ERA	Diff
Don Slaught, Pit	598.2	3.79	3.05	+ 0.74
Jamie Quirk, Oak	385.1	4.27	3.53	+ 0.74
Geno Petralli, Tex	367.2	4.63	3.92	+ 0.71
Charlie O'Brien, Mets	427.1	4.15	3.48	+ 0.67
Carlos Hernandez, LA	434.0	3.86	3.22	+ 0.64
Greg Olson, Atl	754.2	3.43	2.83	+ 0.60
Junior Ortiz, Cle	652.2	4.44	3.85	+ 0.59
Brian Harper, Min	1,114.0	3.85	3.27	+ 0.58
Eddie Taubensee, Hou	804.1	3.99	3.42	+ 0.57
Dave Valle, Sea	972.1	4.68	4.27	+ 0.41

Don Slaught, schizo receiver: in 1991, he was one of the best at coaxing good work out of his pitchers, last year the very worst. Maybe when he hits .345, as he did in 1992, he forgets about taking care of his moundsmen.

Though we like this stat, it does have its limitations. One is obvious: pitchers often have personal catchers, and a receiver's CERA can go up or down depending on who the pitcher is. Greg Maddux of the Cubs loved working with Hector Villanueva, for example, and that gave Villanueva an edge (and a CERA 0.84 lower) over the other Cub catchers. The other limitation comes up when a club has two catchers who are good at handling pitchers: the White Sox with Ron Karkovice and Carlton Fisk, the Cardinals with Tom Pagnozzi and Rich Gedman are two good examples. In that case the receivers will produce similar ERAs, and make neither the leaders or trailers list.

But the number does identify some unsung heroes. Damon Berryhill, formerly of the Cubs, now with the Braves, is one of them. Berryhill was injured in 1990; in the other years since 1989, he's consistently coaxed superior work out of his pitching staffs:

Year	With Berryhill	With Others	Diff
1989	2.88	4.01	- 1.13
1991	3.58	4.09	- 0.51
1992	2.86	3.38	- 0.52

A complete listing for this category can be found on page 322.

WHO'S BEST IN THE INFIELD ZONE?

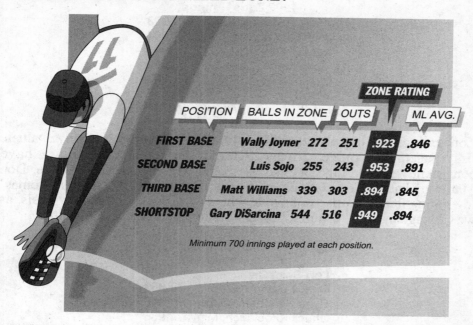

POSITION	BALLS IN ZONE	OUTS	ZONE RATING	ML AVG.
FIRST BASE	Wally Joyner 272	251	.923	.846
SECOND BASE	Luis Sojo 255	243	.953	.891
THIRD BASE	Matt Williams 339	303	.894	.845
SHORTSTOP	Gary DiSarcina 544	516	.949	.894

Minimum 700 innings played at each position.

At STATS, we enjoy being on the cutting edge of statistical analysis; as Tom Wolfe once put it, we like to push "the outside of the envelope." Probably the largest unexplored territory lies in evaluating fielders, and that's where one of our babies, the Zone Rating, comes in. Our play-by-play database permits us to determine, with great accuracy, the location of each ball put into play. From there it's only a small step to measuring the number of balls each fielder could have reasonably been expected to reach (his "zone"), and the number of those balls he actually turned into outs. His "zone rating" is the number of outs divide by the number of balls in his zone.

We'll cheerfully admit that the Zone Rating isn't perfect, but consider its strength in comparison to other defensive measurements. Unlike fielding average, which is a measure only of sure-handedness, the Zone Rating doesn't ignore range; it's all about range. And unlike range factor (putouts plus assists per nine innings), it's not susceptible to variations like a groundball pitching staff, which will automatically give infielders more chances; with zone rating, we'll know when more balls are hit into the fielder's area.

So let's look at the five zone rating leaders, and the trailer, at each of the infield positions for 1992 (minimum 700 innings played):

First Basemen
1992 Zone Ratings

Wally Joyner, KC	.923
John Olerud, Tor	.904
Kent Hrbek, Min	.901
Mark Grace, Cubs	.890
Mark McGwire, Oak	.889
Worst	
Frank Thomas, WSox	.791

Zone ratings are the only measuring system which can objectively evaluate first basemen's range. Joyner, Olerud, Hrbek and McGwire have consistently ranked high, and so has National Leaguer Mark Grace. Don Mattingly has also rated highly in the past, but not in 1992. Frank Thomas' low rating is no surprise to anyone who saw him play on a daily basis, as we Chicagoans did. As a first baseman, Thomas is one hell of a hitter.

Second Basemen
1992 Zone Ratings

Luis Sojo, Cal	.953
Carlos Baerga, Cle	.952
Ryne Sandberg, Cubs	.946
Chuck Knoblauch, Min	.936
Mark Lemke, Atl	.912
Worst	
Craig Biggio, Hou	.842

At second base, the main surprises are the names which are missing: Gold Glovers Roberto Alomar (eighth) and Jose Lind (18th, third from the bottom). We respect them both, but point out that neither has ever rated all that highly in the standard defensive categories, either — something you could never say about Ryne Sandberg. However, we're not about to suggest that Alomar is going to lose his job to Luis Sojo. Craig Biggio's low ranking can be blamed on lack of experience, at least for now.

Third Basemen
1992 Zone Ratings

Matt Williams, SF	.894
Robin Ventura, WSox	.878
Ken Caminiti, Hou	.868
Wade Boggs, Bos	.867
Brook Jacoby, Cle	.866
Worst	
Dean Palmer, Tex	.797

Matt Williams lost his Gold Glove last year when his hitting dropped and he committed 23 errors; our figures, however, indicate that his range was undiminished. Robin Ventura also committed 23 errors, but kept his Gold Glove; of course, he also kept his batting stroke, which matters a lot to the managers and coaches who vote the fielding awards. Terry Pendleton ranked ninth, but his zone rating (.849) wasn't far behind the leaders.

Shortstops
1992 Zone Ratings

Gary DiSarcina, Cal	.949
Manuel Lee, Tor	.943
Cal Ripken, Bal	.936
Craig Grebeck, WSox	.936
Dick Schofield, Cal-Mets	.935
Worst	
Jose Offerman, LA	.845
Walt Weiss, Oak	.845

At shortstop, California's Gary DiSarcina may be a future star — if he can hit enough to keep his job. For now, though, we'll stick with Cal Ripken. Among National Leaguers, Ozzie Smith just missed the top five with a .922 zone rating; there's not much question, though, that the weak-hitting Ducky Schofield is a very fine shortstop.

And now, the annual STATS infield Gold Gloves, which rely on zone ratings, other stats, and careful observation:

First Base: Wally Joyner, AL, and Mark Grace, NL. Grace is automatic, after his outstanding performance last year. We were tempted by Don Mattingly and Mark McGwire in the American League, but felt it was high time to reward Joyner, who's been a good one for some time.

Second Base: Carlos Baerga, AL, and Ryne Sandberg, NL. Sandberg is another easy choice in our estimation; Baerga over Alomar in the AL is more controversial. Baerga led the league in putouts, assists and double plays, and barely lost out to Sojo in the zone ratings. He's a good one.

Third Base: Robin Ventura, AL, and Terry Pendleton, NL. Okay, we know you think we've got a Chicago bias, but Ventura's just outstanding. We don't consider hitting, so we were torn between Pendleton and Matt Williams in the National League. Despite his superior range, we thought Williams' .944 fielding average was too low for a Gold Glover.

Shortstop: Cal Ripken, AL, and Ozzie Smith, NL. Sentimental choices? We don't think so, as both have the numbers (zone rating and others) to back up the choices. We keep waiting for Barry Larkin to pass Smith, but don't see the evidence that he's done so yet. We also considered Schofield.

A complete listing for this category can be found on page 323.

WHO'S BEST IN THE OUTFIELD ZONE?

The zone rating, as we explained in the infield section, measures the number of outs recorded by each fielder against the number of balls hit in his fielding area. So without further ado, here are the 1992 zone ratings leaders at each of the outfield positions:

Left Field 1992 Zone Ratings	
Bernard Gilkey, StL	.897
Greg Vaughn, Mil	.884
Luis Gonzalez, Hou	.880
Jerald Clark, SD	.861
Ron Gant, Atl	.858
Worst	
Billy Hatcher, Cin-Bos	.758

When we looked at the outfield zone ratings a year ago, the top two were Bernard Gilkey and Luis Gonzalez. In 1992 they ranked first and third, so perhaps we can conclude that they're pretty good. There was a glut of left fielders at the .840-860 level: Tim Raines, Dan Gladden, Mel Hall, Rickey Henderson, and Barry Bonds, along with the players listed. Billy Hatcher's low rating is in part due to Fenway, where The Wall tends to wreak havoc on all kinds of statistical measurements (Mike Greenwell usually ranked at the bottom in this category as well — sometimes deservedly). The worst left fielder was probably Kevin Reimer, whose zone rating was .768.

Center Field 1992 Zone Ratings	
Devon White, Tor	.912
Darrin Jackson, SD	.878
Kenny Lofton, Cle	.874
Roberto Kelly, Yanks	.873
Otis Nixon, Atl	.868
Worst	
Howard Johnson, Mets	.798

White and Jackson also ranked high in this category a year ago, which underscores their consistently great defensive work. Other center fielders who ranked above the .850 level include Marquis Grissom (.865), Willie Wilson and Lance Johnson (both .856), Mike Devereaux (.851) and Junior Felix (.850) — all were very good. Andy Van Slyke (.801) has always rated poorly in our system; one theory, that Barry Bonds' good range in left allowed Van Slyke to position himself in a different "zone," will be put to the test this year, with Bonds in San Francisco. We have no qualms about Howard Johnson's low rating, however; we, and everyone else (including, eventually, the Mets), thought that HoJo in center was a disaster.

Right Field
1992 Zone Ratings

Ruben Sierra, Oak-Tex	.884
Pedro Munoz, Min	.878
Dave Justice, Atl	.872
Willie McGee, SF	.867
Tony Gwynn, SD	.857
Worst	
Jay Buhner, Sea	.782

Ruben Sierra has had his ups and downs on defense, and 1992 was an up year for him. As with the left and center fielders, there were a number of players just below the leaders list, in this case in the .830-.850 level: Bobby Bonilla (.850), Mark Whiten (.846), Rob Deer (.842), Paul O'Neill (.841), Larry Walker (.839), Felix Jose (.835) and Joe Carter (.833). There are a lot of good right fielders around, in other words.

Here are the STATS outfield Gold Glove winners, based on zone ratings, other stats and observation:

Left Field: Greg Vaughn, AL and Barry Bonds, NL. We were tempted to go with Bernard Gilkey in the NL, but he didn't play full time all year. Look out for him in future seasons.

Center Field: Devon White, AL and Darrin Jackson, NL. Both players had over 425 putouts, underscoring their superior range along with the zone ratings. There were other good candidates; we like these.

Right Field: Mark Whiten, AL and Larry Walker, NL. In zone ratings, there wasn't much difference between these two and the guys on the top. Whiten and Walker both have superior throwing arms and excellent overall reputations, so they're our choices.

A complete listing for this category can be found on page 325.

WHO ARE THE PRIME PIVOT MEN?

The double play is called "the pitcher's best friend," and why not? — there's nothing like getting two outs on one ball. It would follow, then, that pitchers would feel very friendly towards second basemen who can turn that tough DP. Our data tells us that some second sackers are a lot better friends than others.

What we do, in this study, is to first record all the situations where a double play pivot is possible — man on first, less than two outs, ball hit to another infielder and the second baseman takes the throw. Then we record the number of double plays the second baseman turns. It's so simple, and yet our studies have shown that it reliably identifies the superior pivot men.

When we look at the data, we have to separate it by leagues. The reason is that many more double plays are turned in the American League than in the National. Last year NL hitters grounded into 1.34 DPs per game, AL hitters 1.59 — 19 percent more. That's because they play more "little ball" in the National League: more stolen bases, more sacrifices and, especially important here, more hit-and-runs. Here are the top American League second basemen on the double play pivot for 1992 (minimum 25 opportunities):

Best Pivot Men — 1992 American League

Player, Team	Opp	DP	Pct
Jim Gantner, Mil	37	28	75.7
Carlos Baerga, Cle	109	79	72.5
Mike Gallego, Yanks	25	18	72.0
Mark McLemore, Bal	38	26	68.4
Lance Blankenship, Oak	44	30	68.2
Luis Sojo, Cal	68	46	67.6
Scott Fletcher, Mil	60	40	66.7
Bill Ripken, Bal	55	36	65.5
Mike Bordick, Oak	57	37	64.9
Tony Phillips, Det	39	24	61.5

Nearing the end of his career (in fact, it may have arrived by the time you read this), Jim Gantner has long been recorded as a superior pivot man. However, he now has other significant defensive shortcomings, which is something you can't say about Carlos Baerga and Mike Gallego. One missing name here is Roberto Alomar, who has never been regarded as an exceptional pivot man.

Here are the National League leaders:

Best Pivot Men — 1992 National League

Player, Team	Opp	DP	Pct
Willie Randolph, Mets	37	29	78.4
Robby Thompson, SF	84	55	65.5
Delino DeShields, Mon	66	43	65.2
Geronimo Pena, StL	39	25	64.1
Mickey Morandini, Phi	58	37	63.8
Mike Sharperson, LA	29	18	62.1
Luis Alicea, StL	35	21	60.0
Ryne Sandberg, Cubs	89	50	56.2
Jose Lind, Pit	89	49	55.1
Billy Doran, Cin	53	29	54.7

Whatever league he's in, and whatever age he is (he's now 38), Willie Randolph has always been considered a master at turning the double play. He was head and shoulders above anyone in the National League last year, and even topped all the American League players, which is really a rare feat. The high rating of the Giants' Robby Thompson should be no surprise to readers of this book, and the same is true for Delino DeShields.

One-year studies can be deceptive, so we thought we'd show you the leaders over the last three campaigns (minimum 100 opportunities). Randolph, who's played in both leagues during that time, is still the best:

Prime Pivot Men — 1990-1992

Fielder	Opp	DP	Pct
Willie Randolph	177	129	72.9
Carlos Baerga	172	123	71.5
Scott Fletcher	215	144	67.0
Billy Ripken	201	132	65.7
Luis Sojo	143	93	65.0

Since there's still a league bias at work, we'll point out that National Leaguers Thompson (62.0), DeShields (58.5) and Morandini (56.7) also rank high. Who's been the worst? There was nobody quite like Gregg Jefferies (32.9%), who was to second base what Howard Johnson was to center field.

A complete listing for this category can be found on page 327.

WHO LED THE LEAGUE IN FUMBLES?

It's brutal, isn't it? These major leaguers play on clean, manicured fields. They use fresh, perfect baseballs. They have well-designed gloves which make it easy to catch the ball, even with one hand. They make millions of dollars a year. (We're not sure what that has to do with anything, but like everyone else, we feel obligated to mention it.) And still, they kick the ball away, like a bad Little League team.

Even though fielding averages keep going up, up, up, thanks to the improved conditions stated above, there's a few players who battle against the odds and perform like third-rate butchers (our apologies to all the first-rate butchers out there). We're here to identify them in this article; you can't hide from us, guys, just as you couldn't hide from those two-hoppers you booted into left field.

The annual "Hands of Stone" team is entirely new this year: the torch has been passed to a new generation, and of course they dropped it. This team has it all. There are youngsters like Frank Thomas at first and Jose Offerman at short, still years away from their prime; fumble-fingered veterans like Danny Jackson and Joe Carter; guys who can't hide from a ground ball no matter what position they're shifted to, like Gregg Jefferies. There's even Steve Sax, reliving some of the glories of his misbegotten youth.

This team has bench strength, as well. Among the players who didn't meet the innings requirement were first baseman Mo Vaughn of the Red Sox, who averaged an error every 5.3 games at first base, shortstop Kim Batiste of the Phillies, who committed an error every 2.9 contests at shortstop, third baseman Jim Thome of the Indians, who averaged 3.1 games per error, and had an .882 fielding average, left fielder Kevin Reimer of the Rangers, who booted one every 8.5 games, and catcher Benito Santiago, a long-time member of this team, who proved he still has it by cranking out an error every 8.2 contests.

Best of all, there's the Captain, the man they all look up to: the legendary Matt Young of the Red Sox. Often described as "the worst fielder of all time" by the fawning Boston press, Matt spent 1992 proving that this wasn't just New England hype. In most ways it was a typical Matt Young season: an 0-4 record, a 4.58 ERA, a no-hitter that wasn't a no-hitter (he worked only eight innings, and, of course, lost the game). But in the field, Young really outdid himself. In his 70.2 innings he managed to get his hands on only 16 chances, yet he committed six errors — one more than Roberto Alomar had in 1,276 innings at second base. Young's fielding average last year was .625, which is truly awe-inspiring. Even Matt's lifetime "winning percentage" (.378) has to take second place to that.

HANDS OF STONE		GAMES PER ERROR*	SOFT HANDS		GAMES PER ERROR*
P	Danny Jackson	2.8	P	John Smiley	0 in 26.8
C	Brian Harper	9.5	C	Tom Pagnozzi	132.1
1B	Frank Thomas	12.0	1B	Mark Grace	39.3
2B	Steve Sax	7.0	2B	Roberto Alomar	28.4
3B	Gregg Jefferies	5.5	3B	Kevin Seitzer	11.7
SS	Jose Offerman	3.4	SS	Dick Schofield	18.3
LF	Candy Maldonado	20.8	LF	Tim Raines	62.1
CF	Juan Gonzalez	14.2	CF	Ken Griffey Jr.	131.9
RF	Joe Carter	14.5	RF	Paul O'Neill	134.4

*A 'game' is equivalent to 9 defensive innings played; minimum 1,000 defensive innings (162 for pitchers).

We think we've teased these guys enough. If the youngsters on the "Hands of Stone" team are feeling a little discouraged, all they need to do is look at the "Soft Hands" squad. In 1989, Ken Griffey Jr. was our "Hands of Stone" center fielder after committing 10 errors in only 127 games. A year later he won the first of his three straight Gold Gloves, and last year Griffey committed only one miscue in 1,187 innings in center. He's now one of the best and surest fielders around.

Roberto Alomar is an even more remarkable story. A "Hands of Stone" mainstay in 1989 and 1990, Alomar led the league in errors each year, with 28 boots in '89. But he worked hard to improve, and in '92 Alomar moved over to the "Soft Hands" column after his outstanding five-error campaign. Roberto used to be known as a great fielder who committed too many careless errors. Now he's just known as a great fielder.

Paul O'Neill, who moves from the Reds to the Yankees this year, has made the "Soft Hands" team as the right fielder for three straight seasons. O'Neill's not quite a Gold Glove player, but he's a very steady fielder. We could use a few more of those.

A complete listing for this category can be found on page 328.

HOW IMPORTANT IS AN EFFICIENT DEFENSE?

The Defensive Efficiency Record is a tool invented by Bill James to determine which clubs are the best in the field. Most of us know the limitations of fielding average when determining the best glove men; a player won't make an error on a ball he doesn't reach. It gets even worse when trying to identify the best-fielding teams, because range figures are useless. Every club records three outs an inning.

What Bill did with the DER is simple, but effective. First, he counted the number of balls which were put into play against each team. Then he counted the number of times the club turned those balls into outs. The DER is simply the first number divided by the second . . . a measure of each club's "efficiency" at turning the raw material (the ball in play) into the desired result (the out). As we pointed out a year ago, the DER isn't a perfect stat, as many balls in play simply can't be turned into outs. But of course, most balls can be — even the best hitters make outs much more often than they make hits. What intrigues us about the DER is the high correlation between clubs which do well in the category, and clubs which win.

Here are the 1992 American League rankings in Defensive Efficiency Record:

American League	Balls in Play	Plays Made	DER
Milwaukee Brewers	4766	3354	.704
Toronto Blue Jays	4566	3164	.693
Chicago White Sox	4830	3344	.692
Baltimore Orioles	4791	3312	.691
Oakland Athletics	4718	3252	.689
Minnesota Twins	4656	3201	.688
Kansas City Royals	4786	3268	.683
New York Yankees	4759	3239	.681
Boston Red Sox	4652	3158	.679
California Angels	4691	3167	.675
Detroit Tigers	4971	3355	.675
Seattle Mariners	4735	3190	.674
Cleveland Indians	4835	3237	.669
Texas Rangers	4646	3090	.665

When we looked at this stat a year ago, the best American League clubs in DER were the White Sox, Blue Jays, Twins, Angels and Athletics. Most of them also did well in 1992, and the ones who moved up, especially the

Brewers and Orioles, were clubs who also moved up in the standings. As Bill pointed out long ago, a good defensive outfield generally correlates with a good DER. A left fielder with good range seems particularly important; the Brewers were blessed with the underrated Greg Vaughn, the White Sox with Tim Raines, the Orioles with Brady Anderson. On the other hand, The Texas Rangers, with Kevin Reimer in left last year and an uncertain situation in center, fared very badly in the DER . . . and in the standings.

Here are the National League rankings for 1992:

National League	Balls in Play	Plays Made	DER
Atlanta Braves	4611	3221	.699
Chicago Cubs	4679	3272	.699
Montreal Expos	4552	3172	.697
Pittsburgh Pirates	4837	3363	.695
St. Louis Cardinals	4867	3384	.695
Philadelphia Phillies	4684	3223	.688
Houston Astros	4659	3194	.686
San Francisco Giants	4671	3206	.686
Cincinnati Reds	4486	3070	.684
San Diego Padres	4702	3189	.678
New York Mets	4573	3090	.676
Los Angeles Dodgers	4629	3110	.672

The Cubs are the exception, but the basic relationship — good DER, good ballclub — holds up very well. Once again, the top clubs in the category usually have good, solid defensive outfields.

On the other hand, the low ranking of the Dodgers and Mets can't be a surprise. It's more than errors. Guys playing out of position, guys who couldn't catch the ball . . . that was the 1992 Mets and Dodgers through and through. Defensive ineptitude was a major reason why each club's pitching staff dropped in the ERA rankings last year. And why they couldn't win many ballgames.

So if you're trying to determine whether your club will be a winner this year, don't underestimate the value of defense. And we don't just mean sure-handedness. Clubs which can turn those balls in the gaps into outs are usually going to be clubs which play winning ball.

A complete listing for this category can be found on page 330.

WHOM DO THEY STEAL OFF: THE PITCHER OR THE CATCHER?

One of the most interesting matchups of 1992 took place last August, in the thick of the American League East pennant race. The game: Milwaukee Brewers vs. Toronto Blue Jays. The place: Toronto's SkyDome. The matchup: David Cone, in his first start since being acquired from the Mets, vs. the Brewers baserunners. Through a confluence of mystical forces, fate had pitted the American League's most daring baserunners against one of baseball's easiest pitchers to steal on. The result: the Brewers won the game in a walk, while running Cone ragged, stealing seven bases in just 6.2 innings.

Lost in the shuffle was Blue Jays' catcher Pat Borders, who squatted helplessly as Cone took his big windup, and the Brewers got well on the way to second base before the ball smacked into his mitt. Was Borders a guiltless victim in all this? Is there a catcher anywhere who can throw out baserunners even with David Cone pitching? Without laying complete blame, maybe we can draw some conclusions about whom baserunners **really** steal off — the pitcher or the catcher.

What we did was look at how often runners attempted to steal per 100 opportunities against each pitcher and each catcher. Then, depending upon the rate of steal attempts, we grouped each pitcher and catcher in one of three categories: "Pitchers (or Catchers) They Run On," "Pitchers (or Catchers) They Don't Run On", and "Neutral." Then, we found the stolen base success rate against each group. If one group was more responsible for allowing stolen bases, we'd see a large difference in the stolen base percentages. As it turns out, the data seems to mete out blame fairly equally:

1992 Stolen Base Attempts and Success Rates vs. Pitchers and Catchers

	Attempts per 100 Opportunities	SB%
Pitchers They Run On	15.3	70.9%
Catchers They Run On	13.0	70.3%
Neutral Pitchers	10.6	63.8%
Neutral Catchers	10.3	66.8%
Pitchers They Don't Run On	6.1	61.8%
Catchers They Don't Run On	8.7	61.4%

While the rates are close, it does seem that baserunners consider the pitcher a little more than the catcher before attempting a steal. Other things being equal, they're more willing to take off against a pitcher they can run on (15.3 attempts per 100 opportunities) than they are against a catcher they can victimize (13.0). They're less likely to run if they know there's someone on the mound they can't run on effectively (6.1 attempts per 100) than they are if there's a good-throwing catcher behind the plate (8.7). But while they may run more often on the pitcher, the pitcher and catcher are almost equally to blame for the runners' rate of success (or lack thereof).

Of course, there is wide variance between individual pitchers and catchers, and basestealers certainly are aware of who's on the mound and/or behind the plate when deciding to take off:

1. Lefties are generally tougher to steal off than righties: since 1987, southpaws have held basestealers to a 65% success rate; righthanders 70%. But the left-handedness of Steve Avery and Randy Johnson was no deterrence last year; they led their respective leagues in stolen bases allowed with 42. Among righthanders, you'll always find your David Cones (49 steals allowed to lead the majors), but you'll also find your Ron Darlings (10 SB, 13 CS) and Tim Belchers (6 SB, 11 CS).

2. When the Orioles lost Chris Hoiles in the middle of the season, they may have lost a big bat, but the Orioles pitchers gained an ally in the war against basestealers: Jeff Tackett. With Hoiles catching, the Orioles nabbed only 15.5% of opponent base thieves. With Tackett, they caught 34.0%. Even with Mark Parent, who caught 100 innings, the Birds gunned down 36.4% of basestealers. Apparently, the Orioles hurlers **aren't** helpless; Hoiles just needs to improve his work.

Now, one for the other side:

3. The Reds used one primary catcher for the entire season, Joe Oliver. Overall, Oliver compiled a 29.8% caught stealing rate, not very impressive. However, with Belcher pitching, Oliver threw out 11 in 16 attempts (69%); with Jose Rijo on the mound, he tossed out 12 of 26 (46%). And Belcher and Rijo are righthanders. Oliver had far less success with southpaws Chris Hammond (2 of 6, 33%) and Greg Swindell (8 of 25, 32%) on the mound.

So, a word of advice to pitchers and catchers: blaming each other won't win the war against basestealers; cooperation is the key. And the best way to neutralize the opposition is still the David Cone solution: don't let them get on base in the first place, and keep them from scoring when they do.

WHICH OUTFIELDERS HAVE THE CANNONS?

Few things in baseball are as thrilling as a great throw by an outfielder. Think of Dwight Evans, Roberto Clemente, Carl Furillo . . . great all-around ballplayers, but the first thing people usually remember about them are the great throws they made from right field. Even "The Catch" — Willie Mays off Vic Wertz in Game One of the 1954 World Series — was punctuated by Willie's whirling, falling, amazing throw back to the infield from 460 feet away.

Outfielders' throws can be so dramatic that we hesitate to quantify them; maybe it's better just to wax poetic about them, like some romantic troubadour. But we leave that stuff to Roger Angell, and in this case, putting down some numbers makes more than a little sense. The simplest example of measuring outfielders' throwing arms — the assist totals — isn't all that bad, if you understand its limitations. As we've pointed out before, right fielders with great arms, like Clemente, will usually wind up with a lot of assists; runners **will** challenge them, despite what you might have heard. But as we swing around to center and left, the relationship between great arms and high assist totals becomes more haphazard. Here are the 1992 outfield assist leaders, by position:

1992 Outfield Assist Leaders

Right Field		Center Field		Left Field	
Larry Walker, Mon	16	Darrin Jackson, SD	18	Candy Maldon'do, Tor	13
Jay Buhner, Sea	14	Kenny Lofton, Cle	14	Tim Raines, WSox	12
Mark Whiten, Cle	14	Andy Van Slyke, Pit	11	Brady Anderson, Bal	10
		Lance Johnson, WSox	11		

(Note: in case of ties, players are ranked by innings played)

No one would quarrel with the notion that Larry Walker, Jay Buhner and Mark Whiten are among the best-throwing outfielders in the game. But in center field Lance Johnson does not have a strong arm — he gets his assists through his ability to cut off balls in the gap and get rid of the ball quickly. In left, Tim Raines is definitely a weak thrower. Does he get assists simply because runners take off so often on him? From these raw numbers, we simply can't tell.

That's where STATS comes in. Our exhaustive play-by-play (and pitch-by-pitch) database allows us to calculate a "hold percentage" for each outfielder. This is simply a ratio of extra bases taken on singles and doubles versus the number of opportunities to advance. We've been keeping this number for four seasons now, and we can attest that it works. Perhaps the chart will help convince you.

Let's analyze the data:

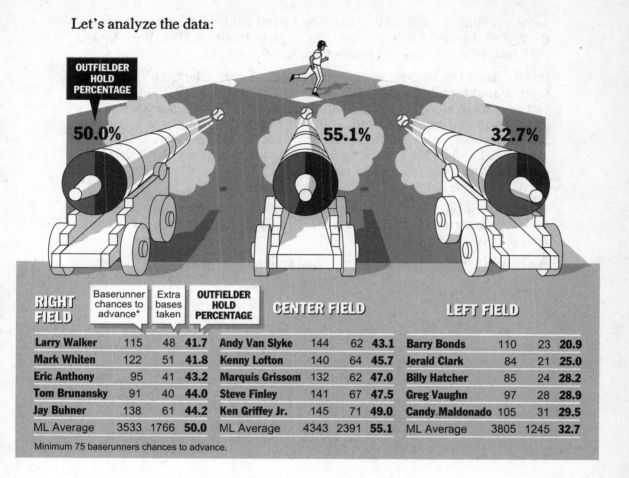

RIGHT FIELD	Baserunner chances to advance*	Extra bases taken	OUTFIELDER HOLD PERCENTAGE	CENTER FIELD				LEFT FIELD			
Larry Walker	115	48	41.7	Andy Van Slyke	144	62	43.1	Barry Bonds	110	23	20.9
Mark Whiten	122	51	41.8	Kenny Lofton	140	64	45.7	Jerald Clark	84	21	25.0
Eric Anthony	95	41	43.2	Marquis Grissom	132	62	47.0	Billy Hatcher	85	24	28.2
Tom Brunansky	91	40	44.0	Steve Finley	141	67	47.5	Greg Vaughn	97	28	28.9
Jay Buhner	138	61	44.2	Ken Griffey Jr.	145	71	49.0	Candy Maldonado	105	31	29.5
ML Average	3533	1766	50.0	ML Average	4343	2391	55.1	ML Average	3805	1245	32.7

Minimum 75 baserunners chances to advance.

In right field, it's a case of the "usual suspects": Walker, Whiten, Tom Brunansky, Buhner. About the only surprise would be Houston's Eric Anthony. Andre Dawson, Felix Jose and Paul O'Neill also rated highly — names you'd expect to see, in other words. The worst right fielder? Joe Orsulak, an Oriole last year, who was probably playing out of position; he rated highly in hold percentage in 1991, when he played left. Danny Tartabull had an even lower ranking than Orsulak, though he didn't have enough opportunities to qualify.

In center field, it's more of the same: Van Slyke, Lofton, Marquis Grissom, Steve Finley and Ken Griffey Jr. all have solid reputations, and the veterans make this list on an annual basis. San Diego's Darrin Jackson, with those 18 assists, could rate only ninth: runners challenged Jackson (179 times) more than any other major league outfielder last year, which helps explain the high assist total. The easiest center fielder to run on was the Mets' Howard Johnson; that's no surprise to either New York fans or the Mets, who have moved Johnson back to the infield.

In left field, the leaders were Barry Bonds, Jerald Clark, Billy Hatcher, Greg Vaughn and Candy Maldonado. Bonds has led left fielders in this category three straight years, which indicates that his low assists total last year (four) can be discounted. Ranking last in left field was rag-armed Kevin Reimer, then of the Rangers, now of the Brewers. Reimer is considered a nice, hard-working fellow . . . but one of the worst defensive outfielders around.

You'll notice that right and center fielders' hold percentages are much lower than those of left fielders. The longer throws from right and center make gunning down a runner difficult despite the strong-arms of those who play those positions.

A complete listing for this category can be found on page 331.

VI. QUESTIONS FROM
PREVIOUS EDITIONS

STATS BASEBALL SCOREBOARD: WHAT HAVE WE LEARNED OVER THE LAST FOUR YEARS?

Each edition of the Scoreboard (this one makes four) has attempted to answer 101 baseball questions. When appropriate, questions are repeated from edition to edition, but most are not. So unless you have all the Scoreboards, you've missed out on some good stuff. With this, the fourth edition, we will provide capsule summaries of some of the most interesting questions and answers of the last three years.

General Baseball Questions

Do Basestealers Have an Advantage on Artificial Turf? Yes, a decided one. In the three-year period from 1987 to 1989, the base-stealing rate on natural grass was 67.1 percent, right at the break-even point in terms of helping or hurting an offense. On turf, however, the success rate was 72.7 percent, significantly better than break-even. We wrote, "The reason for the advantage on artificial turf is pretty simple: you can run faster on it." (Original study appeared in 1990, Page 4)

How Rare is a Two-Strike Homer? Well, rarer than some might have you believe. This question was prompted by those nostalgiasts who say that hitters nowadays refuse to shorten their strokes when they're down in the count. The evidence indicated otherwise: in 1989, only 25.8 percent of all homers were hit with two strikes, 8 percent lower than a natural distribution. (1990, Page 35)

Are Pitchers' Throws to First a Waste of Time? Not at all. Regarding all attempted steals of second base, studies of three years' data found that when the pitcher made no throws to first, runners stole second at a 72 percent success rate. But when pitchers made at least one throw to first, the success rate fell nine points to 63 percent, a significant drop. The effect was even more pronounced for the top basestealers (those with 40 or more stolen bases); their group success rate dropped from 84 percent to 70 percent. (1990, Page 40; 1991, Page 38; 1992, Page 16; see page 78 of this year's book for related study)

Does Artificial Turf Produce More Groundball Hits? Yes, but not a lot more. By comparing each teams' groundball hits, home and road, STATS was able to determine that in 1989, the turf parks only increased the groundball hit percentage by 0.8 percent, which in turn would create just a two percent increase in batting average. (1990, Page 62)

Do Sacrifices Sacrifice Too Much? Well, it depends on when you do it. With a runner on first only, the sacrifice is a losing proposition unless one run (and no more) is badly needed. However, data from 1987 through

1989 indicates that sacrificing with men on first and second is a good percentage move unless a very good hitter is at the plate. (1990, Page 68)

How Does Temperature Affect Offensive Production? In a few words? "Heat equals hitting." STATS records the temperatures of every game, and from 1987 through 1989 the data showed a significant climatic impact on offense. When the temperature was above 90, there were an average of 9.1 runs and 1.83 home runs per game. When the temperature was below 60, there were 8 runs and 1.40 home runs per game. (1990, Page 46)

What Good is an Intentional Walk? Not much. In 1990, nearly one run scored, on average, following an intentional walk. What's more, the batter intentionally walked came around to score 15 percent of the time. But what about walking a batter to set up the double play? When an intentional walk set up a double play situation, a double play actually resulted only 13 percent of the time. As we wrote, "the odds of a double play are lower than the odds of a walked batter eventually scoring!" (1991, Page 6)

Do Free Agents Bust Out With Their New Clubs? No, but they tend to bust their arms or their knees. The entire history of free agency was examined, from 1977 through 1990, and the findings can be described as: "consistency, but not as much of it." Hitters, for example, showed almost identical batting averages and home run rates, but they logged 10 percent fewer at-bats in the first season with their new clubs. And pitchers had identical ERAs from season to season, but worked 8 percent fewer innings. (1991, Page 52)

What's the Opposite of a Grand-Slam Home Run? The name hasn't caught on yet, but we vote for the "grand-slam double play," a double (or triple) play with the bases loaded and no runs scoring. When a team has the bases loaded with less than two out, on average it will score 1.5 runs. So the grand-slam double play saves 1.5 runs for the defensive team, and quite often the game. (1991, Page 62)

Is "Giving Yourself Up" a Give-Up Play? By "giving yourself up," we mean hitting a grounder to the right side of the infield with a man on second and nobody out, allowing the runner to move to third. When it happens, the batter is practically nominated for sainthood by the announcers, but if he doesn't get the runner over, he "didn't do his job." We looked at this play and found two things: 1) Hitting a grounder to the right side on demand is a difficult task, and 2) It only makes strategic sense if one run is critical. To sum up, "Too much is made of this play." (1991, Page 108)

How Does the Wind Affect Run-Scoring at Wrigley? This question was prompted by Cub hitters who like to say, sure, the fences are close and sometimes the wind blows out, but the wind blows in, too, and as a result

Wrigley doesn't really help us. STATS keeps track of wind direction, and we found that the wind blew out 37 percent of the time, blew in 35 percent of the time, and blew across (left to right or right to left) 28 percent of the time. And, to answer the initial question, we wrote: "When the wind blows out, Wrigley is a great hitters' park; when it blows across, it's a very good one; when it blows in, it's a neutral park." So Cubbie hitters, stop whining. (1992, Page 6)

Questions on Offense

Are Power Hitters Pull Hitters? Yes, but not as much as you might think. As you know, STATS records where all balls are hit, including home runs. From 1989 through 1991, only eight players averaged 30 home runs per season, and all of them pulled the majority of their homers. But six of the eight homered to the opposite field more often, percentage-wise, than the average major leaguer. This can probably be explained by the efforts of pitchers to keep the ball away from power hitters. (1992, Page 82)

Can Hitters Cause Errors? Maybe not on purpose, but some hitters are better at it than others. Four characteristics pop up repeatedly when you look at a list of hitters who reach on errors most often. They tend to be right-handed, have good speed, hit the ball hard, and, less importantly, are good bunters. There's one more thing; not surprisingly, they tend to spend half their time in parks with error-prone infield surfaces. (1991, Page 102)

What Kind of Hitters Have Big Platoon Differentials? We took three years of data (1989-1991), and made a list of the 10 batters with the biggest platoon differentials from both sides of the plate. Names on the list included Frank Thomas, Cecil Fielder, Chris Sabo, Hal Morris, Paul O'Neill, and Lou Whitaker. The answer: "All Kinds of Hitters Have Big Platoon Differentials." (1992, Page 92)

Is Patience a Virtue? Apparently so. We drew up a list of the top 10 in first-pitch swinging over three seasons (1989-1991). The list: Mike Marshall, Cory Snyder, Ozzie Guillen, Gary Gaetti, Joe Oliver, Alvaro Espinoza, Matt Williams, Bo Jackson, Kirby Puckett, and Don Slaught. The top 10 in first-pitch taking: Wade Boggs, Randy Ready, Rickey Henderson, Brian Downing, Alvin Davis, Don Mattingly, Frank Thomas, Edgar Martinez, Jody Reed, and Barry Larkin. Defense rests. (1992, Page 106)

Is There Such a Thing as a "Turf Hitter"? No, not as far as we can tell. The supposedly prototypical turf hitter is a fast guy, slaps the ball on the ground a lot. We drew up a list of those hitters (based on 1989-1991 stats), and compared their performance on turf to their performance on grass. The result? "Turf hitters" actually hit five points less on turf than grass (.274 vs. .269), while slugging 20 points more on turf, where triples and doubles go up. "Non-turf hitters" (everybody else) hit almost identically on both surfaces. Conclusion: "Some people may continue to think that there are 'grass' and 'turf' hitters, but the statistical evidence to back those claims has yet to surface." (1992, Page 144)

Questions on Pitching

How Important is a First-Pitch Strike? Very important. In 1989, the batting average following a first-pitch ball was .267, on-base percentage .372. But when the first pitch was a strike, the resultant batting average was .229, on-base percentage .269. There was a caveat; when batters swung and hit the first pitch, they walloped the ball at a .313 clip, .470 slugging. So our advice for a pitcher is, "Get the first one over, but not too over!" (1990, Page 146)

Do They Still Brush 'Em Back? Yep. A study of HBP rates, going all the way back to 1961, found two things. One is that the beanball is almost as popular now as it was in the sixties (when men were men, at least according to Don Drysdale). And the second is that beanball rates tend to rise and fall with seasonal home run rates. (1990, Page 153)

Can a Pitcher Induce a Double Play Grounder? Nope. This study was inspired by Bob Gibson, who claimed he could induce a double play grounder almost at will. STATS identified all GDP situations (runner on first, less than two out), and compared the ground ball rates then with ground ball rates for all situations. It turns out that batters hit ground balls exactly one-third of the time, no matter what the situation. What's more the style of the pitcher made no difference; neither groundball pitchers nor flyball pitchers were able to alter their normal frequencies of ground balls allowed. (1990, Page 162)

What Happens After a Home Run? Based on 1989 data, five things:

1. Batting average for the next hitter drops about 10 points. 2. The home run rate for the next batter goes up about 10 percent. 3. The HBP rate skyrockets, 50 percent in the NL, 100 percent in the AL. 4. The base on balls rate goes up significantly. 5. The strikeout rate rises significantly. Conclusions: about what you'd expect. The pitcher is mad, and so is likely to throw a little harder and a little wilder, which would explain all of the above results except perhaps #2. And the home run rate likely goes up because power hitters are generally followed in the lineup by more power hitters. (1990, Page 192)

What's Lasorda Doing With Ramon Martinez? Now we know. Martinez threw 3,802 total pitches and 115 pitches per start in 1990; both totals led the National League. What's more, he was only 22 at the time, a dangerous age for such a heavy workload. We noted that Fernando Valenzuela assumed a similar burden, and his days as an ace were over at 25. Now it's 1993: Martinez' ERAs have gone up, his strikeout rates have gone down, and at this writing he is recovering from arm surgery. (1991, Page 177)

Do Pitchers Coast With a Big Lead? Yes they do; this is a baseball cliche that actually survives examination. The Scoreboard: "We separated all 1991 plate appearances into those in which the pitcher had at least a three-run lead, and those in which the lead was two runs or less." The differences were just what you'd expect: batting averages went up slightly (more strikes), home runs went up 20 percent (same), walks were down 25 percent (ditto), strikeout rates were down slightly ("let 'em hit it"), and stolen base success rates were way up ("the hell with that guy on first"). (1992, Page 192)

Questions on Defense

Do Good-Throwing Catchers Intimidate Baserunners? Not as much as you would think. We drew up lists of the catchers who had the fewest steal attempts per opportunity against them, for both leagues (based on 1989-1991 data). There were some surprises: Mike Macfarlane, B.J. Surhoff, Mickey Tettleton, Darren Daulton, Mark Parent, Greg Olson — all had little success throwing out runners. We concluded: "Runners try to steal for a variety of reasons: the league, the park, the surface, the pitcher, the catcher. The figures strongly suggest that the catcher is probably one of the least important among all those factors." (1992, Page 221)

Should You Guard the Line in the Late Innings? Yes, but only in a one-run game, and even then it won't matter much. STATS carefully tracks the paths of all balls hit in play, so we can fairly accurately estimate how many hits are saved or lost by guarding the lines. The verdict? Guarding the line will save some doubles (important in a one-run game), but those are offset by the singles the defense gives up, and so increases the chances that multiple runs will be scored. And both effects are marginal.

Previous editions of *STATS Baseball Scoreboard* are available for purchase from STATS, Inc. at 1-800-63-STATS (1-800-637-8287).

APPENDIX

When I was thirteen I received a copy of the Macmillan Baseball Encyclopedia as a gift. Now, this may not have been **every** thirteen year old boy's dream come true, but for a young baseball fan in a prolonged state of pre-pubescence, it was an altogether smart choice, I would say. Armed with a Texas Instruments scientific calculator (a marvel of technology in its day; though they're making laptop computers that size today) and plenty of time on my hands, I could easily spend a winter's evening adding, subtracting, multiplying, and dividing the numbers inside that book, hoping to uncover some undiscovered baseball truths buried in its pages.

Earl Webb's 67 doubles in 1930 is etched in my memory. How **do** you hit 67 doubles in one season? Was everyone hitting a lot of doubles that year? What park did he play in? Did his home field have anything to do with it, and did any of his teammates also hit a lot of doubles? Odd things to have kicking around your head, but those are the kinds of questions this Appendix, and the Scoreboard as a whole, helps you answer. Is there an essay in the book that you think could be approached from a slightly different angle? Another one that you'd like to see more data for? Or just a category that you think just might confirm how great your favorite player is? We've tried to give you all the data we worked with for each essay; maybe you can do a little investigating yourself and come to some conclusions of your own. We don't even mind if you disagree with our conclusions; it's a free country, as they say. Some of our best ideas for subsequent editions came from readers who've done their own calculations from the numbers back here and written us with their own comments and questions. And like "America's Ridiculous Home Videos," we'll even give you credit if we use your idea on the air! Once again, we've spared no expense — just a lot of sleep — to make the 73 data charts, player lists, and statistical summations in the following pages easy to decipher, easy to peruse, and, most importantly, easy to read. For some of the Essays, (28 to be exact) most or all of the figures used for that particular study appear in the Essay itself. In such cases, there is no additional data back here. We put together a whole new section of the Scoreboard this year, the Team Section, so you'll often find appendices which either expand on the team data given in those essays, or give you data on how individual players may have performed in the statistical category covered in the essay.

Each Appendix is keyed twice. The "Title" key serves as a reminder as to what topic is being covered, and corresponds to the title in the Table of Contents. The "Page" key refers to the page where you'll find the appropriate essay. In addition, each Appendix is accompanied by a label describing how the list has been ordered (most alphabetically), a "minimum requirement" telling how much of what a player needed to make the list, and a key for deciphering any obscure abbreviations.

The team abbreviation following a player's name refers to the team with which he finished the season. Here are the abbreviations:

American League Teams		National League Teams	
Bal	Baltimore Orioles	Atl	Atlanta Braves
Bos	Boston Red Sox	ChN	Chicago Cubs
Cal	California Angels	Cin	Cincinnati Reds
ChA	Chicago White Sox	Hou	Houston Astros
Cle	Cleveland Indians	LA	Los Angeles Dodgers
Det	Detroit Tigers	Mon	Montreal Expos
KC	Kansas City Royals	NYN	New York Mets
Mil	Milwaukee Brewers	Phi	Philadelphia Phillies
Min	Minnesota Twins	Pit	Pittsburgh Pirates
NYA	New York Yankees	StL	St. Louis Cardinals
Oak	Oakland Athletics	SD	San Diego Padres
Sea	Seattle Mariners	SF	San Francisco Giants
Tex	Texas Rangers		
Tor	Toronto Blue Jays		

BALTIMORE ORIOLES: WILL THEY UNLOAD THE BASES AGAIN IN 1993? (p. 6)

1992 Team Batting — Bases Loaded

American League

Team	AVG	OBP	SLG	AB	R	H	2B	3B	HR	BB	K
Baltimore	.351	.380	.557	131	140	46	8	2	5	16	20
Boston	.285	.332	.475	158	139	45	9	0	7	17	32
California	.256	.272	.372	78	75	20	4	1	1	5	10
Chicago	.252	.297	.420	131	132	33	8	1	4	15	21
Cleveland	.282	.285	.427	117	96	33	3	1	4	2	24
Detroit	.313	.333	.510	147	143	46	12	1	5	11	32
Kansas City	.174	.215	.233	86	73	15	2	0	1	4	17
Milwaukee	.262	.291	.410	122	124	32	8	2	2	12	17
Minnesota	.348	.337	.522	138	145	48	9	0	5	6	15
New York	.299	.359	.444	117	110	35	3	1	4	16	26
Oakland	.264	.316	.407	140	124	37	8	0	4	17	20
Seattle	.230	.256	.389	113	90	26	3	0	5	8	19
Texas	.211	.255	.317	123	88	26	4	0	3	8	24
Toronto	.252	.315	.382	123	110	31	10	0	2	15	24

National League

Team	AVG	OBP	SLG	AB	R	H	2B	3B	HR	BB	K
Atlanta	.288	.297	.432	111	93	32	8	1	2	6	24
Chicago	.261	.253	.386	88	74	23	2	0	3	1	14
Cincinnati	.222	.220	.326	144	109	32	9	0	2	4	25
Houston	.233	.299	.323	133	92	31	4	1	2	15	29
Los Angeles	.286	.287	.420	119	101	34	4	3	2	5	17
Montreal	.294	.331	.349	109	103	32	3	0	1	11	21
New York	.291	.348	.448	134	132	39	12	0	3	16	21
Philadelphia	.250	.277	.382	136	111	34	1	1	5	6	23
Pittsburgh	.276	.285	.440	134	102	37	6	2	4	4	20
St. Louis	.284	.304	.448	134	109	38	7	3	3	4	28
San Diego	.263	.289	.453	95	88	25	2	2	4	7	13
San Francisco	.206	.229	.330	97	62	20	5	2	1	4	18

BOSTON RED SOX: WAS IT THE LACK OF THE BIG TWO-OUT HIT? (p. 8)

1992 Team Batting — Runners in Scoring Position/2 Outs

American League

Team	AVG	OBP	SLG	AB	R	H	2B	3B	HR	BB	K
Baltimore	.243	.344	.390	667	227	162	33	7	17	98	110
Boston	.212	.325	.299	636	192	135	31	3	6	106	125
California	.220	.310	.307	567	170	125	19	3	8	71	105
Chicago	.219	.332	.327	648	199	142	24	5	12	105	119
Cleveland	.230	.314	.328	643	199	148	16	4	13	72	123
Detroit	.246	.343	.416	658	251	162	30	5	24	97	135
Kansas City	.247	.331	.353	677	211	167	27	6	11	76	91
Milwaukee	.241	.342	.335	701	237	169	31	4	9	101	114
Minnesota	.230	.345	.317	682	218	157	26	3	9	110	107
New York	.217	.335	.343	607	204	132	21	2	17	102	111
Oakland	.233	.365	.357	678	232	158	30	0	18	134	113
Seattle	.221	.306	.361	628	196	139	31	6	15	75	101
Texas	.220	.323	.348	676	222	149	32	3	16	97	146
Toronto	.257	.362	.425	685	254	176	36	8	21	105	113

National League

Team	AVG	OBP	SLG	AB	R	H	2B	3B	HR	BB	K
Atlanta	.222	.322	.360	653	195	145	28	7	16	95	117
Chicago	.235	.329	.318	622	185	146	24	2	8	83	106
Cincinnati	.221	.336	.327	675	198	149	29	5	11	113	121
Houston	.199	.323	.288	649	169	129	20	4	10	108	158
Los Angeles	.219	.321	.312	648	179	142	32	5	6	92	124
Montreal	.231	.333	.320	653	188	151	36	2	6	95	128
New York	.189	.318	.305	604	177	114	31	3	11	113	123
Philadelphia	.228	.341	.332	671	212	153	29	4	11	109	122
Pittsburgh	.228	.349	.322	658	192	150	30	4	8	116	114
St. Louis	.234	.342	.332	743	226	174	36	11	5	114	154
San Diego	.214	.330	.352	585	166	125	22	4	17	100	119
San Francisco	.221	.312	.333	637	179	141	26	6	11	81	149

CALIFORNIA ANGELS: WERE THEY TRAPPED BY THE TRAPPERS? (p. 11)

1992 Major League Equivalencies for Angels AA (Midland) and AAA (Edmonton) Players

Player	G	AB	R	H	2B	3B	HR	RBI	BB	K	SB	CS	Avg	OBP	Slg
Alfonzo, Edgar J.	61	203	23	48	6	0	2	17	12	32	0	2	.236	.279	.296
Anderson, Garret J.	39	135	9	29	3	0	1	11	4	32	1	1	.215	.237	.259
Barbara, Donald J.	118	365	41	87	18	0	2	37	45	81	4	4	.238	.322	.304
Bean, Billy	39	129	10	25	5	0	0	14	4	13	2	3	.194	.218	.233
Billmeyer, Mick	46	125	4	15	3	0	0	10	3	29	0	0	.120	.141	.144
Bradley, Phil	83	253	25	59	12	1	0	15	23	31	3	0	.233	.297	.289
Brooks, Hubie	8	22	1	5	1	0	0	6	0	2	0	0	.227	.227	.273
Brown, Tony	48	170	13	34	6	0	2	10	4	42	1	1	.200	.218	.271
Coachman, Pete	103	329	38	54	9	0	3	22	16	46	5	2	.164	.203	.219
Correia, Rod	123	445	43	103	16	0	3	33	13	77	10	4	.231	.253	.288
Davis, Kevin B.	23	71	12	22	6	1	0	9	2	11	0	2	.310	.329	.423
Easley, Damion	108	396	36	91	12	1	1	26	18	46	13	6	.230	.263	.273
Edmonds, Jim	120	404	47	99	20	0	8	40	28	145	2	5	.245	.294	.354
Flora, Kevin	52	155	20	40	5	1	1	11	16	26	4	8	.258	.327	.323
Gonzales, Lawrence	80	220	22	58	7	0	1	28	22	25	1	1	.264	.331	.309
Gonzalez, Jose	42	120	18	28	8	1	1	10	17	29	7	4	.233	.328	.342
Jackson, John M.	40	139	11	32	2	1	0	9	8	21	5	5	.230	.272	.259
Jones, Bobby	100	296	26	53	10	0	1	17	24	73	2	4	.179	.241	.223
Kapano, Corey	18	57	4	10	3	0	0	3	6	18	0	2	.175	.254	.228
Kipila, Jeff	115	389	37	80	15	1	13	45	23	111	1	4	.206	.250	.350
Lawton, Marcus	46	151	11	31	4	0	0	6	7	23	0	6	.205	.241	.232
Martinez, Ray	118	366	34	81	16	1	2	28	17	85	3	5	.221	.256	.287
McConnell, Walt	99	293	23	60	11	0	0	22	23	46	0	0	.205	.263	.242
McDowell, Oddibe	6	13	0	2	0	0	0	1	2	4	0	1	.154	.267	.154
Morris, John	4	16	1	1	0	0	0	0	0	5	0	0	.063	.063	.063
Musolino, Mike	50	138	9	27	5	0	1	13	11	39	0	1	.196	.255	.254
Oberkfell, Ken	61	186	19	41	9	0	0	20	18	18	1	4	.220	.289	.269
Orton, John	49	138	16	27	6	1	1	14	16	33	1	5	.196	.279	.275
Palacios, Rey	29	85	8	17	3	0	3	5	3	25	0	1	.200	.227	.341
Perez, Eddie	62	221	16	40	5	0	1	13	10	52	9	7	.181	.216	.217
Phillips, J.R.	127	465	34	86	22	1	8	45	15	176	2	3	.185	.210	.288
Romero, Jonathan	15	45	2	3	0	0	0	1	1	11	0	0	.067	.087	.067
Rose, Bobby	20	68	6	14	0	1	1	6	3	13	0	0	.206	.239	.279
Rumsey, Dan	65	202	23	43	7	2	3	19	17	55	2	1	.213	.274	.312
Salmon, Tim	118	372	60	105	27	1	18	62	53	108	4	7	.282	.372	.505
Sojo, Luis	37	133	13	31	6	0	0	14	5	17	2	2	.233	.261	.278
Stark, Matt	16	47	5	14	2	0	1	5	4	6	0	0	.298	.353	.404
Taylor, Terry L.	82	232	22	46	15	0	0	13	27	65	1	2	.198	.282	.263
Tejero, Fausto F.	92	267	12	38	7	0	1	17	7	71	0	4	.142	.164	.180
Vanburkleo, Ty	135	425	49	92	19	2	12	52	43	104	10	4	.216	.288	.355
Wasinger, Mark	58	147	14	27	7	0	0	10	7	23	0	2	.184	.221	.231
Williams, Reggie	139	481	57	103	17	3	1	38	50	115	19	10	.214	.288	.268

CHICAGO WHITE SOX:HOW IMPORTANT IS A SLUGGING OUTFIELD? (p. 14)

1992 Team Batting — By Outfielders

American League

Team	AVG	OBP	SLG	AB	R	H	2B	3B	HR	BB	K
Baltimore	.274	.346	.429	1919	252	526	88	25	53	203	278
Boston	.246	.310	.356	1864	222	458	92	10	31	170	349
California	.246	.312	.338	1809	216	445	68	10	26	173	344
Chicago	.264	.335	.357	1783	238	471	66	21	19	195	226
Cleveland	.269	.337	.389	1914	262	515	69	14	44	191	298
Detroit	.249	.316	.391	1790	256	445	78	9	53	175	378
Kansas City	.245	.310	.347	1770	199	433	76	18	23	165	271
Milwaukee	.267	.326	.399	1873	247	500	102	14	39	164	304
Minnesota	.300	.354	.445	1914	274	574	96	14	51	141	340
New York	.273	.339	.425	1912	267	522	105	7	57	195	295
Oakland	.252	.347	.378	1816	260	458	66	12	46	257	309
Seattle	.269	.333	.430	1857	243	500	92	9	63	173	326
Texas	.260	.317	.438	1874	226	488	94	10	73	148	372
Toronto	.269	.331	.453	1934	291	521	96	23	71	164	388

National League

Team	AVG	OBP	SLG	AB	R	H	2B	3B	HR	BB	K
Atlanta	.270	.337	.419	1916	294	518	69	30	52	189	332
Chicago	.257	.302	.378	1914	209	491	71	13	45	116	270
Cincinnati	.272	.354	.414	1848	262	503	105	17	41	232	309
Houston	.262	.319	.401	1905	212	500	88	20	45	153	331
Los Angeles	.254	.333	.356	1801	201	457	66	20	26	210	337
Montreal	.273	.327	.437	1946	282	532	118	15	57	149	296
New York	.249	.331	.383	1796	237	448	96	6	44	218	328
Philadelphia	.247	.307	.361	1933	230	477	99	10	34	155	318
Pittsburgh	.287	.373	.474	1857	311	533	105	31	60	255	294
St. Louis	.284	.346	.433	1961	255	556	110	18	49	181	384
San Diego	.257	.302	.375	1870	215	480	81	15	37	117	265
San Francisco	.263	.309	.355	1959	223	515	77	11	27	128	349

DETROIT TIGERS:HOW MANY RUNS DO THEY NEED TO WIN? (p. 19)

In this chart, you'll be able to find out how many times a team Won (**W**) or Lost (**L**), and its Winning Percentage (**Pct**) given the number of runs they scored in the game.

Win-Loss Records by #of Runs Scored — 1992

American League

Team	1 W-L	Pct	2 W-L	Pct	3 W-L	Pct	4 W-L	Pct	5 W-L	Pct	6 W-L	Pct	7+ W-L	Pct
Baltimore	1-10	.091	11-20	.355	10-16	.385	15-11	.577	10-6	.625	11-0	1.000	31-4	.886
Boston	4-17	.190	4-22	.154	11-19	.367	10-6	.625	12-7	.632	10-4	.714	22-3	.880
California	2-19	.095	7-24	.226	13-10	.565	9-10	.474	14-5	.737	9-4	.692	18-3	.857
Chicago	2-18	.100	3-14	.176	8-16	.333	14-8	.636	9-4	.692	10-3	.769	40-2	.952
Cleveland	2-17	.105	5-12	.294	8-12	.400	13-10	.565	14-13	.519	9-7	.563	25-4	.862
Detroit	0-16	.000	1-14	.067	5-13	.278	12-12	.500	9-12	.429	13-6	.684	35-5	.875
Kansas City	0-25	.000	8-14	.364	13-17	.433	8-7	.533	10-4	.714	7-7	.500	26-3	.897
Milwaukee	3-25	.107	4-13	.235	10-9	.526	17-11	.607	16-0	1.000	7-1	.875	35-6	.854
Minnesota	2-14	.125	7-12	.368	8-14	.364	14-10	.583	16-6	.727	10-3	.769	33-5	.868
New York	1-14	.067	3-20	.130	6-19	.240	10-6	.625	14-6	.700	10-10	.500	32-3	.914
Oakland	1-13	.071	4-17	.190	7-16	.304	14-7	.667	22-3	.880	13-4	.765	35-0	1.000
Seattle	2-17	.105	7-16	.304	5-11	.313	6-21	.222	6-5	.545	10-6	.625	28-8	.778
Texas	2-16	.111	2-18	.100	9-13	.409	16-6	.727	14-9	.609	12-4	.750	22-5	.815
Toronto	3-14	.176	5-13	.278	13-9	.591	15-10	.600	10-4	.714	11-4	.733	39-2	.951

National League

Team	1 W-L	Pct	2 W-L	Pct	3 W-L	Pct	4 W-L	Pct	5 W-L	Pct	6 W-L	Pct	7+ W-L	Pct
Atlanta	3-10	.231	13-14	.481	14-12	.538	18-10	.643	14-6	.700	9-1	.900	27-3	.900
Chicago	3-14	.176	3-24	.111	15-12	.556	11-6	.647	15-3	.833	11-0	1.000	20-5	.800
Cincinnati	2-16	.111	4-18	.182	12-15	.444	18-6	.750	13-5	.722	13-1	.929	28-1	.966
Houston	3-13	.188	6-18	.250	17-14	.548	10-4	.714	18-9	.667	9-4	.692	18-1	.947
Los Angeles	3-25	.107	6-19	.240	4-20	.167	10-11	.476	11-7	.611	10-1	.909	19-1	.950
Montreal	2-17	.105	2-20	.091	13-11	.542	17-9	.654	10-2	.833	17-2	.895	26-3	.897
New York	4-17	.190	4-26	.133	9-13	.409	14-7	.667	8-3	.727	10-7	.588	23-1	.958
Philadelphia	0-17	0.000	6-22	.214	6-16	.273	10-6	.625	11-10	.524	9-6	.600	28-6	.824
Pittsburgh	4-12	.250	9-14	.391	20-11	.645	12-9	.571	14-5	.737	11-3	.786	26-3	.897
St. Louis	4-23	.148	8-20	.286	12-4	.750	14-8	.636	12-8	.600	9-2	.818	24-3	.889
San Diego	2-19	.095	9-19	.321	12-13	.480	12-9	.571	10-5	.667	7-2	.778	30-1	.968
San Francisco	3-16	.158	8-14	.364	11-21	.344	10-9	.526	9-8	.529	10-3	.769	21-1	.955

OAKLAND ATHLETICS: HOW COSTLY IS A BLOWN SAVE?
(p. 36)

The following charts show the win-loss records of each team following a Blown Save. This Win-Loss record is broken down by the inning in which a Save was blown.

American League

Team	6th W-L	Pct	7th W-L	Pct	8th W-L	Pct	9th W-L	Pct	10th+ W-L	Pct
Baltimore	2-1	.667	2-1	.667	1-2	.333	2-4	.333	0-1	.000
Boston	1-3	.250	3-4	.429	1-5	.167	5-3	.625	0-1	.000
California	1-1	.500	1-3	.250	2-2	.500	0-4	.000	0-0	-
Chicago	1-0	1.000	3-2	.600	2-6	.250	2-5	.286	0-0	-
Cleveland	2-2	.500	4-4	.500	4-1	.800	1-5	.167	0-0	-
Detroit	0-2	.000	1-2	.333	1-4	.200	1-3	.250	0-0	-
Kansas City	3-3	.500	3-7	.300	1-3	.250	2-1	.667	0-0	-
Milwaukee	1-3	.250	1-2	.333	0-3	.000	1-3	.250	1-0	1.000
Minnesota	2-4	.333	1-3	.250	2-1	.667	0-5	.000	0-0	-
New York	1-1	.500	2-3	.400	4-3	.571	0-3	.000	0-0	-
Oakland	1-1	.500	1-2	.333	2-2	.500	1-1	.500	0-0	-
Seattle	0-4	.000	1-4	.200	2-6	.250	0-3	.000	0-1	.000
Texas	0-1	.000	1-5	.167	3-6	.333	2-4	.333	0-0	-
Toronto	0-0	-	0-2	.000	3-2	.600	1-2	.333	0-0	-

National League

Team	6th W-L	Pct	7th W-L	Pct	8th W-L	Pct	9th W-L	Pct	10th+ W-L	Pct
Atlanta	1-1	.500	2-0	1.000	3-2	.600	3-6	.333	0-0	-
Chicago	0-2	.000	2-4	.333	1-5	.167	0-5	.000	0-0	-
Cincinnati	2-2	.500	2-1	.667	4-5	.444	0-6	.000	1-0	1.000
Houston	1-3	.250	1-3	.250	3-2	.600	2-2	.500	0-0	-
Los Angeles	0-1	.000	2-1	.667	1-5	.167	0-7	.000	0-1	.000
Montreal	1-2	.333	1-3	.250	4-2	.667	1-4	.200	0-0	-
New York	0-2	.000	2-1	.667	3-2	.600	0-5	.000	0-2	.000
Philadelphia	1-2	.333	3-5	.375	3-6	.333	1-2	.333	0-0	-
Pittsburgh	5-0	1.000	2-2	.500	4-3	.571	2-2	.500	0-0	-
St. Louis	3-2	.600	0-5	.000	4-2	.667	3-4	.429	0-0	-
San Diego	1-3	.250	1-0	1.000	0-5	.000	2-4	.333	0-2	.000
San Francisco	2-0	1.000	3-1	.750	1-3	.250	2-4	.333	0-0	-

SEATTLE MARINERS: WHO WILL KEN GRIFFEY BE WHEN HE GROWS UP? (p. 33)

Most Runs Created in a Season by Players 22 or Younger
(Minimum 110 Runs Created)

Player	Year	Age	RC	AB	R	H	HR	RBI	SB	BB	Avg
Williams, Ted	1941	22	202.2	456	135	185	37	120	2	145	.406
Kelley, Joe	1894	22	182.3	507	165	199	6	111	46	107	.393
Jackson, Joe	1911	22	174.6	571	126	233	7	83	41	56	.408
DiMaggio, Joe	1937	22	172.8	621	151	215	46	167	3	64	.346
Cobb, Ty	1909	22	158.6	573	116	216	9	107	76	48	.377
Ott, Mel	1929	20	156.9	545	138	179	42	151	6	113	.328
Williams, Ted	1939	20	156.7	565	131	185	31	145	2	107	.327
Mathews, Eddie	1953	21	156.6	579	110	175	47	135	1	99	.302
Foxx, Jimmie	1930	22	154.4	562	127	188	37	156	7	93	.335
Williams, Ted	1940	21	153.8	561	134	193	23	113	4	96	.344
Foxx, Jimmie	1929	21	153.5	517	123	183	33	117	9	103	.354
Williams, Jimmy	1899	22	151.3	617	126	219	9	116	26	60	.355
Keeler, Willie	1894	22	149.1	590	165	219	5	94	32	40	.371
Musial, Stan	1943	22	146.8	617	108	220	13	81	9	72	.357
Trosky, Hal	1934	21	144.5	625	117	206	35	142	2	58	.330
McGraw, John	1894	21	140.8	512	156	174	1	92	78	91	.340
Ott, Mel	1930	21	139.4	521	122	182	25	119	9	103	.349
Sheckard, Jimmy	1901	22	138.4	554	116	196	11	104	35	47	.354
Kaline, Al	1955	20	135.4	588	121	200	27	102	6	82	.340
Vaughan, Arky	1934	22	135.4	558	115	186	12	94	10	94	.333
Allen, Dick	1964	22	134.6	632	125	201	29	91	3	67	.318
Collins, Eddie	1909	22	134.0	572	104	198	3	56	67	62	.346
Lajoie, Nap	1897	22	132.8	545	107	197	9	127	20	15	.361
Mathews, Eddie	1954	22	131.2	476	96	138	40	103	10	113	.290
Cobb, Ty	1907	20	130.8	605	97	212	5	119	49	24	.350
Kaline, Al	1956	21	128.5	617	96	194	27	128	7	70	.314
DiMaggio, Joe	1936	21	127.1	637	132	206	29	125	4	24	.323
Mantle, Mickey	1954	22	126.7	543	129	163	27	102	5	102	.300
Reiser, Pete	1941	22	124.3	536	117	184	14	76	4	46	.343
Pinson, Vada	1959	22	124.0	648	131	205	20	84	21	55	.316
Mantle, Mickey	1952	20	123.0	549	94	171	23	87	4	75	.312
Robinson, Frank	1957	21	121.9	611	97	197	29	75	10	44	.322
Bench, Johnny	1970	22	121.4	605	97	177	45	148	5	54	.293
Robinson, Frank	1956	20	121.4	572	122	166	38	83	8	64	.290
Henderson, Rickey	1980	21	120.2	591	111	179	9	53	100	117	.303
Lindstrom, Freddy	1928	22	120.0	646	99	231	14	107	15	25	.358
Ripken, Cal	1983	22	119.7	663	121	211	27	102	0	58	.318
Chapman, Ben	1931	22	119.0	600	120	189	17	122	61	75	.315
Griffey, Ken	1991	21	118.2	548	76	179	22	100	18	71	.327
Frisch, Frankie	1921	22	117.7	618	121	211	8	100	49	42	.341
Aaron, Hank	1956	22	115.4	609	106	200	26	92	2	37	.328
Cedeno, Cesar	1972	21	115.1	559	103	179	22	82	55	56	.320
Speaker, Tris	1910	22	114.8	538	92	183	7	65	35	52	.340
Aaron, Hank	1955	21	114.0	602	105	189	27	106	3	49	.314
Cobb, Ty	1908	21	113.9	581	88	188	4	108	39	34	.324
McCreery, Tom	1896	21	112.6	441	87	155	7	65	26	42	.352
Cooley, Duff	1895	22	112.6	563	106	191	6	75	27	36	.339
Magee, Sherry	1907	22	112.5	503	75	165	4	85	46	53	.328
Vaughan, Arky	1933	21	112.0	573	85	180	9	97	3	64	.314
Ott, Mel	1931	22	111.4	497	104	145	29	115	10	80	.292
Clarke, Fred	1895	22	111.4	550	96	191	4	82	40	34	.347
McGraw, John	1895	22	111.2	388	110	143	2	48	61	60	.369
Sheckard, Jimmy	1899	20	110.6	536	104	158	3	75	77	56	.295
Magee, Sherry	1905	20	110.3	603	100	180	5	98	48	44	.299
Cepeda, Orlando	1959	21	110.0	605	92	192	27	105	23	33	.317
Crawford, Sam	1901	21	109.8	515	91	170	16	104	13	37	.330

TEXAS RANGERS: ARE THEY BEING KILLED BY THEIR FAILURE TO MAKE CONTACT? (p. 36)

The charts below show how each team's hitters fare in different batting situations: On the First Pitch (**1stP**), with Two Strikes (**2Strk**), Ahead in the Count (**Ahead**), Behind in the Count (**Behind**), versus Groundball Pitchers (**Grd**), versus Flyball Pitchers (**Fly**), versus Power Pitchers (**Pwr**), and versus Finesse Pitchers (**Fin**).

American League

Team	1stP	2Strk	Ahead	Behind	Pwr	Fin	Grd	Fly
Baltimore	.278	.199	.311	.214	.236	.259	.267	.249
Boston	.267	.187	.303	.195	.232	.251	.247	.245
California	.293	.178	.305	.194	.222	.258	.245	.231
Chicago	.287	.186	.332	.196	.242	.264	.264	.268
Cleveland	.307	.191	.332	.219	.242	.287	.276	.259
Detroit	.297	.181	.338	.200	.251	.263	.257	.229
Kansas City	.290	.188	.307	.211	.237	.263	.248	.248
Milwaukee	.328	.206	.303	.224	.270	.276	.286	.268
Minnesota	.331	.210	.342	.223	.261	.291	.295	.264
New York	.313	.188	.320	.193	.259	.271	.245	.265
Oakland	.294	.199	.315	.210	.245	.271	.281	.266
Seattle	.309	.184	.342	.208	.270	.257	.266	.259
Texas	.341	.171	.318	.197	.247	.265	.256	.249
Toronto	.325	.198	.320	.210	.261	.271	.265	.256
AL Averages	**.305**	**.190**	**.321**	**.207**	**.249**	**.268**	**.264**	**.254**

National League

Team	1stP	2Strk	Ahead	Behind	Pwr	Fin	Grd	Fly
Atlanta	.295	.185	.315	.204	.241	.258	.267	.244
Chicago	.303	.195	.318	.202	.233	.254	.268	.242
Cincinnati	.292	.186	.344	.210	.241	.284	.263	.236
Houston	.295	.182	.309	.190	.247	.241	.249	.239
Los Angeles	.300	.184	.303	.196	.234	.259	.259	.242
Montreal	.310	.179	.304	.198	.231	.269	.255	.233
New York	.282	.168	.295	.183	.257	.237	.231	.222
Philadelphia	.290	.192	.318	.211	.254	.262	.257	.227
Pittsburgh	.297	.191	.316	.208	.251	.252	.237	.269
St. Louis	.314	.186	.320	.208	.265	.272	.268	.277
San Diego	.316	.181	.300	.206	.243	.269	.271	.234
San Francisco	.302	.178	.297	.185	.246	.251	.245	.263
NL Averages	**.300**	**.184**	**.312**	**.200**	**.245**	**.259**	**.256**	**.244**
MLB Averages	**.302**	**.187**	**.317**	**.204**	**.247**	**.264**	**.259**	**.250**

ATLANTA BRAVES: IS COX TAKING PROPER CARE OF HIS YOUNG ARMS? (p. 40)

The following charts list the average number of pitches thrown per start for each team, and the top four pitchers for that team based on games started in 1992. For each of those four starters, the number of games started, the average number of innings per start, and the average number of pitches per start are given in parentheses (**GS/IP-GS/Pit-GS**).

American League

Team	Pit/GS	Rotation (GS/IP-GS/Pit-GS)
Baltimore	100	Sutcliffe(36/6.6/106)-McDn'd(35/6.5/104)-Mussina(32/7.5/107)-Milacki(20/5.3/85)
Boston	99	Viola(35/6.8/109)-Clemens(32/7.7/119)-Hesketh(25/5.5/87)-Dopson(25/5.7/83)
California	101	Langston(32/7.2/108)-Finley(31/6.6/109)-Abbott(29/7.3/107)-Valera(28/6.5/103)
Chicago	103	McCaskill(34/6.1/103)-McDowell(34/7.7/117)-Fernandez(29/6.5/102)-Hibbard(28/6.1/87)
Cleveland	95	Nagy(33/7.6/109)-Cook(25/5.5/88)-Armstrong(23/5.9/97)-Scudder(22/4.9/90)
Detroit	88	Gullickson(34/6.5/89)-Tanana(31/6.0/100)-Terrell(14/5.5/90)-King(14/4.8/79)
Kansas City	86	Appier(30/6.9/107)-Pichardo(24/5.4/83)-Gubicza(18/6.2/97)-Reed(18/5.2/74)
Milwaukee	98	Wegman(35/7.5/111)-Navarro(34/7.2/102)-Bosio(33/7.0/95)-Bones(28/5.5/85)
Minnesota	96	Smiley(34/7.1/104)-Tapani(34/6.5/100)-Erickson(32/6.6/97)-Krueger(27/6.0/91)
New York	101	Sandrs'n(33/5.9/95)-Perez(33/7.5/112)-Kamieniecki(28/6.7/106)-Leary(15/6.2/95)
Oakland	96	Moore(36/6.2/105)-Darling(33/6.3/98)-Stewart(31/6.4/103)-Welch(20/6.2/88)
Seattle	99	Fleming(33/6.9/106)-Johnson(31/6.8/122)-Hanson(30/6.1/95)-Fisher(14/5.7/89)
Texas	100	Brown(35/7.6/108)-Guzman(33/6.8/105)-Ryan(27/5.8/101)-Witt(25/6.5/105)
Toronto	101	Morris(34/7.1/105)-Key(33/6.6/103)-Guzman(28/6.5/107)-Stottlemyre(27/6.4/101)

National League

Team	Pit/GS	Rotation (GS/IP-GS/Pit-GS)
Atlanta	98	Smoltz(35/7.0/108)-Avery(35/6.7/98)-Glavine(33/6.8/100)-Leibrandt(31/6.2/92)
Chicago	94	Maddux(35/7.7/106)-Morgan(34/7.1/101)-Castillo(33/6.2/95)-Jackson(19/5.9/91)
Cincinnati	92	Belcher(34/6.7/98)-Rijo(33/6.4/95)-Swindell(30/7.1/102)-Hammond(26/5.6/82)
Houston	88	Harnisch(34/6.1/95)-Henry(28/5.9/87)-Jones(23/5.9/85)-Kile(22/5.7/91)
Los Angeles	98	Hershiser(33/6.4/92)-Candiotti(30/6.7/105)-Gross(30/6.7/98)-Ojeda(29/5.7/93)
Montreal	93	Hill(33/6.6/95)-Martinez(32/7.1/103)-Nabholz(32/6.1/89)-Gardner(30/5.8/97)
New York	99	Fernandez (32/6.7/107)-Gooden(31/6.6/103)-Cone(27/7.3/120)-Schourek(21/6.2/95)
Philadelphia	95	Mulholland(32/7.2/101)-Schilling(26/7.6/108)-Abbott(19/6.2/102)-Rivera(14/6.5/97)
Pittsburgh	91	Drabek(34/7.5/109)-Tomlin(33/6.3/91)-Smith(22/6.3/85)-Walk(19/5.8/87)
St. Louis	89	Tewkb'y(32/7.2/89)-Olivares(30/6.5/97)-Cormier(30/6.2/86)-Osborne(29/5.8/88)
San Diego	91	Benes(34/6.8/102)-Hurst B(32/6.8/96)-Lefferts(27/6.0/83)-Harris(20/5.9/85)
San Francisco	86	Burkett(32/5.9/86)-Black(28/6.3/93)-Wilson(26/5.9/93)-Swift(22/6.6/92)

CHICAGO CUBS: WILL THEY GROUNDBALL THEIR WAY TO SUCCESS? (p. 42)

By looking at the chart below, you'll be able to determine the extent to which each ballpark favors or hurts a certain type of pitcher (Groundball/Neutral/Flyball). The **Home** statistics are the totals of that team and their opponents in that team's home park. The **Road** statistics are the totals of that team and their opponents in that teams's road games. The difference between the ERAs is shown directly below for comparison.

National League

Team		Groundball		Neutral		Flyball	
		IP	ERA	IP	ERA	IP	ERA
Atlanta	Home	943.2	4.47	2686.0	3.87	675.1	4.21
	Road	953.0	4.04	2667.0	3.47	743.2	3.47
	Diff		-0.43		-0.40		-0.74
Chicago	Home	1619.0	3.69	2149.1	4.00	677.1	4.42
	Road	1598.0	3.45	1993.2	3.73	701.1	3.67
	Diff		-0.24		-0.27		-0.75
Cincinnati	Home	1442.2	3.74	1726.0	4.15	1138.1	3.74
	Road	1607.0	3.16	1697.0	3.72	1062.2	3.66
	Diff		-0.58		-0.43		-0.08
Houston	Home	445.0	3.56	698.1	3.17	353.0	3.16
	Road	492.0	3.60	682.1	4.01	253.0	4.52
	Diff		0.04		0.84		1.36
Los Angeles	Home	1441.0	3.49	1875.2	3.22	1023.1	3.30
	Road	1496.0	3.64	1842.1	3.60	977.2	3.73
	Diff		0.15		0.38		0.43
Montreal	Home	887.2	3.04	1223.2	3.53	574.0	3.45
	Road	1175.2	3.09	1366.2	3.83	603.0	3.37
	Diff		0.05		0.30		-0.08
New York	Home	1672.0	3.65	1809.0	3.76	866.2	3.22
	Road	1643.0	3.93	1803.2	3.45	856.1	3.93
	Diff		0.28		-0.31		0.71
Philadelphia	Home	1314.0	4.14	2162.1	3.68	921.1	3.79
	Road	1192.0	3.71	2170.1	3.93	935.2	3.68
	Diff		-0.43		0.25		-0.11
Pittsburgh	Home	1515.1	3.53	1903.2	3.72	953.1	3.90
	Road	1471.1	3.63	1973.1	3.82	906.0	4.33
	Diff		0.10		0.10		0.43
St. Louis	Home	648.0	3.31	527.2	3.62	322.1	3.63
	Road	558.0	3.21	599.0	3.50	307.0	3.72
	Diff		-0.10		0.08		0.09
San Diego	Home	1173.0	3.35	2128.2	3.87	1070.0	3.84
	Road	1178.2	3.44	2126.1	3.51	1073.0	3.25
	Diff		0.09		-0.36		-0.59
San Francisco	Home	1315.0	3.55	2162.1	3.70	888.0	3.57
	Road	1146.1	3.93	2160.0	3.87	1037.0	3.87
	Diff		0.38		0.17		0.30

American League

Team		Groundball		Neutral		Flyball	
		IP	ERA	IP	ERA	IP	ERA
Baltimore	Home	254.2	2.51	939.1	4.25	274.0	4.14
	Road	240.2	4.26	904.0	4.15	307.2	3.39
	Diff		1.75		-0.10		-0.75
Boston	Home	1521.2	4.05	2080.2	3.72	725.0	4.47
	Road	1507.2	4.12	2131.1	3.33	693.0	3.65
	Diff		0.07		-0.39		-0.82
California	Home	1193.0	3.75	2556.2	3.51	620.1	3.53
	Road	1218.2	3.63	2561.1	3.59	545.2	4.34
	Diff		-0.12		0.08		0.81
Chicago	Home	671.0	3.49	1884.1	3.87	381.1	4.96
	Road	670.1	4.24	1849.0	4.00	408.1	4.34
	Diff		0.75		0.13		-0.62
Cleveland	Home	373.0	3.86	708.0	4.25	397.0	4.35
	Road	346.0	3.49	695.2	3.87	424.1	3.46
	Diff		-0.37		-0.38		-0.89
Detroit	Home	1300.0	4.22	2234.1	4.81	752.2	5.01
	Road	1214.2	4.30	2363.1	4.23	777.1	4.70
	Diff		0.08		-0.58		-0.31
Kansas City	Home	811.0	3.84	3039.0	3.76	507.2	4.38
	Road	803.0	4.36	2944.2	3.73	574.1	4.04
	Diff		0.52		-0.03		-0.34
Milwaukee	Home	771.0	5.01	2658.2	3.68	892.0	3.78
	Road	954.2	4.13	2581.1	4.24	867.2	4.09
	Diff		-0.88		0.56		0.31
Minnesota	Home	1056.2	3.93	2409.2	4.14	851.1	4.85
	Road	973.1	3.25	2438.2	3.92	930.0	3.90
	Diff		-0.68		-0.22		-0.95
New York	Home	1290.2	4.29	2091.1	3.72	993.2	4.58
	Road	1297.2	3.83	2072.0	3.98	966.1	4.30
	Diff		-0.46		0.26		-0.28
Oakland	Home	624.2	3.98	2474.2	3.66	1236.1	3.52
	Road	711.1	4.30	2349.0	4.40	1266.0	4.35
	Diff		0.32		0.74		0.83
Seattle	Home	343.2	4.95	845.2	3.83	269.0	4.68
	Road	363.2	4.70	824.0	3.83	259.1	4.27
	Diff		-0.25		0.00		-0.41
Texas	Home	972.0	4.06	2334.2	4.04	1084.0	3.98
	Road	1020.1	4.25	2380.2	4.01	973.0	4.55
	Diff		0.19		-0.03		0.57
Toronto	Home	967.0	4.02	2525.0	4.24	832.2	4.02
	Road	866.0	4.13	2576.1	3.67	916.0	4.16
	Diff		0.11		-0.57		0.14

CINCINNATI REDS: IS THE DUAL-CLOSER SYSTEM DEAD?
(p. 46)

Both Leagues — Listed Alphabetically
(Minimum 40 games in relief in 1992)

Pitcher, Team	Vs. LHB BFP	Vs. LHB Avg	Vs. RHB BFP	Vs. RHB Avg	Pitcher, Team	Vs. LHB BFP	Vs. LHB Avg	Vs. RHB BFP	Vs. RHB Avg
Aguilera, Min	143	.248	130	.228	Maddux M, SD	181	.235	149	.237
Assenmacher, ChN	102	.220	196	.297	Mason R, Pit	190	.216	184	.276
Austin, Mil	95	.220	140	.171	Mathews T, Tex	70	.328	129	.275
Bankhead, Cin	149	.227	150	.211	McClure, StL	103	.198	127	.315
Beck, SF	191	.178	161	.204	McDowell R, LA	192	.318	201	.295
Belinda, Pit	157	.193	142	.256	McElroy, ChN	117	.275	252	.218
Berenguer, KC	158	.341	185	.188	Meacham R, KC	159	.188	253	.261
Boever, Hou	220	.242	259	.252	Melendez J, SD	183	.281	180	.219
Brantley J, SF	231	.181	150	.246	Mercker, Atl	83	.260	206	.185
Candelaria, LA	59	.269	49	.154	Monteleone, NYA	157	.226	223	.241
Carpenter, StL	181	.222	174	.219	Montgomery, KC	165	.205	168	.205
Charlton, Cin	79	.296	262	.251	Munoz M, Det	81	.192	129	.283
Clements, Bal	87	.234	123	.297	Murphy R, Hou	100	.256	142	.264
Crews, LA	171	.331	168	.290	Myers R, SD	81	.270	267	.282
Crim, Cal	148	.241	235	.328	Neagle, Pit	110	.228	270	.254
Davis Storm, Bal	163	.241	209	.246	Nelson Je, Sea	138	.287	214	.220
Dibble, Cin	152	.180	134	.207	Nunez E, Tex	99	.230	164	.291
Eckersley, Oak	157	.262	152	.159	Olin, Cle	162	.324	198	.188
Edens, Min	118	.248	199	.229	Olson Gregg, Bal	123	.195	121	.229
Eichhorn, Tor	146	.341	226	.202	Orosco, Mil	61	.273	97	.207
Farr S, NYA	102	.217	105	.160	Osuna, Hou	88	.247	182	.231
Fassero, Mon	101	.269	267	.241	Parrett, Oak	172	.278	238	.192
Fetters, Mil	88	.225	155	.164	Patterson B, Pit	89	.256	179	.241
Flanagan, Bal	75	.274	105	.384	Pena A, Atl	84	.205	89	.304
Fossas, Bos	62	.214	67	.345	Perez Mi, StL	180	.244	197	.181
Freeman M, Atl	131	.246	145	.256	Plesac, Mil	80	.254	250	.221
Frey, Cal	59	.189	134	.261	Plunk, Cle	128	.237	181	.223
Frohwirth, Bal	166	.246	278	.248	Powell D, Sea	77	.250	166	.232
Gibson P, NYN	82	.338	191	.266	Power, Cle	150	.226	259	.261
Gott, LA	181	.264	188	.192	Radinsky, ChA	76	.182	185	.269
Guetterman, NYN	102	.278	208	.362	Reardon, Atl	115	.306	130	.279
Guthrie, Min	97	.205	206	.220	Righetti, SF	107	.236	233	.283
Habyan, NYA	131	.339	185	.263	Ritchie, Phi	63	.220	111	.330
Harris Greg A., Bos	174	.211	285	.217	Robinson JD, ChN	172	.290	163	.231
Hartley, Phi	126	.252	117	.257	Rodriguez Rich, SD	115	.233	254	.227
Henke, Tor	122	.190	106	.204	Rogers Ken, Tex	96	.261	241	.262
Henneman, Det	157	.278	164	.235	Rojas, Mon	221	.196	178	.203
Henry Do, Mil	124	.208	153	.292	Ruskin, Cin	79	.250	155	.287
Henry Dw, Cin	160	.208	192	.192	Russell Je, Oak	128	.245	148	.206
Hernandez R, ChA	121	.187	156	.175	Sampen, KC	169	.305	179	.247
Hernandez X, Hou	242	.211	212	.190	Scanlan, ChN	185	.231	175	.239
Hickerson, SF	112	.235	233	.236	Schooler, Sea	95	.278	137	.273
Holmes, Mil	73	.224	100	.225	Smith Lee, StL	186	.220	124	.222
Honeycutt, Oak	69	.258	100	.281	Stanton Mike, Atl	90	.237	174	.252
Horsman, Oak	88	.203	92	.296	Swan R, Sea	92	.198	365	.278
Howell Jay, LA	101	.242	102	.218	Thigpen, ChA	98	.338	155	.237
Innis, NYN	197	.289	176	.244	Ward D, Tor	213	.197	201	.217
Jackson M, SF	192	.265	154	.236	Wayne, Min	56	.250	154	.264
Jones Barry, NYN	158	.338	161	.279	Wetteland, Mon	201	.200	146	.230
Jones D, Hou	236	.253	204	.214	Wickander, Cle	74	.278	113	.250
Knudsen, Det	128	.266	185	.263	Williams Mitch, Phi	61	.265	307	.235
Lancaster, Det	153	.358	251	.259	Willis C, Min	113	.231	200	.254
Leach T, ChA	111	.263	181	.187	Wilson S, LA	113	.255	188	.299
Lilliquist, Cle	99	.200	140	.176	Worrell, StL	134	.174	122	.226

LOS ANGELES DODGERS: HOW COSTLY WERE ALL THOSE ERRORS? (p. 56)

In this chart, you'll be able to find out how many times a team Won (**W**) or Lost (**L**), and its Winning Percentage (**Pct**) given the number of errors they made in the game.

Win-Loss Records by #of Errors Made in the Game — 1992

American League

	Errors Made							
	0		**1**		**2**		**3**	
Team	W-L	Pct	W-L	Pct	W-L	Pct	W-L	Pct
Baltimore	65-27	.707	18-33	.353	6-9	.400	0-4	.000
Boston	38-38	.500	20-27	.426	12-15	.444	3-9	.250
California	40-33	.548	21-31	.404	10-21	.323	1-5	.167
Chicago	42-34	.553	34-21	.618	6-17	.261	4-4	.500
Cleveland	38-31	.551	28-30	.483	8-16	.333	2-9	.182
Detroit	37-38	.493	30-35	.462	7-9	.438	1-5	.167
Kansas City	37-36	.507	26-39	.400	8-8	.500	1-7	.125
Milwaukee	58-32	.644	29-28	.509	5-8	.385	0-2	.000
Minnesota	57-33	.633	24-31	.436	8-5	.615	1-3	.250
New York	45-35	.563	20-36	.357	10-11	.476	1-4	.200
Oakland	57-21	.731	31-22	.585	6-17	.261	2-6	.250
Seattle	44-40	.524	16-38	.296	3-16	.158	1-4	.200
Texas	30-30	.500	28-33	.459	15-16	.484	4-6	.400
Toronto	62-39	.614	25-14	.641	7-8	.467	2-5	.286
AL Totals	650-467	.582	350-418	.456	111-176	.387	23-73	.240

National League

	Errors Made							
	0		**1**		**2**		**3**	
Team	W-L	Pct	W-L	Pct	W-L	Pct	W-L	Pct
Atlanta	59-27	.686	25-25	.500	12-8	.600	2-4	.333
Chicago	48-40	.545	23-25	.479	6-9	.400	1-10	.091
Cincinnati	63-36	.636	15-23	.395	8-10	.444	4-3	.571
Houston	50-32	.610	23-35	.397	5-6	.455	3-8	.273
Los Angeles	27-35	.435	23-31	.426	9-23	.281	4-10	.286
Montreal	42-29	.592	37-30	.552	5-12	.294	3-4	.429
New York	49-38	.563	18-28	.391	4-18	.182	1-6	.143
Philadelphia	36-34	.514	26-36	.419	8-16	.333	0-6	.000
Pittsburgh	60-27	.690	27-28	.491	6-10	.375	3-1	.750
St. Louis	51-49	.510	16-18	.471	15-10	.600	1-2	.333
San Diego	50-30	.625	22-34	.393	8-13	.381	2-3	.400
San Francisco	39-43	.476	23-32	.418	10-7	.588	0-8	.000
NL Totals	574-420	.577	278-345	.446	96-142	.403	24-65	.270
ML Totals	1224-887	.580	628-763	.451	207-318	.394	47-138	.254

PHILADELPHIA PHILLES: WERE THEY TOO CONSERVATIVE ON THE BASE PATHS? (p. 62)

Both Leagues — Listed Alphabetically
(Minimum 10 Stolen Base Attempts in 1992)

Player, Team	SB	CS	Pct	Player, Team	SB	CS	Pct	Player, Team	SB	CS	Pct
Alomar R, Tor	49	9	.845	Gant, Atl	32	10	.762	Palmer D, Tex	10	4	.714
Alou, Mon	16	2	.889	Gilkey, StL	18	12	.600	Pecota, NYN	9	3	.750
Amaro, Phi	11	5	.687	Gonzales R, Cal	7	4	.636	Pena G, StL	13	8	.619
Anderson Br, Bal	53	16	.768	Gonzalez L, Hou	7	7	.500	Pettis, Det	14	4	.778
Baerga, Cle	10	2	.833	Goodwin T, LA	7	3	.700	Phillips T, Det	12	10	.545
Bagwell, Hou	10	6	.625	Griffey Jr, Sea	10	5	.666	Polonia, Cal	51	21	.708
Barberie, Mon	9	5	.643	Grissom, Mon	78	13	.857	Puckett, Min	17	7	.708
Bass K, NYN	14	9	.608	Gruber, Tor	7	7	.500	Raines, ChA	45	6	.882
Bell Jay, Pit	7	5	.583	Hamilton D, Mil	41	14	.745	Redus, Pit	11	4	.733
Belle, Cle	8	2	.800	Harris L, LA	19	7	.731	Reed Jody, Bos	7	8	.466
Bichette, Mil	18	7	.720	Hatcher B, Bos	4	8	.333	Reynolds H, Sea	15	12	.555
Biggio, Hou	38	15	.717	Hayes V, Cal	11	6	.647	Roberts B, Cin	44	16	.733
Blankenship, Oak	21	7	.750	Henderson, Oak	48	11	.813	Samuel, KC	8	3	.727
Blauser, Atl	5	5	.500	Hill G, Cle	9	6	.600	Sandberg, ChN	17	6	.739
Bonds Ba, Pit	39	8	.830	Hollins D, Phi	9	6	.600	Sanders D, Atl	26	9	.743
Bordick, Oak	12	6	.666	Howard T, Cle	15	8	.652	Sanders R, Cin	16	7	.695
Boston, NYN	12	6	.666	Huson, Tex	18	6	.750	Sax S, ChA	30	12	.714
Brett G, KC	8	6	.571	Jackson D, SD	14	3	.823	Schofield, NYN	11	4	.733
Briley, Sea	9	2	.818	Jaha, Mil	10	0	1.00	Seitzer, Mil	13	11	.541
Butler, LA	41	21	.661	Javier, Phi	18	3	.857	Sheffield, SD	5	6	.454
Caminiti, Hou	10	4	.714	Jefferies, KC	19	9	.678	Sierra R, Oak	14	4	.778
Cangelosi, Tex	6	5	.545	Johnson H, NYN	22	5	.815	Smith Dw, ChN	9	8	.529
Canseco J, Tex	6	7	.461	Johnson L, ChA	41	14	.745	Smith O, StL	43	9	.827
Carr, StL	10	2	.833	Jose, StL	28	12	.700	Sojo, Cal	7	11	.389
Carter Jo, Tor	12	5	.706	Joyner, KC	11	5	.687	Sosa S, ChN	15	7	.682
Clark W, SF	12	7	.631	Karkovice, ChA	10	4	.714	Stankiewicz, NYA	9	5	.643
Clayton, SF	8	4	.666	Kelly Pat, NYA	8	5	.615	Stubbs, Mil	11	8	.579
Cole A, Pit	16	6	.727	Kelly R, NYA	28	5	.848	Surhoff B, Mil	14	8	.636
Coleman, NYN	24	9	.727	King J, Pit	4	6	.400	Thompson M, StL	18	6	.750
Cora, ChA	10	3	.769	Knoblauch, Min	34	13	.723	Thompson R, SF	5	9	.357
Cotto, Sea	23	2	.920	Lankford, StL	42	24	.636	Thon, Tex	12	2	.857
Curtis C, Cal	43	18	.705	Larkin B, Cin	15	4	.789	Thurman, KC	9	6	.600
Cuyler, Det	8	5	.615	Leius, Min	6	5	.545	Van Slyke, Pit	12	3	.800
Dascenzo, ChN	6	8	.428	Lewis D, SF	28	8	.778	Vaughn G, Mil	15	15	.500
Daulton, Phi	11	2	.846	Listach, Mil	54	18	.750	Vizquel, Sea	15	13	.536
Davis E, LA	19	1	.950	Lofton, Cle	66	12	.846	Walker C, NYN	15	1	.937
DeShields, Mon	46	15	.754	Mack S, Min	26	14	.650	Walker L, Mon	18	6	.750
Devereaux, Bal	10	8	.555	Martinez D, Cin	12	8	.600	Webster M, LA	11	5	.687
DiSarcina, Cal	9	7	.562	Martinez E, Sea	14	4	.778	Whitaker, Det	6	4	.600
Doran, Cin	7	4	.636	McGee, SF	13	4	.765	White D, Tor	37	4	.902
Duncan, Phi	23	3	.884	McGriff F, SD	8	6	.571	Whiten, Cle	16	12	.571
Dykstra, Phi	30	5	.857	McLemore, Bal	11	5	.687	Wilkerson, KC	18	7	.720
Easley D, Cal	9	5	.643	McRae B, KC	18	5	.782	Williams Be, NYA	7	6	.538
Eisenreich, KC	11	6	.647	Miller K, KC	16	6	.727	Williams MD, SF	7	7	.500
Felder, SF	14	4	.778	Molitor, Mil	31	6	.838	Wilson W, Oak	28	8	.778
Felix, Cal	8	8	.500	Morandini, Phi	8	3	.727	Winningham, Bos	6	5	.545
Fernandez T, SD	20	20	.500	Morris H, Cin	6	6	.500	Yount, Mil	15	6	.714
Finley S, Hou	44	9	.830	Newman A, Tex	9	6	.600	Zeile, StL	7	10	.412
Fletcher S, Mil	17	10	.629	Nixon O, Atl	41	18	.695	AL Average	1704	860	.665
Fryman T, Det	8	4	.666	Offerman, LA	23	16	.590	NL Average	1560	741	.678
Gagne, Min	6	7	.461	Owen S, Mon	9	4	.692	MLB Average	3264	1601	.671

SAN DIEGO PADRES: DID THEY UNDERRATE RANDY MYERS? (p. 66)

The chart below lists a relief pitcher's overall Innings Pitched and Earned Run Average, those same two stats minus his worst two relief appearances of the season, and again, those same two stats minus his worst three outings of the season. The final two columns list his total saves for the season and his total number of blown saves for the season.

Both Leagues — Listed Alphabetically
(Minimum 7 Saves)

Reliever, Team	Overall IP	Overall ERA	Without Worst Two IP	Without Worst Two ERA	Without Worst Three IP	Without Worst Three ERA	Season Totals Sv	Season Totals BSv
Aguilera, Min	66.2	2.84	64.2	1.67	64.1	1.26	41	4
Assenmacher, ChN	68.0	4.10	65.2	3.43	64.2	3.20	8	0
Beck, SF	92.0	1.76	90.0	1.00	89.2	0.90	17	1
Belinda, Pit	71.1	3.15	69.0	2.48	68.0	2.25	18	2
Brantley J, SF	91.2	2.95	90.1	2.39	89.0	2.12	7	0
Bullinger, ChN	85.0	4.66	76.1	3.66	72.1	3.24	7	0
Charlton, Cin	81.1	2.99	78.2	2.40	76.2	2.11	26	3
Dibble, Cin	70.1	3.07	69.0	2.35	68.1	2.11	25	4
Eckersley, Oak	80.0	1.91	78.0	1.38	77.0	1.17	51	8
Farr S, NYA	52.0	1.56	50.2	0.89	50.0	0.72	30	2
Franco John, NYN	33.0	1.64	30.1	0.89	29.1	0.61	15	1
Grahe, Cal	94.2	3.52	85.1	2.43	80.0	2.03	21	0
Habyan, NYA	72.2	3.84	71.2	2.76	71.0	2.41	7	0
Harvey, Cal	28.2	2.83	26.2	1.69	25.2	1.40	13	2
Henke, Tor	55.2	2.26	54.1	1.66	53.1	1.35	34	6
Henneman, Det	77.1	3.96	76.2	3.05	76.0	2.61	24	5
Henry Doug, Mil	65.0	4.02	64.1	2.94	63.2	2.54	29	3
Hernandez R, ChA	71.0	1.65	67.2	1.20	67.2	1.06	12	3
Hernandez X, Hou	111.0	2.11	108.0	1.67	106.0	1.44	7	0
Jones D, Hou	111.2	1.85	108.2	1.33	107.0	1.18	36	5
Mason R, Pit	88.0	4.09	81.0	3.11	80.1	2.80	8	1
McDowell R, LA	83.2	4.09	81.0	3.00	80.1	2.69	14	2
Montgomery, KC	82.2	2.18	81.2	1.65	80.2	1.45	39	2
Myers R, SD	79.2	4.29	78.2	3.66	78.0	3.46	38	9
Olin, Cle	88.1	2.34	86.2	1.56	83.0	1.30	29	3
Olson Gregg, Bal	61.1	2.05	60.0	1.50	59.1	1.21	36	1
Patterson B, Pit	64.2	2.92	63.0	2.14	62.2	1.87	9	1
Pena A, Atl	42.0	4.07	40.1	2.68	38.2	2.09	15	0
Radinsky, ChA	59.1	2.73	58.0	1.86	57.2	1.56	15	0
Reardon, Atl	58.0	3.41	57.0	2.68	56.2	2.38	30	3
Rojas, Mon	100.2	1.43	99.2	0.99	99.1	0.91	10	0
Russell Je, Oak	66.1	1.63	65.0	1.25	64.0	1.13	30	2
Scanlan, ChN	87.1	2.89	86.2	2.39	85.2	2.21	14	4
Schooler, Sea	51.2	4.70	50.1	3.22	50.0	2.70	13	0
Smith Le, StL	75.0	3.12	73.1	2.58	72.2	2.35	43	2
Stanton Mike, Atl	63.2	4.10	62.1	3.32	62.0	3.05	8	1
Swan R, Sea	104.1	4.74	99.0	3.73	96.2	3.54	9	1
Thigpen, ChA	55.0	4.75	55.0	3.27	53.1	2.87	22	0
Ward D, Tor	101.1	1.95	98.2	1.46	97.2	1.29	12	0
Wetteland, Mon	83.1	2.92	82.1	2.08	81.2	1.87	37	5
Williams Mitch, Phi	81.0	3.78	80.1	2.91	78.2	2.52	29	2
Young A, NYN	121.0	4.17	115.0	3.76	109.0	3.55	15	2
Totals: Min 5 Saves	4053.0	3.04	3932.0	2.30	3870.1	2.04	977	94

ST. LOUIS CARDINALS: HOW IMPORTANT IS TEWKSBURY'S PINPOINT CONTROL? (p. 68)

Fewest Walks Allowed/9 IP In One Season Since 1901
(Minimum 150 Innings Pitched)

Pitcher	Year	IP	BB	BB/9	W	L	ERA
Adams, Babe	1920	263.0	18	.62	17	13	2.16
Mathewson, Christy	1913	306.0	21	.62	25	11	2.06
Mathewson, Christy	1914	312.0	23	.66	24	13	3.00
Young, Cy	1904	380.0	29	.69	26	16	1.97
Lucas, Red	1933	220.0	18	.74	10	16	3.40
Tewksbury, Bob	1992	233.0	20	.77	16	5	2.16
Young, Cy	1906	287.2	25	.78	13	21	3.19
Adams, Babe	1919	263.0	23	.79	17	10	1.98
Sallee, Slim	1919	228.0	20	.79	21	7	2.05
Adams, Babe	1922	171.0	15	.79	8	11	3.58
Joss, Addie	1908	325.0	30	.83	24	11	1.16
Young, Cy	1905	320.2	30	.84	18	19	1.82
Hoyt, LaMarr	1985	210.1	20	.86	16	8	3.47
Phillippe, Deacon	1902	272.0	26	.86	20	9	2.05
Alexander, Grover	1923	305.0	30	.89	22	12	3.19
Young, Cy	1901	371.1	37	.90	33	10	1.62
Phillippe, Deacon	1903	289.0	29	.90	25	9	2.43
Bonham, Ernie	1942	226.0	24	.96	21	5	2.27
Mathewson, Christy	1908	390.2	42	.97	37	11	1.43
Mathewson, Christy	1915	186.0	20	.97	8	14	3.58
Tannehill, Jesse	1902	231.0	25	.97	20	6	1.95
Young, Cy	1903	341.2	37	.97	28	9	2.08
Burns, Bill	1908	165.0	18	.98	6	11	1.69
Mathewson, Christy	1912	310.0	34	.99	23	12	2.12
Johnson, Walter	1913	346.0	38	.99	36	7	1.14
Eckersley, Dennis	1985	169.1	19	1.01	11	7	3.08
Adams, Babe	1921	160.0	18	1.01	14	5	2.64
Nolan, Gary	1976	239.0	27	1.02	15	9	3.46
Orth, Al	1901	281.2	32	1.02	20	12	2.27
Jenkins, Ferguson	1971	325.0	37	1.02	24	13	2.77
Derringer, Paul	1939	301.0	35	1.05	25	7	2.93
Tannehill, Jesse	1904	281.2	33	1.05	21	11	2.05
Marichal, Juan	1966	307.0	36	1.06	25	6	2.23
Hahn, Noodles	1904	297.2	35	1.06	16	18	2.06
Barnes, Jesse	1919	296.0	35	1.06	25	9	2.40
Hubbell, Carl	1934	313.0	37	1.06	21	12	2.30
Phillippe, Deacon	1906	219.0	26	1.07	15	10	2.47
Hoyt, LaMarr	1983	260.2	31	1.07	24	10	3.66
Walsh, Ed	1908	464.0	56	1.09	40	15	1.42
Burdette, Lew	1961	272.0	33	1.09	18	11	4.00
Swift, Bill	1932	214.0	26	1.09	14	10	3.62
Bonham, Ernie	1945	181.0	22	1.09	8	11	3.28
Newcombe, Don	1959	222.0	27	1.09	13	8	3.16
Rudolph, Dick	1916	312.0	38	1.10	19	12	2.16
Alexander, Grover	1925	236.0	29	1.11	15	11	3.39
Orth, Al	1902	324.0	40	1.11	19	18	3.97
Young, Cy	1908	299.0	37	1.11	21	11	1.26
Mathewson, Christy	1911	307.0	38	1.11	26	13	1.99
Key, Jimmy	1989	216.0	27	1.13	13	14	3.88
Bernhard, Bill	1903	165.2	21	1.14	14	6	2.12
Burdette, Lew	1960	276.0	35	1.14	19	13	3.36
Donahue, Red	1903	267.2	34	1.14	15	16	2.59
Smith, Zane	1991	228.0	29	1.15	16	10	3.20
Joss, Addie	1909	243.0	31	1.15	14	13	1.70
Pennock, Herb	1930	156.0	20	1.15	11	7	4.33

SAN FRANCISCO GIANTS: SHOULD THEY HAVE EXPECTED THE MATT WILLIAMS SLUMP? (p. 71)

Both Leagues — Listed Alphabetically
(Minimum 1250 Plate Appearances Since 1990)

Player, Team	K	BB	K/BB	Player, Team	K	BB	K/BB	Player, Team	K	BB	K/BB
Alomar R, Tor	210	192	1.1	Gonzalez Jua, Tex	279	79	3.5	Olerud, Tor	220	195	1.1
Anderson Br, Bal	188	167	1.1	Grace, ChN	143	201	0.7	Orsulak, Bal	127	102	1.2
Baerga, Cle	207	99	2.1	Greenwell, Bos	97	126	0.8	Owen S, Mon	151	162	0.9
Bagwell, Hou	213	159	1.3	Griffey Jr, Sea	230	178	1.3	Pagnozzi, StL	164	78	2.1
Baines, Oak	208	198	1.1	Grissom, Mon	210	103	2.0	Palmeiro, Tex	214	180	1.2
Bell G, ChA	239	95	2.5	Gruber, Tor	236	105	2.2	Parrish Lan, Sea	294	105	2.8
Bell Jay, Pit	311	172	1.8	Gwynn T, SD	58	124	0.5	Pena T, Bos	185	104	1.8
Bichette, Mil	260	54	4.8	Hall M, NYA	139	61	2.3	Pendleton, Atl	195	110	1.8
Biggio, Hou	245	200	1.2	Harper B, Min	71	59	1.2	Phillips T, Det	273	292	0.9
Boggs W, Bos	131	250	0.5	Harris L, LA	87	90	1.0	Polonia, Cal	181	122	1.5
Bonds Ba, Pit	225	327	0.7	Hatcher B, Bos	149	81	1.8	Puckett, Min	248	132	1.9
Bonilla B, NYN	243	201	1.2	Hayes C, NYA	266	72	3.7	Raines, ChA	159	234	0.7
Brett G, KC	207	149	1.4	Henderson R, Oak	189	290	0.7	Randolph, NYN	106	160	0.7
Brooks, Cal	216	89	2.4	Hrbek, Min	149	207	0.7	Reed Jody, Bos	162	197	0.8
Browne, Oak	115	139	0.8	Incaviglia, Hou	337	106	3.2	Reynolds H, Sea	156	198	0.8
Brunansky, Bos	283	181	1.6	Jacoby, Cle	166	118	1.4	Ripken C, Bal	162	199	0.8
Buechele, ChN	265	128	2.1	James C, SF	177	63	2.8	Roberts B, Cin	190	154	1.2
Buhner, Sea	313	141	2.2	Jefferies, KC	107	136	0.8	Sabo, Cin	191	135	1.4
Burks, Bos	211	112	1.9	Johnson H, NYN	299	202	1.5	Samuel, KC	308	114	2.7
Butler, LA	208	293	0.7	Johnson Lan, ChA	136	93	1.5	Sandberg, ChN	246	205	1.2
Calderon, Mon	165	118	1.4	Jose, StL	294	114	2.6	Santiago, SD	221	71	3.1
Caminiti, Hou	250	138	1.8	Joyner, KC	150	148	1.0	Sax S, ChA	126	133	0.9
Canseco J, Tex	438	213	2.1	Justice, Atl	258	208	1.2	Schofield, NYN	212	163	1.3
Carter Jo, Tor	314	133	2.4	Kelly R, NYA	321	119	2.7	Scioscia, LA	94	134	0.7
Clark Ja, Bos	311	256	1.2	Knoblauch, Min	100	147	0.7	Seitzer, Mil	131	153	0.9
Clark W, SF	270	186	1.5	Kruk, Phi	258	228	1.1	Sheffield, SD	96	111	0.9
Daniels, ChN	274	153	1.8	Lankford, StL	288	126	2.3	Sierra R, Oak	245	150	1.6
Daulton, Phi	241	201	1.2	Larkin B, Cin	171	167	1.0	Smith O, StL	103	203	0.5
Davis C, Min	282	229	1.2	Lee Manuel, Tor	270	100	2.7	Steinbach, Oak	194	86	2.3
Dawson, ChN	215	94	2.3	Lind, Pit	137	91	1.5	Stillwell, SD	174	98	1.8
Deer, Det	453	204	2.2	Mack S, Min	254	127	2.0	Strawberry, LA	269	164	1.6
DeShields, Mon	355	215	1.7	Magadan, NYN	149	213	0.7	Surhoff B, Mil	111	113	1.0
Devereaux, Bal	257	119	2.2	Maldonado C, Tor	322	144	2.2	Tartabull, NYA	329	204	1.6
Doran, Cin	137	189	0.7	Martinez D, Cin	156	86	1.8	Tettleton, Det	428	329	1.3
Downing, Tex	173	170	1.0	Martinez E, Sea	195	212	0.9	Thomas F, ChA	254	304	0.8
Duncan, Phi	232	53	4.4	Mattingly, NYA	105	113	0.9	Thompson R, SF	266	140	1.9
Dykstra, Phi	100	166	0.6	McGee, SF	266	111	2.4	Thon, Tex	201	82	2.5
Eisenreich, KC	122	86	1.4	McGriff F, SD	351	295	1.2	Van Slyke, Pit	273	195	1.4
Felix, Cal	282	89	3.2	McGwire, Oak	337	293	1.2	Vaughn G, Mil	339	155	2.2
Fernandez T, SD	206	182	1.1	McRae B, KC	216	75	2.9	Ventura, ChA	191	228	0.8
Fielder, Det	484	241	2.0	McReynolds, KC	155	187	0.8	Vizquel, Sea	97	95	1.0
Finley S, Hou	181	132	1.4	Milligan, Bal	257	278	0.9	Walker L, Mon	311	132	2.4
Fletcher S, Mil	122	92	1.3	Mitchell Kev, Sea	190	136	1.4	Wallach, Mon	270	142	1.9
Franco Ju, Tex	178	162	1.1	Molitor, Mil	179	187	1.0	Whitaker, Det	162	245	0.7
Fryman T, Det	344	102	3.4	Morris H, Cin	146	112	1.3	White D, Tor	384	146	2.6
Gaetti, Cal	284	90	3.2	Murphy Dal, Phi	236	110	2.1	Williams MD, SF	375	105	3.6
Gagne, Min	231	69	3.3	Murray E, NYN	212	203	1.0	Winfield, Tor	279	190	1.5
Galarraga, StL	324	74	4.4	Nokes, NYA	158	86	1.8	Yount, Mil	249	185	1.3
Gant, Atl	291	166	1.8	O'Brien P, Sea	121	128	0.9	Zeile, StL	241	197	1.2
Gladden, Det	191	92	2.1	O'Neill, Cin	295	203	1.5				

HOW MUCH DIFFERENCE DOES THE UMPIRE MAKE? (p. 74)

In the chart below, you'll find the number of games each umpire worked behind home plate (G), and the number of called strikes per pitches (CS%).

(Minimum 10 Home Plate Assignments in 1992)

American League					National League				
	1992		1990-1992			1992		1990-1992	
Umpire	G	CS%	G	CS%	Umpire	G	CS%	G	CS%
Barnett	29	15.49%	98	15.77%	Barnes	15	16.00%	29	15.34%
Brinkman	34	16.05%	105	15.52%	Bonin	31	15.05%	100	15.16%
Cedarstrom	20	15.72%	57	15.71%	Crawford	36	15.98%	110	14.93%
Clark	36	15.55%	105	15.12%	Cuzzi	11	15.02%	14	15.12%
Coble	36	16.07%	107	15.70%	Darling	35	15.83%	105	15.42%
Cooney	31	15.92%	88	15.20%	Davidson	35	16.15%	107	16.18%
Cousins	33	15.04%	100	14.32%	Davis	36	14.45%	108	14.52%
Craft	34	16.49%	67	16.61%	Demuth	29	15.54%	102	14.93%
Denkinger	35	15.09%	101	14.88%	Froemming	33	14.43%	106	14.06%
Evans	28	16.35%	102	15.70%	Gorman	20	14.20%	26	14.43%
Ford	36	14.85%	109	15.08%	Hallion	36	15.91%	98	15.56%
Garcia	37	15.21%	105	15.46%	Harvey	23	15.75%	95	14.81%
Hendry	36	16.99%	98	16.69%	Hohn	35	15.48%	100	14.99%
Hickox	24	16.57%	45	16.29%	Kellogg	10	16.62%	10	16.62%
Johnson	27	15.43%	91	15.22%	Layne	24	16.67%	91	15.59%
Joyce	35	15.33%	97	15.57%	Marsh	37	14.48%	110	14.13%
Kaiser	36	16.56%	86	15.82%	McSherry	35	14.46%	103	13.98%
Kosc	34	16.20%	107	16.63%	Montague	35	15.58%	104	15.10%
McClelland	35	15.73%	107	14.89%	Poncino	19	15.22%	25	15.03%
McCoy	35	17.17%	104	16.78%	Pulli	35	15.38%	106	15.07%
McKean	19	17.45%	91	16.31%	Quick	28	15.73%	98	15.39%
Meriwether	34	14.92%	76	14.90%	Rapuano	34	16.15%	79	15.31%
Merrill	36	16.90%	107	16.00%	Reliford	32	14.86%	76	14.56%
Morrison	37	15.59%	110	15.06%	Rennert	23	15.25%	84	14.88%
Phillips	32	14.57%	102	14.84%	Rippley	35	15.75%	110	15.09%
Reed	36	15.55%	105	14.92%	Runge	28	16.18%	79	15.87%
Reilly	33	16.28%	103	15.34%	Tata	36	15.85%	108	15.61%
Roe	34	14.73%	104	14.50%	Wendelstedt	36	15.86%	107	15.76%
Scott	36	15.63%	101	15.35%	West	33	15.67%	104	14.88%
Shulock	37	15.25%	107	15.38%	Williams	33	15.32%	104	15.14%
Tschida	34	15.24%	92	15.28%	Winters	36	15.69%	106	15.18%
Voltaggio	33	16.34%	85	15.79%	**NL Totals**	**972**	**15.49%**	**2914**	**15.09%**
Welke	35	16.06%	107	16.05%					
Young	38	15.92%	103	14.94%					
AL Totals	**1134**	**15.79%**	**3401**	**15.48%**					

WHO ARE THE BIGGEST DRAWS? (p. 76)

Both Leagues — Listed By Attendance Increase
(Minimum 20 Games Started in 1992)

Pitcher, Team	GS	Total	Team Avg	Diff	Pitcher, Team	GS	Total	Team Avg	Diff
Ryan N, Tex	27	33664	27646	6018	Tomlin R, Pit	33	23881	23641	240
Erickson S, Min	32	33400	29168	4232	Tewksbury, StL	32	27990	27767	223
Hesketh, Bos	25	33380	30062	3318	Appier, KC	30	26684	26464	220
Clemens, Bos	32	31903	28771	3132	Perez M, NYA	33	25938	25761	177
Swift, SF	22	26033	22955	3078	Krueger, Mon	29	28796	28640	156
Morris Jack, Tor	34	40884	37863	3021	Fernandez S, NYN	32	24480	24411	69
Candiotti, LA	30	29513	26646	2867	McDowell J, ChA	34	28782	28855	-73
Glavine, Atl	33	34932	32139	2793	Sutcliffe, Bal	36	36594	36677	-83
Jones J, Hou	23	24300	21605	2695	Schilling, Phi	26	25572	25670	-98
Rijo, Cin	33	28673	26060	2613	McDonald, Bal	35	35218	35327	-109
Maddux G, ChN	35	28244	25820	2424	McCaskill, ChA	34	31187	31363	-176
Cone, Tor	34	30821	28402	2419	Guzman Jos, Tex	33	27651	27828	-177
Avery, Atl	35	33499	31116	2383	Mussina, Bal	32	35989	36175	-186
Johnson R, Sea	31	26268	23927	2341	Hurst B, SD	32	24350	24577	-227
Gross Kevin, LA	30	31327	29072	2255	Leibrandt, Atl	31	31943	32191	-248
Morgan M, ChN	34	26980	24747	2233	Stottlemyre T, Tor	27	37464	37726	-262
Cormier, StL	30	29093	26915	2178	Mulholland, Phi	32	23927	24190	-263
Nagy, Cle	33	26369	24221	2148	Gooden, NYN	31	24011	24329	-318
Gullickson, Det	34	25011	22931	2080	Pichardo, KC	24	25123	25479	-356
Moore M, Oak	36	32111	30070	2041	Benes, SD	34	23365	23751	-386
Kamieniecki, NYA	28	26068	24112	1956	Jackson Danny, Pit	34	25847	26309	-462
Clark M, StL	20	29960	28158	1802	Abbott J, Cal	29	27472	27942	-470
Dopson, Bos	25	31957	30155	1802	Henry B, Hou	28	19275	19888	-613
Ojeda, LA	29	30368	28581	1787	Blyleven, Cal	24	26986	27618	-632
Schourek, NYN	21	24823	23101	1722	Harnisch, Hou	34	19212	19876	-664
Hough, ChA	27	33855	32225	1630	Tanana, Det	31	22538	23271	-733
Bones, Mil	28	28343	26773	1570	Guzman Ju, Tor	28	36080	36905	-825
Mesa, Cle	27	29635	28075	1560	Valera, Cal	28	27075	28019	-944
Hammond C, Cin	26	27742	26219	1523	Langston, Cal	32	25564	26528	-964
Witt B, Oak	31	30714	29221	1493	Downs, Oak	20	28017	29001	-984
Key, Tor	33	40050	38604	1446	Black, SF	28	21457	22539	-1082
Cook D, Cle	25	22166	20853	1313	Osborne, StL	29	26385	27487	-1102
Darling, Oak	33	29811	28642	1169	Olivares, StL	30	26675	27796	-1121
Martinez D, Mon	32	24880	23744	1136	Harris Greg W., SD	20	21596	22838	-1242
Martinez R, LA	25	30366	29288	1078	Finley C, Cal	31	25323	26633	-1310
Hibbard, ChA	28	31330	30299	1031	Bosio, Mil	33	24035	25353	-1318
Smiley, Min	34	30039	29058	981	Armstrong J, Cle	23	20584	21926	-1342
Castillo F, ChN	33	26825	25852	973	Gardner M, Mon	30	21093	22512	-1419
Hershiser, LA	33	29181	28228	953	Fleming, Sea	33	23257	24688	-1431
Welch, Oak	20	29962	29047	915	Wegman, Mil	35	24465	25944	-1479
Belcher T, Cin	34	28846	27978	868	Milacki, Bal	20	33971	35528	-1557
Smoltz, Atl	35	30919	30157	762	Fernandez A, ChA	29	29035	30643	-1608
Swindell, Cin	30	27892	27254	638	Navarro, Mil	34	25045	26711	-1666
Wilson T, SF	26	22908	22290	618	Nabholz, Mon	32	22640	24354	-1714
Sanderson, NYA	33	26390	25881	509	Brown Kevin, Tex	35	25904	27669	-1765
Drabek, Pit	34	24459	24014	445	Hill K, Mon	33	21433	23386	-1953
Burkett, SF	32	23898	23477	421	Leary, Sea	23	24585	26787	-2202
Viola, Bos	35	30444	30054	390	Scudder, Cle	22	19289	22204	-2915
Stewart D, Oak	31	29337	28958	379	Kile, Hou	22	17049	20317	-3268
Tapani, Min	34	29839	29520	319	Hanson, Sea	30	20935	24653	-3718
Lefferts, Bal	32	24487	24208	279					
Smith Z, Pit	22	24949	24709	240					

DO THEY HAVE TO THROW TO FIRST MORE THAN ONCE?
(p. 78)

Runner, Team	No Throws Made			One Throw Made			2+Throws Made		
	SB	CS	%	SB	CS	%	SB	CS	%
Alomar R, Tor	24	3	89	6	2	75	7	2	78
Anderson Br, Bal	17	4	81	21	6	78	12	2	86
Bass K, NYN	7	3	70	6	3	67	1	2	33
Biggio, Hou	14	5	74	4	3	57	8	6	57
Blankenship L, Oak	6	0	100	4	2	67	9	2	82
Bonds Ba, Pit	13	0	100	10	2	83	9	4	69
Butler, LA	12	9	57	10	4	71	10	8	56
Coleman, NYN	8	2	80	5	1	83	7	3	70
Curtis C, Cal	14	4	78	13	4	76	10	7	59
DeShields, Mon	18	4	82	11	2	85	11	7	61
Duncan, Phi	7	2	78	11	1	92	2	0	100
Dykstra, Phi	11	0	100	5	3	62	11	2	85
Fernandez T, SD	6	7	46	4	5	44	5	7	42
Finley S, Hou	15	1	94	15	4	79	8	4	67
Fletcher S, Mil	10	3	77	1	1	50	5	5	50
Gant, Atl	5	3	62	13	3	81	11	4	73
Gilkey, StL	12	2	86	1	1	50	5	9	36
Grissom, Mon	22	1	96	15	6	71	16	4	80
Hamilton Dar, Mil	17	5	77	6	2	75	15	2	88
Harris L, LA	10	2	83	3	2	60	3	2	60
Henderson R, Oak	17	3	85	11	3	79	11	3	79
Howard T, Cle	7	1	87	2	3	40	4	3	57
Huson, Tex	7	4	64	3	1	75	6	0	100
Jefferies, KC	9	4	69	6	2	75	1	1	50
Johnson H, NYN	12	2	86	3	1	75	3	2	60
Johnson Lan, ChA	16	1	94	10	3	77	6	4	60
Jose, StL	13	1	93	7	4	64	6	7	46
Kelly R, NYA	11	1	92	4	2	67	9	1	90
Knoblauch, Min	8	2	80	9	4	69	12	6	67
Lankford, StL	15	1	94	12	7	63	10	14	42
Lewis D, SF	7	0	100	11	2	85	9	6	60
Listach, Mil	19	8	70	9	5	64	16	5	76
Lofton, Cle	19	2	90	18	0	100	22	8	73
Mack S, Min	8	3	73	9	5	64	8	4	67
McRae B, KC	3	1	75	7	3	70	5	1	83
Molitor, Mil	10	0	100	4	4	50	9	1	90
Nixon O, Atl	15	8	65	5	3	62	16	6	73
Offerman, LA	3	4	43	6	2	75	6	6	50
Pena G, StL	7	4	64	3	1	75	2	3	40
Polonia, Cal	14	7	67	10	5	67	13	6	68
Puckett, Min	7	3	70	7	2	78	2	2	50
Raines, ChA	26	1	96	8	1	89	7	3	70
Reynolds H, Sea	8	4	67	2	3	40	3	2	60
Roberts B, Cin	13	2	87	9	4	69	17	8	68
Sandberg, ChN	8	4	67	5	1	83	3	1	75
Sanders D, Atl	5	1	83	2	0	100	15	6	71
Sanders R, Cin	3	1	75	3	1	75	10	4	71
Sax S, ChA	14	4	78	7	3	70	6	1	86
Seitzer, Mil	7	4	64	3	3	50	1	3	25
Smith O, StL	17	3	85	11	3	79	10	2	83
Sosa S, ChN	6	1	86	3	2	60	6	4	60
Surhoff B, Mil	5	4	56	4	2	67	4	1	80
Thompson M, StL	8	2	80	3	0	100	6	3	67
Vaughn G, Mil	8	6	57	4	5	44	2	2	50
Vizquel, Sea	11	2	85	1	4	20	0	5	0
Walker L, Mon	9	3	75	7	0	100	1	2	33
White D, Tor	10	0	100	12	1	92	7	3	70
Whiten, Cle	6	3	67	5	4	56	3	1	75
Wilkerson, KC	13	3	81	3	1	75	2	3	40
Wilson W, Oak	15	1	94	4	3	57	4	1	67
1992	1505	559	73	675	402	63	651	417	61
1991	1436	560	72	615	361	63	640	425	60
1990	1422	561	72	639	321	67	682	405	63

Note: Steals of second with second base open only

WHAT'S THE LATEST IN PARK FACTORS? (p. 81)

By looking at the chart below, you'll be able to determine the extent to which each ballpark favors or hurts a certain type of statistic or batter type. By dividing the instances of an event (Infield Errors) or the performance of a certain type of hitter (Batting Average or Home Run Rates by left-handed or right-handed batters) in a team's home games by that in a team's road games and multiplying by 100, we can come up with an **Index** by which to judge each park's effects. In these charts, an **Index at 100** indicates a park having little effect; an **Index below 100** indicates a park favorable to that stat; and **Index above 100** indicates a park unfavorable to that type of stat.

American League

Park	Year	Avg	AB	R	H	2B	3B	HR	SO	E	E/I	Avg LHB	HR LHB	Avg RHB	HR RHB
Baltimore	1992	95	100	98	95	85	103	113	95	77	82	94	151	95	99
Boston	90-92	108	103	110	111	123	83	104	98	117	121	113	96	106	107
California	90-92	99	100	98	99	86	70	110	96	105	102	94	99	102	114
Chicago-A	91-92	100	98	94	98	88	88	105	95	90	88	102	112	98	102
Cleveland	1992	108	103	116	111	111	93	116	101	139	140	104	113	111	119
Detroit	90-92	99	99	105	98	92	83	117	104	96	95	101	132	98	111
Kansas City	90-92	100	101	101	101	108	169	62	91	115	112	100	48	101	74
Milwaukee	90-92	96	98	95	93	93	80	92	102	101	98	96	86	95	95
Minnesota	90-92	106	101	109	108	116	180	96	103	86	82	104	102	108	93
NY-A	90-92	99	101	102	100	98	66	111	95	95	98	102	139	98	96
Oakland	90-92	92	97	86	90	83	79	92	105	101	102	92	79	92	98
Seattle	1992	104	102	104	106	136	94	101	106	110	110	107	108	102	97
Texas	90-92	100	99	97	99	97	132	101	111	106	107	96	114	103	94
Toronto	90-92	103	100	105	103	108	117	118	98	89	94	104	87	102	137

National League

Park	Year	Avg	AB	R	H	2B	3B	HR	SO	E	E/I	Avg LHB	HR LHB	Avg RHB	HR RHB
Atlanta	90-92	107	101	113	109	101	63	122	93	125	128	109	135	106	114
Chicago-N	90-92	106	103	113	109	103	108	126	98	114	114	107	114	104	133
Cincinnati	90-92	100	98	107	99	104	83	148	97	80	77	103	138	98	154
Houston	1992	96	103	87	99	94	90	73	113	84	77	93	75	98	71
Los Angeles	90-92	99	100	94	99	80	72	86	101	122	130	99	89	99	84
Montreal	91-92	98	98	96	97	110	107	84	101	99	101	100	83	97	85
NY-N	90-92	98	100	97	97	96	102	92	101	106	107	97	103	99	85
Philadelphia	90-92	100	100	99	100	105	107	101	105	80	79	99	134	100	81
Pittsburgh	90-92	99	97	94	96	108	115	82	104	91	97	99	80	99	85
St. Louis	1992	99	103	102	101	94	103	99	98	105	101	98	104	99	95
San Diego	90-92	101	100	106	102	90	96	123	102	100	96	99	116	104	128
San Francisco	90-92	97	100	94	97	99	88	100	97	101	99	97	98	97	101

DO PLAYERS SUCCUMB TO FATIGUE? (p. 86)

The chart below lists all players who played 30 consecutive games in 1992. The **Before** section contains all statistics up to an including those counting towards the streak; the **After** section lists the statistics of that player over the next 14 calendar dates.

Batter	Before Streak				After Streak			
	AB	H	HR	Avg	AB	H	HR	Avg
Alomar R, Tor	338	107	6	.317	43	12	0	.279
Anderson Br, Bal	118	36	4	.305	41	8	1	.195
Anthony, Hou	132	34	4	.258	18	7	1	.389
Baerga, Cle	120	37	2	.308	46	16	1	.348
Bagwell, Hou	113	24	2	.212	44	9	4	.204
Bell G, ChA	138	38	5	.275	42	7	0	.166
Bell Jay, Pit	116	24	0	.207	46	13	1	.282
Bell Ju, Phi	95	22	0	.231	42	6	1	.143
Belle, Cle	253	66	16	.261	42	10	1	.238
Biggio, Hou	118	34	2	.288	43	14	1	.325
Blankenship L, Oak	102	30	1	.294	21	5	0	.238
Boggs W, Bos	124	33	0	.266	36	11	3	.305
Bonds Ba, Pit	158	48	13	.304	35	9	1	.257
Bonilla B, NYN	107	27	2	.252	40	9	2	.225
Bordick, Oak	101	35	0	.347	33	12	1	.363
Brett G, KC	259	66	3	.255	44	14	1	.318
Brooks, Cal	122	31	5	.254	32	4	1	.125
Brunansky, Bos	248	68	7	.274	41	9	4	.219
Buhner, Sea	420	101	19	.241	31	8	2	.258
Burks, Bos	171	43	5	.251	39	10	2	.256
Butler, LA	120	33	1	.275	36	10	0	.278
Caminiti, Hou	189	60	5	.317	36	11	0	.305
Carter Jo, Tor	130	36	7	.277	45	10	1	.222
Chamberlain W, Phi	269	69	9	.257	6	2	0	.330
Clark Jerald, SD	456	115	11	.252	40	5	1	.125
Clark W, SF	114	39	3	.342	38	12	1	.316
Curtis C, Cal	245	61	8	.249	37	12	0	.324
Cuyler, Det	217	58	3	.267	50	6	0	.120
Dascenzo, ChN	164	37	0	.226	34	10	0	.294
Daulton, Phi	222	65	12	.293	49	8	1	.163
Davis G, Bal	246	73	10	.297	37	6	0	.162
Deer, Det	221	47	21	.213	10	1	0	.100
DeShields, Mon	268	76	2	.284	61	25	2	.410
Devereaux, Bal	118	33	6	.280	37	9	2	.243
DiSarcina, Cal	95	28	0	.295	35	8	0	.228
Duncan, Phi	131	39	2	.298	49	10	0	.204
Dykstra, Phi	125	30	3	.240	48	16	0	.333
Easley D, Cal	106	30	0	.283	38	8	1	.210
Felix, Cal	360	92	6	.256	50	10	2	.200

Batter	Before Streak				After Streak			
	AB	H	HR	Avg	AB	H	HR	Avg
Fernandez T, SD	580	156	4	.269	42	15	0	.357
Fielder, Det	223	50	13	.224	47	15	3	.319
Finley S, Hou	123	36	2	.293	47	13	0	.276
Fryman T, Det	135	43	6	.319	47	9	1	.191
Gant, Atl	113	31	5	.274	48	15	1	.312
Gilkey, StL	275	79	4	.287	38	10	0	.263
Gonzales R, Cal	130	34	6	.262	41	13	1	.317
Gonzalez Juan, Tex	222	59	12	.266	37	11	5	.297
Grace, ChN	101	28	3	.277	46	15	0	.326
Grebeck, ChA	245	64	2	.261	37	13	1	.351
Grissom, Mon	125	31	4	.248	38	12	0	.316
Gruber, Tor	223	49	8	.220	15	6	0	.400
Gwynn T, SD	126	45	1	.357	34	14	1	.412
Hall M, NYA	122	31	5	.254	49	11	1	.224
Hayes C, NYA	107	33	2	.308	37	5	1	.135
Hollins D, Phi	107	24	3	.224	41	16	2	.390
Jackson Darrin, SD	149	34	5	.228	44	12	2	.273
Jefferies, KC	117	25	0	.214	49	11	1	.224
Johnson H, NYN	110	22	4	.200	39	9	0	.231
Johnson Lance, ChA	112	30	0	.268	28	8	1	.286
Jose, StL	117	40	4	.342	48	9	1	.187
Joyner, KC	233	66	5	.283	55	11	1	.200
Justice, Atl	222	50	8	.225	33	13	0	.394
Karros, LA	185	49	9	.265	66	17	1	.257
Kelly R, NYA	120	43	2	.358	45	12	1	.266
King J, Pit	345	76	11	.220	30	8	0	.266
Knoblauch, Min	199	66	1	.332	33	4	0	.121
Kruk, Phi	111	44	2	.396	37	12	2	.324
Lankford, StL	213	61	5	.286	49	14	2	.286
Larkin B, Cin	165	42	3	.255	48	14	1	.291
Lee Manuel, Tor	224	55	3	.246	33	8	0	.242
Leius, Min	235	64	2	.272	34	9	0	.265
Lemke, Atl	145	33	1	.228	36	11	1	.305
Listach, Mil	133	42	0	.316	27	4	0	.148
Lofton, Cle	169	44	1	.260	38	10	0	.263
Mack S, Min	131	44	5	.336	42	11	1	.262
Magadan, NYN	318	90	3	.283	3	1	0	.330
Maldonado C, Tor	322	88	13	.273	44	14	2	.318
Martinez Carlos, Cle	222	59	5	.266	6	1	0	.160
Martinez E, Sea	227	74	8	.326	48	13	4	.271
Mattingly, NYA	210	52	6	.248	42	11	1	.262
McGee, SF	126	35	0	.278	22	8	0	.363
McGriff F, SD	109	33	9	.303	42	14	2	.333
McGwire, Oak	101	32	14	.317	37	10	3	.270
McRae B, KC	121	22	1	.182	37	5	0	.135
McReynolds, KC	194	50	8	.258	44	9	0	.204
Miller K, KC	245	73	3	.298	25	9	0	.360
Molitor, Mil	116	36	1	.310	41	14	4	.341

Batter	Before Streak				After Streak			
	AB	H	HR	Avg	AB	H	HR	Avg
Morris H, Cin	195	61	2	.313	41	9	1	.219
Murray E, NYN	106	29	2	.274	39	11	3	.282
Nixon O, Atl	437	130	2	.298	19	4	0	.210
Offerman, LA	99	22	0	.222	28	6	0	.214
Pagnozzi, StL	350	93	6	.266	34	7	0	.206
Palmeiro, Tex	145	43	6	.297	45	9	0	.200
Palmer Dean, Tex	332	81	16	.244	33	7	1	.212
Pendleton, Atl	122	36	3	.295	49	19	4	.388
Phillips T, Det	156	39	5	.250	42	7	0	.166
Polonia, Cal	116	35	0	.302	39	11	0	.282
Puckett, Min	128	41	5	.320	40	14	2	.350
Raines, ChA	402	116	2	.289	40	10	0	.250
Reed Jody, Bos	130	39	1	.300	37	10	0	.270
Reimer, Tex	182	51	5	.280	35	12	1	.343
Reynolds H, Sea	116	32	1	.276	35	5	0	.143
Ripken C, Bal	112	26	3	.232	38	9	1	.237
Sandberg, ChN	181	49	7	.271	48	18	1	.375
Santiago, SD	318	81	9	.255	38	9	1	.237
Seitzer, Mil	536	145	5	.271	4	1	0	.250
Sheffield, SD	221	69	10	.312	43	12	3	.279
Smith O, StL	150	45	0	.300	45	11	0	.244
Sojo, Cal	196	59	5	.301	46	12	0	.261
Sosa S, ChN	121	28	1	.231	45	11	0	.244
Stankiewicz, NYA	206	61	2	.296	45	11	0	.244
Steinbach, Oak	428	119	12	.278	10	3	0	.300
Tartabull, NYA	146	39	4	.267	30	5	1	.166
Tettleton, Det	105	29	8	.276	36	4	1	.111
Thomas F, ChA	98	27	4	.275	35	12	2	.343
Thompson Ro, SF	350	89	12	.254	37	9	0	.243
Van Slyke, Pit	373	126	7	.338	44	11	2	.250
Velarde, NYA	334	95	5	.284	35	11	2	.314
Ventura, ChA	114	34	1	.298	33	9	2	.273
Vizcaino, ChN	142	29	0	.204	55	14	0	.254
Vizquel, Sea	244	77	0	.316	51	15	0	.294
Walker L, Mon	115	30	6	.261	39	13	3	.333
Wallach, Mon	230	55	3	.239	44	10	0	.227
Weiss W, Oak	160	38	0	.238	29	6	0	.207
White D, Tor	156	37	3	.237	42	10	1	.238
Whiten, Cle	106	29	3	.274	37	13	2	.351
Williams Be, NYA	130	32	4	.246	52	16	0	.307
Williams MD, SF	153	34	11	.222	33	6	0	.182
Wilson W, Oak	153	41	0	.268	25	4	0	.160
Winfield, Tor	114	41	6	.360	42	9	1	.214
Yount, Mil	163	41	3	.252	36	13	1	.361
Zeile, StL	307	80	5	.261	38	8	0	.210

WAS AN ILL WIND BLOWING AT WRIGLEY LAST SUMMER? (p. 88)

Offense by Temperature Chart — 1992

Temperature	Major League Baseball					Wrigley Field				
	G	R/G	HR/G	R	HR	G	R/G	HR/G	R	HR
90- 99	50	8.08	1.74	404	87	0	-	-	-	-
80- 89	357	8.55	1.59	3052	566	8	9.25	1.25	74	10
70- 79	1082	8.20	1.42	8875	1535	25	7.68	1.68	192	42
60- 69	398	8.28	1.46	3294	579	27	6.15	1.04	166	28
50- 59	156	7.61	1.33	1187	208	11	9.36	1.36	103	15
40- 49	59	8.17	1.01	482	60	9	7.89	1.33	71	12
30- 39	2	10.00	1.00	20	2	1	6.00	1.00	6	1
0- 29	2	13.50	0.50	27	1	0	-	-	-	-

Offense by Wind Direction Chart — 1992

Wind Direction	Major League Baseball					Wrigley Field				
	G	R/G	HR/G	R	HR	G	R/G	HR/G	R	HR
Blowing In	389	7.72	1.33	3005	518	42	6.93	1.19	291	50
Blowing Out	548	8.19	1.46	4488	801	18	7.89	1.61	142	29
Blowing Across	799	8.46	1.50	6759	1199	21	8.52	1.38	179	29
Indoors	370	8.35	1.41	3089	520	0	-	-	-	-

WASN'T BIP A PIP IN SEPTEMBER? (p. 96)

The Top Batting and Pitching Months of 1992

Batting (75 or more Plate Appearances)

Player	Month	AVG	SLG	OBP	AB	R	H	2B	3B	HR	RBI	SB	BB
Butler, LA	July	.442	.547	.547	95	23	42	3	2	1	12	18	22
Roberts B, Cin	Sep-Oct	.441	.645	.500	93	21	41	7	3	2	11	8	10
Van Slyke, Pit	May	.415	.606	.486	94	18	39	11	2	1	17	2	12
Daulton, Phi	May	.412	.676	.524	68	13	28	9	0	3	16	4	15
Kruk, Phi	April	.407	.469	.468	81	14	33	3	1	0	16	0	11
Grace, ChN	June	.404	.468	.457	94	14	38	6	0	0	9	1	9
Martinez E, Sea	August	.395	.614	.433	114	22	45	16	0	3	19	2	9
Owen S, Mon	August	.394	.500	.453	66	10	26	5	1	0	10	1	8
McGriff F, SD	May	.392	.680	.478	97	15	38	8	1	6	16	2	16
Gilkey, StL	Sep-Oct	.392	.582	.438	79	16	31	4	1	3	9	4	7
Bonds Ba, Pit	Sep-Oct	.392	.833	.537	102	30	40	10	1	11	27	9	33
Raines, ChA	Sep-Oct	.391	.655	.455	87	21	34	2	3	5	15	7	11
Larkin B, Cin	July	.389	.621	.464	95	13	37	9	2	3	14	3	13
Gwynn T, SD	May	.389	.611	.446	90	19	35	6	1	4	19	3	10
Martinez E, Sea	July	.388	.541	.455	98	22	38	6	0	3	12	4	12
Alomar R, Tor	April	.382	.517	.439	89	19	34	3	0	3	19	8	9
Bagwell, Hou	Sep-Oct	.381	.593	.459	113	20	43	9	0	5	22	1	15
Davis G, Bal	July	.380	.532	.457	79	12	30	3	0	3	14	0	13
Olerud, Tor	July	.378	.541	.452	74	15	28	6	0	2	8	0	10
DeShields, Mon	July	.376	.513	.434	117	22	44	5	1	3	13	11	12
Clark Je, SD	July	.376	.600	.424	85	8	32	6	2	3	17	0	7
Winfield, Tor	April	.375	.545	.424	88	12	33	3	0	4	12	0	9
Puckett, Min	May	.374	.636	.387	107	23	40	5	1	7	25	2	3
Nixon O, Atl	May	.373	.400	.412	75	16	28	2	0	0	2	10	5
Snyder C, SF	June	.372	.649	.388	94	12	35	9	1	5	24	2	2
Hamilton Dar, Mil	June	.372	.453	.433	86	14	32	3	2	0	11	6	10
Mack S, Min	July	.372	.553	.455	94	14	35	4	2	3	17	3	15

Pitching (25 or more Innings Pitched)

Pitcher	Month	ERA	W	L	S	IP	H	R	ER	BB	K
Eldred, Mil	August	0.61	4	0	0	29.2	17	2	2	8	15
Krueger, Mon	April	0.84	4	0	0	32.0	18	3	3	4	16
Smoltz, Atl	July	0.94	3	1	0	38.1	30	4	4	9	32
Ryan N, Tex	Sep-Oct	0.99	0	1	0	27.1	22	4	3	5	20
Brantley J, SF	Sep-Oct	1.01	4	1	0	26.2	15	3	3	9	33
Maddux G, ChN	July	1.13	4	1	0	40.0	29	5	5	11	26
Morgan M, ChN	July	1.18	2	2	0	38.0	31	11	5	11	25
Appier, KC	April	1.27	0	2	0	35.1	18	6	5	12	23
Rijo, Cin	Sep-Oct	1.29	5	1	0	49.0	34	9	7	13	27
Gordon T, KC	July	1.32	2	2	0	27.1	15	5	4	10	26
Smiley, Min	June	1.34	4	0	0	47.0	34	8	7	8	35
Clemens, Bos	April	1.38	3	2	0	39.0	25	8	6	9	45
Martinez De, Mon	August	1.42	4	0	0	38.0	24	9	6	7	25
Glavine, Atl	July	1.42	5	0	0	38.0	33	7	6	12	21
Hill K, Mon	April	1.42	2	2	0	38.0	30	10	6	8	20
Rasmussen, KC	Sep-Oct	1.43	4	1	0	37.2	25	7	6	6	12
Moore M, Oak	April	1.51	4	0	0	35.2	31	7	6	13	19
Johnson R, Sea	April	1.53	3	0	0	29.1	21	9	5	10	30
Martinez De, Mon	Sep-Oct	1.55	2	1	0	40.2	28	8	7	6	27
Swift, SF	April	1.55	4	0	0	40.2	34	8	7	9	17
Appier, KC	July	1.55	4	0	0	46.1	35	8	8	11	33
Cone, Tor	Sep-Oct	1.55	4	2	0	46.1	32	9	8	22	42
Mussina, Bal	Sep-Oct	1.56	5	0	0	52.0	40	9	9	11	32
Black, SF	July	1.59	5	1	0	45.1	34	10	8	10	20
Navarro, Mil	July	1.60	3	0	0	39.1	18	8	7	10	15
Fernandez, NYN	Sep-Oct	1.60	3	2	0	39.1	28	8	7	12	31
Sutcliffe, Bal	August	1.60	4	0	0	45.0	39	8	8	17	19

ARE THERE REALLY RIGHTIES WHO CAN HIT RIGHTHANDERS BETTER? (p. 100)

Both Leagues — Listed Alphabetically
(Active Players/Minimum 1200 PA since 1990)

Right-Handed Batters	Vs. RHP		Vs. LHP		Right-Handed Batters	Vs. RHP		Vs. LHP	
Batter, Team	AB	Avg	AB	Avg	Batter, Team	AB	Avg	AB	Avg
Alomar S, Cle	711	.253	217	.295	King J, Pit	482	.220	478	.255
Bagwell, Hou	724	.271	416	.305	Knoblauch, Min	893	.291	272	.283
Bell G, ChA	1248	.262	499	.283	Lansford C, Oak	759	.249	260	.300
Bell Jay, Pit	1140	.243	683	.296	Larkin B, Cin	1073	.296	538	.314
Belle, Cle	790	.267	279	.269	Lind, Pit	924	.260	560	.245
Bichette, Mil	762	.253	419	.270	Macfarlane, KC	672	.241	397	.272
Biggio, Hou	1092	.296	622	.259	Mack S, Min	944	.305	411	.341
Blauser, Atl	675	.241	406	.300	Maldonado C, Tor	999	.253	368	.307
Borders, Tor	664	.256	453	.256	Martinez E, Sea	1106	.306	453	.347
Brooks, Cal	811	.249	420	.238	McGwire, Oak	1114	.227	359	.256
Brunansky, Bos	982	.246	453	.258	McReynolds, KC	920	.254	496	.268
Buechele, ChN	887	.232	418	.297	Miller K, KC	509	.283	415	.267
Buhner, Sea	762	.245	350	.254	Milligan, Bal	960	.249	347	.274
Burks, Bos	908	.274	389	.267	Mitchell Kev, Sea	879	.264	376	.314
Calderon, Mon	808	.261	439	.321	Molitor, Mil	1274	.301	418	.352
Canseco J, Tex	1139	.263	353	.261	Murphy Dale, Phi	766	.217	403	.295
Carter Joe, Tor	1346	.247	548	.277	Oliver J, Cin	631	.219	487	.277
Clark Ja, Bos	746	.206	326	.334	Olson Greg, Atl	640	.222	371	.288
Clark Je, SD	635	.247	331	.224	Pagnozzi, StL	705	.262	459	.257
Davis E, LA	661	.239	344	.256	Parrish Lan, Sea	822	.236	325	.255
Davis G, Bal	624	.260	277	.253	Pecota, NYN	572	.238	335	.290
Dawson, ChN	1035	.281	599	.294	Pena T, Bos	993	.234	372	.277
Deer, Det	904	.190	377	.257	Puckett, Min	1357	.307	444	.345
Devereaux, Bal	1133	.248	495	.293	Randolph, NYN	736	.260	369	.333
Downing, Tex	678	.263	379	.301	Reed Jo, Bos	1263	.273	503	.276
Duncan, Phi	783	.236	559	.335	Ripken B, Bal	674	.237	349	.275
Dunston, ChN	704	.263	406	.268	Ripken C, Bal	1376	.274	511	.280
Fermin, Cle	760	.254	293	.280	Rivera L, Bos	746	.240	302	.225
Fielder, Det	1320	.245	471	.306	Sabo, Cin	940	.252	553	.316
Fisk, ChA	729	.254	371	.264	Salazar L, ChN	519	.218	479	.271
Fletcher S, Mil	765	.235	378	.265	Samuel, KC	769	.252	541	.272
Franco Ju, Tex	905	.304	373	.330	Sandberg, ChN	1183	.292	629	.316
Fryman T, Det	1050	.257	398	.296	Santiago, SD	860	.252	450	.284
Gaetti, Cal	1170	.233	449	.236	Sax S, ChA	1285	.263	549	.281
Gagne, Min	888	.245	347	.256	Schofield, NYN	811	.231	349	.215
Galarraga, StL	809	.244	470	.238	Seitzer, Mil	993	.261	403	.298
Gallego, NYA	756	.229	288	.243	Sharperson, LA	325	.249	565	.319
Gant, Atl	1135	.267	545	.281	Sheffield, SD	852	.292	367	.305
Gladden, Det	1007	.256	405	.269	Smith Lo, Atl	600	.272	377	.305
Gomez Le, Bal	662	.254	236	.237	Snyder C, SF	573	.239	421	.235
Gonzalez Juan, Tex	890	.260	329	.277	Sosa S, ChN	674	.215	436	.255
Grissom, Mon	895	.270	604	.267	Steinbach, Oak	915	.263	358	.282
Gruber, Tor	1082	.246	385	.275	Tartabull, NYA	851	.281	367	.300
Guerrero P, StL	705	.274	366	.260	Thomas F, ChA	942	.300	381	.375
Harper B, Min	1053	.304	369	.304	Thompson Ro, SF	951	.244	482	.278
Hatcher B, Bos	877	.269	478	.253	Thon, Tex	860	.244	506	.267
Hayes C, NYA	997	.245	533	.259	Trammell, Det	722	.287	314	.268
Henderson D, Oak	784	.237	301	.342	Valle, Sea	663	.205	336	.241
Henderson R, Oak	1002	.293	353	.292	Vaughn G, Mil	1039	.235	386	.223
Incaviglia, Hou	779	.228	436	.252	Wallach, Mon	1153	.245	587	.259
Jackson Darrin, SD	643	.264	416	.238	Williams MD, SF	1198	.256	537	.264
Jacoby, Cle	892	.256	371	.280	Winfield, Tor	1164	.265	462	.297
James C, SF	804	.264	409	.269	Yount, Mil	1237	.253	410	.268
Kelly R, NYA	1183	.269	524	.292	Zeile, StL	956	.248	543	.285

HOW IMPORTANT IS A GOOD "HEART OF THE ORDER"? (p. 102)

Team total statistics for the Number 3, 4, and 5 hitters

American League — Listed by Most RBI

Team	Avg	HR	RBI	Slg	Main 3-4-5 Hitters
Oakland	.254	94	324	.448	Canseco J-Baines-McGwire
Toronto	.279	87	322	.482	Carter Joe-Winfield-Olerud
Chicago	.276	63	321	.443	Thomas F-Bell G-Ventura
Detroit	.250	87	315	.442	Fryman T-Fielder-Tettleton
New York	.280	67	307	.442	Kelly R-Tartabull-Hall
Minnesota	.290	49	291	.430	Puckett-Hrbek-Harper B
Seattle	.275	74	289	.453	Griffey Jr-Mitchell Kev-Buhner
Cleveland	.280	71	288	.444	Baerga-Belle-Sorrento
Texas	.251	78	278	.431	Palmeiro-Sierra R-Reimer
Milwaukee	.264	38	255	.394	Molitor-Vaughn G-Yount
Boston	.250	42	216	.376	Boggs W-Brunansky-Vaughn M
California	.224	36	215	.333	Felix-Brooks-Stevens
Baltimore	.255	51	208	.384	Ripken C-Davis G-Milligan
Kansas City	.262	35	207	.388	Brett G-McReynolds-Joyner
AL Average	**.264**	**62**	**274**	**.421**	

National League — Listed by Most RBI

Team	Avg	HR	RBI	Slg	Main 3-4-5 Hitters
Philadelphia	.288	64	305	.462	Hollins D-Kruk-Daulton
Atlanta	.269	56	291	.423	Pendleton-Justice-Bream
San Diego	.279	81	288	.477	Sheffield-McGriff F-Jackson Darri
Pittsburgh	.280	61	286	.464	Van Slyke-Bonds Ba-Merced
Chicago	.286	54	274	.440	Grace-Dawson-Buechele
Houston	.258	56	273	.409	Bagwell-Anthony-Caminiti
New York	.259	50	265	.406	Johnson H-Murray E-Bonilla B
Montreal	.258	46	264	.402	Alou-Walker L-Wallach
St. Louis	.269	46	264	.405	Lankford-Jose-Zeile
Cincinnati	.269	54	260	.427	Larkin B-O'Neill-Braggs
San Francisco	.267	55	247	.422	Clark W-Snyder C-Williams M
Los Angeles	.232	39	235	.348	Harris L-Karros-Davis E
NL Average	**.268**	**55**	**271**	**.424**	

WHO TAKES 'EM, WHO SWINGS AT 'EM, WHO FOULS 'EM OFF? (p. 108)

The tables below show how hitters reacted to pitches thrown based on the count in 1992.

Listed by League — All Teams Included

American League

Count	Total	Ball	Taken Strike	Swing-ing Strike	Foul	In Play
0-0	86718	38554	22872	4817	9017	11458
Pct	100	44	26	6	10	13
0-1	36649	16568	3909	3265	5773	7134
Pct	100	45	11	9	16	19
0-2	15470	7780	644	1626	2507	2913
Pct	100	50	4	11	16	19
1-0	38393	13564	7966	2885	6124	7854
Pct	100	35	21	8	16	20
1-1	33374	12650	3706	3221	6090	7707
Pct	100	38	11	10	18	23
1-2	26055	9960	1098	3145	5367	6485
Pct	100	38	4	12	21	25
2-0	13470	4272	3443	762	2096	2897
Pct	100	32	26	6	16	22
2-1	18849	5627	1891	1756	4134	5441
Pct	100	30	10	9	22	29
2-2	23105	7058	992	2718	5498	6839
Pct	100	31	4	12	24	30
3-0	4216	1545	2261	57	155	198
Pct	100	37	54	1	4	5
3-1	8441	2312	1149	535	1714	2731
Pct	100	27	14	6	20	32
3-2	14233	3272	579	1429	3862	5091
Pct	100	23	4	10	27	36

National League

Count	Total	Ball	Taken Strike	Swing-ing Strike	Foul	In Play
0-0	73399	30909	18313	4941	8604	10632
Pct	100	42	25	7	12	14
0-1	31794	13523	3350	3422	5201	6298
Pct	100	43	11	11	16	20
0-2	14422	6786	714	1710	2483	2729
Pct	100	47	5	12	17	19
1-0	30741	10600	6476	2588	4819	6258
Pct	100	34	21	8	16	20
1-1	27264	9497	3048	3053	5124	6542
Pct	100	35	11	11	19	24
1-2	22540	8099	1043	2976	4648	5774
Pct	100	36	5	13	21	26
2-0	10522	3361	2814	672	1574	2101
Pct	100	32	27	6	15	20
2-1	14486	4053	1500	1455	3311	4167
Pct	100	28	10	10	23	29
2-2	18854	5380	799	2403	4591	5681
Pct	100	29	4	13	24	30
3-0	3325	1282	1774	34	109	126
Pct	100	39	53	1	3	4
3-1	6228	1688	973	431	1189	1947
Pct	100	27	16	7	19	31
3-2	10948	2352	429	1203	3036	3928
Pct	100	21	4	11	28	36

IF HE SOARED TO THE SKIES IN 1992, WILL HE STAY UP THERE IN '93? (p. 111)

Both Leagues — Listed Alphabetically
(Minimum 350 PA in 1991 and 1992)

Player, Team	91	92	Dff	Player, Team	91	92	Dff	Player, Team	91	92	Dff
Alomar R, Tor	.295	.310	+15	Grissom, Mon	.267	.276	+9	Olerud, Tor	.256	.284	+28
Baerga, Cle	.288	.312	+24	Gruber, Tor	.252	.229	-23	Orsulak, Bal	.278	.289	+11
Bagwell, Hou	.294	.273	-21	Gwynn T, SD	.317	.317	+0	Owen S, Mon	.255	.269	+14
Baines, Oak	.295	.253	-42	Hall M, NYA	.285	.280	-5	Pagnozzi, StL	.264	.249	-15
Bass K, NYN	.233	.269	+36	Hamilton D, Mil	.311	.298	-13	Palmeiro, Tex	.322	.268	-54
Bell G, ChA	.285	.255	-30	Harper B, Min	.311	.307	-4	Pena T, Bos	.231	.241	+10
Bell Jay, Pit	.270	.264	-6	Harris L, LA	.287	.271	-16	Pendleton, Atl	.319	.311	-8
Belle, Cle	.282	.260	-22	Hatcher B, Bos	.262	.249	-13	Phillips T, Det	.284	.276	-8
Bichette, Mil	.238	.287	+49	Hayes C, NYA	.230	.257	+27	Polonia, Cal	.296	.286	-10
Biggio, Hou	.295	.277	-18	Henderson R, Oak	.268	.283	+15	Puckett, Min	.319	.329	+10
Blauser, Atl	.259	.262	+3	Hoiles, Bal	.243	.274	+31	Raines, ChA	.268	.294	+26
Boggs W, Bos	.332	.259	-73	Hrbek, Min	.284	.244	-40	Reed Jo, Bos	.283	.247	-36
Bonds Ba, Pit	.292	.311	+19	Incaviglia, Hou	.214	.266	+52	Reimer, Tex	.269	.267	-2
Bonilla B, NYN	.302	.249	-53	Jackson Darri, SD	.262	.249	-13	Reynolds H, Sea	.254	.247	-7
Brett G, KC	.255	.285	+30	Jefferies, KC	.272	.285	+13	Ripken C, Bal	.323	.251	-72
Brunansky, Bos	.229	.266	+37	Johnson H, NYN	.259	.223	-36	Roberts B, Cin	.281	.323	+42
Buechele, ChN	.262	.261	-1	Johnson L, ChA	.274	.279	+5	Sabo, Cin	.301	.244	-57
Buhner, Sea	.244	.243	-1	Jose, StL	.305	.295	-10	Sandberg, ChN	.291	.304	+13
Butler, LA	.296	.309	+13	Joyner, KC	.301	.269	-32	Santiago, SD	.267	.251	-16
Caminiti, Hou	.253	.294	+41	Justice, Atl	.275	.256	-19	Sax S, ChA	.304	.236	-68
Candaele, Hou	.262	.213	-49	Kelly R, NYA	.267	.272	+5	Schofield, NYN	.225	.206	-19
Canseco J, Tex	.266	.244	-22	Knoblauch, Min	.281	.297	+16	Scioscia, LA	.264	.221	-43
Carter Joe, Tor	.273	.264	-9	Kruk, Phi	.294	.323	+29	Sierra R, Oak	.307	.278	-29
Clark Je, SD	.228	.242	+14	Lankford, StL	.251	.293	+42	Smith O, StL	.285	.295	+10
Clark W, SF	.301	.300	-1	Larkin B, Cin	.302	.304	+2	Sojo, Cal	.258	.272	+14
Davis C, Min	.277	.288	+11	Lee Man, Tor	.234	.263	+29	Steinbach, Oak	.274	.279	+5
Dawson, ChN	.272	.277	+5	Lind, Pit	.265	.235	-30	Stillwell, SD	.265	.227	-38
Deer, Det	.179	.247	+68	Mack S, Min	.310	.315	+5	Surhoff B, Mil	.289	.252	-37
DeShields, Mon	.238	.292	+54	Magadan, NYN	.258	.283	+25	Tartabull, NYA	.316	.266	-50
Devereaux, Bal	.260	.276	+16	Martinez D, Cin	.295	.254	-41	Tettleton, Det	.263	.238	-25
Doran, Cin	.280	.235	-45	Martinez E, Sea	.307	.343	+36	Thomas F, ChA	.318	.323	+5
Downing, Tex	.278	.278	+0	Mattingly, NYA	.288	.288	+0	Thompson Ro, SF	.262	.260	-2
Duncan, Phi	.258	.267	+9	McGee, SF	.312	.297	-15	Valle, Sea	.194	.240	+46
Eisenreich, KC	.301	.269	-32	McGriff F, SD	.278	.286	+8	Van Slyke, Pit	.265	.324	+59
Felder, SF	.264	.286	+22	McGwire, Oak	.201	.268	+67	Vaughn G, Mil	.244	.228	-16
Fernandez T, SD	.272	.275	+3	McRae B, KC	.261	.223	-38	Ventura, ChA	.284	.282	-2
Fielder, Det	.261	.244	-17	McReynolds, KC	.259	.247	-12	Vizquel, Sea	.230	.294	+64
Finley S, Hou	.285	.292	+7	Merced, Pit	.275	.247	-28	Walker L, Mon	.290	.301	+11
Fryman T, Det	.259	.266	+7	Milligan, Bal	.263	.240	-23	Wallach, Mon	.225	.223	-2
Gaetti, Cal	.246	.226	-20	Mitchell Kev, Sea	.256	.286	+30	Whitaker, Det	.279	.278	-1
Gagne, Min	.265	.246	-19	Molitor, Mil	.325	.320	-5	White D, Tor	.282	.248	-34
Gant, Atl	.251	.259	+8	Morandini, Phi	.249	.265	+16	Whiten, Cle	.243	.254	+11
Gladden, Det	.247	.254	+7	Morris H, Cin	.318	.271	-47	Williams MD, SF	.268	.227	-41
Gomez Le, Bal	.233	.265	+32	Murray E, NYN	.260	.261	+1	Winfield, Tor	.262	.290	+28
Gonzalez J, Tex	.264	.260	-4	Nixon O, Atl	.297	.294	-3	Yount, Mil	.260	.264	+4
Gonzalez L, Hou	.254	.243	-11	Nokes, NYA	.268	.224	-44	Zeile, StL	.280	.257	-23
Grace, ChN	.273	.307	+34	O'Brien P, Sea	.248	.222	-26	**AL Avg**	.260	.259	-1
Griffey Jr, Sea	.327	.308	-19	O'Neill, Cin	.256	.246	-10	**NL Avg**	.250	.252	+2

WERE TERRY PENDLETON'S 105 RBI LAST YEAR BETTER THAN CECIL FIELDER'S 124? (p. 113)

Both Leagues — Listed Alphabetically
(minimum 175 RBI Opportunities)

Player, Team	Opp	RBI	Pct	Player, Team	Opp	RBI	Pct
Alicea, StL	177	30	16.9	DeShields, Mon	287	49	17.1
Alomar R, Tor	394	68	17.3	Devereaux, Bal	449	83	18.5
Alomar S, Cle	192	24	12.5	DiSarcina, Cal	302	39	12.9
Alou, Mon	254	47	18.5	Doran, Cin	327	39	11.9
Amaro, Phi	256	27	10.5	Downing, Tex	215	29	13.5
Anderson Br, Bal	400	59	14.8	Duncan, Phi	343	42	12.2
Anthony, Hou	334	61	18.3	Eisenreich, KC	237	26	11.0
Baerga, Cle	437	85	19.5	Felix, Cal	340	63	18.5
Bagwell, Hou	467	78	16.7	Fernandez T, SD	266	33	12.4
Baines, Oak	336	60	17.9	Fielder, Det	499	89	17.8
Barberie, Mon	188	23	12.2	Finley S, Hou	417	50	12.0
Bass K, NYN	280	30	10.7	Fletcher S, Mil	286	48	16.8
Bell G, ChA	557	87	15.6	Fryman T, Det	536	76	14.2
Bell Jay, Pit	329	46	14.0	Gaetti, Cal	284	36	12.7
Belle, Cle	444	78	17.6	Gagne, Min	280	32	11.4
Belliard, Atl	187	14	7.5	Galarraga, StL	220	29	13.2
Benzinger, LA	194	27	13.9	Gant, Atl	397	63	15.9
Berryhill, Atl	222	33	14.9	Gilkey, StL	226	36	15.9
Bichette, Mil	258	36	14.0	Gladden, Det	316	35	11.1
Biggio, Hou	291	33	11.3	Gomez Leo, Bal	394	47	11.9
Blankenship L, Oak	291	31	10.7	Gonzales R, Cal	200	31	15.5
Blauser, Atl	221	32	14.5	Gonzalez Juan, Tex	435	66	15.2
Boggs W, Bos	356	43	12.1	Gonzalez L, Hou	285	45	15.8
Bonds Ba, Pit	407	69	17.0	Grace, ChN	393	70	17.8
Bonilla B, NYN	327	51	15.6	Grebeck, ChA	206	32	15.5
Borders, Tor	329	40	12.2	Griffey Jr, Sea	406	76	18.7
Bordick, Oak	397	45	11.3	Grissom, Mon	380	52	13.7
Braggs, Cin	227	30	13.2	Gruber, Tor	301	32	10.6
Bream, Atl	293	51	17.4	Gwynn T, SD	290	35	12.1
Brett G, KC	366	54	14.8	Hall M, NYA	430	66	15.3
Brooks, Cal	183	28	15.3	Hamilton D, Mil	350	57	16.3
Browne, Oak	259	37	14.3	Hansen D, LA	197	16	8.1
Brunansky, Bos	386	59	15.3	Harper B, Min	400	64	16.0
Buechele, ChN	379	55	14.5	Harris L, LA	224	30	13.4
Buhner, Sea	406	54	13.3	Hatcher B, Bos	259	30	11.6
Burks, Bos	189	22	11.6	Hayes C, NYA	341	48	14.1
Butler, LA	332	36	10.8	Hayes V, Cal	201	25	12.4
Caminiti, Hou	354	49	13.8	Henderson R, Oak	260	31	11.9
Candaele, Hou	204	17	8.3	Hill G, Cle	238	31	13.0
Canseco J, Tex	365	61	16.7	Hoiles, Bal	226	20	8.8
Carreon, Det	250	31	12.4	Hollins D, Phi	437	66	15.1
Carter G, Mon	204	24	11.8	Howard T, Cle	217	30	13.8
Carter Joe, Tor	471	85	18.0	Hrbek, Min	360	43	11.9
Chamberlain W, Phi	212	32	15.1	Hundley, NYN	248	25	10.1
Clark Ja, Bos	238	28	11.8	Huson, Tex	197	20	10.2
Clark Je, SD	296	46	15.5	Incaviglia, Hou	261	33	12.6
Clark W, SF	344	57	16.6	Jackson Darri, SD	382	53	13.9
Clayton, SF	212	20	9.4	Jacoby, Cle	217	32	14.7
Cooper S, Bos	215	28	13.0	James C, SF	180	27	15.0
Cotto, Sea	177	22	12.4	Javier, Phi	195	28	14.4
Curtis C, Cal	274	36	13.1	Jefferies, KC	382	65	17.0
Cuyler, Det	211	25	11.8	Johnson H, NYN	286	36	12.6
Dascenzo, ChN	195	20	10.3	Johnson Lance, ChA	406	44	10.8
Daulton, Phi	431	82	19.0	Jordan R, Phi	199	30	15.1
Davis C, Min	379	54	14.2	Jose, StL	348	61	17.5
Davis E, LA	225	27	12.0	Joyner, KC	378	57	15.1
Davis G, Bal	292	35	12.0	Justice, Atl	380	51	13.4
Dawson, ChN	398	68	17.1	Karkovice, ChA	246	37	15.0
Deer, Det	308	32	10.4	Karros, LA	414	68	16.4

Player, Team	Opp	RBI	Pct
Kelly Pat, NYA	216	20	9.3
Kelly R, NYA	400	56	14.0
Kent, NYN	231	39	16.9
King J, Pit	367	51	13.9
Knoblauch, Min	399	54	13.5
Kruk, Phi	411	60	14.6
Lankford, StL	378	66	17.5
Lansford C, Oak	385	68	17.7
Larkin B, Cin	384	66	17.2
Larkin G, Min	265	36	13.6
LaValliere, Pit	218	27	12.4
Lee Man, Tor	266	36	13.5
Leius, Min	288	33	11.5
Lemke, Atl	298	20	6.7
Lewis M, Cle	258	25	9.7
Lind, Pit	376	39	10.4
Listach, Mil	361	46	12.7
Livingstone, Det	262	42	16.0
Lofton, Cle	307	37	12.1
Maas, NYA	185	24	13.0
Macfarlane, KC	268	31	11.6
Mack S, Min	390	59	15.1
Magadan, NYN	217	25	11.5
Maldonado Candy, Tor	384	46	12.0
Manwaring, SF	212	22	10.4
Martinez Da, Cin	282	28	9.9
Martinez E, Sea	344	55	16.0
Martinez Tino, Sea	352	50	14.2
Mattingly, NYA	404	72	17.8
May D, ChN	250	37	14.8
McGee, SF	254	35	13.8
McGriff F, SD	420	69	16.4
McGwire, Oak	346	62	17.9
McLemore, Bal	194	27	13.9
McRae B, KC	334	48	14.4
McReynolds, KC	249	36	14.5
Merced, Pit	309	54	17.5
Miller K, KC	214	34	15.9
Milligan, Bal	360	42	11.7
Mitchell Kev, Sea	277	58	20.9
Molitor, Mil	445	77	17.3
Morandini, Phi	268	27	10.1
Morris H, Cin	285	47	16.5
Munoz P, Min	308	59	19.2
Murray E, NYN	418	77	18.4
Nixon O, Atl	213	20	9.4
Nokes, NYA	291	37	12.7
O'Brien P, Sea	286	38	13.3
O'Neill, Cin	409	52	12.7
Offerman, LA	303	29	9.6
Olerud, Tor	358	50	14.0
Oliver J, Cin	363	47	12.9
Olson Greg, Atl	208	24	11.5
Orsulak, Bal	268	35	13.1
Owen S, Mon	260	33	12.7
Pagnozzi, StL	321	37	11.5
Palmeiro, Tex	435	63	14.5
Palmer De, Tex	355	46	13.0
Parrish Lan, Sea	193	20	10.4
Pasqua, ChA	204	27	13.2
Pena T, Bos	298	37	12.4
Pendleton, Atl	415	84	20.2
Phillips T, Det	390	54	13.8
Plantier, Bos	280	23	8.2
Polonia, Cal	272	35	12.9
Puckett, Min	495	91	18.4
Raines, ChA	326	47	14.4

Player, Team	Opp	RBI	Pct
Reed Jody, Bos	354	37	10.5
Reimer, Tex	336	42	12.5
Reynolds H, Sea	293	30	10.2
Ripken B, Bal	268	32	11.9
Ripken C, Bal	431	58	13.5
Rivera L, Bos	218	29	13.3
Roberts B, Cin	253	41	16.2
Rodriguez I, Tex	274	29	10.6
Sabo, Cin	282	31	11.0
Sandberg, ChN	368	61	16.6
Sanders R, Cin	259	24	9.3
Santiago, SD	263	32	12.2
Sax S, ChA	352	43	12.2
Schofield, NYN	316	32	10.1
Scioscia, LA	224	21	9.4
Seitzer, Mil	390	66	16.9
Sharperson, LA	274	33	12.0
Sheffield, SD	391	67	17.1
Sierra R, Oak	470	70	14.9
Slaught, Pit	202	33	16.3
Smith O, StL	307	31	10.1
Snyder C, SF	289	43	14.9
Sojo, Cal	220	36	16.4
Sorrento, Cle	316	42	13.3
Stankiewicz, NYA	213	23	10.8
Steinbach, Oak	325	41	12.6
Stevens, Cal	187	30	16.0
Stillwell, SD	228	22	9.6
Stubbs, Mil	204	33	16.2
Surhoff B, Mil	347	58	16.7
Sveum, ChA	188	24	12.8
Tartabull, NYA	336	60	17.9
Taubensee, Hou	203	23	11.3
Tettleton, Det	446	51	11.4
Thomas F, ChA	521	91	17.5
Thompson R, SF	284	35	12.3
Thon, Tex	202	33	16.3
Valle, Sea	239	21	8.8
Van Slyke, Pit	386	75	19.4
Vaughn G, Mil	368	55	14.9
Vaughn M, Bos	298	44	14.8
Velarde, NYA	273	39	14.3
Ventura, ChA	429	77	17.9
Vizquel, Sea	266	21	7.9
Walker C, NYN	197	34	17.3
Walker L, Mon	388	70	18.0
Wallach, Mon	339	50	14.7
Webster M, LA	207	29	14.0
Weiss W, Oak	252	21	8.3
Whitaker, Det	351	52	14.8
White D, Tor	370	43	11.6
Whiten, Cle	343	34	9.9
Wilkerson, KC	186	27	14.5
Wilkins R, ChN	178	14	7.9
Williams MD, SF	366	46	12.6
Wilson W, Oak	309	37	12.0
Winfield, Tor	415	82	19.8
Yount, Mil	420	69	16.4
Zeile, StL	327	41	12.5
Zupcic, Bos	253	40	15.8
MLB Average			**13.4**

ARE THERE TOO MANY AVERAGE GUYS IN YOUR LINEUP?
(p. 118)

1992 Composite League Statistics — Per 600 Plate Appearances

American League

Pos	AVG	OBP	SLG	AB	R	H	2B	3B	HR	RBI	BB	K	SB
As c	.244	.310	.369	537	57	131	23	1	14	60	48	87	3
As 1b	.262	.344	.417	524	68	137	27	2	17	75	65	79	4
As 2b	.264	.336	.361	528	72	139	25	3	7	54	54	58	17
As 3b	.263	.328	.385	534	64	141	27	2	11	66	51	75	8
As ss	.254	.313	.335	537	62	136	23	3	5	49	45	78	13
As lf	.269	.340	.401	531	72	143	24	3	13	62	55	85	21
As cf	.265	.321	.395	544	73	144	25	5	12	65	44	89	21
As rf	.257	.328	.400	533	69	137	24	4	15	66	56	103	11
All DH	.258	.334	.405	529	67	137	25	2	17	73	59	97	7
All PH	.242	.316	.333	525	46	127	23	2	7	80	58	117	5

National League

Pos	AVG	OBP	SLG	AB	R	H	2B	3B	HR	RBI	BB	K	SB
As p	.137	.166	.170	520	30	71	10	1	2	26	18	176	0
As c	.245	.307	.357	540	46	132	25	3	10	58	47	83	3
As 1b	.272	.343	.422	531	65	144	31	3	14	73	57	84	6
As 2b	.259	.326	.361	534	61	138	22	4	8	49	52	76	15
As 3b	.265	.329	.397	538	63	142	26	3	14	67	50	82	7
As ss	.251	.315	.340	536	61	135	23	4	6	42	49	79	13
As lf	.257	.320	.400	540	66	139	29	4	13	64	48	91	20
As cf	.276	.341	.398	535	75	148	25	6	9	51	51	84	32
As rf	.261	.324	.399	542	68	141	23	4	15	68	50	96	11
All PH	.224	.296	.314	529	48	118	17	2	9	72	54	126	8

WHO ARE THE "HUMAN AIR CONDITIONERS"? (p. 120)

The table below shows swings missed (Sw) as a **percentage (%)** of total pitches swung at (**Pit**).

Both Leagues — Listed Alphabetically
(minimum 350 plate appearances)

Player, Team	Sw	Pit	%	Player, Team	Sw	Pit	%	Player, Team	Sw	Pit	%
Alomar R, Tor	108	1108	9.7	Carter Joe, Tor	301	1450	20.8	Gomez Leo, Bal	140	962	14.6
Alou, Mon	149	663	22.5	Clark Je, SD	223	985	22.6	Gonzales R, Cal	125	652	19.2
Amaro, Phi	106	680	15.6	Clark W, SF	199	1052	18.9	Gonzalez J, Tex	346	1203	28.8
Anderson Br, Bal	155	1106	14.0	Clayton, SF	143	667	21.4	Gonzalez L, Hou	151	780	19.4
Anthony, Hou	204	797	25.6	Cooper S, Bos	62	611	10.1	Grace, ChN	91	1003	9.1
Baerga, Cle	214	1279	16.7	Curtis C, Cal	145	837	17.3	Griffey Jr, Sea	175	1109	15.8
Bagwell, Hou	224	1125	19.9	Dascenzo, ChN	45	619	7.3	Grissom, Mon	187	1145	16.3
Baines, Oak	152	846	18.0	Daulton, Phi	201	903	22.3	Gruber, Tor	205	884	23.2
Bass K, NYN	167	775	21.5	Davis C, Min	196	914	21.4	Gwynn T, SD	53	812	6.5
Bell G, ChA	261	1250	20.9	Davis G, Bal	145	737	19.7	Hall M, NYA	151	1066	14.2
Bell Jay, Pit	213	1134	18.8	Dawson, ChN	224	1125	19.9	Hamilton D, Mil	78	842	9.3
Belle, Cle	302	1196	25.3	Deer, Det	284	883	32.2	Hansen D, LA	101	631	16.0
Bichette, Mil	196	784	25.0	DeShields, Mon	190	952	20.0	Harper B, Min	97	925	10.5
Biggio, Hou	159	1081	14.7	Devereaux, Bal	203	1146	17.7	Harris L, LA	66	608	10.9
Blankenship, Oak	80	563	14.2	DiSarcina, Cal	107	864	12.4	Hatcher B, Bos	107	733	14.6
Blauser, Atl	142	680	20.9	Doran, Cin	98	726	13.5	Hayes C, NYA	227	1027	22.1
Boggs W, Bos	34	820	4.1	Downing, Tex	92	591	15.6	Hayes V, Cal	92	586	15.7
Bonds Ba, Pit	124	868	14.3	Duncan, Phi	249	1159	21.5	Henderson, Oak	73	699	10.4
Bonilla B, NYN	172	865	19.9	Dykstra, Phi	50	609	8.2	Hill G, Cle	196	721	27.2
Borders, Tor	160	890	18.0	Eisenreich, KC	68	588	11.6	Hoiles, Bal	115	619	18.6
Bordick, Oak	93	811	11.5	Felder, SF	72	558	12.9	Hollins D, Phi	204	1143	17.8
Bream, Atl	110	657	16.7	Felix, Cal	294	1052	27.9	Howard T, Cle	143	718	19.9
Brett G, KC	229	1132	20.2	Fernandez T, SD	125	1208	10.3	Hrbek, Min	124	739	16.8
Browne, Oak	68	544	12.5	Fielder, Det	400	1295	30.9	Hundley, NYN	153	724	21.1
Brunansky, Bos	164	804	20.4	Finley S, Hou	151	1059	14.3	Huson, Tex	84	604	13.9
Buechele, ChN	203	980	20.7	Fletcher S, Mil	64	643	10.0	Incaviglia, Hou	245	753	32.5
Buhner, Sea	351	1090	32.2	Fryman T, Det	289	1294	22.3	Jackson D, SD	307	1204	25.5
Butler, LA	95	1072	8.9	Gaetti, Cal	243	952	25.5	Javier, Phi	118	670	17.6
Caminiti, Hou	150	928	16.2	Gagne, Min	183	900	20.3	Jefferies, KC	75	933	8.0
Candaele, Hou	91	625	14.6	Gant, Atl	238	1020	23.3	Johnson H, NYN	178	718	24.8
Canseco J, Tex	237	842	28.1	Gilkey, StL	118	643	18.4	Johnson L, ChA	66	922	7.2
Carreon, Det	130	695	18.7	Gladden, Det	124	749	16.6	Jose, StL	256	1058	24.2

Player, Team	Sw	Pit	%	Player, Team	Sw	Pit	%	Player, Team	Sw	Pit	%
Joyner, KC	134	987	13.6	Milligan, Bal	173	892	19.4	Scioscia, LA	53	582	9.1
Justice, Atl	252	1011	24.9	Mitchell Kev, Sea	141	700	20.1	Seitzer, Mil	98	979	10.0
Karkovice, ChA	180	657	27.4	Molitor, Mil	166	1164	14.3	Sharperson, LA	60	569	10.5
Karros, LA	233	1058	22.0	Morandini, Phi	129	824	15.7	Sheffield, SD	172	1032	16.7
Kelly Pat, NYA	148	698	21.2	Morris H, Cin	98	722	13.6	Sierra R, Oak	183	1052	17.4
Kelly R, NYA	259	1168	22.2	Munoz P, Min	241	885	27.2	Smith O, StL	80	932	8.6
King J, Pit	120	861	13.9	Murray E, NYN	229	1152	19.9	Snyder C, SF	253	854	29.6
Knoblauch, Min	92	1024	9.0	Nixon O, Atl	92	741	12.4	Sojo, Cal	62	613	10.1
Kruk, Phi	202	949	21.3	Nokes, NYA	158	768	20.6	Sorrento, Cle	168	836	20.1
Lankford, StL	294	1193	24.6	O'Brien P, Sea	73	659	11.1	Stankiewicz, NYA	84	705	11.9
Lansford C, Oak	94	872	10.8	O'Neill, Cin	157	880	17.8	Steinbach, Oak	152	862	17.6
Larkin B, Cin	144	940	15.3	Offerman, LA	157	1001	15.7	Stillwell, SD	114	682	16.7
Larkin G, Min	111	634	17.5	Olerud, Tor	102	808	12.6	Surhoff B, Mil	73	800	9.1
Lee Manuel, Tor	130	777	16.7	Oliver J, Cin	181	998	18.1	Tartabull, NYA	274	915	29.9
Leius, Min	102	663	15.4	Orsulak, Bal	75	720	10.4	Tettleton, Det	210	974	21.6
Lemke, Atl	73	670	10.9	Owen S, Mon	64	649	9.9	Thomas F, ChA	151	1015	14.9
Lewis D, SF	52	554	9.4	Pagnozzi, StL	173	905	19.1	Thompson R, SF	165	858	19.2
Lewis M, Cle	114	728	15.7	Palmeiro, Tex	190	1172	16.2	Valle, Sea	110	667	16.5
Lind, Pit	91	882	10.3	Palmer D, Tex	345	1144	30.2	Van Slyke, Pit	171	1144	14.9
Listach, Mil	183	1130	16.2	Pena T, Bos	113	786	14.4	Vaughn G, Mil	285	1054	27.0
Livingstone, Det	79	613	12.9	Pendleton, Atl	200	1258	15.9	Vaughn M, Bos	147	676	21.7
Lofton, Cle	76	908	8.4	Phillips T, Det	170	1133	15.0	Velarde, NYA	156	776	20.1
Macfarlane, KC	190	756	25.1	Plantier, Bos	202	727	27.8	Ventura, ChA	132	1026	12.9
Mack S, Min	243	1165	20.9	Polonia, Cal	120	1115	10.8	Vizquel, Sea	74	941	7.9
Magadan, NYN	54	566	9.5	Puckett, Min	236	1252	18.8	Walker L, Mon	273	1045	26.1
Maldonado, Tor	252	979	25.7	Raines, ChA	81	944	8.6	Wallach, Mon	275	1129	24.4
Manwaring, SF	114	684	16.7	Reed Jo, Bos	61	807	7.6	Weiss W, Oak	56	564	9.9
Martinez D, Cin	96	701	13.7	Reimer, Tex	281	1075	26.1	Whitaker, Det	95	828	11.5
Martinez E, Sea	82	856	9.6	Reynolds H, Sea	60	747	8.0	White D, Tor	334	1353	24.7
Martinez T, Sea	142	812	17.5	Ripken B, Bal	76	549	13.8	Whiten, Cle	219	920	23.8
Mattingly, NYA	107	1083	9.9	Ripken C, Bal	110	1088	10.1	Williams M, SF	293	1102	26.6
May D, ChN	112	641	17.5	Roberts B, Cin	153	1061	14.4	Wilson W, Oak	156	802	19.5
McGee, SF	234	1015	23.1	Rodriguez I, Tex	170	902	18.8	Winfield, Tor	248	1060	23.4
McGriff F, SD	235	1007	23.3	Sabo, Cin	136	676	20.1	Yount, Mil	203	1101	18.4
McGwire, Oak	226	903	25.0	Sandberg, ChN	190	1105	17.2	Zeile, StL	126	786	16.0
McRae B, KC	179	1050	17.0	Sanders R, Cin	204	794	25.7	Zupcic, Bos	112	630	17.8
McReynolds, KC	97	675	14.4	Santiago, SD	158	750	21.1	**MLB Average**			18.9
Merced, Pit	151	723	20.9	Sax S, ChA	101	920	11.0				
Miller K, KC	86	715	12.0	Schofield, NYN	171	848	20.2				

WHO GETS THOSE CRUCIAL GO-AHEAD RBI? (p. 122)

Both Leagues — Listed Alphabetically
(Minimum 50 RBI total in 1992)

Player, Team	GA RBI	Occ	RBI	%	Player, Team	GA RBI	Occ	RBI	%
Alomar R, Tor	15	59	76	25	Knoblauch, Min	15	52	56	29
Alou, Mon	17	43	56	40	Kruk, Phi	25	60	70	42
Anderson Br, Bal	16	66	80	24	Lankford, StL	28	66	86	42
Anthony, Hou	20	62	80	32	Lansford C, Oak	12	58	75	21
Baerga, Cle	42	87	105	48	Larkin B, Cin	23	69	78	33
Bagwell, Hou	28	76	96	37	Mack S, Min	17	60	75	28
Baines, Oak	17	54	76	31	Maldonado C, Tor	8	54	66	15
Bell G, ChA	25	83	112	30	Martinez E, Sea	17	53	73	32
Bell Jay, Pit	15	44	55	34	Martinez Tino, Sea	12	52	66	23
Belle, Cle	31	78	112	40	Mattingly, NYA	21	69	86	30
Boggs W, Bos	13	40	50	33	McGriff F, SD	26	76	104	34
Bonds Ba, Pit	19	74	103	26	McGwire, Oak	26	77	104	34
Bonilla B, NYN	18	50	70	36	McRae B, KC	11	43	52	26
Borders, Tor	9	41	53	22	Merced, Pit	18	46	60	39
Bream, Atl	12	50	61	24	Milligan, Bal	14	42	53	33
Brett G, KC	15	56	61	27	Mitchell Kev, Sea	17	48	67	35
Brunansky, Bos	19	55	74	35	Molitor, Mil	28	74	89	38
Buechele, ChN	13	53	64	25	Morris H, Cin	14	40	53	35
Buhner, Sea	15	58	79	26	Munoz P, Min	18	51	71	35
Caminiti, Hou	9	51	62	18	Murray E, NYN	26	63	93	41
Canseco J, Tex	15	67	87	22	Nokes, NYA	11	41	59	27
Carter Jo, Tor	26	85	119	31	O'Brien P, Sea	8	41	52	20
Clark Je, SD	12	44	58	27	O'Neill, Cin	14	58	66	24
Clark W, SF	23	61	73	38	Olerud, Tor	14	52	66	27
Daulton, Phi	21	78	109	27	Oliver J, Cin	15	43	57	35
Davis C, Min	14	54	66	26	Palmeiro, Tex	19	65	85	29
Dawson, ChN	24	74	90	32	Palmer Dean, Tex	8	53	72	15
Deer, Det	10	47	64	21	Pendleton, Atl	35	82	105	43
DeShields, Mon	16	49	56	33	Phillips T, Det	11	49	64	22
Devereaux, Bal	24	79	107	30	Puckett, Min	28	87	110	32
Duncan, Phi	12	39	50	31	Raines, ChA	8	45	54	18
Felix, Cal	25	64	72	39	Reimer, Tex	15	44	58	34
Fielder, Det	27	88	124	31	Ripken C, Bal	22	60	72	37
Finley S, Hou	16	52	55	31	Sandberg, ChN	29	66	87	44
Fletcher S, Mil	11	42	51	26	Seitzer, Mil	13	61	71	21
Fryman T, Det	18	76	96	24	Sheffield, SD	32	69	100	46
Gant, Atl	18	66	80	27	Sierra R, Oak	26	69	87	38
Gomez Le, Bal	14	45	64	31	Snyder C, SF	20	45	57	44
Gonzalez Juan, Tex	33	83	109	40	Sorrento, Cle	8	48	60	17
Gonzalez L, Hou	15	43	55	35	Steinbach, Oak	11	43	53	26
Grace, ChN	19	66	79	29	Surhoff B, Mil	17	53	62	32
Griffey Jr, Sea	22	72	103	31	Tartabull, NYA	17	55	85	31
Grissom, Mon	13	55	66	24	Tettleton, Det	19	57	83	33
Hall M, NYA	19	69	81	28	Thomas F, ChA	39	97	115	40
Hamilton D, Mil	5	52	62	10	Van Slyke, Pit	33	80	89	41
Harper B, Min	15	61	73	25	Vaughn G, Mil	20	56	78	36
Hayes C, NYA	11	55	66	20	Vaughn M, Bos	7	42	57	17
Hollins D, Phi	25	68	93	37	Ventura, ChA	25	79	93	32
Hrbek, Min	17	45	58	38	Walker L, Mon	30	77	93	39
Jackson Darrin, SD	11	52	70	21	Wallach, Mon	7	51	59	14
Jefferies, KC	24	66	75	36	Whitaker, Det	8	53	71	15
Jose, StL	21	58	75	36	White D, Tor	15	49	60	31
Joyner, KC	20	54	66	37	Williams MD, SF	18	45	66	40
Justice, Atl	17	52	72	33	Winfield, Tor	17	78	108	22
Karkovice, ChA	13	36	50	36	Yount, Mil	18	67	77	27
Karros, LA	23	64	88	36					
Kelly R, NYA	16	56	66	29					
Kent, NYN	14	37	50	38					
King J, Pit	14	57	65	25					

WHO GETS RUNG UP? (p. 124)

Both Leagues — Listed Alphabetically
(Minimum 50 strike outs in 1992)

Player	Tot	Look	%	Player	Tot	Look	%
Alomar R, Tor	52	20	38.5	Davis C, Min	76	24	31.6
Amaro, Phi	54	15	27.8	Davis E, LA	71	20	28.2
Anderson Br, Bal	98	30	30.6	Davis G, Bal	65	13	20.0
Anthony, Hou	98	31	31.6	Dawson, ChN	70	9	12.9
Baerga, Cle	76	13	17.1	Deer, Det	131	26	19.8
Bagwell, Hou	97	31	32.0	DeShields, Mon	108	26	24.1
Baines, Oak	61	21	34.4	Devereaux, Bal	94	19	20.2
Barberie, Mon	62	15	24.2	DiSarcina, Cal	50	19	38.0
Bass K, NYN	70	13	18.6	Downing, Tex	58	18	31.0
Bell G, ChA	97	14	14.4	Duncan, Phi	108	23	21.3
Bell Jay, Pit	103	23	22.3	Fariss, Tex	51	18	35.3
Belle, Cle	128	37	28.9	Felix, Cal	128	28	21.9
Benzinger, LA	54	8	14.8	Fernandez T, SD	62	16	25.8
Berryhill, Atl	67	13	19.4	Fielder, Det	151	22	14.6
Bichette, Mil	74	9	12.2	Finley S, Hou	63	15	23.8
Biggio, Hou	95	32	33.7	Fryman T, Det	144	33	22.9
Blankenship L, Oak	57	34	59.6	Gaetti, Cal	79	9	11.4
Blauser, Atl	82	28	34.1	Gagne, Min	83	14	16.9
Bonds Ba, Pit	69	27	39.1	Galarraga, StL	69	11	15.9
Bonilla B, NYN	73	30	41.1	Gant, Atl	101	31	30.7
Borders, Tor	75	18	24.0	Gilkey, StL	52	15	28.8
Bordick, Oak	59	12	20.3	Gladden, Det	64	15	23.4
Boston, NYN	60	12	20.0	Gomez Leo, Bal	78	29	37.2
Bream, Atl	51	12	23.5	Gonzalez Juan, Tex	143	16	11.2
Brett G, KC	69	17	24.6	Gonzalez L, Hou	52	9	17.3
Brunansky, Bos	96	35	36.5	Griffey Jr, Sea	67	12	17.9
Buechele, ChN	105	17	16.2	Grissom, Mon	81	18	22.2
Buhner, Sea	146	27	18.5	Gruber, Tor	72	10	13.9
Butler, LA	67	21	31.3	Hall M, NYA	53	6	11.3
Caminiti, Hou	68	21	30.9	Hatcher B, Bos	52	12	23.1
Canseco J, Tex	128	40	31.3	Hayes C, NYA	100	28	28.0
Carreon, Det	57	5	8.8	Hayes V, Cal	54	14	25.9
Carter Joe, Tor	109	6	5.5	Henderson R, Oak	56	24	42.9
Cedeno A, Hou	71	19	26.8	Hill G, Cle	73	14	19.2
Chamberlain W, Phi	55	6	10.9	Hoiles, Bal	60	27	45.0
Cianfrocco, Mon	66	7	10.6	Hollins D, Phi	110	30	27.3
Clark Ja, Bos	87	38	43.7	Horn, Bal	60	8	13.3
Clark Je, SD	97	19	19.6	Howard T, Cle	60	9	15.0
Clark W, SF	82	12	14.6	Hrbek, Min	56	17	30.4
Clayton, SF	63	12	19.0	Hundley, NYN	76	17	22.4
Cole A, Pit	67	33	49.3	Hunter B, Atl	50	8	16.0
Curtis C, Cal	71	23	32.4	Incaviglia, Hou	99	19	19.2
Cuyler, Det	62	17	27.4	Jackson Darrin, SD	106	17	16.0
Daniels, ChN	54	23	42.6	Jacoby, Cle	54	17	31.5
Daulton, Phi	103	27	26.2	Javier, Phi	54	17	31.5

Player	Tot	Look	%	Player	Tot	Look	%
Johnson H, NYN	79	20	25.3	Plantier, Bos	83	8	9.6
Jose, StL	100	19	19.0	Polonia, Cal	64	22	34.4
Joyner, KC	50	15	30.0	Puckett, Min	97	17	17.5
Justice, Atl	85	23	27.1	Reimer, Tex	103	23	22.3
Karkovice, ChA	89	23	25.8	Ripken C, Bal	50	22	44.0
Karros, LA	103	32	31.1	Rivera L, Bos	56	18	32.1
Kelly Pat, NYA	72	26	36.1	Roberts B, Cin	54	8	14.8
Kelly R, NYA	96	17	17.7	Rodriguez I, Tex	73	12	16.4
Kent, NYN	76	21	27.6	Sabo, Cin	54	5	9.3
King J, Pit	56	16	28.6	Sandberg, ChN	73	15	20.5
Knoblauch, Min	60	23	38.3	Sanders D, Atl	52	10	19.2
Kruk, Phi	88	24	27.3	Sanders R, Cin	98	29	29.6
Lankford, StL	147	33	22.4	Santiago, SD	52	11	21.2
Larkin B, Cin	58	12	20.7	Schofield, NYN	82	23	28.0
Lee Manuel, Tor	73	18	24.7	Sierra R, Oak	68	11	16.2
Leius, Min	61	33	54.1	Snyder C, SF	96	20	20.8
Lewis M, Cle	69	26	37.7	Sorrento, Cle	89	29	32.6
Listach, Mil	124	39	31.5	Sosa S, ChN	63	22	34.9
Lofton, Cle	54	30	55.6	Steinbach, Oak	58	12	20.7
Maas, NYA	63	13	20.6	Stevens, Cal	64	16	25.0
Macfarlane, KC	89	21	23.6	Stillwell, SD	58	17	29.3
Mack S, Min	106	22	20.8	Stubbs, Mil	68	15	22.1
Maldonado C, Tor	112	31	27.7	Sveum, ChA	68	24	35.3
Martinez D, Cin	54	17	31.5	Tartabull, NYA	115	29	25.2
Martinez E, Sea	61	25	41.0	Taubensee, Hou	78	21	26.9
Martinez Tino, Sea	77	21	27.3	Tettleton, Det	137	42	30.7
McGee, SF	88	16	18.2	Thomas F, ChA	88	35	39.8
McGriff F, SD	108	37	34.3	Thompson Ro, SF	75	20	26.7
McGwire, Oak	105	40	38.1	Valle, Sea	58	19	32.8
McRae B, KC	88	30	34.1	Van Slyke, Pit	99	27	27.3
Merced, Pit	63	17	27.0	Vaughn G, Mil	123	27	22.0
Milligan, Bal	81	31	38.3	Vaughn M, Bos	67	14	20.9
Molitor, Mil	66	18	27.3	Velarde, NYA	78	22	28.2
Morandini, Phi	64	17	26.6	Ventura, ChA	71	21	29.6
Morris H, Cin	53	16	30.2	Walker C, NYN	50	14	28.0
Munoz P, Min	90	16	17.8	Walker L, Mon	97	17	17.5
Murray E, NYN	74	12	16.2	Wallach, Mon	90	18	20.0
Nixon O, Atl	54	16	29.6	White D, Tor	133	23	17.3
Nokes, NYA	62	11	17.7	Whiten, Cle	102	35	34.3
O'Neill, Cin	85	37	43.5	Wilkins R, ChN	53	14	26.4
Offerman, LA	98	40	40.8	Williams MD, SF	109	16	14.7
Olerud, Tor	61	20	32.8	Wilson W, Oak	65	15	23.1
Oliver J, Cin	75	14	18.7	Winfield, Tor	89	22	24.7
Pagnozzi, StL	64	12	18.8	Winningham, Bos	53	16	30.2
Palmeiro, Tex	83	19	22.9	Yount, Mil	81	17	21.0
Palmer De, Tex	154	33	21.4	Zeile, StL	70	26	37.1
Parrish Lance, Sea	70	22	31.4	Zupcic, Bos	60	22	36.7
Pasqua, ChA	57	18	31.6	**MLB Average**	**23538**	**6298**	**26.8**
Pena T, Bos	61	17	27.9				
Pendleton, Atl	67	9	13.4				
Phillips T, Det	93	28	30.1				

IS FRANK THOMAS UNDERRATED? (p. 126)

Both Leagues — Listed Alphabetically
(minimum 400 plate appearances in 1992)

Player, Team	RC	OW%	Player, Team	RC	OW%	Player, Team	RC	OW%
Alomar R, Tor	111.3	.733	Griffey Jr, Sea	104.5	.713	O'Neill, Cin	67.4	.584
Amaro, Phi	39.6	.435	Grissom, Mon	93.7	.625	Offerman, LA	60.7	.499
Anderson Br, Bal	117.7	.692	Gruber, Tor	39.3	.306	Olerud, Tor	78.4	.661
Anthony, Hou	53.0	.527	Gwynn T, SD	76.9	.669	Oliver J, Cin	57.0	.519
Baerga, Cle	105.4	.653	Hall M, NYA	75.4	.530	Orsulak, Bal	52.0	.556
Bagwell, Hou	98.5	.686	Hamilton D, Mil	69.8	.588	Owen S, Mon	53.1	.593
Baines, Oak	62.5	.517	Harper B, Min	68.4	.565	Pagnozzi, StL	46.0	.399
Bass K, NYN	48.9	.539	Hatcher B, Bos	35.9	.308	Palmeiro, Tex	96.0	.620
Bell G, ChA	68.2	.417	Hayes C, NYA	58.7	.452	Palmer D, Tex	72.8	.521
Bell Jay, Pit	79.8	.550	Henderson R, Oak	91.6	.781	Pena T, Bos	34.7	.291
Belle, Cle	87.1	.581	Hollins D, Phi	106.6	.735	Pendleton, Atl	101.1	.691
Bichette, Mil	46.3	.480	Hrbek, Min	59.0	.573	Phillips T, Det	97.8	.624
Biggio, Hou	95.2	.665	Jackson Darri, SD	60.5	.439	Polonia, Cal	63.2	.421
Blankenship L, Oak	54.5	.578	Jefferies, KC	74.9	.494	Puckett, Min	113.6	.704
Blauser, Atl	58.5	.695	Johnson H, NYN	43.4	.525	Raines, ChA	98.2	.689
Boggs W, Bos	67.2	.524	Johnson L, ChA	62.5	.427	Reed Jody, Bos	55.4	.369
Bonds Ba, Pit	147.7	.896	Jose, StL	75.2	.654	Reimer, Tex	71.4	.583
Bonilla B, NYN	66.1	.641	Joyner, KC	72.3	.508	Reynolds H, Sea	47.0	.369
Borders, Tor	52.5	.425	Justice, Atl	83.8	.712	Ripken C, Bal	76.2	.476
Bordick, Oak	69.3	.554	Karros, LA	66.6	.538	Roberts B, Cin	96.1	.748
Bream, Atl	57.1	.660	Kelly R, NYA	71.3	.492	Rodriguez I, Tex	42.4	.384
Brett G, KC	74.3	.518	King J, Pit	46.7	.403	Sandberg, ChN	117.1	.766
Brunansky, Bos	73.0	.615	Knoblauch, Min	93.3	.619	Sanders R, Cin	65.2	.703
Buechele, ChN	66.0	.561	Kruk, Phi	103.0	.793	Santiago, SD	37.7	.414
Buhner, Sea	76.9	.546	Lankford, StL	107.7	.727	Sax S, ChA	51.3	.309
Butler, LA	99.4	.719	Lansford C, Oak	60.6	.477	Schofield, NYN	41.1	.382
Caminiti, Hou	75.7	.657	Larkin B, Cin	93.9	.731	Seitzer, Mil	65.8	.470
Canseco J, Tex	66.5	.573	Lee Man, Tor	46.3	.460	Sheffield, SD	117.9	.804
Carter Joe, Tor	94.1	.589	Leius, Min	39.3	.361	Sierra R, Oak	86.2	.579
Clark Je, SD	52.8	.474	Lemke, Atl	40.5	.386	Smith O, StL	71.7	.612
Clark W, SF	98.4	.763	Lewis M, Cle	42.2	.395	Snyder C, SF	50.7	.574
Curtis C, Cal	57.9	.497	Lind, Pit	33.1	.264	Sorrento, Cle	67.1	.582
Dascenzo, ChN	35.5	.410	Listach, Mil	78.8	.549	Stankiewicz, NYA	46.5	.454
Daulton, Phi	107.0	.806	Lofton, Cle	87.3	.610	Steinbach, Oak	57.7	.526
Davis C, Min	77.7	.670	Macfarlane, KC	53.8	.519	Stillwell, SD	31.8	.338
Davis G, Bal	56.0	.568	Mack S, Min	114.0	.718	Surhoff B, Mil	50.2	.392
Dawson, ChN	75.5	.618	Maldonado C, Tor	80.8	.643	Tartabull, NYA	90.6	.758
Deer, Det	72.8	.687	Martinez D, Cin	46.1	.506	Tettleton, Det	100.2	.693
DeShields, Mon	79.6	.644	Martinez E, Sea	115.9	.791	Thomas F, ChA	141.7	.815
Devereaux, Bal	94.3	.578	Martinez Tino, Sea	54.4	.450	Thompson Ro, SF	60.6	.584
DiSarcina, Cal	41.3	.274	Mattingly, NYA	86.7	.567	Valle, Sea	41.3	.435
Doran, Cin	47.8	.525	McGee, SF	58.0	.571	Van Slyke, Pit	122.1	.792
Duncan, Phi	63.7	.495	McGriff F, SD	116.1	.801	Vaughn G, Mil	63.5	.475
Felix, Cal	52.1	.381	McGwire, Oak	109.5	.781	Vaughn M, Bos	46.7	.510
Fernandez T, SD	75.1	.533	McRae B, KC	49.1	.327	Velarde, NYA	52.7	.508
Fielder, Det	89.3	.585	McReynolds, KC	61.1	.629	Ventura, ChA	98.5	.650
Finley S, Hou	93.7	.661	Merced, Pit	53.8	.576	Vizquel, Sea	54.2	.446
Fletcher S, Mil	48.4	.497	Miller K, KC	61.7	.610	Walker L, Mon	95.1	.740
Fryman, Det	86.1	.524	Milligan, Bal	70.4	.583	Wallach, Mon	54.4	.430
Gaetti, Cal	40.8	.326	Mitchell Kev, Sea	55.4	.627	Whitaker, Det	84.9	.698
Gagne, Min	39.3	.315	Molitor, Mil	115.8	.723	White D, Tor	80.9	.507
Gant, Atl	74.1	.591	Morandini, Phi	45.5	.487	Whiten, Cle	64.3	.491
Gilkey, StL	60.4	.674	Morris H, Cin	51.0	.568	Williams M, SF	53.8	.428
Gladden, Det	45.2	.418	Munoz P, Min	44.1	.409	Wilson W, Oak	44.8	.445
Gomez Leo, Bal	72.3	.593	Murray E, NYN	78.5	.616	Winfield, Tor	109.9	.717
Gonzalez Juan, Tex	89.5	.600	Nixon O, Atl	58.1	.570	Yount, Mil	73.3	.519
Gonzalez L, Hou	41.2	.463	Nokes, NYA	45.2	.441	Zeile, StL	57.3	.559
Grace, ChN	101.8	.719	O'Brien P, Sea	43.0	.406	Zupcic, Bos	45.4	.467

SHOULD THEY BE LEAVING THOSE "FLYBALL HITTERS" ALONE? (p. 129)

The table below lists the number of groundballs hit (**Grd**), the number of flyballs hit (**Fly**), and the ratio of the two (**G/F**).

Both Leagues — Listed Alphabetically
(minimum 600 balls hit in play, excluding Bunts and Line Drives, from 1990 through 1992)

Player, Team	Grd	Fly	G/F	Player, Team	Grd	Fly	G/F	Player, Team	Grd	Fly	G/F
Alomar R, Tor	734	460	1.60	Candaele, Hou	406	291	1.40	Fryman T, Det	379	427	0.89
Alomar S, Cle	354	308	1.15	Canseco J, Tex	401	450	0.89	Gaetti, Cal	547	543	1.01
Anderson Br, Bal	394	328	1.20	Carter Joe, Tor	536	726	0.74	Gagne, Min	402	388	1.04
Baerga, Cle	692	377	1.84	Clark W, SF	528	539	0.98	Galarraga, StL	448	310	1.45
Bagwell, Hou	377	340	1.11	Coleman, NYN	403	226	1.78	Gallego, NYA	376	328	1.15
Baines, Oak	557	366	1.52	Daniels, ChN	427	257	1.66	Gant, Atl	535	598	0.89
Bass K, NYN	389	277	1.40	Daulton, Phi	375	421	0.89	Gantner, Mil	479	312	1.54
Bell G, ChA	526	663	0.79	Davis A, Cal	313	406	0.77	Gladden, Det	469	457	1.03
Bell Jay, Pit	620	576	1.08	Davis C, Min	513	380	1.35	Gonzalez J, Tex	358	422	0.85
Belle, Cle	364	320	1.14	Davis E, LA	362	258	1.40	Grace, ChN	729	493	1.48
Benzinger, LA	390	337	1.16	Davis G, Bal	307	316	0.97	Greenwell, Bos	595	402	1.48
Bichette, Mil	396	336	1.18	Dawson, ChN	597	512	1.17	Griffey Jr, Sea	615	515	1.19
Biggio, Hou	652	457	1.43	Deer, Det	241	424	0.57	Griffin A, Tor	358	276	1.30
Blauser, Atl	326	359	0.91	DeShields, Mon	650	318	2.04	Grissom, Mon	627	420	1.49
Boggs W, Bos	747	399	1.87	Devereaux, Bal	564	561	1.01	Gruber, Tor	527	509	1.04
Bonds Ba, Pit	466	573	0.81	Doran, Cin	415	381	1.09	Guerrero P, StL	408	351	1.16
Bonilla B, NYN	527	610	0.86	Downing, Tex	363	346	1.05	Guillen, ChA	460	322	1.43
Borders, Tor	414	333	1.24	Duncan, Phi	561	338	1.66	Gwynn T, SD	771	354	2.18
Bream, Atl	338	362	0.93	Dunston, ChN	344	387	0.89	Hall M, NYA	533	515	1.04
Brett G, KC	648	482	1.34	Dykstra, Phi	471	341	1.38	Hamilton Dar, Mil	456	221	2.06
Briley, Sea	407	233	1.75	Eisenreich, KC	549	325	1.69	Harper B, Min	559	489	1.14
Brooks, Cal	482	368	1.31	Felder, SF	393	244	1.61	Harris L, LA	628	255	2.46
Browne, Oak	469	338	1.39	Felix, Cal	477	269	1.77	Hatcher B, Bos	570	363	1.57
Brunansky, Bos	401	511	0.78	Fermin, Cle	540	217	2.49	Hayes C, NYA	555	462	1.20
Buechele, ChN	423	395	1.07	Fernandez T, SD	745	450	1.66	Hayes V, Cal	369	304	1.21
Buhner, Sea	307	362	0.85	Fielder, Det	481	543	0.89	Henderson D, Oak	294	361	0.81
Burks, Bos	448	402	1.11	Finley S, Hou	733	405	1.81	Henderson R, Oak	455	462	0.98
Butler, LA	824	311	2.65	Fisk, ChA	366	361	1.01	Hrbek, Min	538	437	1.23
Calderon, Mon	487	381	1.28	Fletcher S, Mil	432	357	1.21	Huson, Tex	382	279	1.37
Caminiti, Hou	586	467	1.26	Franco Ju, Tex	562	285	1.97	Incaviglia, Hou	365	334	1.09

Player, Team	Grd	Fly	G/F	Player, Team	Grd	Fly	G/F	Player, Team	Grd	Fly	G/F
Jackson D, SD	327	332	0.98	Murray E, NYN	625	543	1.15	Seitzer, Mil	602	397	1.52
Jacoby, Cle	453	420	1.08	Newman A, Tex	428	219	1.95	Sheffield, SD	412	450	0.92
James C, SF	480	357	1.34	Nixon O, Atl	471	207	2.28	Sierra R, Oak	709	596	1.19
Jefferies, KC	660	597	1.11	Nokes, NYA	368	462	0.80	Smith Lo, Atl	302	324	0.93
Johnson H, NYN	346	613	0.56	O'Brien P, Sea	492	492	1.00	Smith O, StL	806	371	2.17
Johnson L, ChA	846	355	2.38	O'Neill, Cin	519	463	1.12	Snyder C, SF	293	308	0.95
Jose, StL	618	330	1.87	Olerud, Tor	495	326	1.52	Sosa S, ChN	350	275	1.27
Joyner, KC	524	491	1.07	Oliver J, Cin	364	365	1.00	Steinbach, Oak	479	377	1.27
Justice, Atl	371	436	0.85	Olson Greg, Atl	419	290	1.45	Stillwell, SD	495	388	1.28
Kelly R, NYA	603	490	1.23	Oquendo, StL	324	289	1.12	Strawberry, LA	375	378	0.99
King J, Pit	334	370	0.90	Orsulak, Bal	491	376	1.31	Stubbs, Mil	314	345	0.91
Knoblauch, Min	530	321	1.65	Owen S, Mon	500	390	1.28	Surhoff B, Mil	669	366	1.83
Kruk, Phi	583	342	1.70	Pagnozzi, StL	438	327	1.34	Tartabull, NYA	404	310	1.30
Lankford, StL	410	364	1.13	Palmeiro, Tex	624	615	1.01	Tettleton, Det	383	443	0.86
Lansford C, Oak	441	312	1.41	Parrish Lan, Sea	344	349	0.99	Thomas F, ChA	395	417	0.95
Larkin B, Cin	711	460	1.55	Pasqua, ChA	288	348	0.83	Thompson M, StL	466	168	2.77
Larkin G, Min	346	337	1.03	Pecota, NYN	351	266	1.32	Thompson Ro, SF	503	440	1.14
LaValliere, Pit	360	307	1.17	Pena T, Bos	636	301	2.11	Thon, Tex	517	400	1.29
Lee Man, Tor	525	240	2.19	Pendleton, Atl	679	486	1.40	Trammell, Det	352	335	1.05
Lemke, Atl	370	294	1.26	Perry Ge, StL	348	256	1.36	Treadway, Atl	301	317	0.95
Lind, Pit	690	413	1.67	Phillips T, Det	658	460	1.43	Valle, Sea	410	290	1.41
Maas, NYA	241	394	0.61	Polonia, Cal	723	315	2.30	Van Slyke, Pit	519	526	0.99
Macfarlane, KC	328	354	0.93	Puckett, Min	795	424	1.88	Vaughn G, Mil	379	496	0.76
Mack S, Min	575	302	1.90	Raines, ChA	654	454	1.44	Ventura, ChA	672	510	1.32
Magadan, NYN	451	300	1.50	Randolph, NYN	507	257	1.97	Vizquel, Sea	494	319	1.55
Maldonado, Tor	424	401	1.06	Reed Jo, Bos	651	545	1.19	Walker L, Mon	551	352	1.57
Martinez Da, Cin	450	355	1.27	Reynolds H, Sea	654	536	1.22	Wallach, Mon	571	598	0.95
Martinez E, Sea	586	447	1.31	Ripken B, Bal	444	275	1.61	Weiss W, Oak	384	237	1.62
Mattingly, NYA	596	601	0.99	Ripken C, Bal	762	613	1.24	Whitaker, Det	424	509	0.83
McGee, SF	834	223	3.74	Rivera L, Bos	329	310	1.06	White D, Tor	637	419	1.52
McGriff F, SD	546	432	1.26	Roberts B, Cin	699	294	2.38	Whiten, Cle	376	247	1.52
McGwire, Oak	316	639	0.49	Sabo, Cin	469	594	0.79	Williams M, SF	539	573	0.94
McRae B, KC	535	307	1.74	Salazar L, ChN	336	341	0.99	Wilson W, Oak	427	230	1.86
McReynolds, KC	410	607	0.68	Samuel, KC	484	295	1.64	Winfield, Tor	643	453	1.42
Milligan, Bal	440	396	1.11	Sandberg, ChN	675	554	1.22	Yount, Mil	540	563	0.96
Mitchell Kev, Sea	389	494	0.79	Santiago, SD	414	404	1.03	Zeile, StL	570	446	1.28
Molitor, Mil	631	495	1.28	Sax S, ChA	994	404	2.46				
Morris H, Cin	489	305	1.60	Schofield, NYN	375	355	1.06				
Murphy Dal, Phi	441	319	1.38	Scioscia, LA	469	351	1.34				

CAN YOU LEARN TO HIT LEFTIES? (p. 132)

Both Leagues — Listed Alphabetically
(Active Players/Minimum 400 PA since 1990)

Left-Handed Batters	Vs. LHP		Vs. RHP		Left-Handed Batters	Vs. LHP		Vs. RHP	
Batter, Team	AB	Avg	AB	Avg	Batter, Team	AB	Avg	AB	Avg
Anderson Br, Bal	272	.202	841	.270	Lofton, Cle	142	.352	508	.254
Anthony, Hou	269	.204	528	.216	Lyons S, Bos	43	.140	370	.227
Azocar, SD	67	.209	372	.228	Maas, NYA	302	.202	738	.249
Backman, Phi	56	.143	492	.289	Magadan, NYN	439	.267	751	.306
Baines, Oak	227	.269	1154	.279	Martinez Ch, Bal	68	.265	346	.269
Bergman, Det	46	.130	534	.260	Martinez D, Cin	230	.248	954	.283
Boggs W, Bos	554	.271	1125	.312	Martinez Tino, Sea	151	.238	489	.245
Bonds Ba, Pit	663	.300	839	.302	Mattingly, NYA	557	.271	1064	.285
Boston, NYN	138	.261	773	.266	May D, ChN	82	.256	352	.270
Bradley S, NYN	36	.167	375	.221	Mayne, KC	44	.114	413	.252
Bream, Atl	169	.231	857	.268	McGriff F, SD	620	.271	996	.299
Brett G, KC	538	.277	1103	.297	Morandini, Phi	201	.189	625	.278
Briley, Sea	77	.208	841	.263	Morris H, Cin	318	.245	864	.331
Bush, Min	14	.071	514	.257	Mulliniks, Tor	20	.250	319	.263
Butler, LA	724	.293	1066	.312	Myers G, Cal	63	.159	574	.258
Clark W, SF	651	.290	1027	.304	Nokes, NYA	196	.230	995	.251
Cole A, Pit	163	.313	753	.276	O'Brien P, Sea	365	.219	957	.239
Cooper S, Bos	47	.319	326	.288	O'Neill, Cin	485	.227	1046	.272
Daniels, ChN	422	.261	701	.270	Olerud, Tor	253	.269	1017	.268
Daulton, Phi	411	.231	818	.263	Orsulak, Bal	216	.245	1074	.285
Davis A, Cal	281	.246	779	.255	Pagliarulo, Min	123	.236	745	.262
DeShields, Mon	567	.265	1025	.276	Palmeiro, Tex	553	.298	1284	.305
Dykstra, Phi	440	.305	741	.317	Pasqua, ChA	98	.214	909	.255
Eisenreich, KC	318	.255	906	.294	Perry Ge, StL	263	.221	587	.259
Finley S, Hou	524	.250	1143	.293	Petralli, Tex	51	.196	665	.248
Fletcher D, Mon	40	.275	341	.226	Plantier, Bos	96	.198	416	.284
Foley T, Mon	57	.193	390	.203	Polonia, Cal	351	.242	1233	.320
Gantner, Mil	261	.272	844	.268	Quirk, Oak	66	.348	435	.237
Gibson K, Pit	241	.216	592	.253	Reed Jef, Cin	55	.255	415	.255
Gonzalez L, Hou	203	.241	678	.249	Reimer, Tex	130	.231	858	.273
Grace, ChN	662	.284	1149	.303	Riles, Hou	35	.143	462	.221
Greenwell, Bos	428	.280	906	.294	Sanders D, Atl	86	.221	460	.250
Gregg, Atl	28	.071	337	.255	Sasser, NYN	100	.200	539	.295
Griffey Jr, Sea	551	.325	1159	.305	Scioscia, LA	306	.219	822	.263
Guillen, ChA	386	.238	694	.293	Smith Dw, ChN	61	.197	613	.264
Gwynn T, SD	644	.300	979	.324	Sorrento, Cle	53	.189	573	.262
Hall M, NYA	399	.271	1036	.278	Spiers, Mil	201	.224	592	.279
Hamilton Dar, Mil	185	.254	846	.313	Stevens, Cal	115	.200	503	.231
Hansen D, LA	53	.189	351	.225	Strawberry, LA	511	.258	692	.273
Harris L, LA	165	.218	1042	.299	Stubbs, Mil	289	.246	809	.234
Hayes V, Cal	311	.251	747	.237	Surhoff B, Mil	332	.280	1127	.271
Horn, Bal	37	.081	688	.247	Taubensee, Hou	57	.263	306	.219
Hrbek, Min	340	.279	1008	.271	Thompson M, StL	216	.204	736	.283
Huson, Tex	105	.219	877	.242	Treadway, Atl	149	.282	757	.288
James D, NYA	23	.174	370	.276	Van Slyke, Pit	642	.257	956	.318
Johnson Lan, ChA	478	.276	1218	.280	Varsho, Pit	20	.200	377	.252
Joyner, KC	487	.251	946	.297	Vaughn M, Bos	112	.196	462	.255
Justice, Atl	445	.306	874	.253	Ventura, ChA	528	.248	1163	.285
Kruk, Phi	529	.287	959	.312	Walker L, Mon	485	.280	949	.279
Lankford, StL	481	.252	809	.287	Whitaker, Det	258	.240	1137	.270
LaValliere, Pit	141	.270	767	.269	Wilkins R, ChN	88	.261	359	.245
Livingstone, Det	57	.316	424	.281	Winningham, Bos	62	.145	501	.250

WHO GETS THE "SLIDIN' BILLY" TROPHY FOR LEADOFF MEN? (p. 134)

Both Leagues — Listed Alphabetically
(Players with 100+ Plate Appearances batting Leadoff in 1992)

Player, Team	OBP	AB	R	H	BB	HBP	SB
Amaro, Phi	.284	130	20	24	13	5	1
Anderson Br, Bal	.374	622	100	169	98	9	53
Biggio, Hou	.378	602	94	166	93	7	37
Blankenship L, Oak	.400	77	8	17	21	2	3
Boggs W, Bos	.315	221	21	49	31	1	0
Boston, NYN	.372	98	17	29	12	1	2
Butler, LA	.374	324	46	87	53	2	17
Cole A, Pit	.341	223	36	62	21	1	15
Coleman, NYN	.356	223	35	61	27	2	22
Cotto, Sea	.337	184	29	53	13	1	16
Dascenzo, ChN	.285	179	21	47	6	0	2
DeShields, Mon	.366	343	54	106	28	3	25
Downing, Tex	.414	202	41	59	37	5	0
Dykstra, Phi	.375	345	53	104	40	3	30
Felder, SF	.328	213	32	60	14	1	11
Fernandez T, SD	.336	620	84	170	55	4	20
Gilkey, StL	.320	193	27	45	24	1	7
Grissom, Mon	.343	320	53	95	22	1	41
Hatcher B, Bos	.250	207	24	43	10	2	3
Henderson R, Oak	.426	392	77	111	94	6	47
Huson, Tex	.276	106	14	24	8	0	2
Javier, Phi	.314	167	25	38	21	1	9
Jefferies, KC	.377	145	17	45	15	1	6
Knoblauch, Min	.377	264	42	79	34	2	12
Lankford, StL	.375	236	36	68	30	3	19
Lewis D, SF	.287	255	28	56	25	0	21
Listach, Mil	.351	443	72	129	40	1	42
Lofton, Cle	.360	551	91	155	66	2	64
Mack S, Min	.369	365	63	109	34	7	16
McGee, SF	.346	130	13	41	5	1	7
McRae B, KC	.291	104	14	21	10	3	5
Merced, Pit	.379	87	14	24	15	0	1
Miller K, KC	.362	286	44	84	23	8	10
Molitor, Mil	.383	133	18	42	17	0	9
Nixon O, Atl	.344	445	76	129	38	0	41
Offerman, LA	.332	268	42	71	28	0	14
Pena G, StL	.378	97	18	28	11	3	6
Phillips T, Det	.377	550	103	152	92	1	10
Polonia, Cal	.338	569	82	163	45	1	49
Raines, ChA	.350	345	54	88	53	0	30
Randolph, NYN	.339	94	12	22	15	0	1
Redus, Pit	.287	157	17	38	10	0	9
Reed Jody, Bos	.294	191	27	45	17	0	3
Reynolds H, Sea	.307	136	16	31	16	0	6
Roberts B, Cin	.396	505	85	164	60	2	44
Sanders D, Atl	.336	229	40	70	11	0	18
Sax S, ChA	.289	234	34	58	14	0	13
Sosa S, ChN	.323	113	17	31	8	1	5
Stankiewicz, NYA	.337	259	38	71	23	2	6
Vizcaino, ChN	.233	166	12	34	6	0	1
Vizquel, Sea	.366	266	34	86	16	2	7
White D, Tor	.304	640	98	159	47	5	37
Williams Be, NYA	.352	260	38	72	29	1	7
AL Team Avg	**.345**	**667**	**101**	**180**	**75**	**5**	**36**
NL Team Avg	**.338**	**670**	**95**	**181**	**66**	**4**	**39**

WILL JOSE LIGHT UP THE ARLINGTON SKY? (p. 136)

The table below lists the number of opposite field home runs hit (**Opp**), the total home runs hit (**HR**), and the percentage hit to the opposite field (**%**).

Both Leagues — Listed Alphabetically
(Active players with a 50+ home runs hit from 1988 through 1992)

Player, Team	HR	Opp	%	Player, Team	HR	Opp	%
Baines, Oak	81	27	33	Johnson H, NYN	128	3	2
Barfield Je, NYA	85	16	19	Joyner, KC	67	7	10
Bell G, ChA	113	2	2	Justice, Atl	71	8	11
Belle, Cle	70	4	6	Kelly R, NYA	55	22	40
Bonds Ba, Pit	135	20	15	Kruk, Phi	55	22	40
Bonilla B, NYN	117	14	12	Larkin B, Cin	55	7	13
Braggs, Cin	53	2	4	Maas, NYA	55	1	2
Brett G, KC	67	23	34	Maldonado C, Tor	75	5	7
Brooks, Cal	78	7	9	Mattingly, NYA	69	2	3
Brunansky, Bos	90	10	11	McGriff F, SD	171	45	26
Buechele, ChN	70	9	13	McGwire, Oak	168	21	13
Buhner, Sea	81	23	28	McReynolds, KC	102	0	0
Burks, Bos	73	3	4	Milligan, Bal	62	9	15
Calderon, Mon	64	9	14	Mitchell Kev, Sea	137	16	12
Canseco J, Tex	166	22	13	Molitor, Mil	65	4	6
Carter Jo, Tor	153	6	4	Murphy Dale, Phi	88	24	27
Clark Ja, Bos	111	17	15	Murray E, NYN	109	10	9
Clark W, SF	116	27	23	Nokes, NYA	82	0	0
Daniels, ChN	72	33	46	O'Brien P, Sea	64	1	2
Daulton, Phi	60	5	8	O'Neill, Cin	89	8	9
Davis A, Cal	68	0	0	Palmeiro, Tex	78	5	6
Davis C, Min	96	20	21	Parrish Lan, Sea	87	11	13
Davis E, LA	100	25	25	Pasqua, ChA	68	12	18
Davis G, Bal	109	8	7	Pendleton, Atl	68	6	9
Dawson, ChN	125	8	6	Puckett, Min	79	19	24
Deer, Det	133	9	7	Ripken C, Bal	113	4	4
Devereaux, Bal	63	7	11	Sabo, Cin	80	1	1
Downing, Tex	80	5	6	Salazar L, ChN	52	4	8
Fielder, Det	139	18	13	Sandberg, ChN	141	2	1
Fisk, ChA	71	0	0	Santiago, SD	64	12	19
Franco Ju, Tex	51	19	37	Sheffield, SD	54	1	2
Fryman T, Det	50	2	4	Sierra R, Oak	110	9	8
Gaetti, Cal	93	10	11	Snyder C, SF	75	7	9
Galarraga, StL	91	16	18	Strawberry, LA	138	25	18
Gant, Atl	109	1	1	Stubbs, Mil	55	5	9
Gibson K, Pit	60	7	12	Tartabull, NYA	115	35	30
Gonzalez Juan, Tex	75	9	12	Tettleton, Det	115	10	9
Greenwell, Bos	61	2	3	Thomas F, ChA	63	15	24
Griffey Jr, Sea	87	16	18	Thompson Ro, SF	68	3	4
Gruber, Tor	96	10	10	Van Slyke, Pit	82	7	9
Hall M, NYA	69	1	1	Vaughn G, Mil	72	3	4
Hayes V, Cal	53	1	2	Walker L, Mon	58	13	22
Henderson D, Oak	84	9	11	Wallach, Mon	68	4	6
Henderson R, Oak	79	3	4	Whitaker, Det	100	1	1
Hrbek, Min	107	13	12	White D, Tor	68	7	10
Incaviglia, Hou	89	17	19	Williams MD, SF	113	13	12
Jackson Darrin, SD	51	3	6	Winfield, Tor	100	13	13
James C, SF	54	5	9	Yount, Mil	69	32	46
Jefferies, KC	52	2	4	**Major League Avg**	**16001**	**1632**	**10**

WHO BEATS OUT THOSE INFIELD HITS? (p. 142)

Both Leagues — Listed Alphabetically
(Minimum 10 infield hits or 100 total hits in 1992)

Player	H	IH	%	Player	H	IH	%	Player	H	IH	%
Alomar R, Tor	177	14	8	Griffey Jr, Sea	174	14	8	Offerman, LA	139	16	12
Anderson Br, Bal	169	12	7	Grissom, Mon	180	34	19	Olerud, Tor	130	12	9
Anthony, Hou	105	8	8	Gruber, Tor	102	12	12	Oliver J, Cin	131	13	10
Baerga, Cle	205	22	11	Gwynn T, SD	165	16	10	Orsulak, Bal	113	10	9
Bagwell, Hou	160	12	8	Hall M, NYA	163	11	7	Ortiz Ju, Cle	61	11	18
Baines, Oak	121	11	9	Hamilton D, Mil	140	11	8	Owen S, Mon	104	17	16
Bass K, NYN	108	10	9	Harper B, Min	154	7	5	Pagnozzi, StL	121	9	7
Bell G, ChA	160	7	4	Harris L, LA	94	18	19	Palmeiro, Tex	163	10	6
Bell Jay, Pit	167	19	11	Hatcher B, Bos	102	17	17	Palmer D, Tex	124	5	4
Belle, Cle	152	7	5	Hayes C, NYA	131	11	8	Pendleton, Atl	199	18	9
Bichette, Mil	111	14	13	Henderson, Oak	112	16	14	Phillips T, Det	167	23	14
Biggio, Hou	170	41	24	Hollins D, Phi	158	22	14	Polonia, Cal	165	23	14
Boggs W, Bos	133	13	10	Howard T, Cle	100	12	12	Puckett, Min	210	28	13
Bonds Ba, Pit	147	7	5	Jackson D, SD	146	16	11	Raines, ChA	162	15	9
Bonilla B, NYN	109	5	5	Javier, Phi	83	14	17	Reed Jody, Bos	136	10	7
Borders, Tor	116	9	8	Jefferies, KC	172	15	9	Reimer, Tex	132	4	3
Bordick, Oak	151	17	11	Johnson L, ChA	158	31	20	Reynolds H, Sea	113	5	4
Brett G, KC	169	9	5	Jordan R, Phi	84	10	12	Ripken C, Bal	160	12	8
Brunansky, Bos	122	5	4	Jose, StL	150	22	15	Roberts B, Cin	172	22	13
Buechele, ChN	137	13	9	Joyner, KC	154	8	5	Rodriguez I, Tex	109	13	12
Buhner, Sea	132	17	13	Justice, Atl	124	6	5	Sandberg, ChN	186	30	16
Butler, LA	171	29	17	Karros, LA	140	10	7	Sanders R, Cin	104	11	11
Caminiti, Hou	149	13	9	Kelly R, NYA	158	10	6	Santiago, SD	97	14	14
Canseco J, Tex	107	10	9	King J, Pit	111	9	8	Sax S, ChA	134	19	14
Carter Joe, Tor	164	12	7	Knoblauch, Min	178	16	9	Seitzer, Mil	146	14	10
Chamberlain, Phi	71	10	14	Kruk, Phi	164	18	11	Sheffield, SD	184	18	10
Clark Je, SD	120	16	13	Lankford, StL	175	7	4	Sierra R, Oak	167	19	11
Clark W, SF	154	8	5	Lansford C, Oak	130	9	7	Smith O, StL	153	24	16
Cole A, Pit	77	13	17	Larkin B, Cin	162	18	11	Snyder C, SF	105	8	8
Cotto, Sea	76	10	13	Larkin G, Min	83	11	13	Sojo, Cal	100	7	7
Curtis C, Cal	114	17	15	Lee Man, Tor	104	16	15	Sorrento, Cle	123	5	4
Dascenzo, ChN	96	17	18	Leius, Min	102	12	12	Stankiewicz, NYA	107	16	15
Daulton, Phi	131	10	8	Lewis D, SF	74	10	14	Steinbach, Oak	122	6	5
Davis C, Min	128	9	7	Lewis M, Cle	109	6	6	Stevens, Cal	69	10	15
Davis G, Bal	110	10	9	Lind, Pit	110	17	15	Stillwell, SD	86	15	17
Dawson, ChN	150	14	9	Listach, Mil	168	23	14	Surhoff B, Mil	121	11	9
Deer, Det	97	11	11	Livingstone, Det	100	5	5	Tartabull, NYA	112	10	9
DeShields, Mon	155	15	10	Lofton, Cle	164	16	10	Tettleton, Det	125	8	6
Devereaux, Bal	180	17	9	Mack S, Min	189	39	21	Thomas F, ChA	185	14	8
DiSarcina, Cal	128	8	6	Maldonado C, Tor	133	7	5	Thompson M, StL	61	11	18
Duncan, Phi	153	26	17	Martinez D, Cin	100	10	10	Thompson R, SF	115	8	7
Dykstra, Phi	104	10	10	Martinez E, Sea	181	14	8	Van Slyke, Pit	199	11	6
Eisenreich, KC	95	14	15	Martinez T, Sea	118	5	4	Vaughn G, Mil	114	9	8
Felder, SF	92	11	12	Mattingly, NYA	184	13	7	Velarde, NYA	112	6	5
Felix, Cal	125	20	16	McGee, SF	141	33	23	Ventura, ChA	167	7	4
Fernandez T, SD	171	20	12	McGriff F, SD	152	15	10	Vizquel, Sea	142	19	13
Fielder, Det	145	5	3	McGwire, Oak	125	3	2	Walker C, NYN	73	11	15
Finley S, Hou	177	21	12	McRae B, KC	119	12	10	Walker L, Mon	159	19	12
Fletcher S, Mil	106	12	11	Merced, Pit	100	8	8	Wallach, Mon	120	8	7
Fryman T, Det	175	14	8	Miller K, KC	118	9	8	Whitaker, Det	126	6	5
Gaetti, Cal	103	11	11	Milligan, Bal	111	7	6	White D, Tor	159	20	13
Gagne, Min	108	12	11	Mitchell Kev, Sea	103	12	12	Whiten, Cle	129	9	7
Gant, Atl	141	16	11	Molitor, Mil	195	25	13	Williams M, SF	120	12	10
Gilkey, StL	116	12	10	Morandini, Phi	112	17	15	Wilson W, Oak	107	12	11
Girardi, ChN	73	15	21	Morris H, Cin	107	6	6	Winfield, Tor	169	15	9
Gladden, Det	106	9	8	Munoz P, Min	113	9	8	Yount, Mil	147	12	8
Gomez Leo, Bal	124	12	10	Murray E, NYN	144	6	4	Zeile, StL	113	7	6
Gonzalez J, Tex	152	16	11	Nixon O, Atl	134	22	16	Zupcic, Bos	108	10	9
Grace, ChN	185	12	6	O'Neill, Cin	122	9	7	**MLB Average**			**10**

WHO ARE THE MOST PRODUCTIVE BASERUNNERS? (p. 144)

Both Leagues — Listed Alphabetically
(Minimum 100 times on base in 1992)

In the chart below, **TOB** = times on base, **R** = Runs Scored, **%** = the percentage of Runs Scored per Times On Base

Player	TOB	R	%	Player	TOB	R	%	Player	TOB	R	%
Alicea, StL	102	24	.235	Canseco J, Tex	167	48	.287	Gant, Atl	220	57	.259
Alomar R, Tor	290	97	.335	Carreon, Det	107	24	.224	Gilkey, StL	168	49	.292
Alomar S, Cle	109	20	.184	Carter Joe, Tor	201	63	.313	Girardi, ChN	108	18	.167
Alou, Mon	126	44	.349	Clark Ja, Bos	122	27	.221	Gladden, Det	152	50	.329
Amaro, Phi	140	36	.257	Clark Je, SD	154	33	.214	Gomez Leo, Bal	201	45	.224
Anderson Br, Bal	273	79	.289	Clark W, SF	230	53	.230	Gonzales R, Cal	146	40	.274
Anthony, Hou	144	26	.181	Clayton, SF	122	27	.221	Gonzalez J, Tex	168	34	.202
Baerga, Cle	265	72	.272	Cole A, Pit	116	44	.379	Gonzalez L, Hou	127	30	.236
Bagwell, Hou	266	69	.259	Cooper S, Bos	138	29	.210	Grace, ChN	270	63	.233
Baines, Oak	183	42	.230	Cotto, Sea	106	37	.349	Grebeck, ChA	117	21	.180
Barberie, Mon	130	25	.192	Curtis C, Cal	182	49	.269	Griffey Jr, Sea	217	56	.258
Bass K, NYN	141	31	.220	Cuyler, Det	101	36	.356	Grissom, Mon	258	85	.329
Bell G, ChA	198	49	.248	Dascenzo, ChN	143	37	.259	Gruber, Tor	146	31	.212
Bell Jay, Pit	236	78	.331	Daulton, Phi	213	53	.249	Gwynn T, SD	224	71	.317
Belle, Cle	205	47	.229	Davis C, Min	214	51	.238	Hall M, NYA	204	52	.255
Belliard, Atl	103	20	.194	Davis E, LA	117	16	.137	Hamilton Dar, Mil	210	62	.295
Benzinger, LA	100	20	.200	Davis G, Bal	153	33	.216	Hansen D, LA	115	24	.209
Bichette, Mil	138	32	.232	Dawson, ChN	200	38	.190	Harper B, Min	201	49	.244
Biggio, Hou	298	90	.302	Deer, Det	132	34	.258	Harris L, LA	136	28	.206
Blankenship, Oak	182	56	.308	DeShields, Mon	216	75	.347	Hatcher B, Bos	138	44	.319
Blauser, Atl	136	47	.346	Devereaux, Bal	227	52	.229	Hayes C, NYA	164	34	.207
Boggs W, Bos	229	55	.240	DiSarcina, Cal	174	45	.259	Hayes V, Cal	115	31	.270
Bonds Ba, Pit	258	75	.291	Doran, Cin	161	40	.248	Henderson, Oak	211	62	.294
Bonilla B, NYN	174	43	.247	Downing, Tex	159	43	.270	Hill G, Cle	112	20	.179
Borders, Tor	165	34	.206	Duncan, Phi	195	63	.323	Hoiles, Bal	132	29	.220
Bordick, Oak	225	59	.262	Dykstra, Phi	153	47	.307	Hollins D, Phi	252	77	.306
Boston, NYN	107	26	.243	Eisenreich, KC	136	29	.213	Howard T, Cle	131	35	.267
Braggs, Cin	110	32	.291	Felder, SF	124	40	.323	Hrbek, Min	160	37	.231
Bream, Atl	150	20	.133	Felix, Cal	178	54	.303	Huson, Tex	130	45	.346
Brett G, KC	222	48	.216	Fernandez T, SD	246	80	.325	Incaviglia, Hou	118	20	.170
Browne, Oak	144	40	.278	Fielder, Det	211	45	.213	Jackson D, SD	179	55	.307
Brunansky, Bos	196	32	.163	Finley S, Hou	259	79	.305	Jacoby, Cle	108	26	.241
Buechele, ChN	216	43	.199	Fletcher S, Mil	164	50	.305	Javier, Phi	143	41	.287
Buhner, Sea	206	44	.214	Fryman T, Det	244	67	.275	Jefferies, KC	233	56	.240
Butler, LA	303	83	.274	Gaetti, Cal	138	29	.210	Johnson H, NYN	146	41	.281
Caminiti, Hou	200	55	.275	Gagne, Min	141	46	.326	Johnson L, ChA	237	64	.270
Candaele, Hou	109	18	.165	Galarraga, StL	100	28	.280	Jordan R, Phi	109	29	.266

Player	TOB	R	%	Player	TOB	R	%	Player	TOB	R	%
Jose, StL	194	48	.247	Morandini, Phi	157	44	.280	Sheffield, SD	224	54	.241
Joyner, KC	226	57	.252	Morris H, Cin	164	35	.213	Sierra R, Oak	214	66	.308
Justice, Atl	200	57	.285	Munoz P, Min	141	32	.227	Slaught, Pit	115	22	.191
Karkovice, ChA	111	26	.234	Murray E, NYN	211	48	.228	Smith O, StL	236	73	.309
Karros, LA	183	43	.235	Newman A, Tex	105	25	.238	Snyder C, SF	129	34	.264
Kelly Pat, NYA	119	31	.261	Nixon O, Atl	203	77	.379	Sojo, Cal	124	30	.242
Kelly R, NYA	233	71	.305	Nokes, NYA	112	20	.179	Sorrento, Cle	168	34	.202
Kent, NYN	115	41	.357	O'Brien P, Sea	126	26	.206	Stankiewicz, NYA	165	50	.303
King J, Pit	149	42	.282	O'Neill, Cin	210	45	.214	Steinbach, Oak	179	36	.201
Knoblauch, Min	294	102	.347	Offerman, LA	225	66	.293	Stevens, Cal	104	18	.173
Kruk, Phi	269	76	.283	Olerud, Tor	204	52	.255	Stillwell, SD	124	33	.266
Lankford, StL	240	67	.279	Oliver J, Cin	178	32	.180	Surhoff B, Mil	183	59	.322
Lansford C, Oak	210	58	.276	Olson Greg, Atl	115	24	.209	Tartabull, NYA	210	47	.224
Larkin B, Cin	245	64	.261	Orsulak, Bal	165	41	.249	Taubensee, Hou	105	18	.171
Larkin G, Min	118	32	.271	Owen S, Mon	163	45	.276	Tettleton, Det	228	50	.219
LaValliere, Pit	125	20	.160	Pagnozzi, StL	162	26	.161	Thomas F, ChA	303	84	.277
Lee Manuel, Tor	172	46	.267	Palmeiro, Tex	236	62	.263	Thompson R, SF	182	40	.220
Leius, Min	154	48	.312	Palmer De, Tex	189	48	.254	Thon, Tex	105	26	.248
Lemke, Atl	175	32	.183	Pecota, NYN	103	26	.252	Valle, Sea	132	30	.227
Lewis D, SF	115	37	.322	Pena T, Bos	142	38	.268	Van Slyke, Pit	264	89	.337
Lewis M, Cle	152	39	.257	Pendleton, Atl	240	77	.321	Vaughn G, Mil	175	54	.309
Lind, Pit	172	38	.221	Phillips T, Det	297	104	.350	Vaughn M, Bos	130	29	.223
Listach, Mil	258	92	.357	Plantier, Bos	134	39	.291	Velarde, NYA	167	50	.299
Livingstone, Det	132	39	.295	Polonia, Cal	238	83	.349	Ventura, ChA	262	69	.263
Lofton, Cle	267	91	.341	Puckett, Min	295	85	.288	Vizquel, Sea	199	49	.246
Macfarlane, KC	141	34	.241	Raines, ChA	264	95	.360	Walker C, NYN	106	22	.208
Mack S, Min	283	85	.300	Randolph, NYN	129	27	.209	Walker L, Mon	201	62	.308
Magadan, NYN	153	30	.196	Reed Jo, Bos	221	61	.276	Wallach, Mon	186	44	.237
Maldonado, Tor	202	44	.218	Reimer, Tex	176	40	.227	Webster M, LA	103	27	.262
Manwaring, SF	136	20	.147	Reynolds H, Sea	180	52	.289	Weiss W, Oak	130	36	.277
Martinez D, Cin	155	44	.284	Ripken B, Bal	108	31	.287	Whitaker, Det	206	58	.282
Martinez E, Sea	246	82	.333	Ripken C, Bal	250	59	.236	White D, Tor	233	81	.348
Martinez T, Sea	158	37	.234	Rivera L, Bos	106	17	.160	Whiten, Cle	216	64	.296
Mattingly, NYA	234	75	.321	Roberts B, Cin	251	88	.351	Wilkerson, KC	111	25	.225
May D, ChN	117	25	.214	Rodriguez I, Tex	141	31	.220	Williams Be, NYA	111	34	.306
McGee, SF	188	55	.293	Sabo, Cin	118	30	.254	Williams MD, SF	166	38	.229
McGriff F, SD	242	44	.182	Sandberg, ChN	263	74	.281	Wilson W, Oak	165	38	.230
McGwire, Oak	197	45	.228	Sanders D, Atl	117	46	.393	Winfield, Tor	258	66	.256
McRae B, KC	188	59	.314	Sanders R, Cin	166	50	.301	Yount, Mil	229	63	.275
McReynolds, KC	164	32	.195	Santiago, SD	129	27	.209	Zeile, StL	187	44	.235
Merced, Pit	161	44	.273	Sax S, ChA	208	70	.337	Zupcic, Bos	153	43	.281
Miller K, KC	185	53	.287	Schofield, NYN	172	48	.279	**MLB Avg**			**.277**
Milligan, Bal	235	60	.255	Scioscia, LA	117	16	.137				
Mitchell Kev, Sea	147	39	.265	Seitzer, Mil	225	69	.307				
Molitor, Mil	294	77	.262	Sharperson, LA	156	45	.288				

WHY IS BARRY BONDS SECOND(ARY) TO NONE? (p. 146)

Both Leagues — Listed Alphabetically
(minimum 350 plate appearances in 1992)

Player, Team	SA	Player, Team	SA	Player, Team	SA	Player, Team	SA
Alomar R, Tor	.340	Fernandez T, SD	.174	Larkin G, Min	.211	Reimer, Tex	.251
Alou, Mon	.287	Fielder, Det	.337	Lee Manuel, Tor	.189	Reynolds H, Sea	.188
Amaro, Phi	.243	Finley S, Hou	.269	Leius, Min	.154	Ripken B, Bal	.133
Anderson Br, Bal	.395	Fletcher S, Mil	.181	Lemke, Atl	.187	Ripken C, Bal	.217
Anthony, Hou	.257	Fryman T, Det	.225	Lewis D, SF	.194	Roberts B, Cin	.278
Baerga, Cle	.209	Gaetti, Cal	.167	Lewis M, Cle	.145	Rodriguez I, Tex	.157
Bagwell, Hou	.321	Gagne, Min	.141	Lind, Pit	.094	Sabo, Cin	.262
Baines, Oak	.257	Gant, Atl	.279	Listach, Mil	.216	Sandberg, ChN	.335
Bass K, NYN	.219	Gilkey, StL	.242	Livingstone, Det	.147	Sanders R, Cin	.340
Bell G, ChA	.217	Gladden, Det	.180	Lofton, Cle	.292	Santiago, SD	.179
Bell Jay, Pit	.209	Gomez Leo, Bal	.293	Macfarlane, KC	.276	Sax S, ChA	.189
Belle, Cle	.316	Gonzales R, Cal	.255	Mack S, Min	.278	Schofield, NYN	.241
Bichette, Mil	.189	Gonzalez J, Tex	.327	Magadan, NYN	.240	Scioscia, LA	.155
Biggio, Hou	.282	Gonzalez L, Hou	.204	Maldonado, Tor	.311	Seitzer, Mil	.206
Blankenship, Oak	.375	Grace, ChN	.250	Manwaring, SF	.178	Sharperson, LA	.243
Blauser, Atl	.329	Griffey Jr, Sea	.313	Martinez D, Cin	.216	Sheffield, SD	.334
Boggs W, Bos	.239	Grissom, Mon	.306	Martinez E, Sea	.322	Sierra R, Oak	.256
Bonds Ba, Pit	.647	Gruber, Tor	.182	Martinez T, Sea	.248	Smith O, StL	.226
Bonilla B, NYN	.336	Gwynn T, SD	.181	Mattingly, NYA	.194	Snyder C, SF	.233
Borders, Tor	.213	Hall M, NYA	.202	May D, ChN	.145	Sojo, Cal	.133
Bordick, Oak	.163	Hamilton D, Mil	.255	McGee, SF	.137	Sorrento, Cle	.279
Bream, Atl	.293	Hansen D, LA	.179	McGriff F, SD	.454	Stankiewicz, NYA	.185
Brett G, KC	.174	Harper B, Min	.153	McGwire, Oak	.507	Steinbach, Oak	.233
Browne, Oak	.201	Harris L, LA	.135	McRae B, KC	.188	Stillwell, SD	.148
Brunansky, Bos	.317	Hatcher B, Bos	.122	McReynolds, KC	.367	Surhoff B, Mil	.177
Buechele, ChN	.206	Hayes C, NYA	.202	Merced, Pit	.269	Tartabull, NYA	.468
Buhner, Sea	.298	Hayes V, Cal	.238	Miller K, KC	.204	Tettleton, Det	.451
Butler, LA	.289	Henderson R, Oak	.508	Milligan, Bal	.348	Thomas F, ChA	.431
Caminiti, Hou	.245	Hill G, Cle	.257	Mitchell Kev, Sea	.233	Thompson Ro, SF	.244
Candaele, Hou	.147	Hoiles, Bal	.403	Molitor, Mil	.302	Valle, Sea	.196
Canseco J, Tex	.353	Hollins D, Phi	.334	Morandini, Phi	.149	Van Slyke, Pit	.290
Carreon, Det	.199	Howard T, Cle	.136	Morris H, Cin	.228	Vaughn G, Mil	.301
Carter Joe, Tor	.304	Hrbek, Min	.353	Munoz P, Min	.177	Vaughn M, Bos	.299
Clark Je, SD	.192	Hundley, NYN	.168	Murray E, NYN	.285	Velarde, NYA	.218
Clark W, SF	.327	Huson, Tex	.267	Nixon O, Atl	.189	Ventura, ChA	.302
Clayton, SF	.178	Incaviglia, Hou	.235	Nokes, NYA	.294	Vizquel, Sea	.128
Cooper S, Bos	.217	Jackson Darri, SD	.206	O'Brien P, Sea	.253	Walker L, Mon	.305
Curtis C, Cal	.286	Javier, Phi	.222	O'Neill, Cin	.288	Wallach, Mon	.201
Dascenzo, ChN	.122	Jefferies, KC	.207	Offerman, LA	.193	Weiss W, Oak	.174
Daulton, Phi	.454	Johnson H, NYN	.320	Olerud, Tor	.321	Whitaker, Det	.366
Davis C, Min	.313	Johnson Lan, ChA	.192	Oliver J, Cin	.188	White D, Tor	.267
Davis G, Bal	.241	Jose, StL	.248	Orsulak, Bal	.166	Whiten, Cle	.256
Dawson, ChN	.242	Joyner, KC	.224	Owen S, Mon	.254	Williams MD, SF	.231
Deer, Det	.435	Justice, Atl	.349	Pagnozzi, StL	.161	Wilson W, Oak	.202
DeShields, Mon	.266	Karkovice, ChA	.260	Palmeiro, Tex	.283	Winfield, Tor	.340
Devereaux, Bal	.259	Karros, LA	.233	Palmer De, Tex	.316	Yount, Mil	.237
DiSarcina, Cal	.097	Kelly Pat, NYA	.236	Pena T, Bos	.124	Zeile, StL	.255
Doran, Cin	.287	Kelly R, NYA	.222	Pendleton, Atl	.225	Zupcic, Bos	.140
Downing, Tex	.347	King J, Pit	.192	Phillips T, Det	.304	**MLB Average**	**.229**
Duncan, Phi	.186	Knoblauch, Min	.243	Plantier, Bos	.238		
Dykstra, Phi	.293	Kruk, Phi	.312	Polonia, Cal	.173		
Eisenreich, KC	.153	Lankford, StL	.338	Puckett, Min	.246		
Felder, SF	.193	Lansford C, Oak	.204	Raines, ChA	.328		
Felix, Cal	.181	Larkin B, Cin	.289	Reed Jo, Bos	.180		

WHY DIDN'T CECIL "GO TO THE MOON" IN 1992? (p. 148)

Both Leagues — 1992 Home Runs Listed by Distance (440+ Feet)

Dir	Dis	Batter	Pitcher	When?	Where?
G	480	Deer, Det	McDonald, Bal	6/11	@Det
H	470	Clark Ja, Bos	Magnante, KC	5/10	@KC
H	460	Thomas F, ChA	Milacki, Bal	5/16	@ChA
H	460	Sheffield, SD	Burkett, SF	8/4	@SD
R	460	Jose, StL	Carter L, SF	9/6	@StL
H	460	Belle, Cle	DeLucia, Sea	9/6	@Cle
F	460	Tartabull, NYA	Reed Ri, KC	9/20	@KC
G	450	Davis E, LA	Henry B, Hou	4/14	@Hou
T	450	Strawberry, LA	Swift, SF	4/26	@SF
E	450	Karkovice, ChA	Ruffin, Mil	5/4	@ChA
N	450	McGriff F, SD	Belinda, Pit	5/16	@Pit
G	450	Belle, Cle	Horsman, Oak	5/25	@Oak
N	450	Maldonado C, Tor	Leary, Sea	6/9	@NYA
N	450	Gonzalez Juan, Tex	Mussina, Bal	7/26	@Bal
P	450	McGriff F, SD	Williams Br, Hou	8/6	@SD
Q	450	Vaughn M, Bos	DeLucia, Sea	9/2	@Sea
K	440	Hoiles, Bal	Smiley, Min	4/29	@Min
H	440	Gonzalez Juan, Tex	Hibbard, ChA	5/1	@ChA
V	440	Justice, Atl	Innis, NYN	5/1	@Atl
P	440	Thomas F, ChA	Mussina, Bal	5/8	@Bal
N	440	Sheffield, SD	Walk, Pit	5/16	@Pit
T	440	Murray E, NYN	Harris Greg W., SD	5/21	@SD
R	440	Stevens, Cal	Sutcliffe, Bal	5/23	@Bal
O	440	Davis C, Min	Lancaster, Det	5/29	@Min
K	440	Milligan, Bal	Valera, Cal	6/1	@Cal
G	440	Gonzalez Juan, Tex	Parker C, Sea	6/8	@Tex
X	440	Merced, Pit	Worrell, StL	6/23	@Pit
I	440	Fielder, Det	Young Ma, Bos	6/23	@Det
G	440	Canseco J, Tex	Smiley, Min	6/27	@Oak
G	440	McGwire, Oak	Smiley, Min	6/27	@Oak
U	440	Reimer, Tex	Leiter M, Det	6/28	@Det
R	440	Williams Be, NYA	Doherty, Det	8/10	@Det
P	440	Fielder, Det	Habyan, NYA	8/10	@Det
Q	440	Reimer, Tex	Appier, KC	8/25	@Tex
P	440	McGriff F, SD	Drabek, Pit	8/28	@SD
F	440	Jackson Darrin, SD	Drabek, Pit	8/28	@SD
L	440	Bonds Ba, Pit	Howell Jay, LA	9/6	@Pit
G	440	Canseco J, Tex	Kiely, Det	9/15	@Det
K	440	Hill G, Cle	Wells D, Tor	9/16	@Tor

WHO'S THE BEST BUNTER? (p. 150)

The following table shows: **SH** = Sac Hits, **FSH** = Failed Sac Hits; and **BH**= Bunt Hits, **FBH** = Failed Bunt Hits

Both Leagues — Listed Alphabetically
(minimum 10 bunts in play)

Batter, Team	SH	FSH	%	BH	FBH	%	Batter, Team	SH	FSH	%	BH	FBH	%
Alomar R, Tor	6	3	67	10	2	83	Lemke, Atl	12	2	86	1	4	20
Anderson Br, Bal	10	2	83	2	3	40	Lewis D, SF	10	3	77	7	12	37
Avery, Atl	9	2	82	1	0	100	Listach, Mil	12	3	80	11	17	39
Baerga, Cle	2	2	50	4	2	67	Lofton, Cle	4	3	57	32	32	50
Barnes B, Mon	6	1	86	2	1	67	Mack S, Min	11	1	92	2	1	67
Belcher T, Cin	7	2	78	0	1	0	Maddux G, ChN	13	4	76	0	0	0
Bell Jay, Pit	19	0	100	0	0	0	Martinez D, Mon	10	0	100	0	0	0
Belliard, Atl	13	0	100	1	3	25	McLemore, Bal	6	0	100	2	5	29
Biggio, Hou	5	1	83	9	11	45	McRae B, KC	7	2	78	13	19	41
Black, SF	10	1	91	0	0	0	Molitor, Mil	4	1	80	5	2	71
Blankenship L, Oak	8	1	89	6	0	100	Morandini, Phi	6	2	75	0	2	0
Blauser, Atl	7	1	87	1	2	33	Morgan M, ChN	11	3	79	0	0	0
Bordick, Oak	14	1	93	2	1	67	Nabholz, Mon	7	4	64	1	0	100
Browne, Oak	16	2	89	5	3	62	Newman A, Tex	8	1	89	5	3	62
Butler, LA	24	2	92	42	28	60	Nixon O, Atl	5	2	71	17	21	45
Candaele, Hou	7	0	100	0	3	0	Offerman, LA	5	1	83	9	9	50
Candiotti, LA	12	3	80	0	0	0	Oliver J, Cin	6	2	75	2	1	67
Cole A, Pit	1	1	50	9	8	53	Pena T, Bos	13	1	93	0	4	0
Coleman, NYN	2	0	100	5	7	42	Pettis, Det	3	1	75	3	4	43
Cormier, StL	10	4	71	0	0	0	Phillips T, Det	5	1	83	4	3	57
Cuyler, Det	8	1	89	11	9	55	Polonia, Cal	8	1	89	7	8	47
Dascenzo, ChN	4	1	80	4	6	40	Portugal, Hou	6	3	67	0	1	0
DeShields, Mon	9	2	82	6	8	43	Puckett, Min	1	1	50	13	4	76
DiSarcina, Cal	5	3	62	2	3	40	Raines, ChA	4	1	80	19	13	59
Drabek, Pit	8	4	67	0	0	0	Randolph, NYN	6	1	86	2	1	67
Felder, SF	3	1	75	6	5	55	Reed Jody, Bos	10	1	91	1	0	100
Fermin, Cle	9	0	100	3	0	100	Reynolds H, Sea	11	2	85	4	10	29
Fernandez S, NYN	7	5	58	0	0	0	Ripken B, Bal	10	3	77	3	2	60
Fernandez T, SD	9	1	90	5	4	56	Rivera L, Bos	5	2	71	3	2	60
Finley S, Hou	16	1	94	10	13	43	Rodriguez I, Tex	7	0	100	5	2	71
Fletcher S, Mil	6	1	86	3	6	33	Rossy, KC	7	2	78	1	1	50
Fox, Oak	6	1	86	5	1	83	Sax S, ChA	12	2	86	2	1	67
Frye, Tex	11	0	100	1	1	50	Schofield, NYN	10	0	100	3	4	43
Gagne, Min	12	3	80	4	5	44	Scioscia, LA	5	1	83	4	0	100
Glavine, Atl	9	4	69	2	1	67	Seitzer, Mil	7	1	87	2	7	22
Grebeck, ChA	10	0	100	0	2	0	Sharperson, LA	5	2	71	3	0	100
Hamilton Dar, Mil	4	1	80	6	8	43	Slaught, Pit	6	0	100	6	3	67
Harnisch, Hou	5	6	45	3	0	100	Smith O, StL	12	0	100	3	2	60
Harris L, LA	6	3	67	3	1	75	Smoltz, Atl	10	0	100	0	0	0
Hershiser, LA	6	4	60	0	0	0	Sojo, Cal	2	0	100	5	5	50
Hill K, Mon	10	2	83	0	0	0	Sosa S, ChN	4	2	67	5	2	71
Howard D, KC	8	2	80	3	5	37	Stankiewicz, NYA	7	1	87	5	5	50
Howard T, Cle	11	1	92	2	3	40	Stillwell, SD	4	0	100	3	3	50
Hundley, NYN	7	1	87	1	4	20	Thurman, KC	6	1	86	1	4	20
Hurst B, SD	9	1	90	0	0	0	Tomlin R, Pit	7	5	58	1	1	50
Huson, Tex	8	1	89	4	1	80	Vaughn G, Mil	2	3	40	3	2	60
Jackson Dan, Pit	9	2	82	0	0	0	Vizcaino, ChN	5	0	100	4	4	50
Jackson Darrin, SD	6	2	75	6	4	60	Vizquel, Sea	9	0	100	5	7	42
Javier, Phi	3	0	100	2	7	22	Webster M, LA	8	1	89	3	5	37
Johnson L, ChA	4	2	67	5	3	62	Weiss W, Oak	11	0	100	2	1	67
Jones J, Hou	9	1	90	0	0	0	Whitaker, Det	5	1	83	4	1	80
Karkovice, ChA	4	3	57	3	3	50	White D, Tor	0	2	0	6	3	67
Kelly Pat, NYA	6	1	86	8	11	42	Wilkerson, KC	7	0	100	2	8	20
King J, Pit	8	1	89	5	2	71	Wilson Tr, SF	7	2	78	0	1	0
Lee Man, Tor	8	1	89	0	1	0	Wilson W, Oak	2	1	67	5	4	56
Lefferts, Bal	9	2	82	1	1	50	Young E, LA	4	0	100	1	5	17
Leibrandt, Atl	8	3	73	1	0	100	MLB Avg.	1665	382	81	695	628	53

DO THEY STEAL WITH A BIG LEAD THESE DAYS? (p. 154)

Stolen Base Attempts/Opportunity Chart — 1992

In this chart, you'll be able to find out how many times a team Attempted to Steal Second Base (**Att**) per Opportunity to Steal Second Base (**O**) given the score (behind by -5 or more through ahead by 5 or more)

American League

Team	-5 Att/O	-4 Att/O	-3 Att/O	-2 Att/O	-1 Att/O	0 Att/O	1 Att/O	2 Att/O	3 Att/O	4 Att/O	5 Att/O
Baltimore	2/109	0/58	4/67	6/110	18/174	47/484	23/200	7/146	10/99	3/56	5/106
Boston	0/78	0/38	3/87	11/140	7/186	30/488	17/204	7/115	4/71	1/41	0/47
California	2/65	1/55	9/86	19/131	33/182	73/390	33/177	34/129	14/78	8/51	3/59
Chicago	4/80	4/52	10/74	15/117	24/185	64/460	20/203	18/135	11/86	8/68	7/105
Cleveland	5/135	4/70	2/96	14/146	20/175	73/416	25/194	18/134	7/76	9/56	1/62
Detroit	0/124	0/86	0/89	4/128	13/211	41/396	10/152	10/119	6/92	10/68	1/137
Kansas City	1/93	0/57	1/73	7/147	19/182	74/445	29/211	17/95	12/78	10/50	4/48
Milwaukee	9/73	4/62	7/76	14/100	33/164	95/438	55/195	37/125	21/88	24/84	20/156
Minnesota	2/74	1/80	3/85	4/102	21/162	71/446	31/217	16/142	19/105	10/70	4/105
New York	1/114	3/53	3/98	5/171	10/191	31/358	16/142	8/118	12/109	3/75	4/109
Oakland	6/88	7/70	9/66	10/131	21/207	43/442	23/193	15/143	15/120	7/72	2/77
Seattle	3/121	1/59	9/114	8/151	8/165	33/337	31/219	16/116	6/58	7/51	7/109
Texas	1/99	3/58	4/82	4/123	12/151	31/415	23/199	12/146	12/78	6/62	1/74
Toronto	4/122	3/47	5/71	13/119	26/177	29/344	17/214	10/134	11/105	6/47	12/154
AL Att%	3	4	6	7	11	13	13	13	13	13	5

National League

Team	-5 Att/O	-4 Att/O	-3 Att/O	-2 Att/O	-1 Att/O	0 Att/O	1 Att/O	2 Att/O	3 Att/O	4 Att/O	5 Att/O
Atlanta	3/72	0/37	4/53	5/59	16/187	59/374	29/185	23/149	19/111	6/83	3/119
Chicago	0/74	0/60	1/80	2/142	9/158	53/494	24/225	15/139	8/87	7/43	3/76
Cincinnati	1/63	3/55	7/90	11/116	15/175	64/384	24/208	18/138	16/107	7/74	2/104
Houston	4/120	4/59	7/94	10/94	20/176	64/454	17/170	22/131	10/73	4/35	2/59
Los Angeles	1/85	2/61	8/87	12/156	23/230	67/431	16/152	24/133	10/74	10/55	3/43
Montreal	3/65	1/52	7/80	12/122	21/179	73/413	33/160	25/131	24/104	15/63	5/81
New York	5/99	6/60	5/67	15/110	13/223	54/402	15/132	14/97	12/72	8/47	7/59
Philadelphia	3/111	2/69	1/135	10/145	15/201	54/346	28/223	8/82	8/80	9/46	1/101
Pittsburgh	0/43	1/49	6/66	12/94	22/199	46/450	21/216	10/128	12/107	7/45	3/81
St. Louis	8/68	7/32	13/99	27/131	50/245	109/437	38/187	17/91	14/66	10/51	6/61
San Diego	3/73	4/76	3/96	5/99	5/177	33/374	22/186	16/126	8/68	3/49	4/74
San Francisco	0/94	1/70	7/106	4/115	27/192	62/443	15/142	22/116	15/75	6/31	1/36
NL Att%	3	5	7	9	10	15	13	15	15	15	4

Stolen Bases/Caught Stealing by Score Chart — 1992

In this chart, you'll be able to find out how many times a team Stole Any Base (S) or were Caught Stealing Any Base (C) given the score (behind by -5 or more through ahead by 5 or more)

American League

Team	-5 S/C	-4 S/C	-3 S/C	-2 S/C	-1 S/C	0 S/C	1 S/C	2 S/C	3 S/C	4 S/C	5 S/C
Baltimore	1/1	0/0	3/1	4/2	14/6	39/15	14/9	4/3	5/7	2/2	3/2
Boston	0/0	0/0	0/3	5/6	6/2	11/20	13/12	6/3	3/1	0/1	0/0
California	2/0	1/1	6/4	16/7	19/18	57/26	20/15	15/20	13/6	8/4	3/0
Chicago	4/0	4/0	7/3	14/3	21/6	51/24	19/7	17/3	10/4	8/3	5/4
Cleveland	6/0	4/0	2/0	17/1	16/8	61/25	15/14	11/12	3/4	8/3	1/0
Detroit	0/0	0/0	0/0	6/0	7/7	31/17	6/6	7/7	1/5	8/2	0/1
Kansas City	0/1	0/1	1/0	7/2	15/6	58/29	19/14	10/7	9/6	8/4	4/1
Milwaukee	8/1	4/0	9/1	13/7	30/6	68/38	40/26	33/14	15/8	22/6	14/8
Minnesota	2/0	1/0	1/2	2/2	15/9	47/27	14/21	13/6	13/7	10/0	5/0
New York	2/0	3/0	4/0	4/3	8/4	23/11	11/6	10/4	7/7	4/0	2/2
Oakland	4/2	6/1	12/1	11/1	12/10	41/17	20/13	11/7	16/4	9/2	1/1
Seattle	3/0	1/0	7/3	8/2	4/5	22/15	27/13	14/6	6/3	2/5	6/3
Texas	1/0	3/0	4/0	3/1	10/2	21/15	20/8	8/8	8/5	2/5	1/0
Toronto	7/0	3/0	9/2	12/3	20/8	26/8	16/7	11/3	11/3	5/2	9/3
AL SB%	**89**	**91**	**76**	**75**	**67**	**66**	**60**	**62**	**63**	**71**	**68**

National League

Team	-5 S/C	-4 S/C	-3 S/C	-2 S/C	-1 S/C	0 S/C	1 S/C	2 S/C	3 S/C	4 S/C	5 S/C
Atlanta	3/0	0/0	3/1	3/3	14/7	47/17	21/12	15/9	12/9	5/1	3/1
Chicago	0/0	0/0	1/0	1/1	8/2	34/20	14/12	9/8	6/2	3/4	1/2
Cincinnati	1/0	3/0	8/0	7/6	10/5	49/21	16/11	12/9	10/11	8/1	1/1
Houston	6/0	4/0	6/2	16/0	17/7	45/27	13/5	18/8	7/4	3/1	4/0
Los Angeles	1/0	4/0	6/3	9/5	27/7	51/31	8/11	20/11	7/5	7/4	2/1
Montreal	3/0	1/0	8/0	12/2	20/7	65/24	26/13	17/8	27/4	13/4	4/1
New York	5/0	6/0	5/0	16/2	9/6	45/19	13/6	14/6	7/5	5/4	4/4
Philadelphia	3/0	2/0	1/0	9/2	12/4	51/9	24/11	9/0	7/3	7/2	2/0
Pittsburgh	0/0	2/0	6/1	12/1	12/11	34/20	17/9	10/1	10/6	4/3	3/1
St. Louis	8/0	7/0	15/2	20/8	39/15	64/50	24/19	12/8	10/7	4/7	5/2
San Diego	3/0	2/2	2/1	4/2	3/2	23/14	14/13	8/9	6/4	2/3	2/2
San Francisco	0/0	1/1	6/2	4/1	20/9	41/25	9/9	15/8	11/5	4/4	1/0
NL SB%	**100**	**91**	**85**	**77**	**70**	**66**	**60**	**65**	**65**	**63**	**68**

How Will Winfield Do In '93? (p. 156)

Most Runs Created in a Season by Players 40 or Older
(Minimum 50 Runs Created)

Player	Year	Age	RC	AB	R	H	HR	RBI	SB	BB	Avg
Rice, Sam	1930	40	111.3	593	121	207	1	73	13	55	.349
Winfield, Dave	1992	40	109.9	583	92	169	26	108	2	82	.290
Cobb, Ty	1927	40	104.1	490	104	175	5	93	22	67	.357
Evans, Darrell	1987	40	103.2	499	90	128	34	99	6	100	.257
Mays, Willie	1971	40	98.0	417	82	113	18	61	23	112	.271
Williams, Ted	1960	41	94.8	310	56	98	29	72	1	75	.316
Anson, Cap	1894	42	94.3	340	82	132	5	99	17	40	.388
Musial, Stan	1962	41	93.8	433	57	143	19	82	3	64	.330
Anson, Cap	1895	43	90.4	474	87	159	2	91	12	55	.335
Appling, Luke	1949	42	89.6	492	82	148	5	58	7	121	.301
Appling, Luke	1948	41	81.6	497	63	156	0	47	10	94	.314
Appling, Luke	1947	40	81.5	503	67	154	8	49	8	64	.306
Wagner, Honus	1915	41	81.0	566	68	155	6	78	22	39	.274
Fisk, Carlton	1990	42	78.6	452	65	129	18	65	7	61	.285
Anson, Cap	1896	44	77.9	402	72	133	2	90	24	49	.331
Rose, Pete	1982	41	75.4	634	80	172	3	54	8	66	.271
Downing, Brian	1991	40	72.7	407	76	113	17	49	1	58	.278
Yastrzemski, Carl	1982	42	71.6	459	53	126	16	72	0	59	.275
Nettles, Graig	1985	40	70.1	440	66	115	15	61	0	72	.261
Musial, Stan	1961	40	69.0	372	46	107	15	70	0	52	.288
Jackson, Reggie	1986	40	68.2	419	65	101	18	58	1	92	.241
Sauer, Hank	1957	40	67.2	378	46	98	26	76	1	49	.259
Rose, Pete	1981	40	67.1	431	73	140	0	33	4	46	.325
Cramer, Doc	1945	40	65.1	541	62	149	6	58	2	35	.275
Anson, Cap	1897	45	65.1	424	67	121	3	75	11	60	.285
Rice, Sam	1931	41	60.8	413	81	128	0	42	6	35	.310
Fisk, Carlton	1989	41	60.5	375	47	110	13	68	1	36	.293
Downing, Brian	1992	41	60.5	320	53	89	10	39	1	62	.278
Wagner, Honus	1914	40	59.9	552	60	139	1	50	23	51	.252
Cooney, Johnny	1941	40	58.9	442	52	141	0	29	3	27	.319
Rose, Pete	1985	44	58.7	405	60	107	2	46	8	86	.264
Cobb, Ty	1928	41	58.2	353	54	114	1	40	5	34	.323
Yastrzemski, Carl	1980	40	58.2	364	49	100	15	50	0	44	.275
Wagner, Honus	1916	42	57.8	432	45	124	1	39	11	34	.287
Aaron, Hank	1974	40	57.7	340	47	91	20	69	1	39	.268
Vernon, Mickey	1958	40	57.6	355	49	104	8	55	0	44	.293
Evans, Darrell	1988	41	56.8	437	48	91	22	64	1	84	.208
Aaron, Hank	1975	41	56.3	465	45	109	12	60	0	70	.234
Yastrzemski, Carl	1983	43	55.1	380	38	101	10	56	0	54	.266
Brock, Lou	1979	40	54.0	405	56	123	5	38	21	23	.304
Lajoie, Nap	1915	40	53.4	490	40	137	1	61	10	11	.280
Ryan, Jimmy	1903	40	52.4	437	42	109	7	46	9	17	.249
Fisk, Carlton	1988	40	52.3	253	37	70	19	50	0	37	.277
Lopes, Davey	1985	40	52.3	275	52	78	11	44	47	46	.284
Parker, Dave	1991	40	52.1	502	47	120	11	59	3	33	.239
Fisk, Carlton	1991	43	51.7	460	42	111	18	74	1	32	.241
Maranville, Rabbit	1932	40	51.1	571	67	134	0	37	4	46	.235
Morgan, Joe	1984	40	50.9	365	50	89	6	43	8	66	.244
Rice, Sam	1932	42	50.2	288	58	93	1	34	7	32	.323

ARE HIGH-PITCH OUTINGS DANGEROUS? (p. 162)

Most Pitches In a Game By Starting Pitchers in 1992

Date	Opp	Score	Pitcher	W/L	IP	H	R	ER	BB	SO	#Pit	Time
7/17	SF	1- 0	Cone, Tor	W	9.0	6	0	0	4	13	166	2:44:00
9/27	@Tex	2- 3	Johnson R, Sea	-	8.0	6	2	2	4	18	160	3:10:00
8/15	Min	3- 2	Johnson R, Sea	W	9.0	4	2	2	7	13	159	3:05:00
6/21	@Tex	2- 3	Clemens, Bos	L	6.2	5	3	3	6	4	151	3:07:00
8/26	Oak	2- 1	Viola, Bos	W	10.0	6	1	1	3	4	151	3:04:00
6/4	Det	2- 6	Sanderson, NYA	L	7.1	8	6	6	6	7	148	3:33:00
7/8	@Bal	3- 5	Hough, ChA	L	7.2	8	5	4	6	5	148	2:49:00
10/2	Tex	6- 3	Langston, Cal	W	9.0	6	3	0	1	13	147	2:36:00
7/9	@NYA	6- 7	Johnson R, Sea	L	7.0	5	7	1	9	3	146	3:04:00
7/31	StL	3- 2	Wakefield, Pit	W	9.0	6	2	0	5	10	146	2:17:00
9/13	@Bal	3- 1	Eldred, Mil	W	9.0	4	1	1	1	12	146	2:58:00
4/17	@Mon	10- 2	Cone, Tor	W	9.0	7	2	2	5	3	145	3:22:00
7/26	NYA	8- 5	Johnson R, Sea	W	6.0	7	4	4	6	8	145	3:04:00
9/5	@Cle	4- 5	Johnson R, Sea	-	7.2	7	4	4	7	8	145	2:58:00
4/6	@Det	4- 2	Morris Ja, Tor	W	9.0	5	2	2	3	7	144	2:46:00
5/4	Min	1- 6	Clemens, Bos	L	9.0	12	6	6	3	6	144	2:46:00
7/3	Phi	2- 0	Astacio, LA	W	9.0	3	0	0	4	10	144	2:33:00
7/7	Oak	3- 2	Ritz, Det	W	6.2	4	2	2	5	3	144	3:10:00
8/5	NYN	6- 2	Wakefield, Pit	W	8.0	7	2	2	4	7	144	2:39:00
8/7	@Cal	1- 3	McDowell J, ChA	L	8.0	11	3	2	5	6	144	2:49:00
8/28	Bos	1- 7	Finley C, Cal	L	7.0	6	5	3	6	7	144	3:26:00

Fewest Pitches In a Game By Starting Pitchers in 1992

Date	Opp	Score	Pitcher	W/L	IP	H	R	ER	BB	SO	#Pit	Time
9/18	@Pit	2- 5	Mulholland, Phi	L	5.0	8	5	5	0	3	80	1:42:00
10/2	@KC	5- 1	Smiley, Min	W	9.0	4	1	1	0	4	80	2:08:00
5/26	KC	8- 1	Gullickson, Det	W	9.0	6	1	1	0	0	84	2:11:00
6/23	SF	7- 0	Glavine, Atl	W	9.0	5	0	0	0	4	84	2:56:00
4/17	@ChA	7- 0	Krueger, Mon	W	9.0	5	0	0	0	5	85	2:21:00
7/27	@Cle	4- 0	Navarro, Mil	W	9.0	3	0	0	0	5	85	2:17:00
5/30	SD	5- 1	Tewksbury, StL	W	9.0	4	1	1	0	2	86	2:22:00
6/30	KC	6- 0	Sanderson, NYA	W	9.0	4	0	0	0	4	86	2:15:00
9/12	NYN	4- 1	Martinez De, Mon	W	9.0	5	1	1	1	4	88	2:23:00
9/24	Cal	4- 0	Bosio, Mil	W	9.0	5	0	0	0	9	88	2:16:00
10/3	Pit	2- 1	Gooden, NYN	W	9.0	4	1	1	1	3	88	2:06:00
10/2	@StL	1- 2	Schilling, Phi	L	8.0	4	2	2	0	2	89	2:04:00
6/12	NYA	3- 0	Nagy, Cle	W	9.0	5	0	0	0	5	90	2:00:00
7/9	@SD	1- 3	Mulholland, Phi	L	8.0	8	3	3	0	6	90	2:29:00
6/6	@SD	5- 1	Glavine, Atl	W	9.0	2	1	1	2	7	92	2:25:00
4/24	@Bos	1- 3	Guzman Jos, Tex	L	5.0	8	3	3	2	5	93	1:55:00
6/1	SD	6- 1	Maddux G, ChN	W	9.0	4	1	1	0	6	93	2:13:00
6/20	@NYN	6- 1	Tewksbury, StL	W	9.0	5	1	1	0	4	93	2:27:00
7/30	@Min	5- 3	Bosio, Mil	W	9.0	7	3	3	0	1	93	2:41:00
5/3	@SD	7- 1	Tewksbury, StL	W	9.0	6	1	1	0	4	94	2:15:00
6/5	Cal	7- 1	Bosio, Mil	W	9.0	5	1	1	0	4	94	2:39:00
7/11	Cle	5- 1	Brown Kevin, Tex	W	9.0	6	1	1	2	3	94	2:09:00
9/10	@ChA	8- 0	Haas D, Det	W	9.0	4	0	0	0	2	94	2:37:00
5/7	@StL	2- 0	Swift, SF	W	9.0	4	0	0	1	4	95	2:04:00
9/9	NYN	2- 1	Schilling, Phi	W	9.0	1	1	1	0	8	95	2:07:00

WHICH RELIEVERS TIRE EASILY? (p. 164)

Both Leagues — Listed Alphabetically
(Minimum 25 games in relief in 1992)

Pitcher	1-15	16-30	31+	Pitcher	1-15	16-30	31+	Pitcher	1-15	16-30	31+
Agosto, Sea	.365	.250	.306	Guthrie, Min	.209	.259	.139	Olin, Cle	.249	.253	.240
Aguilera, Min	.238	.200	.750	Habyan, NYA	.286	.329	.269	Olson G, Bal	.222	.167	.333
Alvarez W, ChA	.198	.338	.281	Harris Greg, Bos	.197	.284	.176	Orosco, Mil	.234	.222	.000
Andersen, SD	.185	.235	.333	Hartley, Phi	.274	.228	.111	Osuna, Hou	.209	.276	.444
Assenm'ch'r, Ch	.242	.333	.500	Harvey, Cal	.228	.160	.000	Pall, ChA	.291	.258	.258
Austin, Mil	.157	.259	.222	Heaton, Mil	.280	.277	.200	Parrett, Oak	.223	.203	.302
Ayrault, Phi	.225	.196	.167	Henke, Tor	.203	.167	.000	Patterson B, Pit	.265	.200	.214
Bailes, Cal	.375	.286	.387	Henneman, Det	.266	.242	.154	Patterson K, Ch	.313	.196	.263
Bankhead, Cin	.242	.145	.300	Henry Do, Mil	.262	.240	.222	Pena A, Atl	.211	.333	.750
Bannister F, Tex	.247	.349	.267	Henry Dw, Cin	.186	.200	.257	Perez Mi, StL	.188	.264	.235
Beck, SF	.150	.250	.286	Hentgen, Tor	.275	.218	.259	Plesac, Mil	.274	.167	.211
Belinda, Pit	.217	.194	.462	HernandezJ, SD	.291	.262	.500	Plunk, Cle	.242	.207	.233
Berenguer, KC	.243	.282	.254	HernandezR, Ch	.193	.167	.171	Powell D, Sea	.198	.339	.206
Boever, Hou	.225	.277	.321	HernandezX, Ho	.213	.179	.172	Power, Cle	.234	.287	.218
Bolton, Cin	.314	.197	.305	Hickerson, SF	.195	.295	.323	Quantrill, Bos	.247	.317	.333
Brantley J, SF	.209	.215	.195	Holmes, Mil	.215	.250	.333	Radinsky, ChA	.264	.167	.400
Bullinger, ChN	.239	.290	.201	Honeycutt, Oak	.275	.182	.444	Reardon, Atl	.317	.175	.000
Burke, NYA	.339	.176	.231	Horsman, Oak	.266	.214	.000	Righetti, SF	.270	.241	.304
Burns T, Tex	.267	.240	.243	Howell Jay, LA	.211	.298	.125	Ritchie, Phi	.259	.414	.250
Cadaret, NYA	.296	.179	.280	Innis, NYN	.251	.330	.125	Robinson J, Ch	.270	.253	.261
Campbell, Oak	.289	.250	.258	Jackson M, SF	.266	.208	.385	Rodriguez R, SD	.226	.226	.246
Candelaria, LA	.226	.143	.000	Jones Ba, NYN	.301	.324	.333	Rogers Ken, Tex	.265	.231	.444
Carpenter, StL	.242	.190	.071	Jones Ca, Sea	.196	.250	.250	Rojas, Mon	.183	.213	.250
Charlton, Cin	.257	.277	.200	Jones D, Hou	.256	.198	.200	Ruskin, Cin	.276	.318	.000
Clements, Bal	.268	.190	.538	Kiely, Det	.234	.241	.161	Russell Je, Oak	.200	.305	.143
Corsi, Oak	.330	.191	.154	Kipper, Min	.299	.245	.211	Sampen, KC	.265	.267	.314
Crews, LA	.262	.357	.371	Knudsen, Det	.266	.250	.281	Scanlan, ChN	.228	.247	.263
Crim, Cal	.299	.290	.281	Lancaster, Det	.285	.280	.316	Schooler, Sea	.267	.304	.250
Darwin, Bos	.266	.205	.270	Leach T, ChA	.214	.217	.214	Scott Ti, SD	.248	.278	.444
Davis Sto, Bal	.232	.220	.291	Lilliquist, Cle	.206	.095	.286	Shifflett, KC	.299	.218	.320
Dibble, Cin	.175	.227	.250	MacDonald, Tor	.226	.286	.349	Slocumb, ChN	.329	.348	.435
Doherty, Det	.273	.300	.292	Maddux M, SD	.253	.193	.250	Smith Le, StL	.213	.250	.200
Eckersley, Oak	.226	.156	.250	Magnante, KC	.315	.353	.317	Stanton M, Atl	.267	.208	.000
Edens, Min	.305	.133	.241	Mason R, Pit	.215	.226	.439	Swan R, Sea	.271	.226	.272
Eichhorn, Tor	.245	.253	.364	Mathews T, Tex	.290	.362	.125	Thigpen, ChA	.284	.215	.800
Farr S, NYA	.193	.194	.000	McClure, StL	.261	.241	.308	Timlin, Tor	.256	.283	.289
Fassero, Mon	.269	.242	.115	McDowell R, LA	.296	.302	.400	Valdez S, Mon	.171	.200	.250
Fetters, Mil	.170	.213	.222	McElroy, ChN	.231	.260	.176	Ward D, Tor	.232	.170	.125
Flanagan, Bal	.348	.282	.400	Meacham R, KC	.224	.230	.273	Wayne, Min	.234	.255	.391
Fossas, Bos	.299	.143	.000	Melendez J, SD	.268	.186	.283	Wells D, Tor	.273	.314	.286
Foster S, Cin	.272	.291	.262	Mercker, Atl	.155	.273	.313	Wetteland, Mon	.222	.208	.150
Franco, NY	.215	.100	1.00	Mills A, Bal	.179	.301	.191	Whitehurst, NYN	.286	.253	.250
Freeman M, Atl	.235	.286	.286	Monteleone, NY	.275	.157	.259	Wickander, Cle	.330	.146	.167
Frey, Cal	.261	.190	.143	Montgomery, KC	.215	.186	.182	Williams Mit, Phi	.242	.242	.229
Frohwirth, Bal	.292	.193	.210	Munoz M, Det	.237	.303	.182	Willis C, Min	.235	.269	.250
Gibson P, NYN	.287	.262	.313	Murphy R, Hou	.276	.229	.000	Wilson S, LA	.320	.254	.196
Gordon T, KC	.177	.271	.296	Myers R, SD	.298	.253	.217	Wohlers, Atl	.256	.194	.000
Gossage, Oak	.247	.205	.167	Neagle, Pit	.234	.270	.245	Worrell, StL	.217	.143	.000
Gott, LA	.238	.220	.071	Nelson G, Oak	.306	.400	.320	Young A, NYN	.262	.250	.320
Grahe, Cal	.221	.217	.288	Nelson Je, Sea	.272	.176	.200				
Guetterman, NY	.303	.406	.364	Nunez E, Tex	.263	.270	.286				

WHICH STARTING STAFFS STAR, AND WHICH RELIEF STAFFS REEK? (p. 167)

American League Starters

Team	ERA	W	L	IP	H	R	ER	HR	BB	K	BA
Baltimore	4.11	66	59	1034.00	1042	495	472	106	321	584	.263
Boston	3.65	51	63	1028.67	985	480	417	77	353	662	.252
California	3.80	47	68	1057.33	1058	483	446	91	377	662	.265
Chicago	4.03	60	54	1057.33	1032	523	473	98	374	559	.256
Cleveland	4.55	44	65	955.33	1042	541	483	107	349	557	.279
Detroit	5.08	52	63	901.67	1025	542	509	115	338	396	.290
Kansas City	4.15	47	59	896.33	927	443	413	69	313	473	.269
Milwaukee	3.67	68	52	1071.67	1035	470	437	101	273	517	.253
Minnesota	3.86	65	51	1020.00	987	469	438	85	333	605	.257
New York	4.30	54	66	1032.33	1042	546	493	95	432	597	.266
Oakland	3.88	67	52	962.67	939	467	415	94	411	497	.258
Seattle	4.58	50	70	975.67	1008	553	497	81	420	613	.268
Texas	3.92	59	61	1031.67	1027	512	449	66	398	737	.263
Toronto	4.09	75	54	1037.67	972	510	472	96	379	638	.249

National League Starters

Team	ERA	W	L	IP	H	R	ER	HR	BB	K	BA
Atlanta	2.95	72	42	1066.00	958	396	349	53	323	688	.240
Chicago	3.21	59	56	1028.00	896	417	367	72	354	599	.237
Cincinnati	3.55	63	54	1008.33	994	429	398	78	292	639	.261
Houston	4.23	42	60	924.33	923	472	434	84	340	586	.262
Los Angeles	3.35	48	70	1036.33	975	454	386	60	376	687	.250
Montreal	3.23	65	55	998.67	871	397	358	66	347	652	.235
New York	3.52	49	59	1031.67	968	444	404	67	327	792	.249
Philadelphia	4.10	45	64	1005.67	980	500	458	82	323	552	.256
Pittsburgh	3.25	59	47	1010.00	977	403	365	56	263	529	.257
St. Louis	3.58	50	51	1007.33	1011	438	401	85	235	547	.262
San Diego	3.83	57	58	994.67	1017	462	423	84	278	605	.267
San Francisco	3.91	46	63	925.00	918	447	402	90	317	487	.262

American League Relievers

Team	ERA	W	L	IP	H	R	ER	HR	BB	K	BA
Baltimore	3.03	23	14	430.00	377	161	145	18	197	262	.241
Boston	3.60	22	26	420.00	418	189	168	30	182	281	.264
California	3.96	25	22	388.67	391	188	171	39	155	226	.263
Chicago	3.34	26	22	404.33	368	167	150	25	176	251	.243
Cleveland	3.31	32	21	514.67	465	205	189	52	217	333	.247
Detroit	3.83	23	24	534.00	509	252	227	40	226	297	.253
Kansas City	3.27	25	31	551.00	499	224	200	37	199	361	.243
Milwaukee	2.78	24	18	385.33	309	134	119	26	162	276	.224
Minnesota	3.37	25	21	433.00	404	184	162	36	146	318	.248
New York	4.03	22	20	420.33	411	200	188	34	180	254	.257
Oakland	3.42	29	14	484.33	457	205	184	35	190	346	.252
Seattle	4.47	14	28	469.33	459	246	233	48	241	281	.261
Texas	4.53	18	24	428.67	444	241	216	47	200	297	.267
Toronto	3.46	21	12	403.00	374	172	155	28	162	316	.245

National League Relievers

Team	ERA	W	L	IP	H	R	ER	HR	BB	K	BA
Atlanta	3.68	26	22	394.00	363	173	161	36	166	260	.247
Chicago	3.82	19	28	441.00	441	207	187	35	221	302	.266
Cincinnati	3.26	27	18	441.33	368	180	160	31	178	421	.229
Houston	2.89	39	21	535.00	463	196	172	30	199	392	.234
Los Angeles	3.56	15	29	401.67	426	182	159	22	177	294	.274
Montreal	3.30	22	20	469.33	425	184	172	26	178	362	.243
New York	4.06	23	31	415.00	436	209	187	31	155	233	.274
Philadelphia	4.20	25	28	422.33	407	217	197	31	226	299	.257
Pittsburgh	3.56	37	19	469.67	433	192	186	45	192	315	.247
St. Louis	2.95	33	28	472.67	394	166	155	33	165	295	.228
San Diego	3.05	25	22	466.67	427	174	158	27	161	366	.247
San Francisco	3.09	26	27	536.00	467	200	184	38	185	440	.238

WHICH PITCHERS ARE HOT WHEN IT'S COLD? (p. 170)

(Active pitchers with 25+ IP in <50 degree weather, 1989-1992)

Pitcher	G	W	L	IP	ER	ERA	Opp ERA	Other Games
Tim Leary	4	3	1	32.0	4	1.13	2.57	4.30
Dave Stewart	5	4	1	37.2	5	1.19	2.74	3.61
Jose Guzman	4	3	1	28.0	4	1.29	3.00	3.62
Alex Fernandez	4	3	0	31.1	5	1.44	4.77	4.48
Dave Stieb	9	7	0	69.1	13	1.69	4.62	3.51
Roger Clemens	14	10	3	114.1	22	1.73	3.37	2.71
Charles Nagy	5	4	0	38.2	9	2.10	6.00	3.85
John Smiley	8	5	3	56.0	14	2.25	3.26	3.38
Dwight Gooden	4	3	0	27.0	7	2.33	5.03	3.51
John Candelaria	6	3	1	38.1	10	2.35	3.35	3.90
Frank Viola	5	3	1	33.1	9	2.43	3.92	3.29
Greg Maddux	13	8	4	103.0	29	2.53	3.58	3.05
Danny Jackson	6	1	1	38.1	11	2.58	3.52	4.03
Greg Harris	12	1	2	27.2	8	2.60	3.29	3.39
Jack McDowell	8	5	1	61.0	18	2.66	6.75	3.60
Bill Wegman	7	3	2	44.0	13	2.66	4.13	3.73
Greg Swindell	10	4	2	74.2	23	2.77	3.58	3.47
Jimmy Key	6	4	2	41.1	13	2.83	3.06	3.62
Tom Candiotti	8	6	2	62.2	20	2.87	6.31	3.14
Neal Heaton	10	4	1	40.0	13	2.93	5.84	3.88
Scott Bailes	7	1	2	27.2	9	2.93	4.13	5.17
Greg Cadaret	13	1	2	27.2	9	2.93	4.27	3.91
Rick Sutcliffe	4	3	1	33.1	11	2.97	5.82	4.11
Greg Hibbard	5	3	1	33.0	11	3.00	2.74	3.82
Bret Saberhagen	7	3	2	44.2	15	3.02	3.30	3.09
Eric King	6	3	1	32.2	11	3.03	4.56	3.95
Kirk McCaskill	6	3	2	37.0	13	3.16	4.25	3.77
Bruce Ruffin	8	2	1	36.1	13	3.22	2.28	4.86
Mike Flanagan	9	1	2	38.1	14	3.29	5.20	4.12
Chris Bosio	16	9	5	112.0	42	3.38	3.69	3.39
Charlie Leibrandt	7	2	5	45.0	17	3.40	3.63	3.61
Bob Walk	9	3	3	52.2	20	3.42	3.35	3.52
Duane Ward	21	0	4	26.2	11	3.71	3.88	3.06
Mike Morgan	4	0	2	31.1	13	3.73	1.64	3.09
Mike Bielecki	8	2	1	36.0	15	3.75	4.07	3.87
Melido Perez	5	2	1	31.0	13	3.77	3.61	3.86
Bobby Witt	6	4	1	38.0	16	3.79	5.14	4.38
Don Carman	6	2	2	26.0	11	3.81	4.19	4.70
Bud Black	14	3	5	67.0	29	3.90	2.36	3.82
Nolan Ryan	5	3	1	33.2	15	4.01	3.60	3.33
Jose DeLeon	7	1	4	40.1	18	4.02	2.97	3.56
Walt Terrell	5	0	2	31.0	14	4.06	2.05	4.57
Zane Smith	7	3	3	41.0	19	4.17	6.86	3.20
Mark Gubicza	8	2	3	48.1	23	4.28	2.96	3.55
Paul Gibson	13	2	1	29.0	15	4.66	4.66	4.02
Mike Boddicker	11	4	4	50.0	26	4.68	4.59	3.75
Les Lancaster	19	2	2	40.2	22	4.87	3.26	3.89
Charlie Hough	4	1	1	25.2	14	4.91	3.41	3.88
Bryn Smith	5	3	1	31.0	17	4.94	5.00	3.39
Chuck Crim	19	1	2	29.0	16	4.97	3.32	3.64
Jeff M. Robinson	7	2	1	38.0	21	4.97	5.70	4.64
Jack Armstrong	5	1	3	29.2	17	5.16	3.77	4.59
Scott Sanderson	7	2	3	43.0	25	5.23	2.71	4.10
Jack Morris	10	4	5	63.1	38	5.40	3.52	4.04
Jaime Navarro	6	3	1	35.2	22	5.55	5.67	3.62
Sid Fernandez	5	0	3	26.2	18	6.08	2.81	2.88
Todd Stottlemyre	11	1	4	37.2	27	6.45	3.69	4.21
Frank Tanana	8	1	5	44.1	32	6.50	3.73	4.08
MLB Average	333			5960.1	2398	3.62		3.80

WHAT KIND OF PITCHER HAS TROUBLE IN THE FIRST? (p. 172)

Both Leagues — Listed Alphabetically
(Minimum 10 Games Started)

Pitcher	IP	ERA	Pitcher	IP	ERA	Pitcher	IP	ERA
Abbott J, Cal	29.0	2.48	Greene T, Phi	12.0	6.75	Otto, Cle	16.0	5.06
Abbott K, Phi	19.0	6.63	Gross Ke, LA	30.0	4.80	Pavlik, Tex	10.1	6.97
Aldred, Det	13.0	5.54	Gubicza, KC	18.0	1.00	Perez M, NYA	33.0	4.64
Appier, KC	30.0	2.70	Gullickson, Det	33.0	5.73	Pichardo, KC	24.0	3.38
Aquino, KC	13.0	5.54	Guzman Jose, Tex	33.0	3.27	Portugal, Hou	16.0	5.63
Armstrong J, Cle	23.0	8.22	Guzman Ju, Tor	28.0	1.61	Reed Ri, KC	17.0	3.18
Astacio, LA	11.0	3.27	Haas D, Det	11.0	5.73	Rhodes A, Bal	15.0	2.40
Avery, Atl	35.0	3.86	Hammond C, Cin	26.0	5.19	Rijo, Cin	33.0	1.64
Banks, Min	12.0	4.50	Haney C, KC	13.0	9.69	Ritz, Det	11.0	7.36
Barnes B, Mon	17.0	0.53	Hanson, Sea	30.0	2.10	Rivera Ben, Phi	14.0	2.57
Belcher T, Cin	33.2	6.15	Harnisch, Hou	33.2	3.74	Robinson D, Phi	11.0	14.73
Benes, SD	34.0	2.38	Harris Greg W., SD	20.0	3.60	Robinson JM, Pit	11.0	5.73
Bielecki, Atl	13.1	3.38	Henry B, Hou	27.1	3.29	Ryan N, Tex	26.0	4.85
Black, SF	28.0	0.64	Hershiser, LA	33.0	4.36	Saberhagen, NYN	15.0	5.40
Blyleven, Cal	23.1	6.17	Hesketh, Bos	25.0	2.52	Sanderson, NYA	33.0	4.64
Bones, Mil	28.0	2.25	Hibbard, ChA	28.0	3.54	Schilling, Phi	26.0	3.12
Bosio, Mil	33.0	2.73	Hill K, Mon	33.0	5.45	Schourek, NYN	21.0	3.00
Boskie, ChN	16.2	9.72	Hough, ChA	26.2	6.75	Scudder, Cle	19.2	10.07
Brown Kevin, Tex	35.0	5.66	Hurst B, SD	32.0	4.22	Seminara, SD	18.0	2.50
Browning, Cin	15.2	9.19	Jackson Dan, Pit	34.0	5.03	Slusarski, Oak	14.0	3.21
Burba, SF	10.1	8.71	Johnson R, Sea	31.0	3.48	Smiley, Min	34.0	3.10
Burkett, SF	32.0	3.94	Jones J, Hou	23.0	7.83	Smith P, Atl	11.0	1.63
Burns T, Tex	10.0	1.80	Kamieniecki, NYA	28.0	4.82	Smith Z, Pit	21.1	3.80
Cadaret, NYA	11.0	7.36	Key, Tor	33.0	4.09	Smoltz, Atl	35.0	3.86
Candiotti, LA	29.2	5.76	Kile, Hou	22.0	2.86	Stewart D, Oak	31.0	3.77
Castillo F, ChN	33.0	1.36	King E, Det	14.0	5.79	Stieb, Tor	14.0	2.57
Clark M, StL	20.0	3.15	Krueger, Mon	29.0	4.34	Stottlemyre T, Tor	27.0	5.33
Clemens, Bos	32.0	3.09	Langston, Cal	32.0	5.34	Sutcliffe, Bal	36.0	5.25
Cone, Tor	34.0	1.32	Leary, Sea	23.0	7.04	Swift, SF	22.0	5.32
Cook D, Cle	25.0	4.32	Lefferts, Bal	31.1	4.60	Swindell, Cin	30.0	2.70
Cormier, StL	30.0	3.30	Leibrandt, Atl	31.0	3.48	Tanana, Det	31.0	5.52
Darling, Oak	33.0	4.91	Leiter M, Det	14.0	3.86	Tapani, Min	34.0	2.38
Darwin, Bos	15.0	5.40	Maddux G, ChN	35.0	2.06	Terrell W, Det	13.0	6.92
DeLeon J, Phi	18.0	4.00	Magnante, KC	11.2	6.17	Tewksbury, StL	32.0	4.50
DeLucia, Sea	10.0	10.80	Mahomes, Min	13.0	6.23	Tomlin R, Pit	33.0	3.00
Deshaies, SD	15.0	0.00	Martinez De, Mon	32.0	1.13	Valera, Cal	28.0	2.89
Doherty, Det	10.1	4.36	Martinez R, LA	25.0	3.60	Viola, Bos	35.0	3.34
Dopson, Bos	25.0	3.60	McCaskill, ChA	34.0	2.91	Wakefield, Pit	13.0	1.38
Downs, Oak	20.0	4.05	McDonald, Bal	35.0	1.80	Walk, Pit	19.0	3.79
Drabek, Pit	34.0	5.03	McDowell J, ChA	34.0	4.76	Wegman, Mil	35.0	1.80
Eldred, Mil	14.0	1.28	Mesa, Cle	27.0	3.67	Welch, Oak	20.0	3.15
Erickson S, Min	32.0	3.94	Milacki, Bal	20.0	8.55	Wells D, Tor	14.0	3.86
Fernandez A, ChA	29.0	4.97	Moore M, Oak	36.0	4.00	Whitehurst, NYN	11.0	8.18
Fernandez S, NYN	32.0	4.22	Morgan M, ChN	34.0	0.53	Williams Br, Hou	16.0	6.75
Finley C, Cal	31.0	4.36	Morris Ja, Tor	34.0	6.88	Wilson Tr, SF	26.0	3.81
Fisher, Sea	14.0	5.14	Mulholland, Phi	32.0	3.94	Witt B, Oak	31.0	3.77
Fleming, Sea	33.0	3.82	Mussina, Bal	32.0	1.69	Young A, NYN	13.0	2.77
Gardiner, Bos	18.0	2.50	Nabholz, Mon	32.0	2.81	MLB Average		4.23
Gardner M, Mon	30.0	6.00	Nagy, Cle	33.0	1.91			
Glavine, Atl	33.0	5.45	Navarro, Mil	34.0	3.18			
Gooden, NYN	31.0	3.77	Ojeda, LA	29.0	3.72			
Gordon T, KC	10.2	6.75	Olivares, StL	30.0	4.50			
Grant M, Sea	10.0	5.40	Osborne, StL	29.0	5.90			

WHY CAN'T PITCHERS HIT ANYMORE? (p. 174)

1992 Active Pitchers — Listed Alphabetically
(minimum 100 plate appearances lifetime)

Pitcher, Team	AVG	AB	H	HR	RBI	Pitcher, Team	AVG	AB	H	HR	RBI
Aguilera, Min	.203	138	28	3	11	Jackson Dan, Pit	.122	246	30	0	13
Armstrong J, Cle	.092	119	11	0	5	Jones J, Hou	.168	184	31	2	11
Avery, Atl	.184	185	34	0	6	Kipper, Min	.137	95	13	0	2
Barnes B, Mon	.138	87	12	0	2	Lamp, Pit	.164	201	33	0	7
Belcher T, Cin	.112	322	36	2	18	Lancaster, Det	.102	128	13	0	5
Benes, SD	.113	213	24	3	10	Leary, Sea	.221	163	36	1	19
Bielecki, Atl	.079	267	21	0	12	Lefferts, Bal	.121	132	16	1	3
Black, SF	.128	125	16	0	8	Leibrandt, Atl	.120	267	32	0	14
Blyleven, Cal	.131	451	59	0	25	Lilliquist, Cle	.213	108	23	2	8
Boskie, ChN	.192	104	20	1	6	Maddux G, ChN	.184	490	90	2	29
Browning, Cin	.149	570	85	1	28	Maddux M, SD	.073	82	6	0	4
Burkett, SF	.052	174	9	0	6	Magrane, StL	.143	245	35	4	12
Candelaria, LA	.174	596	104	1	48	Martinez D, Mon	.141	440	62	0	26
Carman, Tex	.057	209	12	0	5	Martinez R, LA	.124	251	31	1	20
Castillo F, ChN	.110	100	11	0	2	Mathews G, Phi	.136	162	22	0	5
Charlton, Cin	.082	85	7	0	0	Morgan M, ChN	.101	257	26	0	11
Combs, Phi	.147	95	14	0	4	Mulholland, Phi	.082	294	24	0	6
Cone, Tor	.154	395	61	0	20	Nabholz, Mon	.101	138	14	0	3
Cook D, Cle	.250	96	24	1	7	Ojeda, LA	.127	347	44	1	9
Cox D, Pit	.109	359	39	0	12	Olivares, StL	.225	138	31	2	14
Darling, Oak	.145	525	76	2	21	Pena A, Atl	.112	179	20	1	7
Darwin, Bos	.124	193	24	1	16	Portugal, Hou	.161	174	28	1	10
Davis MW, Atl	.153	163	25	1	9	Power, Cle	.089	157	14	1	7
DeLeon J, Phi	.092	413	38	0	9	Rasmussen D, KC	.193	259	50	0	14
Deshaies, SD	.090	367	33	0	12	Rijo, Cin	.174	276	48	1	15
Downs, Oak	.123	211	26	0	11	Robinson D, Phi	.231	631	146	13	69
Drabek, Pit	.160	469	75	1	26	Robinson JD, ChN	.137	161	22	2	10
Dunne, ChA	.101	109	11	0	6	Robinson R, Mil	.153	144	22	0	6
Eckersley, Oak	.133	180	24	3	12	Ruffin, Mil	.080	263	21	0	6
Fernandez S, NYN	.198	464	92	1	29	Ryan N, Tex	.110	852	94	2	36
Fisher, Sea	.124	105	13	2	10	Sanderson, NYA	.100	460	46	2	26
Gardner M, Mon	.116	155	18	0	7	Smiley, Min	.110	254	28	0	15
Glavine, Atl	.185	356	66	0	27	Smith Bry, StL	.155	490	76	3	37
Gooden, NYN	.198	648	128	5	54	Smith P, Atl	.096	166	16	0	5
Grant M, Sea	.067	104	7	0	2	Smith Z, Pit	.156	443	69	0	27
Greene T, Phi	.214	117	25	2	7	Smoltz, Atl	.137	293	40	2	17
Gross Ke, LA	.157	548	86	4	26	Sutcliffe, Bal	.184	539	99	4	54
Gullickson, Det	.141	576	81	3	27	Terrell W, Det	.120	192	23	3	10
Harkey, ChN	.241	87	21	0	4	Tewksbury, StL	.124	185	23	0	8
Harnisch, Hou	.132	129	17	0	12	Tomlin R, Pit	.141	142	20	0	3
Harris Greg W., SD	.086	105	9	0	3	Viola, Bos	.140	179	25	0	6
Heaton, Mil	.171	187	32	0	12	Walk, Pit	.148	452	67	1	46
Hershiser, LA	.196	555	109	0	36	Welch, Oak	.151	581	88	2	30
Hesketh, Bos	.070	86	6	0	2	Wilson Tr, SF	.172	134	23	1	9
Hill K, Mon	.150	193	29	1	11	**MLB Totals, 1992**	**.138**	**4110**	**567**	**12**	**204**
Honeycutt, Oak	.133	181	24	0	8						
Hough, ChA	.208	130	27	1	12						
Hurst B, SD	.114	273	31	0	8						

WHAT HAPPENS TO ROOKIE PITCHERS THE SECOND TIME AROUND THE LEAGUE? (p. 176)

The following charts lists how rookie pitchers fared the First, Second, and Third time they faced teams. The totals reflect ALL rookies of that type in 1992, not just those listed.

Relief Pitcher Chart — 1992

Reliever	First Time			Second Time			Third Time		
	G	IP	ERA	G	IP	ERA	G	IP	ERA
Austin, Mil	12	15.2	3.45	12	15.0	6.00	28	36.1	0.99
Ayrault, Phi	11	15.2	5.74	8	11.1	1.59	11	16.1	1.65
Barton, Sea	6	7.2	3.52	4	3.0	3.00	4	1.2	0.00
Bottenfield, Mon	7	23.1	1.93	3	9.0	3.00	0	0.0	-
Brantley C, Phi	9	45.1	4.57	7	23.1	4.63	18	39.1	3.66
Bullinger, ChN	11	12.1	5.84	11	32.0	3.38	17	40.2	5.31
Butcher M, Cal	10	14.0	3.21	7	11.1	1.59	2	2.1	11.57
Campbell K, Oak	13	29.0	3.72	13	22.0	5.73	20	37.0	4.38
Christopher, Cle	10	15.0	1.80	2	3.1	2.70	1	3.2	4.91
Cooke, Pit	7	17.0	4.76	2	3.2	0.00	2	2.1	0.00
Dewey, NYN	10	19.0	2.37	9	15.2	3.45	15	21.1	5.06
Doherty, Det	13	31.1	2.01	12	23.1	6.94	22	61.1	3.67
Fortugno, Cal	11	33.2	5.08	3	8.0	5.63	0	0.0	-
Foster S, Cin	11	22.0	6.14	9	10.0	0.90	22	32.0	0.84
Hentgen, Tor	13	21.0	3.86	10	25.1	4.97	8	11.1	7.15
Heredia G, Mon	9	33.2	3.74	8	23.0	2.35	10	21.0	6.43
Hernandez Je, SD	9	13.2	0.00	8	14.0	3.86	18	23.1	4.24
Hill Mi, Cin	9	14.2	1.23	8	12.2	2.13	19	26.0	5.54
Horsman, Oak	13	12.2	1.42	13	12.0	0.75	36	22.2	3.57
Kiely, Det	13	18.0	3.50	13	22.1	3.63	20	21.1	3.38
Knudsen, Det	13	18.2	2.41	13	21.0	5.57	22	31.0	5.23
Leon, Tex	9	13.2	3.29	3	2.0	18.00	3	2.2	10.13
Meacham R, KC	14	33.0	4.36	13	22.0	3.27	47	74.1	2.78
Neagle, Pit	17	48.0	4.50	12	16.2	4.86	33	41.2	4.10
Nelson Je, Sea	13	14.1	3.14	13	13.1	4.05	40	53.1	3.38
Nielsen J, NYA	11	12.2	2.84	8	6.2	8.10	1	0.1	0.00
Pena J, SF	11	22.1	3.22	9	16.2	2.70	5	5.0	7.20
Perez Mi, StL	11	15.0	4.80	11	14.1	1.26	82	94.1	2.48
Quantrill, Bos	11	18.2	1.93	9	17.1	3.12	7	13.1	1.35
Reed S, SF	8	7.1	1.23	6	5.2	3.18	4	2.2	3.38
Scott Tim, SD	11	13.1	2.03	10	9.2	10.24	15	15.2	5.17
Shepherd K, Phi	6	13.1	2.03	3	3.1	2.70	3	5.1	6.75
Shifflett, KC	13	17.0	2.12	12	19.2	3.66	9	15.1	1.76
Springer R, NYA	9	12.2	5.68	5	3.1	8.10	0	0.0	-
Whiteside, Tex	10	15.1	2.93	5	6.2	0.00	5	6.0	1.50
Wohlers, Atl	11	9.2	1.86	9	10.0	4.50	29	35.1	2.55
Young A, NYN	11	56.0	4.66	10	34.0	2.65	41	80.1	3.81
Young P, Mon	9	13.2	4.61	3	5.2	3.18	1	1.0	0.00
Totals	405	769.1	3.57	316	528.1	3.87	620	897.2	3.56

Starting Pitcher Chart — 1992

Starter	First Time			Second Time			Third Time		
	G	IP	ERA	G	IP	ERA	G	IP	ERA
Abbott K, Phi	15	67.0	5.78	10	47.2	4.91	11	38.1	3.99
Ashby Andy, Phi	7	36.1	6.69	6	27.0	5.33	5	15.2	9.19
Astacio, LA	8	59.0	1.83	2	14.0	3.86	1	9.0	0.00
Banks, Min	11	49.2	5.98	6	26.0	6.23	4	12.2	3.55
Clark M, StL	9	35.2	4.54	8	51.2	2.26	10	48.1	6.52
Eldred, Mil	11	74.2	2.65	5	33.2	1.60	1	8.0	0.00
Fleming, Sea	13	48.0	5.06	13	83.0	2.60	16	115.0	3.76
Groom, Det	9	32.1	6.12	2	6.0	4.50	1	0.1	0.00
Haas D, Det	10	38.0	3.32	7	29.0	4.03	6	5.1	13.50
Henry B, Hou	11	70.0	4.37	10	55.2	3.72	7	40.0	3.83
Hillman, NYN	9	49.2	3.99	2	2.2	30.38	0	0.0	-
Mahomes, Min	10	50.2	5.15	4	19.0	4.74	0	0.0	-
Osborne, StL	11	66.2	3.51	10	45.0	5.20	13	67.1	3.07
Pavlik, Tex	8	40.2	4.20	4	15.1	4.11	1	6.0	4.50
Pichardo, KC	13	47.1	4.18	9	40.2	4.87	9	55.2	3.07
Rhodes A, Bal	10	46.2	7.14	7	45.0	3.80	6	38.2	3.26
Rivera Ben, Phi	10	17.0	3.71	8	42.2	2.74	10	57.2	3.12
Seminara, SD	9	53.0	2.89	5	22.1	4.43	5	25.0	4.68
Trombley, Min	8	35.1	3.31	2	11.0	3.27	0	0.0	-
Valera, Cal	18	94.2	3.71	10	66.2	4.05	7	41.2	4.10
Wakefield, Pit	8	57.1	2.51	4	29.2	1.82	1	5.0	0.00
Williams Br, Hou	9	61.2	2.34	6	34.0	3.71	3	12.2	12.08
Totals	227	1131.1	4.10	140	747.2	3.84	117	602.1	4.09
Starters+ Relievers	632	1900.2	3.88	456	1276.0	3.85	737	1500.0	3.77

WHO PITCHED BETTER IN 1992 — TOM GLAVINE OR MELIDO PEREZ? (p. 178)

In the table below, **Sup** stands for Run Support Per Nine Innigs. **RS** is the total Runs In Support for that pitcher while he was in the game.

Both Leagues — Listed Alphabetically
(minimum 20 games started in 1992)

Pitcher, Team	W/L	ERA	Sup	IP	RS
Abbott J, Cal	7-15	2.77	2.64	211.0	62
Appier, KC	15-8	2.46	4.02	208.1	93
Armstrong J, Cle	3-15	5.44	3.85	135.2	58
Avery, Atl	11-11	3.20	3.93	233.2	102
Belcher T, Cin	15-13	3.85	4.45	226.2	112
Benes, SD	13-14	3.35	3.03	231.1	78
Black, SF	10-12	3.97	3.41	177.0	67
Blyleven, Cal	8-12	4.77	3.75	132.0	55
Bones, Mil	9-10	4.76	4.30	155.0	74
Bosio, Mil	16-6	3.62	5.21	231.1	134
Brown Kevin, Tex	21-11	3.32	4.74	265.2	140
Burkett, SF	13-9	3.84	4.70	189.2	99
Candiotti, LA	10-15	3.03	3.21	202.0	72
Castillo F, ChN	10-11	3.46	3.46	205.1	79
Clark M, StL	3-10	4.45	3.18	113.1	40
Clemens, Bos	18-11	2.41	4.23	246.2	116
Cone, Tor	17-10	2.83	4.40	247.2	121
Cook D, Cle	5-6	3.91	4.30	138.0	66
Cormier, StL	10-10	3.70	3.94	185.0	81
Darling, Oak	15-10	3.66	4.89	206.1	112
Dopson, Bos	7-11	4.08	4.01	141.1	63
Downs, Oak	4-7	3.65	2.97	106.0	35
Drabek, Pit	15-11	2.77	3.93	256.2	112
Erickson S, Min	13-12	3.40	4.37	212.0	103
Fernandez A, ChA	8-11	4.27	4.17	187.2	87
Fernandez S, NYN	14-11	2.73	4.40	214.2	105
Finley C, Cal	7-12	3.96	3.74	204.1	85
Fleming, Sea	17-10	3.39	4.34	228.1	110
Gardner M, Mon	11-10	4.26	4.36	175.1	85
Glavine, Atl	20-8	2.76	5.32	225.0	133
Gooden, NYN	10-13	3.67	3.58	206.0	82
Gross Ke, LA	8-13	3.18	3.41	200.2	76
Gullickson, Det	14-13	4.34	5.32	221.2	131
Guzman Jose, Tex	16-11	3.66	5.46	224.0	136
Guzman Ju, Tor	16-5	2.64	4.88	180.2	98
Hammond C, Cin	7-10	4.24	3.87	144.1	62
Hanson, Sea	7-17	4.85	3.82	183.2	78
Harnisch, Hou	9-10	3.70	4.27	206.2	98
Harris Greg, SD	4-8	4.12	4.35	118.0	57
Henry B, Hou	6-9	4.02	3.37	165.2	62
Hershiser, LA	10-15	3.67	3.29	210.2	77
Hesketh, Bos	7-9	4.29	4.75	138.1	73
Hibbard, ChA	10-7	4.55	3.86	170.0	73
Hill K, Mon	16-9	2.68	4.50	218.0	109
Hough, ChA	7-12	3.93	3.73	176.1	73
Hurst B, SD	14-9	3.85	3.81	217.1	92
Jackson Dan, Pit	8-13	3.84	3.84	201.1	86
Johnson R, Sea	12-14	3.77	4.32	210.1	101
Jones J, Hou	8-6	4.15	4.54	136.2	69
Kamieniecki, NYA	6-14	4.36	4.40	188.0	92
Key, Tor	13-13	3.53	5.36	216.2	129
Kile, Hou	5-10	3.95	3.23	125.1	45
Krueger, Mon	10-7	4.51	6.10	169.2	115
Langston, Cal	13-14	3.66	3.69	229.0	94
Leary, Sea	8-10	5.12	4.93	137.0	75
Lefferts, Bal	14-12	3.76	4.45	196.1	97
Leibrandt, Atl	15-7	3.39	4.34	191.0	92
Maddux G, ChN	20-11	2.18	3.96	268.0	118
Martinez D, Mon	16-11	2.47	4.02	226.1	101
Martinez R, LA	8-11	4.00	3.52	150.2	59
McCaskill, ChA	12-13	4.18	4.74	209.0	110
McDonald, Bal	13-13	4.24	4.64	227.0	117
McDowell J, ChA	20-10	3.18	5.46	260.2	158
Mesa, Cle	7-12	4.60	4.60	158.1	81
Milacki, Bal	6-8	5.92	5.25	106.1	62
Moore M, Oak	17-12	4.12	4.96	223.0	123
Morgan M, ChN	16-8	2.55	4.13	240.0	110
Morris Ja, Tor	21-6	4.04	5.98	240.2	160
Mulholland, Phi	13-11	3.81	4.99	229.0	127
Mussina, Bal	18-5	2.54	4.78	241.0	128
Nabholz, Mon	11-12	3.32	4.29	195.0	93
Nagy, Cle	17-10	2.96	4.36	252.0	122
Navarro, Mil	17-11	3.33	4.65	246.0	127
Ojeda, LA	6-9	3.63	3.90	166.1	72
Olivares, StL	9-9	3.85	3.94	194.0	85
Osborne, StL	10-8	3.78	3.78	169.0	71
Perez Me, NYA	13-16	2.87	4.07	247.2	112
Pichardo, KC	9-5	3.87	5.25	130.1	76
Rijo, Cin	15-10	2.56	4.31	211.0	101
Ryan N, Tex	5-9	3.72	4.12	157.1	72
Sanderson, NYA	12-11	4.93	6.24	193.1	134
Schilling, Phi	12-9	2.27	3.41	198.0	75
Schourek, NYN	5-8	3.78	3.16	131.0	46
Scudder, Cle	6-10	4.83	4.08	108.0	49
Smiley, Min	16-9	3.21	4.44	241.0	119
Smith Z, Pit	8-8	3.11	3.69	139.0	57
Smoltz, Atl	15-12	2.85	4.27	246.2	117
Stewart D, Oak	12-10	3.66	4.61	199.1	102
Stottlemyre T, Tor	11-11	4.53	5.93	173.0	114
Sutcliffe, Bal	16-15	4.47	4.21	237.1	111
Swift, SF	9-3	2.18	4.04	144.2	65
Swindell, Cin	12-8	2.71	4.82	212.2	114
Tanana, Det	12-11	4.44	4.24	184.2	87
Tapani, Min	16-11	3.97	6.05	220.0	148
Tewksbury, StL	15-5	2.18	4.09	231.0	105
Tomlin R, Pit	14-9	3.44	3.96	206.2	91
Valera, Cal	7-11	3.76	4.01	182.0	81
Viola, Bos	13-12	3.44	3.63	238.0	96
Wegman, Mil	13-14	3.20	4.85	261.2	141
Welch, Oak	11-7	3.27	5.31	123.2	73
Wilson Tr, SF	8-14	4.21	2.81	154.0	48
Witt B, Oak	10-14	4.29	4.24	193.0	91
MLB Average		3.85	4.32		

WAS MEL ROJAS BETTER THAN THE ECK LAST YEAR?
(p.182)

The table below lists a relievers Holds (H), Saves (Sv), Blown Saves (BS), and Hold + Save Percentage (%), which is Holds plus Saves divided by Holds plus Saves plus Blown Saves.

Both Leagues — Listed Alphabetically
(minimum 5 Holds+Saves+Blown Saves in 1992)

Pitcher	H	Sv	BS	%	Pitcher	H	Sv	BS	%	Pitcher	H	Sv	BS	%
Aguilera, Min	0	41	7	85	Harris Greg, Bos	19	4	6	79	Nunez E, Tex	5	3	1	89
Andersen, SD	8	2	0	100	Hartley, Phi	8	0	4	67	Olin, Cle	0	29	7	81
Assenmacher, Ch	20	8	5	85	Harvey, Cal	0	13	3	81	Olson Gregg, Bal	0	36	8	82
Austin, Mil	9	0	1	90	Heaton, Mil	8	0	2	80	Orosco, Mil	11	1	1	92
Bankhead, Cin	14	1	4	79	Henke, Tor	4	34	3	93	Osuna, Hou	6	0	2	75
Beck, SF	4	17	6	78	Henneman, Det	0	24	4	86	Parrett, Oak	19	0	1	95
Belinda, Pit	0	18	6	75	Henry Do, Mil	1	29	4	88	Patterson B, Pit	10	9	4	83
Berenguer, KC	6	1	3	70	Henry Dw, Cin	6	0	2	75	Pena A, Atl	4	15	3	86
Boever, Hou	7	2	4	69	Hernandez Je, SD	3	1	1	80	Perez Mi, StL	9	0	3	75
Brantley J, SF	3	7	2	83	Hernandez, ChA	6	12	4	82	Plunk, Cle	7	4	4	73
Bullinger, ChN	4	7	0	100	Hernandez X, Hou	8	7	3	83	Powell D, Sea	6	0	0	100
Burke, NYA	5	0	2	71	Hickerson, SF	8	0	5	62	Power, Cle	14	6	5	80
Cadaret, NYA	7	1	2	80	Holmes, Mil	2	6	2	80	Quantrill, Bos	3	1	4	50
Campbell K, Oak	4	1	0	100	Honeycutt, Oak	18	3	4	84	Radinsky, ChA	16	15	8	79
Candelaria, LA	12	5	2	89	Horsman, Oak	10	1	1	92	Reardon, Atl	0	30	10	75
Carpenter, StL	7	1	7	53	Howe S, NYA	5	6	1	92	Righetti, SF	2	3	2	71
Charlton, Cin	7	26	8	80	Howell Jay, LA	5	4	2	82	Ritchie, Phi	3	1	1	80
Clements, Bal	5	0	1	83	Innis, NYN	16	1	3	85	Robinson JD, Ch	7	1	3	73
Cox D, Pit	2	3	2	71	Irvine, Bos	2	0	3	40	Rodriguez R, SD	5	0	1	83
Crim, Cal	8	1	2	82	Jackson M, SF	9	2	1	92	Rogers Ken, Tex	16	6	4	85
Darwin, Bos	1	3	3	57	Jones Ba, NYN	8	1	6	60	Rojas, Mon	13	10	1	96
Davis Storm, Bal	5	4	3	75	Jones Ca, Sea	3	0	2	60	Ruskin, Cin	5	0	3	63
DeLucia, Sea	3	1	2	67	Jones D, Hou	0	36	6	86	Russell Je, Oak	1	30	9	78
Dibble, Cin	4	25	5	85	Kiely, Det	7	0	1	88	Sampen, KC	6	0	1	86
Doherty, Det	10	3	1	93	Knudsen, Det	8	5	2	87	Scanlan, ChN	7	14	4	84
Eckersley, Oak	0	51	3	94	Leach T, ChA	6	0	0	100	Schooler, Sea	3	13	5	76
Edens, Min	11	3	2	88	Lewis S, Cal	5	0	0	100	Scott Ti, SD	4	0	1	80
Eichhorn, Tor	5	2	4	64	Lilliquist, Cle	15	6	5	81	Shepherd K, Phi	0	2	4	33
Farr S, NYA	0	30	6	83	Maddux M, SD	8	5	4	76	Smith Le, StL	0	43	8	84
Fassero, Mon	12	1	6	68	Magnante, KC	4	0	3	57	Stanton Mike, Atl	15	8	3	88
Fetters, Mil	8	2	3	77	Mason R, Pit	11	8	2	90	Swan R, Sea	7	9	2	89
Fisher, Sea	4	1	0	100	Mathews T, Tex	6	0	4	60	Thigpen, ChA	3	22	7	78
Flanagan, Bal	10	0	0	100	McClure, Cal	14	0	0	100	Ward D, Tor	25	12	4	90
Fossas, Bos	14	2	1	94	McDowell R, LA	5	14	8	70	Wayne, Min	9	0	3	75
Foster S, Cin	4	2	1	86	McElroy, ChN	3	6	5	64	Wells D, Tor	3	2	2	71
Franco Jo, NYN	1	15	2	89	Meacham R, KC	15	2	4	81	Wetteland, Mon	0	37	9	80
Freeman M, Atl	16	3	3	86	Melendez J, SD	4	0	2	67	Whitehurst, NYN	4	0	3	57
Frey, Cal	4	4	1	89	Mercker, Atl	6	6	3	80	Wickander, Cle	7	1	2	80
Frohwirth, Bal	15	4	3	86	Mills A, Bal	2	2	1	80	Williams Mit, Phi	0	29	7	81
Gibson P, NYN	5	0	0	100	Monteleone, NYA	7	0	2	78	Willis C, Min	10	1	2	85
Gossage, Oak	5	0	1	83	Montgomery, KC	0	39	7	85	Wilson S, LA	6	0	4	60
Gott, LA	11	6	1	94	Munoz M, Det	15	2	1	94	Wohlers, Atl	2	4	2	75
Grahe, Cal	1	21	3	88	Murphy R, Hou	9	0	2	82	Worrell, StL	25	3	4	88
Guetterman, NYN	9	2	1	92	Myers R, SD	0	38	8	83	Young A, NYN	2	15	5	77
Guthrie, Min	19	5	2	92	Neagle, Pit	5	2	2	78	**MLB Avg**				**82**
Habyan, NYA	16	7	5	82	Nelson Je, Sea	6	6	8	60					

DID BELINDA SQUANDER THE BUCS' INHERITANCE? (p. 184)

The table below shows the percentage (%) of Inherited Runners (IR) each relief pitcher allowed to score (SC).

Both Leagues — Listed Alphabetically
(minimum 15 inherited runners)

Pitcher, Team	IR	SC	%	Pitcher, Team	IR	SC	%	Pitcher, Team	IR	SC	%
Agosto, Sea	33	14	42.4	Gott, LA	38	12	31.6	Olin, Cle	49	11	22.4
Aguilera, Min	40	7	17.5	Grahe, Cal	18	3	16.7	Olson Gregg, Bal	31	5	16.1
Alvarez W, ChA	25	3	12.0	Guetterman, NYN	32	10	31.3	Orosco, Mil	64	14	21.9
Andersen, SD	17	7	41.2	Guthrie, Min	57	9	15.8	Osuna, Hou	40	6	15.0
Assenmacher, ChN	62	13	21.0	Habyan, NYA	36	17	47.2	Pall, ChA	16	4	25.0
Austin, Mil	43	13	30.2	Harris Greg A., Bos	73	18	24.7	Parrett, Oak	65	21	32.3
Ayrault, Phi	16	8	50.0	Hartley, Phi	17	7	41.2	Patterson B, Pit	36	13	36.1
Bailes, Cal	28	12	42.9	Heaton, Mil	22	7	31.8	Patterson K, ChN	23	7	30.4
Bankhead, Cin	28	4	14.3	Henry Do, Mil	26	9	34.6	Perez Mi, StL	45	10	22.2
Bannister F, Tex	32	12	37.5	Henry Dw, Cin	37	14	37.8	Plesac, Mil	28	12	42.9
Barton, Sea	19	4	21.1	Hernandez R, ChA	38	13	34.2	Plunk, Cle	44	11	25.0
Beck, SF	41	9	22.0	Hernandez X, Hou	48	12	25.0	Powell D, Sea	50	6	12.0
Belinda, Pit	28	18	64.3	Hickerson, SF	39	11	28.2	Power, Cle	84	25	29.8
Berenguer, KC	36	8	22.2	Holmes, Mil	35	6	17.1	Quantrill, Bos	17	7	41.2
Boddicker, KC	16	10	62.5	Honeycutt, Oak	48	14	29.2	Raczka, Oak	15	6	40.0
Boever, Hou	61	10	16.4	Horsman, Oak	48	11	22.9	Radinsky, ChA	65	22	33.8
Bohanon, Tex	17	8	47.1	Howe S, NYA	24	5	20.8	Reardon, Atl	30	15	50.0
Bolton, Cin	21	5	23.8	Howell Jay, LA	18	7	38.9	Reed S, SF	22	8	36.4
Brantley J, SF	32	11	34.4	Innis, NYN	50	15	30.0	Righetti, SF	17	5	29.4
Bullinger, ChN	21	5	23.8	Irvine, Bos	28	12	42.9	Ritchie, Phi	38	16	42.1
Burke, NYA	21	6	28.6	Jackson M, SF	28	8	28.6	Robinson JD, ChN	24	7	29.2
Burns T, Tex	16	2	12.5	Jones Ba, NYN	33	18	54.5	Robinson JM, Pit	16	9	56.3
Butcher M, Cal	22	11	50.0	Jones Ca, Sea	25	4	16.0	Rodriguez Rich, SD	43	13	30.2
Cadaret, NYA	36	12	33.3	Jones D, Hou	37	11	29.7	Rogers Ken, Tex	66	29	43.9
Campbell K, Oak	22	3	13.6	Kiely, Det	36	14	38.9	Rojas, Mon	58	10	17.2
Candelaria, LA	64	15	23.4	Kipper, Min	16	4	25.0	Ruffin, Mil	18	11	61.1
Carpenter, StL	64	19	29.7	Knudsen, Det	42	13	31.0	Ruskin, Cin	37	15	40.5
Charlton, Cin	27	10	37.0	Lancaster, Det	38	24	63.2	Russell Je, Oak	43	12	27.9
Clements, Bal	54	11	20.4	Leach T, ChA	35	11	31.4	Sampen, KC	42	13	31.0
Corsi, Oak	24	9	37.5	Leiter M, Det	16	2	12.5	Scanlan, ChN	41	12	29.3
Cox D, Pit	17	8	47.1	Lilliquist, Cle	54	12	22.2	Schooler, Sea	40	17	42.5
Crews, LA	37	9	24.3	Maddux M, SD	26	11	42.3	Slocumb, ChN	22	6	27.3
Crim, Cal	55	23	41.8	Magnante, KC	18	4	22.2	Stanton WMike, Atl	40	10	25.0
Darwin, Bos	36	13	36.1	Mallicoat, Hou	18	4	22.2	Swan R, Sea	44	11	25.0
Davis Storm, Bal	51	11	21.6	Mason R, Pit	44	9	20.5	Terrell W, Det	16	6	37.5
DeLucia, Sea	21	8	38.1	Mathews T, Tex	31	14	45.2	Thigpen, ChA	39	12	30.8
Dibble, Cin	41	10	24.4	McClure, StL	67	15	22.4	Timlin, Tor	23	8	34.8
Doherty, Det	33	11	33.3	McDowell R, LA	42	10	23.8	Valdez S, Mon	18	9	50.0
Eckersley, Oak	31	2	6.5	McElroy, ChN	51	15	29.4	Ward D, Tor	30	9	30.0
Edens, Min	47	11	23.4	Meacham R, KC	55	17	30.9	Wayne, Min	34	10	29.4
Eichhorn, Tor	44	19	43.2	Melendez J, SD	38	16	42.1	Wells D, Tor	22	6	27.3
Farr S, NYA	18	8	44.4	Mercker, Atl	22	9	40.9	Wetteland, Mon	37	8	21.6
Fassero, Mon	51	13	25.5	Mills A, Bal	32	9	28.1	Whitehurst, NYN	34	13	38.2
Fetters, Mil	58	18	31.0	Monteleone, NYA	23	14	60.9	Whiteside, Tex	18	2	11.1
Flanagan, Bal	36	10	27.8	Montgomery, KC	20	7	35.0	Wickander, Cle	38	9	23.7
Fossas, Bos	70	20	28.6	Munoz M, Det	55	11	20.0	Williamson, Bal	22	13	59.1
Foster S, Cin	23	7	30.4	Murphy R, Hou	37	9	24.3	Willis C, Min	50	21	42.0
Freeman M, Atl	42	20	47.6	Myers R, SD	40	16	40.0	Wilson S, LA	48	11	22.9
Frey, Cal	50	5	10.0	Neagle, Pit	26	4	15.4	Young A, NYN	17	4	23.5
Frohwirth, Bal	64	26	40.6	Nelson G, Oak	26	7	26.9	Young Ma, Bos	24	8	33.3
Gardiner, Bos	21	4	19.0	Nelson Je, Sea	63	18	28.6	**MLB Average**			**30.8**
Gibson P, NYN	20	11	55.0	Nichols Ro, Cle	20	10	50.0				
Gordon T, KC	19	5	26.3	Nunez E, Tex	37	13	35.1				

WHY DON'T SOUTHPAWS WHO CAN HANDLE LEFTIES HAVE IT MADE? (p. 187)

Both Leagues — Listed Alphabetically
(minimum 1 relief game in 1992)

Left-Handed Relievers	Vs. LHB		Vs. RHB		Left-Handed Relievers	Vs. LHB		Vs. RHB	
Pitcher, Team	BFP	Avg	BFP	Avg	Pitcher, Team	BFP	Avg	BFP	Avg
Abbott K, Phi	140	.326	437	.269	Lilliquist, Cle	99	.200	140	.176
Agosto, Sea	72	.349	155	.314	MacDonald, Tor	64	.143	140	.336
Aldred, Det	53	.280	251	.313	Magnante, KC	80	.375	323	.312
Alvarez W, ChA	110	.225	345	.286	Mallicoat, Hou	40	.353	80	.241
Assenmacher, ChN	102	.220	196	.297	Mathews G, Phi	56	.313	172	.257
Bailes, Cal	59	.360	141	.347	McClure, StL	103	.198	127	.315
Bannister F, Tex	60	.174	113	.333	McElroy, ChN	117	.275	252	.218
Barnes B, Mon	73	.233	344	.209	Mercker, Atl	83	.260	206	.185
Barton, Sea	20	.389	30	.125	Munoz M, Det	81	.192	129	.283
Bell E, Cle	19	.133	56	.417	Murphy R, Hou	100	.256	142	.264
Bohanon, Tex	40	.235	180	.310	Myers R, SD	81	.270	267	.282
Bolton, Cin	93	.256	252	.295	Neagle, Pit	110	.228	270	.254
Borbon PF, Atl	4	.250	3	.500	Nielsen J, NYA	29	.273	61	.229
Brown Kevin D, Sea	4	.500	11	.250	Orosco, Mil	61	.273	97	.207
Cadaret, NYA	103	.227	368	.279	Osborne, StL	162	.318	592	.263
Candelaria, LA	59	.269	49	.154	Osuna, Hou	88	.247	182	.231
Carman, Tex	3	.333	8	.375	Otto, Cle	59	.352	309	.330
Casian, Min	12	.083	16	.400	Patterson B, Pit	89	.256	179	.241
Charlton, Cin	79	.296	262	.251	Patterson K, ChN	78	.266	113	.270
Clements, Bal	87	.234	123	.297	Pena J, SF	62	.296	142	.275
Cook D, Cle	102	.235	567	.259	Plesac, Mil	80	.254	250	.221
Cooke, Pit	23	.217	68	.266	Poole, Bal	7	.286	7	.167
Davis MW, Atl	68	.305	193	.299	Powell D, Sea	77	.250	166	.232
DiPino, StL	17	.188	28	.240	Raczka, Oak	16	.273	17	.333
Fassero, Mon	101	.269	267	.241	Radinsky, ChA	76	.182	185	.269
Flanagan, Bal	75	.274	105	.384	Rasmussen D, KC	22	.200	136	.220
Fortugno, Cal	33	.286	144	.225	Righetti, SF	107	.236	233	.283
Fossas, Bos	62	.214	67	.345	Ritchie, Phi	63	.220	111	.330
Franco Jo, NYN	36	.250	92	.195	Rodriguez Rich, SD	115	.233	254	.227
Frey, Cal	59	.189	134	.261	Rogers Ken, Tex	96	.261	241	.262
Gibson P, NYN	82	.338	191	.266	Ruffin, Mil	84	.221	188	.325
Gleaton, Pit	49	.286	93	.282	Ruskin, Cin	79	.250	155	.287
Groom, Det	38	.355	139	.311	Sauveur, KC	18	.200	47	.300
Guetterman, NYN	102	.278	208	.362	Scheid, Hou	12	.200	44	.300
Gunderson, Sea	14	.385	31	.292	Searcy, LA	15	.231	35	.370
Guthrie, Min	97	.205	206	.220	Simons, Mon	12	.444	23	.524
Guzman Johnny, Oak	5	.400	13	.500	Smith Dan, Tex	8	.143	59	.347
Hammond C, Cin	132	.291	495	.259	Stanton Mike, Atl	90	.237	174	.252
Haney C, KC	69	.258	270	.245	Swan R, Sea	92	.198	365	.278
Heaton, Mil	65	.222	124	.292	Taylor S, Bos	15	.286	42	.231
Hesketh, Bos	105	.255	554	.280	Tomlin R, Pit	163	.250	703	.289
Hibbard, ChA	99	.224	656	.285	Wayne, Min	56	.250	154	.264
Hickerson, SF	112	.235	233	.236	Wells D, Tor	103	.293	426	.288
Hillman, NYN	42	.297	185	.322	West, Min	25	.238	114	.284
Honeycutt, Oak	69	.258	100	.281	Wickander, Cle	74	.278	113	.250
Horsman, Oak	88	.203	92	.296	Williams Mitch, Phi	61	.265	307	.235
Howe S, NYA	20	.200	59	.093	Wilson S, LA	113	.255	188	.299
Jeffcoat, Tex	22	.350	67	.350	Young Cu, NYA	53	.392	242	.274
Johnson Jeff, NYA	45	.308	200	.333	Young Ma, Bos	68	.269	253	.253
Kipper, Min	48	.250	120	.276					
Krueger, Mon	110	.308	655	.262					

WHAT'S THE BEST PREDICTOR OF A PITCHER'S ERA? (p. 192)

Both Leagues — Listed Alphabetically
(Active Pitchers/Minimum 5 GS Before and After the All Star Break, 1992)

Pitcher, Team	1st Half IP	ERA	2nd Half IP	ERA	Pitcher, Team	1st Half IP	ERA	2nd Half IP	ERA
Abbott J, Cal	134.0	2.96	77.0	2.45	Krueger, Mon	118.2	3.19	60.0	7.20
Abbott K, Phi	80.1	5.15	53.0	5.09	Langston, Cal	116.1	4.02	112.2	3.28
Appier, KC	135.0	2.33	73.1	2.70	Leary, Sea	93.0	5.23	48.0	5.63
Armstrong J, Cle	106.2	5.40	60.0	3.30	Lefferts, Bal	109.1	3.54	87.0	4.03
Avery, Atl	127.1	2.62	106.1	3.89	Leibrandt, Atl	94.0	3.64	99.0	3.09
Belcher T, Cin	126.1	3.42	101.1	4.53	Maddux G, ChN	142.1	2.40	125.2	1.93
Benes, SD	131.0	3.71	100.1	2.87	Mahomes, Min	41.1	5.23	28.1	4.77
Black, SF	87.0	3.00	90.0	4.90	Martinez D, Mon	125.0	2.88	101.1	1.95
Blyleven, Cal	46.2	5.21	86.1	4.48	Martinez R, LA	105.0	3.51	45.2	5.12
Bones, Mil	92.2	4.95	70.2	4.08	McCaskill, ChA	115.0	4.15	94.0	4.21
Bosio, Mil	117.0	4.23	114.1	2.99	McDonald, Bal	120.2	5.00	106.1	3.39
Boskie, ChN	68.1	3.95	23.1	8.10	McDowell J, ChA	133.2	3.50	127.0	2.83
Brown Kevin, Tex	146.2	3.01	119.0	3.71	Mesa, Cle	67.2	5.19	93.0	4.16
Burkett, SF	101.2	4.07	88.0	3.58	Moore M, Oak	124.1	4.42	98.2	3.74
Candiotti, LA	121.0	3.05	82.2	2.94	Morgan M, ChN	122.0	2.66	118.0	2.44
Castillo F, ChN	106.2	3.21	98.2	3.74	Morris Ja, Tor	126.2	4.41	114.0	3.63
Clark M, StL	51.2	2.79	61.2	5.84	Mulholland, Phi	135.1	3.52	93.2	4.23
Clemens, Bos	140.0	2.31	106.2	2.53	Mussina, Bal	120.0	2.40	121.0	2.68
Cone, Tor	140.2	2.56	109.0	3.14	Nabholz, Mon	101.2	3.90	93.1	2.70
Cook D, Cle	73.0	4.19	85.0	3.49	Nagy, Cle	138.2	2.40	113.1	3.65
Cormier, StL	86.0	4.60	100.0	2.88	Navarro, Mil	130.0	3.95	116.0	2.64
Darling, Oak	107.0	4.37	99.1	2.90	Ojeda, LA	95.2	3.01	70.2	4.46
DeLeon J, Phi	79.1	4.20	38.0	4.74	Olivares, StL	98.2	3.83	98.1	3.84
Dopson, Bos	69.0	3.39	72.1	4.73	Osborne, StL	110.0	3.19	69.0	4.70
Downs, Oak	70.1	3.58	74.0	3.16	Perez M, NYA	127.1	3.11	120.1	2.62
Drabek, Pit	140.0	2.76	116.2	2.78	Pichardo, KC	70.0	3.60	73.2	4.28
Erickson S, Min	101.2	4.16	110.1	2.69	Reed Ri, KC	34.2	4.15	65.2	3.43
Fernandez A, ChA	93.2	4.23	94.0	4.31	Rijo, Cin	102.0	3.18	109.0	1.98
Fernandez S, NYN	113.0	3.19	101.2	2.21	Ryan N, Tex	76.2	3.76	80.2	3.68
Finley C, Cal	92.2	5.44	111.2	2.74	Saberhagen, NYN	52.0	3.81	45.2	3.15
Fleming, Sea	118.0	3.20	110.1	3.59	Sanderson, NYA	115.1	4.60	78.0	5.42
Gardner M, Mon	109.2	3.61	70.0	5.53	Schilling, Phi	104.2	2.75	121.2	2.00
Glavine, Atl	140.1	2.57	84.2	3.08	Schourek, NYN	47.1	2.85	88.2	4.06
Gooden, NYN	118.0	3.81	88.0	3.48	Scudder, Cle	93.0	4.94	16.0	7.31
Greene T, Phi	31.1	6.32	33.0	4.36	Seminara, SD	45.1	3.97	55.0	3.44
Gross Ke, LA	108.0	3.67	96.2	2.61	Smiley, Min	121.2	3.48	119.1	2.94
Gullickson, Det	126.0	3.36	95.2	5.64	Smoltz, Atl	139.0	3.04	107.2	2.59
Guzman Jose, Tex	119.0	3.93	105.0	3.34	Stewart D, Oak	111.1	3.96	88.0	3.27
Guzman Ju, Tor	127.2	2.12	53.0	3.91	Stottlemyre T, Tor	88.0	5.32	86.0	3.66
Hammond C, Cin	89.2	3.71	57.2	4.99	Sutcliffe, Bal	139.1	4.00	98.0	5.14
Haney C, KC	38.0	5.45	42.0	3.86	Swift, SF	92.1	2.53	72.1	1.49
Hanson, Sea	131.2	3.96	55.0	6.87	Swindell, Cin	128.2	2.94	85.0	2.33
Harnisch, Hou	117.1	3.76	89.1	3.63	Tanana, Det	95.2	4.70	91.0	4.05
Harris Greg W., SD	66.2	4.05	51.1	4.21	Tapani, Min	117.1	3.84	102.2	4.12
Henry B, Hou	98.1	4.58	67.1	3.21	Terrell W, Det	79.1	4.54	57.1	6.12
Hershiser, LA	115.1	3.43	95.1	3.97	Tewksbury, StL	134.2	1.87	98.1	2.56
Hesketh, Bos	96.2	3.82	52.0	5.37	Tomlin R, Pit	109.0	3.47	99.2	3.34
Hibbard, ChA	115.2	4.20	60.1	4.77	Valera, Cal	100.1	3.59	87.2	3.90
Hill K, Mon	118.0	2.59	100.0	2.79	Viola, Bos	129.2	3.12	108.1	3.82
Hough, ChA	95.2	3.29	80.2	4.69	Walk, Pit	52.0	3.98	83.0	2.71
Hurst B, SD	135.2	3.25	81.2	4.85	Wegman, Mil	145.1	3.28	116.1	3.09
Jackson Danny, Pit	113.0	4.22	88.1	3.36	Welch, Oak	73.1	2.70	50.1	4.11
Johnson R, Sea	93.2	4.04	116.2	3.55	Wells D, Tor	68.1	3.29	51.2	8.19
Jones Ji, Hou	69.2	4.39	69.2	3.75	Wilson Tr, SF	101.0	4.19	53.0	4.25
Kamieniecki, NYA	85.1	4.64	102.2	4.12	Witt B, Oak	111.2	3.79	81.1	4.98
Key, Tor	120.1	2.84	96.1	4.39					
Kile, Hou	65.1	4.13	60.0	3.75					
King E, Det	38.1	7.51	41.0	3.07					

CAN A CLOSER RACK UP THOSE SAVES, WITHOUT A MAN TO HOLD THE FORT? (p. 194)

A Hold (**H**) is a Save Opportunity passed on to the next pitcher. If a pitcher comes into the game in a Save Situation and leaves the game having gotten at least one out and without having blown the lead, this is a "passed on" Save Opportunity and the pitcher is credited with a Hold.

Both Leagues — Listed By Most Holds
(minumum 1 Hold in 1992)

Pitcher, Team	H	Pitcher, Team	H	Pitcher, Team	H	Pitcher, Team	H
Ward D, Tor	25	Jones Ba, NYN	8	Foster S, Cin	4	Wohlers, Atl	2
Worrell, StL	25	Knudsen, Det	8	Frey, Cal	4	Young A, NYN	2
Assenmacher, ChN	20	Maddux M, SD	8	Henke, Tor	4	Acker, Sea	1
Guthrie, Min	19	Boever, Hou	7	Magnante, KC	4	Agosto, Sea	1
Harris Greg A., Bos	19	Cadaret, NYA	7	Melendez J, SD	4	Arnsberg, Cle	1
Parrett, Oak	19	Carpenter, StL	7	Pena A, Atl	4	Baller, Phi	1
Honeycutt, Oak	18	Charlton, Cin	7	Scott Tim, SD	4	Bell E, Cle	1
Freeman M, Atl	16	Kiely, Det	7	Whitehurst, NYN	4	Bielecki, Atl	1
Habyan, NYA	16	Monteleone, NYA	7	Alvarez W, ChA	3	Blair W, Hou	1
Innis, NYN	16	Plunk, Cle	7	Bannister F, Tex	3	Boddicker, KC	1
Radinsky, ChA	16	Robinson JD, ChN	7	Brantley J, SF	3	Bottenfield, Mon	1
Rogers Ken, Tex	16	Scanlan, ChN	7	DeLucia, Sea	3	Casian, Min	1
Frohwirth, Bal	15	Swan R, Sea	7	Hernandez Je, SD	3	Christopher, Cle	1
Lilliquist, Cle	15	Wickander, Cle	7	Jones Ca, Sea	3	Cooke, Pit	1
Meacham R, KC	15	Berenguer, KC	6	Lamp, Pit	3	Crews, LA	1
Munoz M, Det	15	Henry Dw, Cin	6	Leiter M, Det	3	Darwin, Bos	1
Stanton Mike, Atl	15	Hernandez R, ChA	6	McElroy, ChN	3	Dewey, NYN	1
Bankhead, Cin	14	Leach T, ChA	6	Quantrill, Bos	3	DiPino, StL	1
Fossas, Bos	14	Mathews T, Tex	6	Ritchie, Phi	3	Franco Jo, NYN	1
McClure, StL	14	Mercker, Atl	6	Schooler, Sea	3	Grahe, Cal	1
Power, Cle	14	Nelson Je, Sea	6	Smith Bry, StL	3	Henry Do, Mil	1
Rojas, Mon	13	Osuna, Hou	6	Swift, SF	3	Hentgen, Tor	1
Candelaria, LA	12	Powell D, Sea	6	Thigpen, ChA	3	Heredia G, Mon	1
Fassero, Mon	12	Sampen, KC	6	Wells D, Tor	3	Hill Mi, Cin	1
Edens, Min	11	Wilson S, LA	6	Cox D, Pit	2	Hoy, Bos	1
Gott, LA	11	Burke, NYA	5	Downs, Oak	2	Lancaster, Det	1
Mason R, Pit	11	Clements, Bal	5	Drahman, ChA	2	Mallicoat, Hou	1
Orosco, Mil	11	Davis Storm, Bal	5	Gleaton, Pit	2	Nichols Ro, Cle	1
Doherty, Det	10	Eichhorn, Tor	5	Grant M, Sea	2	Osborne, StL	1
Flanagan, Bal	10	Gibson P, NYN	5	Gross Ke, LA	2	Pena J, SF	1
Horsman, Oak	10	Gossage, Oak	5	Gross Ki, LA	2	Plesac, Mil	1
Patterson B, Pit	10	Howe S, NYA	5	Harris Ge, SD	2	Reed S, SF	1
Willis C, Min	10	Howell Jay, LA	5	Holmes, Mil	2	Ruffin, Mil	1
Austin, Mil	9	Lewis S, Cal	5	Irvine, Bos	2	Russell Je, Oak	1
Guetterman, NYN	9	McDowell R, LA	5	Kipper, Min	2	Sauveur, KC	1
Jackson M, SF	9	Neagle, Pit	5	Landrum B, Mon	2	Service, Mon	1
Murphy R, Hou	9	Nunez E, Tex	5	MacDonald, Tor	2	Shifflett, KC	1
Perez Mi, StL	9	Rodriguez Rich, SD	5	Mills A, Bal	2	Slocumb, ChN	1
Wayne, Min	9	Ruskin, Cin	5	Nelson G, Oak	2	Smith Dan, Tex	1
Andersen, SD	8	Bailes, Cal	4	Pall, ChA	2	Smith Dave, ChN	1
Crim, Cal	8	Beck, SF	4	Patterson K, ChN	2	Smith Z, Pit	1
Fetters, Mil	8	Bullinger, ChN	4	Raczka, Oak	2	Timlin, Tor	1
Hartley, Phi	8	Campbell K, Oak	4	Righetti, SF	2	Walk, Pit	1
Heaton, Mil	8	Corsi, Oak	4	Springer R, NYA	2	Woodson K, Sea	1
Hernandez X, Hou	8	Dibble, Cin	4	Terrell W, Det	2	Young Ma, Bos	1
Hickerson, SF	8	Fisher, Sea	4	Walton B, Oak	2		

DO SOME PITCHERS TURN IT ON WITH RUNNERS IN SCORING POSITION? (p. 196)

Both Leagues — Listed Alphabetically
(Minimum 350 Innings Pitched since 1990)

Pitcher, Team	Overall AB	Avg	RISP AB	Avg	Pitcher, Team	Overall AB	Avg	RISP AB	Avg
Abbott J, Cal	2532	.267	542	.258	Leibrandt, Atl	2233	.254	485	.266
Appier, KC	2283	.241	513	.220	Maddux G, ChN	2851	.237	632	.248
Armstrong J, Cle	1819	.267	429	.303	Martinez D, Mon	2482	.222	549	.209
Avery, Atl	2067	.254	499	.259	Martinez R, LA	2269	.230	523	.241
Belcher T, Cin	2198	.239	481	.247	McCaskill, ChA	2137	.256	476	.277
Benes, SD	2436	.247	532	.227	McDonald, Bal	1775	.241	345	.258
Bielecki, Atl	1610	.271	395	.276	McDowell J, ChA	2689	.241	563	.245
Black, SF	2255	.248	442	.240	Milacki, Bal	1687	.271	381	.299
Boddicker, KC	1906	.265	498	.261	Moore M, Oak	2384	.255	583	.256
Bosio, Mil	2152	.251	440	.252	Morgan M, ChN	2550	.242	523	.237
Brown Kevin, Tex	2513	.267	628	.261	Morris Ja, Tor	2777	.245	646	.262
Browning, Cin	2135	.274	441	.283	Mulholland, Phi	2441	.258	521	.290
Burkett, SF	2320	.266	535	.290	Nabholz, Mon	1533	.230	322	.242
Candiotti, LA	2421	.242	571	.235	Nagy, Cle	1956	.271	463	.266
Clemens, Bos	2747	.224	594	.202	Navarro, Mil	2420	.263	545	.259
Cone, Tor	2568	.227	630	.197	Ojeda, LA	1788	.265	451	.244
Darling, Oak	2005	.258	482	.263	Olivares, StL	1526	.250	314	.232
Darwin, Bos	1493	.245	359	.220	Perez Me, NYA	2131	.235	476	.239
DeLeon J, Phi	1730	.245	433	.231	Portugal, Hou	1741	.245	383	.274
Deshaies, SD	1718	.253	382	.267	Rasmussen D, KC	1461	.277	312	.279
Drabek, Pit	2685	.243	570	.214	Rijo, Cin	2243	.223	478	.218
Erickson S, Min	1965	.251	449	.229	Ryan N, Tex	1903	.198	408	.203
Fernandez A, ChA	1791	.265	403	.273	Saberhagen, NYN	1608	.246	319	.248
Fernandez S, NYN	1583	.207	305	.203	Sanderson, NYA	2367	.264	484	.275
Finley C, Cal	2465	.254	559	.242	Smiley, Min	2245	.249	476	.279
Gardner M, Mon	1855	.241	430	.267	Smith Bryn, StL	1389	.265	327	.278
Glavine, Atl	2571	.245	554	.260	Smith Z, Pit	2203	.258	442	.296
Gooden, NYN	2382	.257	645	.250	Smoltz, Atl	2628	.235	571	.240
Gordon T, KC	1779	.246	475	.242	Stewart D, Oak	2597	.249	579	.250
Gross Ke, LA	1831	.260	447	.262	Stieb, Tor	1349	.244	311	.267
Gullickson, Det	2512	.281	535	.279	Stottlemyre T, Tor	2276	.256	505	.285
Guzman Jos, Tex	1489	.256	362	.210	Sutcliffe, Bal	1366	.272	332	.253
Hanson, Sea	2287	.261	478	.270	Swift, SF	1428	.247	349	.203
Harnisch, Hou	2298	.235	537	.235	Swindell, Cin	2574	.270	533	.278
Harris Greg A., Bos	1730	.246	422	.249	Tanana, Det	2200	.270	476	.246
Harris Greg W., SD	1365	.235	310	.206	Tapani, Min	2377	.259	504	.262
Hesketh, Bos	1398	.267	358	.226	Terrell W, Det	2029	.298	508	.309
Hibbard, ChA	2204	.265	435	.292	Tewksbury, StL	2174	.264	463	.266
Hill K, Mon	1767	.234	432	.231	Tomlin R, Pit	1750	.262	391	.271
Hough, ChA	2206	.234	484	.233	Viola, Bos	2729	.257	600	.243
Hurst B, SD	2493	.245	517	.251	Walk, Pit	1448	.257	347	.262
Jackson Dan, Pit	1511	.277	426	.279	Wegman, Mil	1856	.250	377	.244
Johnson R, Sea	2263	.212	595	.203	Welch, Oak	2182	.251	457	.278
Key, Tor	2245	.259	432	.243	Wells D, Tor	1926	.255	398	.271
King E, Det	1480	.264	336	.274	Wilson Tr, SF	1713	.241	379	.277
Krueger, Mon	1871	.278	438	.267	Witt B, Oak	1875	.247	471	.238
Lancaster, Det	1358	.274	371	.305	Young Ma, Bos	1451	.247	379	.261
Langston, Cal	2565	.238	525	.267					
Leary, Sea	1777	.272	433	.277					

WHICH PITCHERS CAN REST IN PEACE? (p. 198)

The following table lists the Percentage (%) of baserunners that a pitcher "bequeathed" to his bullpen (**Left**), and those that subsequently scored (**Sc**).

Both Leagues — Listed Alphabetically
(minimum 20 runners bequeathed)

Pitcher	Left	Sc	Sc	Pitcher	Left	Sc	Sc	Pitcher	Left	Sc	Sc
Agosto, Sea	23	5	21.7	Gullickson, Det	28	11	39.3	Nunez E, Tex	28	5	17.9
Armstrong J, Cle	27	8	29.6	Guthrie, Min	37	13	35.1	Ojeda, LA	22	1	4.5
Assenmacher, ChN	36	4	11.1	Guzman Jose, Tex	23	13	56.5	Olivares, StL	23	7	30.4
Austin, Mil	25	6	24.0	Habyan, NYA	21	5	23.8	Orosco, Mil	42	5	11.9
Avery, Atl	25	9	36.0	Hammond C, Cin	25	7	28.0	Osuna, Hou	39	7	17.9
Bankhead, Cin	23	5	21.7	Hanson, Sea	28	6	21.4	Parrett, Oak	38	7	18.4
Bannister F, Tex	26	8	30.8	Harris Greg A., Bos	42	11	26.2	Patterson B, Pit	24	4	16.7
Barnes B, Mon	20	4	20.0	Henry B, Hou	24	8	33.3	Perez Mi, StL	22	6	27.3
Benes, SD	21	3	14.3	Henry Dw, Cin	30	7	23.3	Plesac, Mil	21	1	4.8
Black, SF	27	13	48.1	Hesketh, Bos	33	12	36.4	Plunk, Cle	29	9	31.0
Boever, Hou	38	6	15.8	Hibbard, ChA	26	9	34.6	Powell D, Sea	35	10	28.6
Bolton, Cin	32	9	28.1	Hickerson, SF	27	5	18.5	Power, Cle	28	5	17.9
Bones, Mil	36	15	41.7	Honeycutt, Oak	24	4	16.7	Quantrill, Bos	23	8	34.8
Bullinger, ChN	25	8	32.0	Horsman, Oak	37	7	18.9	Radinsky, ChA	40	7	17.5
Cadaret, NYA	33	7	21.2	Howell Jay, LA	22	1	4.5	Righetti, SF	24	14	58.3
Campbell K, Oak	30	13	43.3	Innis, NYN	23	8	34.8	Robinson JD, ChN	25	5	20.0
Candelaria, LA	30	7	23.3	Irvine, Bos	25	14	56.0	Rodriguez Rich, SD	22	7	31.8
Castillo F, ChN	35	13	37.1	Jackson Dan, Pit	31	11	35.5	Rogers Ken, Tex	33	8	24.2
Clements, Bal	36	6	16.7	Jackson M, SF	26	8	30.8	Rojas, Mon	20	3	15.0
Cook D, Cle	27	4	14.8	Jones Ba, NYN	23	12	52.2	Ruskin, Cin	29	9	31.0
Crews, LA	20	6	30.0	Jones Ca, Sea	21	11	52.4	Sampen, KC	23	2	8.7
Crim, Cal	26	7	26.9	Key, Tor	26	5	19.2	Sanderson, NYA	24	8	33.3
Darling, Oak	21	9	42.9	Knudsen, Det	24	5	20.8	Scudder, Cle	34	17	50.0
Darwin, Bos	28	15	53.6	Krueger, Mon	28	18	64.3	Stanton Mike, Atl	27	11	40.7
DeLucia, Sea	20	4	20.0	Langston, Cal	21	12	57.1	Stewart D, Oak	20	7	35.0
Doherty, Det	27	11	40.7	Leary, Sea	24	13	54.2	Stottlemyre T, Tor	23	4	17.4
Dopson, Bos	22	8	36.4	Lefferts, Bal	27	12	44.4	Sutcliffe, Bal	39	21	53.8
Downs, Oak	30	9	30.0	Lilliquist, Cle	38	5	13.2	Swan R, Sea	31	11	35.5
Edens, Min	36	8	22.2	Magnante, KC	31	3	9.7	Tapani, Min	22	3	13.6
Eichhorn, Tor	22	6	27.3	Mason R, Pit	23	8	34.8	Valera, Cal	27	7	25.9
Fassero, Mon	34	8	23.5	Mathews T, Tex	29	12	41.4	Viola, Bos	24	7	29.2
Fernandez A, ChA	24	6	25.0	McCaskill, ChA	26	11	42.3	Wayne, Min	31	4	12.9
Fernandez S, NYN	22	5	22.7	McClure, StL	43	5	11.6	Wegman, Mil	21	7	33.3
Finley C, Cal	22	7	31.8	McDonald, Bal	37	9	24.3	Wickander, Cle	38	9	23.7
Fisher, Sea	20	10	50.0	McDowell R, LA	22	8	36.4	Willis C, Min	30	8	26.7
Flanagan, Bal	28	5	17.9	McElroy, ChN	30	11	36.7	Wilson S, LA	37	5	13.5
Fossas, Bos	41	5	12.2	Mesa, Cle	29	13	44.8	Witt B, Oak	23	12	52.2
Freeman M, Atl	22	2	9.1	Milacki, Bal	23	7	30.4	Young Ma, Bos	31	4	12.9
Frohwirth, Bal	31	6	19.4	Moore M, Oak	34	5	14.7	**MLB Avg.**			30.8
Gardiner, Bos	24	12	50.0	Munoz M, Det	41	8	19.5				
Gardner M, Mon	29	11	37.9	Murphy R, Hou	34	3	8.8				
Gibson P, NYN	24	8	33.3	Nabholz, Mon	34	11	32.4				
Gordon T, KC	20	5	25.0	Nagy, Cle	22	9	40.9				
Gott, LA	33	9	27.3	Navarro, Mil	30	13	43.3				
Gross Ke, LA	26	9	34.6	Neagle, Pit	28	10	35.7				
Guetterman, NYN	28	7	25.0	Nelson Je, Sea	32	11	34.4				

HOW IMPORTANT IS THE "QUALITY START"? (p. 200)

Both leagues — Listed Alphabetically
(minimum 15 games started in 1992)

Player,Team	Games Started	Quality Starts	Pct.	Player,Team	Games Started	Quality Starts	Pct.
Abbott J, Cal	29	19	65.5	Langston, Cal	32	20	62.5
Abbott K, Phi	19	10	52.6	Leary, Sea	23	7	30.4
Appier, KC	30	23	76.7	Lefferts, Bal	32	19	59.4
Armstrong J, Cle	23	7	30.4	Leibrandt, Atl	31	18	58.1
Avery, Atl	35	23	65.7	Maddux G, ChN	35	30	85.7
Barnes B, Mon	17	7	41.2	Martinez D, Mon	32	25	78.1
Belcher T, Cin	34	21	61.8	Martinez R, LA	25	14	56.0
Benes, SD	34	23	67.6	McCaskill, ChA	34	15	44.1
Black, SF	28	16	57.1	McDonald, Bal	35	19	54.3
Blyleven, Cal	24	13	54.2	McDowell J, ChA	34	22	64.7
Bones, Mil	28	12	42.9	Mesa, Cle	27	13	48.1
Bosio, Mil	33	22	66.7	Milacki, Bal	20	7	35.0
Boskie, ChN	18	5	27.8	Moore M, Oak	36	19	52.8
Brown Kevin, Tex	35	23	65.7	Morgan M, ChN	34	27	79.4
Browning, Cin	16	7	43.8	Morris Ja, Tor	34	19	55.9
Burkett, SF	32	15	46.9	Mulholland, Phi	32	17	53.1
Candiotti, LA	30	19	63.3	Mussina, Bal	32	24	75.0
Castillo F, ChN	33	21	63.6	Nabholz, Mon	32	17	53.1
Clark M, StL	20	10	50.0	Nagy, Cle	33	24	72.7
Clemens, Bos	32	23	71.9	Navarro, Mil	34	23	67.6
Cone, Tor	34	24	70.6	Ojeda, LA	29	14	48.3
Cook D, Cle	25	10	40.0	Olivares, StL	30	18	60.0
Cormier, StL	30	17	56.7	Osborne, StL	29	16	55.2
Darling, Oak	33	19	57.6	Otto, Cle	16	5	31.3
Darwin, Bos	15	9	60.0	Perez Me, NYA	33	23	69.7
DeLeon J, Phi	18	7	38.9	Pichardo, KC	24	12	50.0
Deshaies, SD	15	9	60.0	Portugal, Hou	16	11	68.8
Dopson, Bos	25	11	44.0	Reed R, KC	18	6	33.3
Downs, Oak	20	7	35.0	Rhodes A, Bal	15	10	66.7
Drabek, Pit	34	25	73.5	Rijo, Cin	33	23	69.7
Erickson S, Min	32	18	56.3	Ryan N, Tex	27	18	66.7
Fernandez A, ChA	29	14	48.3	Saberhagen, NYN	15	7	46.7
Fernandez S, NYN	32	26	81.3	Sanderson, NYA	33	17	51.5
Finley C, Cal	31	17	54.8	Schilling, Phi	26	22	84.6
Fleming, Sea	33	22	66.7	Schourek, NYN	21	11	52.4
Gardiner, Bos	18	7	38.9	Scudder, Cle	22	12	54.5
Gardner M, Mon	30	17	56.7	Seminara, SD	18	10	55.6
Glavine, Atl	33	21	63.6	Smiley, Min	34	22	64.7
Gooden, NYN	31	21	67.7	Smith Z, Pit	22	14	63.6
Gross Ke, LA	30	21	70.0	Smoltz, Atl	35	23	65.7
Gubicza, KC	18	8	44.4	Stewart D, Oak	31	17	54.8
Gullickson, Det	34	17	50.0	Stottlemyre T, Tor	27	13	48.1
Guzman Jose, Tex	33	21	63.6	Sutcliffe, Bal	36	18	50.0
Guzman Ju, Tor	28	20	71.4	Swift, SF	22	17	77.3
Hammond C, Cin	26	13	50.0	Swindell, Cin	30	21	70.0
Hanson, Sea	30	15	50.0	Tanana, Det	31	18	58.1
Harnisch, Hou	34	15	44.1	Tapani, Min	34	19	55.9
Harris Greg W., SD	20	8	40.0	Tewksbury, StL	32	27	84.4
Henry B, Hou	28	10	35.7	Tomlin R, Pit	33	20	60.6
Hershiser, LA	33	19	57.6	Valera, Cal	28	14	50.0
Hesketh, Bos	25	11	44.0	Viola, Bos	35	23	65.7
Hibbard, ChA	28	16	57.1	Walk, Pit	19	10	52.6
Hill K, Mon	33	24	72.7	Wegman, Mil	35	21	60.0
Hough, ChA	27	15	55.6	Welch, Oak	20	10	50.0
Hurst B, SD	32	22	68.8	Williams Br, Hou	16	11	68.8
Jackson Dan, Pit	34	19	55.9	Wilson Tr, SF	26	12	46.2
Johnson R, Sea	31	19	61.3	Witt B, Oak	31	15	48.4
Jones Ji, Hou	23	10	43.5	**MLB Avg**	**4212**	**2257**	**53.6**
Kamieniecki, NYA	28	12	42.9				
Key, Tor	33	21	63.6				
Kile, Hou	22	11	50.0				
Krueger, Mon	29	13	44.8				

WHOSE HEATER IS THE HOTTEST? (p. 204)

Both Leagues — Listed Alphabetically
(minimum 81 innings pitched or 50 relief games)

Pitcher,Team	IP	K	K/9	Pitcher,Team	IP	K	K/9
Abbott J, Cal	211.0	130	5.5	Erickson S, Min	212.0	101	4.3
Abbott K, Phi	133.1	88	5.9	Farr S, NYA	52.0	37	6.4
Aguilera, Min	66.2	52	7.0	Fassero, Mon	85.2	63	6.6
Alvarez W, ChA	100.1	66	5.9	Fernandez A, ChA	187.2	95	4.6
Appier, KC	208.1	150	6.5	Fernandez S, NYN	214.2	193	8.1
Armstrong J, Cle	166.2	114	6.2	Fetters, Mil	62.2	43	6.2
Assenmacher, ChN	68.0	67	8.9	Finley C, Cal	204.1	124	5.5
Astacio, LA	82.0	43	4.7	Fisher, Sea	91.1	26	2.6
Avery, Atl	233.2	129	5.0	Fleming, Sea	228.1	112	4.4
Bankhead, Cin	70.2	53	6.8	Fossas, Bos	29.2	19	5.8
Barnes B, Mon	100.0	65	5.8	Freeman M, Atl	64.1	41	5.7
Beck, SF	92.0	87	8.5	Frey, Cal	45.1	24	4.8
Belcher T, Cin	227.2	149	5.9	Frohwirth, Bal	106.0	58	4.9
Belinda, Pit	71.1	57	7.2	Gardiner, Bos	130.2	79	5.4
Benes, SD	231.1	169	6.6	Gardner M, Mon	179.2	132	6.6
Black, SF	177.0	82	4.2	Glavine, Atl	225.0	129	5.2
Blyleven, Cal	133.0	70	4.7	Gooden, NYN	206.0	145	6.3
Boddicker, KC	86.2	47	4.9	Gordon T, KC	117.2	98	7.5
Boever, Hou	111.1	67	5.4	Gott, LA	88.0	75	7.7
Bones, Mil	163.1	65	3.6	Grahe, Cal	94.2	39	3.7
Bosio, Mil	231.1	120	4.7	Grant M, Sea	81.0	42	4.7
Boskie, ChN	91.2	39	3.8	Gross Ke, LA	204.2	158	6.9
Brantley J, SF	91.2	86	8.4	Gubicza, KC	111.1	81	6.5
Brown Kevin, Tex	265.2	173	5.9	Guetterman, NYN	66.0	20	2.7
Browning, Cin	87.0	33	3.4	Gullickson, Det	221.2	64	2.6
Bullinger, ChN	85.0	36	3.8	Guthrie, Min	75.0	76	9.1
Burkett, SF	189.2	107	5.1	Guzman Jose, Tex	224.0	179	7.2
Burns T, Tex	103.0	55	4.8	Guzman Ju, Tor	180.2	165	8.2
Cadaret, NYA	103.2	73	6.3	Habyan, NYA	72.2	44	5.4
Candelaria, LA	25.1	23	8.2	Hammond C, Cin	147.1	79	4.8
Candiotti, LA	203.2	152	6.7	Hanson, Sea	186.2	112	5.4
Carpenter, StL	88.0	46	4.7	Harnisch, Hou	206.2	164	7.1
Castillo F, ChN	205.1	135	5.9	Harris Greg A., Bos	107.2	73	6.1
Charlton, Cin	81.1	90	10.0	Harris Greg W., SD	118.0	66	5.0
Clark M, StL	113.1	44	3.5	Henke, Tor	55.2	46	7.4
Clemens, Bos	246.2	208	7.6	Henneman, Det	77.1	58	6.8
Clements, Bal	48.1	20	3.7	Henry B, Hou	165.2	96	5.2
Cone, Tor	249.2	261	9.4	Henry Do, Mil	65.0	52	7.2
Cook D, Cle	158.0	96	5.5	Henry Dw, Cin	83.2	72	7.7
Cormier, StL	186.0	117	5.7	Hernandez X, Hou	111.0	96	7.8
Crim, Cal	87.0	30	3.1	Hershiser, LA	210.2	130	5.6
Darling, Oak	206.1	99	4.3	Hesketh, Bos	148.2	104	6.3
Darwin, Bos	161.1	124	6.9	Hibbard, ChA	176.0	69	3.5
Davis Storm, Bal	89.1	53	5.3	Hickerson, SF	87.1	68	7.0
DeLeon J, Phi	117.1	79	6.1	Hill K, Mon	218.0	150	6.2
DeLucia, Sea	83.2	66	7.1	Hillegas, Oak	86.0	49	5.1
Deshaies, SD	96.0	46	4.3	Honeycutt, Oak	39.0	32	7.4
Dibble, Cin	70.1	110	14.1	Horsman, Oak	43.1	18	3.7
Doherty, Det	116.0	37	2.9	Hough, ChA	176.1	76	3.9
Dopson, Bos	141.1	55	3.5	Hurst B, SD	217.1	131	5.4
Downs, Oak	144.1	71	4.4	Innis, NYN	88.0	39	4.0
Drabek, Pit	256.2	177	6.2	Jackson Dan, Pit	201.1	97	4.3
Eckersley, Oak	80.0	93	10.5	Jackson M, SF	82.0	80	8.8
Edens, Min	76.1	57	6.7	Johnson R, Sea	210.1	241	10.3
Eichhorn, Tor	87.2	61	6.3	Jones Ba, NYN	69.2	30	3.9
Eldred, Mil	100.1	62	5.6	Jones D, Hou	111.2	93	7.5

Pitcher,Team	IP	K	K/9	Pitcher,Team	IP	K	K/9
Jones J, Hou	139.1	69	4.5	Reardon, Atl	58.0	39	6.1
Kamieniecki, NYA	188.0	88	4.2	Reed R, KC	100.1	49	4.4
Key, Tor	216.2	117	4.9	Rhodes A, Bal	94.1	77	7.3
Kile, Hou	125.1	90	6.5	Righetti, SF	78.1	47	5.4
Krueger, Mon	178.2	99	5.0	Rijo, Cin	211.0	171	7.3
Lancaster, Det	86.2	35	3.6	Rivera Ben, Phi	117.1	77	5.9
Langston, Cal	229.0	174	6.8	Robinson JM, Pit	82.0	32	3.5
Leach T, ChA	73.2	22	2.7	Rodriguez Rich, SD	91.0	64	6.3
Leary, Sea	141.0	46	2.9	Rogers Ken, Tex	78.2	70	8.0
Lefferts, Bal	196.1	104	4.8	Rojas, Mon	100.2	70	6.3
Leibrandt, Atl	193.0	104	4.8	Ruskin, Cin	53.2	43	7.2
Leiter M, Det	112.0	75	6.0	Russell Je, Oak	66.1	48	6.5
Lilliquist, Cle	61.2	47	6.9	Ryan N, Tex	157.1	157	9.0
Maddux G, ChN	268.0	199	6.7	Saberhagen, NYN	97.2	81	7.5
Magnante, KC	89.1	31	3.1	Sampen, KC	83.0	37	4.0
Martinez De, Mon	226.1	147	5.8	Sanderson, NYA	193.1	104	4.8
Martinez R, LA	150.2	101	6.0	Scanlan, ChN	87.1	42	4.3
Mason R, Pit	88.0	56	5.7	Schilling, Phi	226.1	147	5.8
McCaskill, ChA	209.0	109	4.7	Schooler, Sea	51.2	33	5.7
McClure, StL	54.0	24	4.0	Schourek, NYN	136.0	60	4.0
McDonald, Bal	227.0	158	6.3	Scudder, Cle	109.0	66	5.4
McDowell J, ChA	260.2	178	6.1	Seminara, SD	100.1	61	5.5
McDowell R, LA	83.2	50	5.4	Smiley, Min	241.0	163	6.1
McElroy, ChN	83.2	83	8.9	Smith Le, StL	75.0	60	7.2
Meacham R, KC	101.2	64	5.7	Smith Z, Pit	141.0	56	3.6
Melendez J, SD	89.1	82	8.3	Smoltz, Atl	246.2	215	7.8
Mercker, Atl	68.1	49	6.5	Stanton Mike, Atl	63.2	44	6.2
Mesa, Cle	160.2	62	3.5	Stewart D, Oak	199.1	130	5.9
Milacki, Bal	115.2	51	4.0	Stieb, Tor	96.1	45	4.2
Mills A, Bal	103.1	60	5.2	Stottlemyre T, Tor	174.0	98	5.1
Monteleone, NYA	92.2	62	6.0	Sutcliffe, Bal	237.1	109	4.1
Montgomery, KC	82.2	69	7.5	Swan R, Sea	104.1	45	3.9
Moore M, Oak	223.0	117	4.7	Swift, SF	164.2	77	4.2
Morgan M, ChN	240.0	123	4.6	Swindell, Cin	213.2	138	5.8
Morris Ja, Tor	240.2	132	4.9	Tanana, Det	186.2	91	4.4
Mulholland, Phi	229.0	125	4.9	Tapani, Min	220.0	138	5.6
Munoz M, Det	48.0	23	4.3	Terrell W, Det	136.2	61	4.0
Murphy R, Hou	55.2	42	6.8	Tewksbury, StL	233.0	91	3.5
Mussina, Bal	241.0	130	4.9	Thigpen, ChA	55.0	45	7.4
Myers R, SD	79.2	66	7.5	Tomlin R, Pit	208.2	90	3.9
Nabholz, Mon	195.0	130	6.0	Valera, Cal	188.0	113	5.4
Nagy, Cle	252.0	169	6.0	Viola, Bos	238.0	121	4.6
Navarro, Mil	246.0	100	3.7	Wakefield, Pit	92.0	51	5.0
Neagle, Pit	86.1	77	8.0	Walk, Pit	135.0	60	4.0
Nelson Je, Sea	81.0	46	5.1	Ward D, Tor	101.1	103	9.1
Nichols Ro, Cle	105.1	56	4.8	Wegman, Mil	261.2	127	4.4
Ojeda, LA	166.1	94	5.1	Welch, Oak	123.2	47	3.4
Olin, Cle	88.1	47	4.8	Wells D, Tor	120.0	62	4.7
Olivares, StL	197.0	124	5.7	Wetteland, Mon	83.1	99	10.7
Olson Gregg, Bal	61.1	58	8.5	Whitehurst, NYN	97.0	70	6.5
Orosco, Mil	39.0	40	9.2	Williams Br, Hou	96.1	54	5.0
Osborne, StL	179.0	104	5.2	Williams Mit, Phi	81.0	74	8.2
Osuna, Hou	61.2	37	5.4	Willis C, Min	79.1	45	5.1
Parrett, Oak	98.1	78	7.1	Wilson S, LA	66.2	54	7.3
Patterson B, Pit	64.2	43	6.0	Wilson Tr, SF	154.0	88	5.1
Perez Me, NYA	247.2	218	7.9	Witt B, Oak	193.0	125	5.8
Perez Mi, StL	93.0	46	4.5	Worrell, StL	64.0	64	9.0
Pichardo, KC	143.2	59	3.7	Young A, NYN	121.0	64	4.8
Plunk, Cle	71.2	50	6.3				
Portugal, Hou	101.1	62	5.5				
Power, Cle	99.1	51	4.6				
Radinsky, ChA	59.1	48	7.3				

IF THEY THROW GROUNDBALLS IN THE FIRST, WILL IT BE FLYBALLS IN THE SEVENTH? (p. 206)

Both Leagues — Listed Alphabetically
(Minimum 10 Games Started)

Pitcher	Innings 1-3	4-6	7+	Pitcher	Innings 1-3	4-6	7+	Pitcher	Innings 1-3	4-6	7+
Abbott J, Cal	2.17	1.80	1.45	Gross Ke, LA	1.77	1.62	1.50	Perez Me, NYA	1.21	1.23	1.24
Abbott K, Phi	1.22	0.94	0.46	Gubicza, KC	1.87	1.11	1.44	Pichardo, KC	1.72	1.23	2.67
Aldred, Det	0.79	1.21	1.00	Gullickson, Det	0.85	0.85	0.95	Portugal, Hou	1.31	1.67	1.70
Appier, KC	1.09	1.01	0.84	Guzman J, Tex	1.17	1.42	1.29	Reed Ri, KC	1.19	1.55	0.44
Aquino, KC	1.28	1.26	1.50	Guzman Ju, Tor	0.97	1.11	0.74	Rhodes A, Bal	0.94	0.80	1.79
Armstrong J, Cle	1.20	1.05	1.30	Haas D, Det	0.98	1.24	1.57	Rijo, Cin	2.14	1.94	1.65
Astacio, LA	1.89	1.74	1.61	Hammond C, Cin	1.64	1.64	3.25	Ritz, Det	1.58	1.50	5.00
Avery, Atl	1.05	1.51	1.41	Haney C, KC	0.75	1.18	0.36	Rivera Be, Phi	1.13	1.00	0.92
Banks, Min	1.11	1.28	1.25	Hanson, Sea	2.25	2.07	2.36	Robinson D, Phi	0.75	0.75	2.00
Barnes B, Mon	1.06	1.02	0.75	Harnisch, Hou	1.03	0.79	0.58	Robinson JM, Pit	0.93	0.86	0.75
Belcher T, Cin	1.02	0.95	0.85	Harris Greg, SD	1.52	1.14	1.00	Ryan N, Tex	0.61	1.06	0.58
Benes, SD	1.02	1.07	1.13	Henry B, Hou	1.36	1.27	1.32	Saberhagen, NY	2.15	0.82	1.05
Bielecki, Atl	1.96	1.65	0.83	Hershiser, LA	2.17	1.84	1.39	Sanderson, NYA	0.90	0.87	0.52
Black, SF	0.99	1.13	0.73	Hesketh, Bos	1.45	1.88	1.15	Schilling, Phi	1.19	1.15	1.04
Blyleven, Cal	1.02	1.17	0.83	Hibbard, ChA	3.29	1.95	2.71	Schourek, NYN	1.12	1.14	0.58
Bones, Mil	1.11	1.06	1.26	Hill K, Mon	1.95	1.73	1.09	Scudder, Cle	1.46	1.23	1.22
Bosio, Mil	1.13	1.20	1.63	Hough, ChA	1.02	1.04	1.19	Seminara, SD	1.90	1.94	1.60
Boskie, ChN	0.79	0.95	2.67	Hurst B, SD	1.60	1.68	1.12	Slusarski, Oak	1.34	0.65	1.00
Brown K, Tex	2.70	2.36	2.06	Jackson Dan, Pit	1.88	1.71	2.64	Smiley, Min	1.07	1.07	0.85
Browning, Cin	0.94	0.83	1.17	Johnson R, Sea	0.82	0.94	1.09	Smith P, Atl	1.20	0.95	0.56
Burba, SF	1.05	1.22	0.00	Jones Ji, Hou	2.08	1.76	1.62	Smith Z, Pit	2.46	2.13	2.04
Burkett, SF	1.43	1.21	1.33	Kamieniecki, NY	1.30	1.23	1.63	Smoltz, Atl	1.33	1.49	0.67
Burns T, Tex	1.03	0.55	0.77	Key, Tor	1.16	1.20	1.28	Stewart D, Oak	0.72	0.74	0.55
Cadaret, NYA	1.34	1.53	1.25	Kile, Hou	1.09	1.15	0.35	Stieb, Tor	1.86	1.08	1.00
Candiotti, LA	1.65	1.27	1.07	King E, Det	1.38	1.50	1.25	Stottlemyre, Tor	1.30	1.02	1.09
Castillo F, ChN	1.18	1.15	1.17	Krueger, Mon	0.88	0.82	1.04	Sutcliffe, Bal	0.85	0.93	0.96
Clark M, StL	1.03	1.09	1.15	Langston, Cal	1.42	1.49	1.66	Swift, SF	2.32	2.82	3.29
Clemens, Bos	1.69	2.12	2.14	Leary, Sea	1.83	1.15	1.60	Swindell, Cin	0.98	0.84	0.81
Cone, Tor	0.97	1.04	0.76	Lefferts, Bal	1.14	1.49	1.24	Tanana, Det	1.04	1.08	1.06
Cook D, Cle	0.82	0.65	0.79	Leibrandt, Atl	1.42	1.30	1.33	Tapani, Min	1.53	1.04	1.48
Cormier, StL	1.83	1.52	1.64	Leiter M, Det	0.93	0.80	0.75	Terrell W, Det	1.90	1.93	1.33
Darling, Oak	1.13	1.02	0.92	Maddux G, ChN	3.33	2.30	2.19	Tewksbury, StL	1.81	1.83	1.56
Darwin, Bos	0.70	0.92	1.20	Magnante, KC	0.96	1.19	0.50	Tomlin R, Pit	1.94	1.57	1.56
DeLeon J, Phi	0.68	0.96	0.44	Mahomes, Min	0.58	1.17	0.33	Valera, Cal	1.07	1.13	0.86
DeLucia, Sea	0.83	1.19	0.00	Martinez D, Mon	2.07	1.58	1.58	Viola, Bos	2.41	1.86	1.33
Deshaies, SD	0.82	0.47	0.93	Martinez R, LA	1.16	0.96	2.00	Wakefield, Pit	0.93	1.35	0.96
Doherty, Det	3.23	2.45	2.00	McCaskill, ChA	1.99	1.28	0.85	Walk, Pit	2.06	1.72	1.33
Dopson, Bos	2.28	2.19	2.23	McDonald, Bal	1.11	1.13	0.84	Wegman, Mil	2.10	1.60	1.26
Downs, Oak	0.86	1.06	0.54	McDowell J, ChA	0.84	0.98	1.44	Welch, Oak	0.96	0.88	1.18
Drabek, Pit	1.77	2.10	1.52	Mesa, Cle	0.88	0.94	0.80	Wells D, Tor	0.83	0.73	0.14
Eldred, Mil	0.96	0.57	1.26	Milacki, Bal	1.10	1.30	1.25	Whitehurst, NYN	1.84	1.15	-
Erickson S, Min	2.88	2.12	2.28	Moore M, Oak	1.83	1.24	1.52	Williams Br, Hou	1.23	1.13	1.25
Fernandez A, Ch	0.91	0.93	0.89	Morgan M, ChN	3.00	2.23	2.03	Wilson Tr, SF	1.28	1.23	1.00
Fernandez S, NY	0.59	0.44	0.45	Morris Ja, Tor	1.29	1.49	1.24	Witt B, Oak	1.35	1.36	1.95
Finley C, Cal	1.13	1.16	0.95	Mulholland, Phi	1.60	1.15	1.39	Young A, NYN	2.06	1.76	2.00
Fisher, Sea	0.72	0.55	0.25	Mussina, Bal	0.96	0.86	0.73	**MLB Avg**	**1.32**	**1.25**	**1.20**
Fleming, Sea	1.60	1.03	0.84	Nabholz, Mon	1.66	2.32	1.67	**Groundball Pit.**	**2.06**	**1.77**	**1.80**
Gardiner, Bos	1.00	1.56	1.11	Nagy, Cle	3.00	2.21	2.13	**Neutral Pit.**	**1.23**	**1.20**	**1.12**
Gardner M, Mon	0.97	0.89	0.69	Navarro, Mil	1.43	1.31	1.06	**Flyball Pit.**	**0.86**	**0.83**	**0.77**
Glavine, Atl	1.74	1.30	1.23	Ojeda, LA	1.38	1.29	1.38				
Gooden, NYN	1.84	1.64	1.15	Olivares, StL	1.39	1.86	2.18				
Gordon T, KC	1.40	1.12	4.00	Osborne, StL	1.28	1.02	1.05				
Grant M, Sea	1.00	0.85	2.00	Otto, Cle	1.91	1.66	1.50				
Greene T, Phi	1.02	1.09	1.67	Pavlik, Tex	0.76	1.19	1.80				

WHICH PITCHERS GET CHEAP STRIKEOUTS? (p. 208)

National League Pitchers — Listed Alphabetically
(minimum 15 Total Strikeouts in 1992)

Pitcher	K	P-K	Pct	Pitcher	K	P-K	Pct	Pitcher	K	P-K	Pct
Abbott K, Phi	88	18	20	Gibson P, NYN	49	9	18	Neagle, Pit	77	10	13
Andersen, SD	35	3	9	Glavine, Atl	129	22	17	Nied, Atl	19	3	16
Ashby An, Phi	24	4	17	Gleaton, Pit	18	5	28	Ojeda, LA	94	18	19
Assenmacher, ChN	67	4	6	Gooden, NYN	145	27	19	Olivares, StL	124	22	18
Astacio, LA	43	7	16	Gott, LA	75	3	4	Oliveras, SF	17	2	12
Avery, Atl	129	20	16	Greene T, Phi	39	5	13	Osborne, StL	104	18	17
Ayala Bo, Cin	23	4	17	Gross Ke, LA	158	20	13	Osuna, Hou	37	4	11
Ayrault, Phi	27	3	11	Guetterman, NYN	15	2	13	Palacios V, Pit	33	7	21
Bankhead, Cin	53	5	9	Hammond C, Cin	79	19	24	Patterson B, Pit	43	1	2
Barnes B, Mon	65	7	11	Haney C, KC	27	5	19	Patterson K, ChN	23	2	9
Beck, SF	87	3	3	Harkey, ChN	21	2	10	Pena A, Atl	34	1	3
Belcher T, Cin	149	21	14	Harnisch, Hou	164	29	18	Pena J, SF	32	6	19
Belinda, Pit	57	0	0	Harris Ge, SD	19	2	11	Perez Mi, StL	46	8	17
Benes, SD	169	27	16	Harris Greg W., SD	66	12	18	Portugal, Hou	62	12	19
Berenguer, KC	19	1	5	Hartley, Phi	53	1	2	Pugh, Cin	18	2	11
Bielecki, Atl	62	7	11	Henry B, Hou	96	16	17	Righetti, SF	47	4	9
Black, SF	82	12	15	Henry Dw, Cin	72	10	14	Rijo, Cin	171	29	17
Blair W, Hou	48	4	8	Heredia G, Mon	22	2	9	Ritchie, Phi	19	3	16
Boever, Hou	67	3	4	Hernandez Je, SD	25	0	0	Rivera Be, Phi	77	11	14
Bolton, Cin	27	7	26	Hernandez X, Hou	96	7	7	Robinson Do, Phi	17	1	6
Boskie, ChN	39	8	21	Hershiser, LA	130	24	18	Robinson JD, ChN	46	7	15
Bowen R, Hou	22	4	18	Hickerson, SF	68	4	6	Rodriguez Rich, SD	64	7	11
Brantley C, Phi	32	4	13	Hill K, Mon	150	19	13	Rogers Kev, SF	26	4	15
Brantley J, SF	86	4	5	Hillman, NYN	16	3	19	Rojas, Mon	70	2	3
Brink, Phi	16	6	38	Howell Jay, LA	36	5	14	Ruskin, Cin	43	3	7
Brocail, SD	15	3	20	Hurst B, SD	131	14	11	Saberhagen, NYN	81	11	14
Browning, Cin	33	8	24	Innis, NYN	39	5	13	Sampen, KC	23	1	4
Bullinger, ChN	36	4	11	Jackson Dan, Pit	97	19	20	Scanlan, ChN	42	4	10
Burba, SF	47	12	26	Jackson M, SF	80	3	4	Schilling, Phi	147	17	12
Burkett, SF	107	11	10	Jones Ba, NYN	30	2	7	Schourek, NYN	60	8	13
Candelaria, LA	23	0	0	Jones D, Hou	93	0	0	Scott Ti, SD	30	3	10
Candiotti, LA	152	14	9	Jones Ji, Hou	69	8	12	Seminara, SD	61	11	18
Carpenter, StL	46	4	9	Kile, Hou	90	10	11	Slocumb, ChN	27	1	4
Carter L, SF	21	3	14	Lamp, Pit	15	0	0	Smith Le, StL	60	0	0
Castillo F, ChN	135	17	13	Lefferts, Bal	81	16	20	Smith P, Atl	43	3	7
Charlton, Cin	90	1	1	Leibrandt, Atl	104	14	13	Smith Z, Pit	56	10	18
Clark M, StL	44	5	11	Maddux G, ChN	199	14	7	Smoltz, Atl	215	28	13
Cone, Tor	214	28	13	Maddux M, SD	60	3	5	Stanton WMike, Atl	44	2	5
Cormier, StL	117	13	11	Magrane, StL	20	3	15	Swift, SF	77	9	12
Cox D, Pit	48	6	13	Mallicoat, Hou	20	2	10	Swindell, Cin	138	19	14
Crews, LA	43	9	21	Martinez De, Mon	147	16	11	Tewksbury, StL	91	10	11
Davis MW, Atl	15	3	20	Martinez R, LA	101	11	11	Tomlin R, Pit	90	16	18
DeLeon J, Phi	79	6	8	Mason R, Pit	56	2	4	Valdez S, Mon	32	3	9
Deshaies, SD	46	9	20	Mathews G, Phi	27	4	15	Wakefield, Pit	51	7	14
Dewey, NYN	24	1	4	McClure, StL	24	5	21	Walk, Pit	60	12	20
Dibble, Cin	110	0	0	McDowell R, LA	50	0	0	Wetteland, Mon	99	1	1
Downs, Oak	33	5	15	McElroy, ChN	83	2	2	Whitehurst, NYN	70	9	13
Drabek, Pit	177	21	12	Melendez J, SD	82	7	9	Williams Br, Hou	54	6	11
Fassero, Mon	63	5	8	Mercker, Atl	49	7	14	Williams Mit, Phi	74	2	3
Fernandez S, NYN	193	35	18	Morgan M, ChN	123	17	14	Wilson S, LA	54	7	13
Foster S, Cin	34	2	6	Mulholland, Phi	125	22	18	Wilson Tr, SF	88	12	14
Franco Jo, NYN	20	0	0	Murphy R, Hou	42	3	7	Wohlers, Atl	17	2	12
Freeman M, Atl	41	1	2	Myers R, SD	66	2	3	Worrell, StL	64	3	5
Gardner M, Mon	132	23	17	Nabholz, Mon	130	23	18	Young A, NYN	64	9	14

WHO SHOULD (AND SHOULDN'T) BE A CLOSER? (p. 210)

Both Leagues — Listed Alphabetically
(minimum 20 Games in relief in 1992)

Pitcher, Team	Late & Close ERA	Avg	Pitcher, Team	Late & Close ERA	Avg	Pitcher, Team	Late & Close ERA	Avg
Agosto, Sea	2.31	.311	Guthrie, Min	2.33	.208	Nichols Ro, Cle	3.27	.306
Aguilera, Min	2.49	.214	Habyan, NYA	0.92	.296	Nielsen J, NYA	0.00	.294
Alvarez W, ChA	2.57	.375	Harris Ge, SD	1.17	.207	Nunez E, Tex	4.15	.287
Andersen, SD	5.27	.231	Harris Greg A., Bos	1.31	.207	Olin, Cle	1.34	.246
Assenmacher, ChN	2.47	.239	Hartley, Phi	3.62	.231	Olson Gregg, Bal	2.22	.228
Austin, Mil	1.76	.176	Harvey, Cal	2.08	.222	Orosco, Mil	1.80	.192
Ayrault, Phi	0.00	.111	Heaton, Mil	2.75	.233	Osuna, Hou	3.48	.250
Bailes, Cal	0.00	.370	Henke, Tor	2.94	.222	Pall, ChA	3.54	.269
Bankhead, Cin	3.09	.244	Henneman, Det	3.11	.269	Parrett, Oak	4.02	.214
Bannister F, Tex	9.00	.368	Henry Do, Mil	2.79	.248	Patterson B, Pit	1.80	.269
Beck, SF	1.49	.193	Henry Dw, Cin	2.82	.151	Patterson K, ChN	1.50	.286
Belinda, Pit	2.65	.224	Hentgen, Tor	3.24	.222	Pena A, Atl	3.18	.267
Berenguer, KC	4.96	.292	Hernandez Je, SD	2.94	.327	Pena J, SF	1.17	.167
Blair W, Hou	1.08	.226	Hernandez R, ChA	2.12	.191	Perez Mi, StL	1.81	.226
Boddicker, KC	3.17	.292	Hernandez X, Hou	2.13	.207	Plesac, Mil	2.57	.275
Boever, Hou	0.71	.270	Hickerson, SF	2.23	.241	Plunk, Cle	2.70	.200
Bolton, Cin	1.74	.275	Holmes, Mil	1.74	.237	Powell D, Sea	2.65	.241
Brantley J, SF	1.14	.252	Honeycutt, Oak	2.66	.261	Power, Cle	1.67	.238
Bullinger, ChN	1.65	.200	Horsman, Oak	0.96	.138	Quantrill, Bos	3.06	.348
Burke, NYA	3.86	.238	Howe S, NYA	1.44	.141	Radinsky, ChA	1.43	.231
Burns T, Tex	2.05	.299	Howell Jay, LA	1.64	.295	Reardon, Atl	3.59	.281
Cadaret, NYA	5.68	.320	Innis, NYN	1.62	.313	Righetti, SF	3.42	.296
Campbell K, Oak	2.45	.192	Irvine, Bos	4.22	.347	Ritchie, Phi	1.93	.341
Candelaria, LA	2.21	.230	Jackson M, SF	3.07	.240	Robinson JD, ChN	1.50	.264
Carpenter, StL	2.78	.256	Jones Ba, NYN	4.31	.309	Rodriguez Rich, SD	3.77	.216
Charlton, Cin	3.00	.249	Jones Ca, Sea	7.94	.268	Rogers Ken, Tex	2.22	.289
Clements, Bal	0.84	.194	Jones D, Hou	1.43	.239	Rojas, Mon	1.32	.238
Corsi, Oak	0.00	.351	Kiely, Det	2.30	.250	Ruskin, Cin	2.29	.299
Crews, LA	0.84	.279	Kipper, Min	1.23	.235	Russell Je, Oak	1.59	.230
Crim, Cal	3.80	.318	Knudsen, Det	3.51	.281	Sampen, KC	3.15	.359
Darwin, Bos	2.82	.250	Lamp, Pit	8.31	.316	Scanlan, ChN	3.42	.249
Davis MW, Atl	0.00	.500	Lancaster, Det	4.50	.372	Schooler, Sea	5.40	.327
Davis Sto, Bal	0.28	.221	Leach T, ChA	1.52	.272	Scott Ti, SD	2.87	.245
Dewey, NYN	4.05	.280	Leiter M, Det	3.00	.143	Shifflett, KC	1.62	.286
Dibble, Cin	3.61	.178	Lilliquist, Cle	1.93	.231	Slocumb, ChN	3.68	.419
Doherty, Det	5.02	.390	MacDonald, Tor	0.00	.115	Smith Le, StL	2.06	.204
Eckersley, Oak	1.80	.172	Maddux M, SD	2.39	.267	Stanton WMike, Atl	2.70	.245
Edens, Min	2.64	.211	Magnante, KC	2.30	.391	Swan R, Sea	1.86	.239
Eichhorn, Tor	2.51	.309	Mallicoat, Hou	3.00	.190	Terrell W, Det	1.47	.282
Farr S, NYA	1.00	.184	Mason R, Pit	4.15	.272	Thigpen, ChA	3.23	.252
Fassero, Mon	1.06	.236	Mathews T, Tex	6.59	.393	Timlin, Tor	1.59	.304
Fetters, Mil	1.20	.146	McClure, StL	0.86	.247	Valdez S, Mon	0.00	.167
Flanagan, Bal	20.77	.421	McDowell R, LA	2.86	.279	Ward D, Tor	0.84	.199
Fossas, Bos	3.09	.295	McElroy, ChN	2.44	.253	Wayne, Min	1.37	.253
Foster S, Cin	1.20	.174	Meacham R, KC	1.93	.237	Wells D, Tor	1.62	.313
Franco Jo, NYN	1.71	.220	Melendez J, SD	1.15	.215	Wetteland, Mon	2.05	.227
Freeman M, Atl	2.51	.227	Mercker, Atl	1.63	.202	Whitehurst, NYN	3.57	.329
Frey, Cal	1.26	.234	Mills A, Bal	0.59	.183	Whiteside, Tex	0.84	.195
Frohwirth, Bal	0.61	.226	Monteleone, NYA	1.77	.218	Wickander, Cle	3.09	.295
Gibson P, NYN	3.11	.314	Montgomery, KC	2.10	.244	Williams Mit, Phi	2.11	.250
Gleaton, Pit	9.00	.091	Munoz M, Det	0.00	.218	Willis C, Min	2.36	.238
Gordon T, KC	5.14	.316	Murphy R, Hou	1.56	.292	Wilson S, LA	6.35	.415
Gossage, Oak	4.32	.224	Myers R, SD	4.36	.275	Wohlers, Atl	3.06	.290
Gott, LA	1.74	.200	Neagle, Pit	1.86	.194	Worrell, StL	0.73	.189
Grahe, Cal	1.05	.200	Nelson G, Oak	3.86	.267	Young A, NYN	3.74	.248
Guetterman, NYN	4.23	.324	Nelson Je, Sea	1.53	.244	Young Ma, Bos	1.80	.118

DO SAVES COME EASY FOR DENNIS ECKERSLEY? (p. 212)

Both Leagues — Listed Alphabetically
(1992 Relievers with a minimum of 3 Save Opportunities)

Reliever	Easy	Regular	Tough	Reliever	Easy	Regular	Tough
Aguilera, Min	22/24	14/17	5/7	Lilliquist, Cle	2/2	4/5	0/4
Assenmacher, ChN	2/2	4/5	2/6	Maddux M, SD	0/0	5/5	0/4
Bankhead, Cin	0/0	1/2	0/3	Magnante, KC	0/1	0/2	0/0
Beck, SF	1/1	13/16	3/6	Mason R, Pit	1/1	5/6	2/3
Belinda, Pit	4/4	8/12	6/8	Mathews T, Tex	0/0	0/1	0/3
Berenguer, KC	0/1	0/1	1/2	McDowell R, LA	3/5	7/9	4/8
Boddicker, KC	0/0	3/3	0/0	McElroy, ChN	1/1	2/3	3/7
Boever, Hou	0/0	1/1	1/5	Meacham R, KC	0/0	2/4	0/2
Brantley J, SF	3/3	3/4	1/2	Mercker, Atl	1/1	2/2	3/6
Bullinger, ChN	2/2	4/4	1/1	Mills A, Bal	0/0	1/1	1/2
Cadaret, NYA	0/0	0/0	1/3	Montgomery, KC	16/16	21/24	2/6
Candelaria, LA	1/1	3/4	1/2	Munoz M, Det	1/1	1/1	0/1
Carpenter, StL	0/0	1/3	0/5	Myers R, SD	13/15	19/22	6/9
Charlton, Cin	6/6	16/20	4/8	Neagle, Pit	1/1	1/3	0/0
Cox D, Pit	0/0	2/2	1/3	Nelson Je, Sea	0/0	5/8	1/6
Crim, Cal	0/0	1/1	0/2	Nunez E, Tex	0/0	1/1	2/3
Darwin, Bos	0/0	3/5	0/1	Olin, Cle	8/8	15/18	6/10
Davis Sto, Bal	0/0	2/4	2/3	Olson Gregg, Bal	18/18	14/20	4/6
DeLucia, Sea	0/0	1/2	0/1	Patterson B, Pit	2/2	5/6	2/5
Dibble, Cin	13/14	8/12	4/4	Pena A, Atl	7/7	5/7	3/4
Doherty, Det	0/0	2/3	1/1	Perez Mi, StL	0/0	0/1	0/2
Eckersley, Oak	28/28	22/24	1/2	Plesac, Mil	0/0	1/2	0/1
Edens, Min	0/0	3/4	0/1	Plunk, Cle	0/0	3/5	1/3
Eichhorn, Tor	0/0	1/2	1/4	Power, Cle	0/1	5/7	1/3
Farr S, NYA	16/16	13/15	1/5	Quantrill, Bos	0/0	0/2	1/3
Fassero, Mon	0/0	1/5	0/2	Radinsky, ChA	2/2	9/10	4/11
Fetters, Mil	0/0	1/1	1/4	Reardon, Atl	19/21	10/15	1/4
Fossas, Bos	0/0	0/0	2/3	Righetti, SF	1/1	2/3	0/1
Foster S, Cin	1/1	0/1	1/1	Robinson JD, ChN	0/0	1/2	0/2
Franco Jo, NYN	10/10	5/7	0/0	Rogers Ken, Tex	1/1	3/3	2/6
Freeman M, Atl	1/1	1/3	1/2	Rojas, Mon	1/1	7/7	2/3
Frey, Cal	0/0	2/3	2/2	Ruskin, Cin	0/0	0/1	0/2
Frohwirth, Bal	1/1	3/4	0/2	Russell Je, Oak	12/12	8/11	10/16
Gott, LA	0/0	3/3	3/4	Scanlan, ChN	2/2	9/11	3/5
Grahe, Cal	1/1	18/21	2/2	Schilling, Phi	1/1	1/2	0/0
Guetterman, NYN	1/1	1/1	0/1	Schooler, Sea	3/4	4/6	6/8
Guthrie, Min	1/1	4/4	0/2	Shepherd K, Phi	0/0	1/4	1/2
Habyan, NYA	1/2	5/6	1/4	Smith Le, StL	21/21	19/25	3/5
Harris Greg A., Bos	1/1	3/4	0/5	Stanton WMike, Atl	2/2	2/2	4/7
Hartley, Phi	0/1	0/2	0/1	Swan R, Sea	2/2	7/8	0/1
Harvey, Cal	6/6	7/9	0/1	Thigpen, ChA	4/4	11/14	7/11
Henke, Tor	20/21	12/14	2/2	Walk, Pit	1/2	1/1	0/0
Henneman, Det	10/12	13/15	1/1	Ward D, Tor	4/4	6/9	2/3
Henry Do, Mil	10/11	15/17	4/5	Wayne, Min	0/0	0/1	0/2
Hernandez R, ChA	1/1	9/11	2/4	Wells D, Tor	0/0	2/3	0/1
Hernandez X, Hou	1/2	6/6	0/2	Wetteland, Mon	12/12	18/23	7/11
Hickerson, SF	0/0	0/1	0/4	Whitehurst, NYN	0/0	0/1	0/2
Holmes, Mil	2/2	3/3	1/3	Whiteside, Tex	0/0	2/2	2/2
Honeycutt, Oak	2/3	0/0	1/4	Wickander, Cle	0/0	0/0	1/3
Howe S, NYA	1/1	2/2	3/4	Williams Mit, Phi	11/11	17/23	1/2
Howell Jay, LA	2/2	1/1	1/3	Willis C, Min	0/0	1/2	0/1
Innis, NYN	0/0	1/2	0/2	Wilson S, LA	0/1	0/1	0/2
Irvine, Bos	0/0	0/2	0/1	Wohlers, Atl	1/1	2/3	1/2
Jackson M, SF	0/0	2/3	0/0	Worrell, StL	1/1	1/4	1/2
Jones Ba, NYN	1/1	0/3	0/3	Young A, NYN	8/8	4/8	3/4
Jones D, Hou	8/8	26/31	2/3	AL Average	214/231	313/407	92/232
Knudsen, Det	1/1	3/4	1/2	NL Average	152/162	254/359	84/199
Lancaster, Det	0/0	0/2	0/1	MLB Totals	366/393	567/766	176/431

ARE CATCHERS' THROWING STATS DECEPTIVE? (p. 216)

The chart below lists the number of Stolen Bases (**SB**) while this catcher was behind the plate, the number of runners he caught stealing (**CCS**), his caught stealing percentage (**CS%**), the number of runners he picked off (**CPk**), the number of stolen bases allowed per 9 innings caught (**SB/9**), the number of runners caught stealing (**PCS**) and picked off (**PPk**) by the pitcher while this catcher was catching.

Both Leagues — Listed Alphabetically
(Minimum 250 Innings Caught)

Catcher, Team	SB	CCS	CS%	CPk	SB/9	PCS	PPk
Alomar S, Cle	43	30	41.1	0	0.53	5	6
Berryhill, Atl	71	15	17.4	0	0.97	5	6
Borders, Tor	116	48	29.3	3	0.90	3	2
Carter G, Mon	98	35	26.3	1	1.33	3	4
Daulton, Phi	88	39	30.7	0	0.66	10	16
Fisk, ChA	41	16	28.1	0	0.86	4	3
Fitzgerald MR, Cal	41	10	19.6	0	0.79	8	4
Fletcher D, Mon	70	15	17.6	0	1.22	9	4
Gedman, StL	37	3	7.5	0	1.14	0	1
Girardi, ChN	46	28	37.8	0	0.64	4	2
Harper B, Min	118	36	23.4	0	0.95	16	3
Hernandez Ca, LA	44	15	25.4	1	0.91	0	1
Hoiles, Bal	87	16	15.5	0	0.96	6	3
Hundley, NYN	89	26	22.6	1	0.90	7	4
Karkovice, ChA	69	29	29.6	2	0.68	4	6
Kreuter, Det	26	17	39.5	1	0.49	5	1
LaValliere, Pit	71	35	33.0	2	0.83	9	5
Macfarlane, KC	67	23	25.6	2	0.71	5	1
Manwaring, SF	46	36	43.9	1	0.47	11	0
Mayne, KC	26	12	31.6	0	0.51	6	4
Nilsson, Mil	21	12	36.4	0	0.49	0	0
Nokes, NYA	108	25	18.8	1	1.08	8	8
O'Brien C, NYN	36	25	41.0	1	0.76	5	3
Oliver J, Cin	87	37	29.8	1	0.65	10	12
Olson Greg, Atl	70	25	26.3	0	0.83	20	6
Ortiz Ju, Cle	59	25	29.8	2	0.81	2	2
Orton, Cal	22	12	35.3	0	0.58	6	6
Pagnozzi, StL	87	33	27.5	0	0.66	3	5
Parrish Lan, Sea	59	18	23.4	1	1.28	5	0
Pena T, Bos	80	32	28.6	2	0.66	7	2
Petralli, Tex	22	19	46.3	0	0.54	1	2
Quirk, Oak	41	19	31.7	0	0.96	1	3
Rodriguez I, Tex	53	51	49.0	5	0.49	6	2
Santiago, SD	73	27	27.0	0	0.74	15	5
Scioscia, LA	87	32	26.9	1	0.91	11	1
Servais, Hou	48	12	20.0	1	0.82	3	1
Slaught, Pit	45	19	29.7	0	0.68	6	4
Stanley M, NYA	41	17	29.3	0	0.86	2	10
Steinbach, Oak	68	50	42.4	1	0.61	3	1
Surhoff B, Mil	57	35	38.0	1	0.55	4	4
Tackett, Bal	33	17	34.0	2	0.57	1	0
Taubensee, Hou	67	33	33.0	2	0.75	2	1
Tettleton, Det	74	29	28.2	0	0.71	10	3
Tingley, Cal	28	19	40.4	1	0.61	4	0
Valle, Sea	84	27	24.3	1	0.78	13	2
Walters D, SD	47	16	25.4	0	0.98	2	3
Webster L, Min	29	6	17.1	1	0.83	3	1
Wilkins R, ChN	49	26	34.7	1	0.75	3	2

WHICH CATCHERS ARE THE BEST HANDLERS OF PITCHERS? (p. 219)

Both Leagues — Listed Alphabetically
(minimum 250 innings caught)

Catcher	Innings	Own ERA	Others ERA	Diff
Alomar S, Cle	729.2	3.81	4.41	- 0.60
Berryhill, Atl	661.1	2.86	3.38	- 0.52
Borders, Tor	1160.2	3.82	4.31	- 0.49
Carter G, Mon	665.0	3.14	3.34	- 0.20
Daulton, Phi	1200.2	4.17	3.92	+ 0.25
Fisk, ChA	429.2	3.98	3.78	+ 0.20
Fitzgerald MR, Cal	468.0	3.73	3.89	- 0.16
Fletcher D, Mon	518.0	2.97	3.40	- 0.43
Gedman, StL	291.0	3.46	3.36	+ 0.10
Girardi, ChN	651.1	3.61	3.23	+ 0.38
Harper B, Min	1114.0	3.85	3.27	+ 0.58
Hernandez Ca, LA	434.0	3.86	3.22	+ 0.64
Hoiles, Bal	817.1	3.83	3.74	+ 0.09
Hundley, NYN	892.1	3.31	4.27	- 0.96
Karkovice, ChA	915.0	3.77	3.95	- 0.18
Kreuter, Det	475.2	4.75	4.55	+ 0.20
LaValliere, Pit	767.0	2.97	3.76	- 0.79
Macfarlane, KC	845.0	3.93	3.65	+ 0.28
Manwaring, SF	874.1	3.64	3.56	+ 0.08
Mayne, KC	458.1	3.30	4.05	- 0.75
Nilsson, Mil	388.0	3.60	3.38	+ 0.22
Nokes, NYA	903.0	4.24	4.19	+ 0.05
O'Brien C, NYN	427.1	4.15	3.48	+ 0.67
Oliver J, Cin	1200.0	3.42	3.68	- 0.26
Olson Greg, Atl	754.2	3.43	2.83	+ 0.60
Ortiz Ju, Cle	652.2	4.44	3.85	+ 0.59
Orton, Cal	344.1	3.79	3.86	- 0.07
Pagnozzi, StL	1189.0	3.36	3.46	- 0.10
Parrish Lan, Sea	416.0	3.98	3.80	+ 0.18
Pena T, Bos	1084.0	3.49	4.07	- 0.58
Petralli, Tex	367.2	4.63	3.92	+ 0.71
Quirk, Oak	385.1	4.27	3.53	+ 0.74
Rodriguez I, Tex	982.2	3.81	4.69	- 0.88
Santiago, SD	885.1	3.73	3.34	+ 0.39
Scioscia, LA	864.2	3.14	3.81	- 0.67
Servais, Hou	524.0	3.38	3.94	- 0.56
Slaught, Pit	598.2	3.79	3.05	+ 0.74
Stanley M, NYA	428.0	4.10	4.27	- 0.17
Steinbach, Oak	998.2	3.50	4.24	- 0.74
Surhoff B, Mil	926.0	3.16	3.92	- 0.76
Tackett, Bal	516.2	3.73	3.83	- 0.10
Taubensee, Hou	804.1	3.99	3.42	+ 0.57
Tettleton, Det	943.0	4.52	4.79	- 0.27
Tingley, Cal	412.2	3.42	4.01	- 0.59
Valle, Sea	972.1	4.68	4.27	+ 0.41
Walters D, SD	432.1	3.50	3.61	- 0.11
Webster L, Min	315.0	3.31	3.83	- 0.52
Wilkins R, ChN	589.0	3.41	3.39	+ 0.02

WHO'S BEST IN THE INFIELD ZONE? (p. 221)

Zone Ratings — Infielders
(minimum 600 defensive innings in 1992)

FIRST BASE		1992			1990-92		
Player, Team	Innings	In Zone	Outs	Zone Rating	In Zone	Outs	Zone Rating
Joyner, KC	1262.1	272	251	.923	617	546	.885
Olerud, Tor	1095.2	218	197	.904	458	413	.902
Hrbek, Min	903.1	161	145	.901	526	469	.892
Grace, ChN	1414.0	347	309	.890	1081	952	.881
McGwire, Oak	1181.2	217	193	.889	738	663	.898
Martinez Tin, Sea	663.2	128	112	.875	212	172	.811
Morris H, Cin	908.2	158	138	.873	464	392	.845
Fielder, Det	954.1	188	164	.872	615	521	.847
Stevens, Cal	738.0	126	109	.865	248	206	.831
Mattingly, NYA	1223.2	274	237	.865	647	578	.893
Bream, Atl	907.1	138	119	.862	435	379	.871
Bagwell, Hou	1401.1	321	276	.860	604	509	.843
Merced, Pit	834.1	178	152	.854	327	268	.820
Palmeiro, Tex	1382.2	311	263	.846	814	694	.853
Vaughn M, Bos	720.1	125	105	.840	195	165	.846
McGriff F, SD	1334.2	235	197	.838	735	615	.837
Milligan, Bal	1061.0	201	167	.831	589	495	.840
Clark W, SF	1229.2	238	197	.828	782	648	.829
Karros, LA	1201.1	298	246	.826	302	249	.825
Sorrento, Cle	1016.2	207	170	.821	240	194	.808
Galarraga, StL	754.1	170	139	.818	619	521	.842
Murray E, NYN	1308.1	251	205	.817	799	672	.841
Kruk, Phi	958.0	166	135	.813	403	344	.854
Thomas F, ChA	1406.0	268	212	.791	445	349	.784
O'Brien P, Sea	625.1	121	95	.785	482	409	.849
MLB Average				**.846**			**.845**

SECOND BASE		1992			1990-92		
Player, Team	Innings	In Zone	Outs	Zone Rating	In Zone	Outs	Zone Rating
Sojo, Cal	761.0	255	243	.953	603	566	.939
Baerga, Cle	1434.0	495	471	.952	784	718	.916
Sandberg, ChN	1379.1	573	542	.946	1666	1563	.938
Knoblauch, Min	1339.2	452	423	.936	954	873	.915
Alicea, StL	635.2	252	230	.913	276	254	.920
Lemke, Atl	1065.0	376	343	.912	735	673	.916
Fletcher S, Mil	855.1	350	319	.911	1023	910	.890
Reed Jo, Bos	1256.0	509	461	.906	1399	1287	.920
Randolph, NYN	651.2	228	205	.899	966	873	.904
Blankenship L, Oak	613.2	250	224	.896	390	351	.900
Ripken B, Bal	893.2	354	316	.893	1034	941	.910
Alomar R, Tor	1276.0	420	374	.890	1364	1216	.891
Morandini, Phi	944.1	366	325	.888	727	643	.884
Thompson Ro, SF	1051.0	421	373	.886	1401	1224	.874
Miller K, KC	786.1	279	247	.885	468	410	.876
DeShields, Mon	1183.1	407	359	.882	1317	1142	.867
Kelly Pat, NYA	864.0	328	286	.872	372	327	.879
Sax S, ChA	1251.1	458	397	.867	1492	1312	.879
Whitaker, Det	978.1	360	312	.867	1148	1044	.909
Bordick, Oak	733.2	306	264	.863	314	270	.860
Stillwell, SD	938.1	319	274	.859	319	274	.859
Lind, Pit	1190.2	481	412	.857	1480	1293	.874
Reynolds H, Sea	1107.1	400	342	.855	1453	1299	.894
Doran, Cin	792.0	285	241	.846	886	752	.849
Biggio, Hou	1407.2	506	426	.842	515	433	.841
MLB Average				**.891**			**.891**

THIRD BASE

Player, Team	Innings	1992 In Zone	Outs	Zone Rating	1990-92 In Zone	Outs	Zone Rating
Williams MD, SF	1247.2	339	303	.894	1053	931	.884
Ventura, ChA	1395.1	441	387	.878	1139	1008	.885
Caminiti, Hou	1140.2	266	231	.868	934	816	.874
Boggs W, Bos	993.2	294	255	.867	946	823	.870
Jacoby, Cle	731.1	217	188	.866	552	470	.851
Wallach, Mon	700.2	230	199	.865	995	857	.861
Zeile, StL	1079.0	302	259	.858	746	615	.824
Livingstone, Det	841.1	236	202	.856	315	276	.876
Hansen D, LA	832.1	229	196	.856	258	217	.841
Gruber, Tor	1021.2	275	234	.851	929	791	.851
Pendleton, Atl	1389.0	424	360	.849	1163	1010	.868
Lansford C, Oak	963.1	216	183	.847	495	411	.830
Leius, Min	1025.1	311	263	.846	440	375	.852
Sheffield, SD	1247.2	386	326	.845	833	672	.807
Hayes C, NYA	1211.2	325	274	.843	1045	907	.868
Hollins D, Phi	1367.2	346	290	.838	473	391	.827
Martinez E, Sea	869.2	287	240	.836	1006	851	.846
Jefferies, KC	1288.1	410	342	.834	615	509	.828
Magadan, NYN	755.0	168	140	.833	202	168	.832
Seitzer, Mil	1265.0	353	290	.822	865	716	.828
Buechele, ChN	1240.1	365	299	.819	943	802	.851
Gomez Le, Bal	1221.2	322	262	.814	602	483	.802
Sabo, Cin	790.0	195	156	.800	857	710	.829
Palmer De, Tex	1272.0	349	278	.797	455	363	.798
MLB Average				**.845**			**.842**

SHORTSTOP

Player, Team	Innings	1992 In Zone	Outs	Zone Rating	1990-92 In Zone	Outs	Zone Rating
DiSarcina, Cal	1376.1	544	516	.949	624	586	.939
Lee Manuel, Tor	1079.1	387	365	.943	850	771	.907
Stankiewicz, NYA	696.0	281	264	.940	281	264	.940
Ripken C, Bal	1440.0	487	456	.936	1554	1485	.956
Grebeck, ChA	728.2	329	308	.936	404	375	.928
Schofield, NYN	1153.2	444	415	.935	1259	1173	.932
Velarde, NYA	606.1	258	239	.926	360	334	.928
Smith O, StL	1156.1	485	447	.922	1365	1251	.916
Fryman T, Det	1202.2	498	458	.920	785	736	.938
Rivera L, Bos	732.0	332	301	.907	1173	1029	.877
Vizquel, Sea	1152.0	486	436	.897	1250	1135	.908
Howard D, KC	616.0	230	206	.896	457	400	.875
Listach, Mil	1279.0	531	475	.895	531	475	.895
Gagne, Min	1146.1	507	451	.890	1386	1224	.883
Larkin B, Cin	1207.2	458	407	.889	1449	1292	.892
Bell Ja, Pit	1411.1	642	569	.886	1856	1599	.862
Clayton, SF	787.2	308	272	.883	326	282	.865
Belliard, Atl	860.1	339	296	.873	779	702	.901
Lewis M, Cle	1017.1	421	366	.869	546	474	.868
Owen S, Mon	972.0	374	323	.864	1243	1080	.869
Fernandez T, SD	1348.1	489	421	.861	1558	1386	.890
Thon, Tex	678.2	268	229	.854	1273	1113	.874
Offerman, LA	1290.0	511	432	.845	721	614	.852
Weiss W, Oak	859.2	336	284	.845	897	786	.876
MLB Average				**.894**			**.885**

WHO'S BEST IN THE OUTFIELD ZONE? (p. 224)

Zone Ratings — Outfielders
(minimum 600 defensive innings in 1992)

LEFT FIELD	1992				1990-92		
Player, Team	Innings	In Zone	Outs	Zone Rating	In Zone	Outs	Zone Rating
Gilkey, StL	814.0	232	208	.897	453	408	.901
Vaughn G, Mil	1147.0	311	275	.884	914	768	.840
Gonzalez L, Hou	859.1	266	234	.880	600	523	.872
Clark Je, SD	958.0	267	230	.861	448	376	.839
Gant, Atl	1096.2	267	229	.858	370	308	.832
Raines, ChA	1118.1	352	300	.852	956	784	.820
Gladden, Det	754.2	234	199	.850	844	714	.846
Hall M, NYA	860.0	247	209	.846	453	362	.799
Henderson R, Oak	883.1	258	218	.845	882	741	.840
Anderson Br, Bal	1330.0	404	339	.839	630	522	.829
Bonds Ba, Pit	1240.2	351	294	.838	1123	921	.820
May D, ChN	667.2	160	134	.837	210	173	.824
Mack S, Min	1265.0	350	284	.811	501	414	.826
McReynolds, KC	818.0	220	178	.809	804	639	.795
Bass K, NYN	603.2	165	133	.806	206	169	.820
Maldonado C, Tor	1123.0	318	254	.799	702	574	.818
Polonia, Cal	841.0	233	185	.794	686	540	.787
Reimer, Tex	840.2	250	192	.768	381	302	.793
Hatcher B, Bos	701.2	190	144	.758	496	400	.806
MLB Average				**.831**			**.813**

CENTER FIELD	1992				1990-92		
Player, Team	Innings	In Zone	Outs	Zone Rating	In Zone	Outs	Zone Rating
White D, Tor	1307.0	465	424	.912	1314	1150	.875
Dascenzo, ChN	634.2	201	177	.881	428	356	.832
Jackson Darrin, SD	1338.1	468	411	.878	771	676	.877
Lofton, Cle	1256.1	470	411	.874	517	452	.874
Kelly R, NYA	877.1	314	274	.873	996	831	.834
Nixon O, Atl	826.0	325	282	.868	508	440	.866
Grissom, Mon	1402.1	444	384	.865	968	814	.841
Wilson W, Oak	903.0	403	345	.856	592	499	.843
Johnson Lan, ChA	1364.0	478	409	.856	1368	1172	.857
Devereaux, Bal	1396.0	497	423	.851	1276	1096	.859
Sanders R, Cin	600.2	241	205	.851	269	227	.844
Felix, Cal	1076.2	387	329	.850	615	516	.839
Butler, LA	1318.1	411	345	.839	1334	1107	.830
Finley S, Hou	1352.1	478	401	.839	933	775	.831
McRae B, KC	1283.1	484	406	.839	1109	925	.834
Martinez Da, Cin	718.2	248	207	.835	628	510	.812
Puckett, Min	1274.2	459	382	.832	1273	1036	.814
Lewis D, SF	720.1	261	217	.831	477	396	.830
Gonzalez Jua, Tex	1023.1	361	299	.828	628	518	.825
Griffey Jr, Sea	1187.0	419	345	.823	1278	1025	.802
Lankford, StL	1369.0	515	424	.823	1080	860	.796
Dykstra, Phi	750.2	303	249	.822	1007	839	.833
Yount, Mil	1196.0	441	362	.821	1352	1087	.804
Cuyler, Det	733.2	282	230	.816	822	677	.824
Van Slyke, Pit	1373.2	507	406	.801	1231	978	.794
Johnson H, NYN	713.0	218	174	.798	218	174	.798
MLB Average				**.846**			**.827**

RIGHT FIELD		1992			1990-92		
Player, Team	Innings	In Zone	Outs	Zone Rating	In Zone	Outs	Zone Rating
Sierra R, Oak	1269.1	311	275	.884	1005	850	.846
Munoz P, Min	920.1	238	209	.878	371	315	.849
Justice, Atl	1198.0	351	306	.872	759	623	.821
McGee, SF	721.0	180	156	.867	269	234	.870
Gwynn T, SD	1127.2	301	258	.857	1029	864	.840
Bonilla B, NYN	988.0	267	227	.850	810	663	.819
Whiten, Cle	1278.1	358	303	.846	715	594	.831
Hayes V, Cal	681.2	191	161	.843	391	337	.862
Deer, Det	919.0	272	229	.842	961	768	.799
O'Neill, Cin	1209.2	327	275	.841	995	829	.833
Pasqua, ChA	622.0	182	153	.841	296	242	.818
Walker L, Mon	1216.2	310	260	.839	852	715	.839
Jose, StL	1117.1	309	258	.835	730	628	.860
Carter Jo, Tor	1043.2	287	239	.833	494	423	.856
Bichette, Mil	846.0	216	178	.824	615	497	.808
Orsulak, Bal	812.1	242	197	.814	625	512	.819
Anthony, Hou	900.1	206	165	.801	406	328	.808
Dawson, ChN	1182.1	271	216	.797	864	675	.781
Canseco J, Tex	766.2	230	183	.796	767	598	.780
Brunansky, Bos	784.1	232	184	.793	931	745	.800
Buhner, Sea	1325.1	367	287	.782	734	567	.773
MLB Average				.829			.816

WHO ARE THE PRIME PIVOT MEN? (p. 226)

Both Leagues — Listed Alphabetically
1992 Second Basemen over 3 seasons (1990-1992) with 10 or more DP Opportunities

Player, Team	DP Opp	DP	Pct.	Player, Team	DP Opp	DP	Pct.
Alicea, StL	36	22	.611	Lemke, Atl	124	64	.516
Alomar R, Tor	223	128	.574	Lewis M, Cle	29	19	.655
Backman, Phi	28	11	.393	Lind, Pit	261	135	.517
Baerga, Cle	172	123	.715	Litton, SF	31	25	.806
Barberie, Mon	16	7	.438	Lyons S, Bos	13	7	.538
Bell Ju, Phi	39	28	.718	McKnight, NYN	10	4	.400
Benavides, Cin	14	6	.429	McLemore, Bal	49	34	.694
Biggio, Hou	81	43	.531	Miller K, KC	100	55	.550
Blankenship L, Oak	72	48	.667	Molitor, Mil	41	19	.463
Blauser, Atl	30	16	.533	Morandini, Phi	120	68	.567
Boone Br, Sea	17	13	.765	Naehring, Bos	17	7	.412
Bordick, Oak	61	39	.639	Newman A, Tex	88	55	.625
Branson, Cin	21	12	.571	Noboa, NYN	17	9	.529
Browne, Oak	97	45	.464	Oberkfell, Cal	13	5	.385
Candaele, Hou	72	45	.625	Oquendo, StL	130	68	.523
Cora, ChA	55	36	.655	Pecota, NYN	48	24	.500
DeShields, Mon	193	113	.585	Pena G, StL	67	47	.701
Doran, Cin	143	81	.566	Phillips T, Det	113	71	.628
Duncan, Phi	106	54	.509	Quinones L, Min	24	14	.583
Faries, SD	21	10	.476	Randolph, NYN	177	129	.729
Fletcher S, Mil	215	144	.670	Ready, Oak	41	16	.390
Foley T, Mon	10	5	.500	Reed Jo, Bos	263	168	.639
Franco Ju, Tex	169	89	.527	Reynolds H, Sea	315	180	.571
Frye, Tex	43	26	.605	Riles, Hou	13	5	.385
Gallego, NYA	131	78	.595	Ripken B, Bal	201	132	.657
Gantner, Mil	126	81	.643	Roberts B, Cin	58	25	.431
Garcia C, Pit	10	4	.400	Rose B, Cal	22	15	.682
Gonzales R, Cal	40	29	.725	Samuel, KC	176	73	.415
Grebeck, ChA	15	11	.733	Sandberg, ChN	216	120	.556
Harris L, LA	69	32	.464	Sax S, ChA	270	153	.567
Hill D, Min	71	47	.662	Sharperson, LA	32	20	.625
Howard D, KC	10	5	.500	Shumpert, KC	104	65	.625
Hudler, StL	10	5	.500	Sojo, Cal	143	93	.650
Hulett, Bal	21	12	.571	Stankiewicz, NYA	18	11	.611
Huson, Tex	20	12	.600	Stillwell, SD	60	30	.500
Jefferies, KC	79	26	.329	Teufel, SD	59	25	.424
Jones Ti, StL	12	8	.667	Thompson Ro, SF	242	150	.620
Kelly Pat, NYA	81	48	.593	Treadway, Atl	127	65	.512
Kent, NYN	17	8	.471	Whitaker, Det	243	143	.588
King J, Pit	14	9	.643	Wilkerson, KC	51	26	.510
Knoblauch, Min	177	109	.616	Young E, LA	20	11	.550
Lee Manuel, Tor	62	28	.452	**MLB Avg**	**7666**	**4470**	**.583**

WHO LED THE LEAGUE IN FUMBLES? (p. 228)

Both Leagues — Listed by Most games per Error (G/E) — 1992
(minimum 600 defensive innings played)

Name	Inn	E	G/E	Name	Inn	E	G/E
				Bagwell, Hou	1401.1	7	22.2
Catchers				O'Brien P, Sea	625.1	3	23.2
Rodriguez I, Tex	982.2	15	7.3	Hrbek, Min	903.1	3	33.5
Santiago, SD	885.1	12	8.2	Mattingly, NYA	1223.2	4	34.0
Harper B, Min	1114.0	13	9.5	Grace, ChN	1414.0	4	39.3
Scioscia, LA	864.2	9	10.7	Morris H, Cin	908.2	1	101.0
Steinbach, Oak	998.2	10	11.1				
Daulton, Phi	1200.2	11	12.1	**Second Basemen**			
Carter G, Mon	665.0	6	12.3	Stillwell, SD	938.1	16	6.5
Ortiz Ju, Cle	652.2	5	14.5	Miller K, KC	786.1	13	6.7
Valle, Sea	972.1	7	15.4	Sax S, ChA	1251.1	20	7.0
Borders, Tor	1160.2	8	16.1	Thompson Ro, SF	1051.0	15	7.8
Oliver J, Cin	1199.2	8	16.7	Baerga, Cle	1434.0	19	8.4
Karkovice, ChA	915.0	6	16.9	Kelly Pat, NYA	864.0	11	8.7
Surhoff B, Mil	926.0	6	17.1	DeShields, Mon	1183.1	15	8.8
Taubensee, Hou	804.1	5	17.9	Randolph, NYN	651.2	8	9.1
Girardi, ChN	651.1	4	18.1	Reed Jo, Bos	1256.0	14	10.0
Pena T, Bos	1084.0	6	20.1	Reynolds H, Sea	1107.1	12	10.3
Macfarlane, KC	845.0	4	23.5	Whitaker, Det	978.1	9	12.1
Manwaring, SF	874.0	4	24.3	Sojo, Cal	761.0	7	12.1
Nokes, NYA	903.0	4	25.1	Biggio, Hou	1407.2	12	13.0
LaValliere, Pit	767.0	3	28.4	Lemke, Atl	1065.0	9	13.1
Hoiles, Bal	817.1	3	30.3	Bordick, Oak	733.2	6	13.6
Hundley, NYN	892.1	3	33.0	Doran, Cin	792.0	5	17.6
Alomar S, Cle	729.2	2	40.5	Alicea, StL	635.2	4	17.7
Tettleton, Det	943.0	2	52.4	Sandberg, ChN	1379.1	8	19.2
Berryhill, Atl	661.0	1	73.4	Morandini, Phi	944.1	5	21.0
Olson Greg, Atl	754.2	1	83.9	Lind, Pit	1190.2	6	22.0
Pagnozzi, StL	1189.0	1	132.1	Blankenship L, Oak	613.2	3	22.7
				Fletcher S, Mil	855.1	4	23.8
First Basemen				Knoblauch, Min	1339.2	6	24.8
Vaughn M, Bos	720.1	15	5.3	Ripken B, Bal	893.2	4	24.8
Bream, Atl	907.1	10	10.1	Alomar R, Tor	1276.0	5	28.4
Galarraga, StL	754.1	8	10.5				
Fielder, Det	954.1	10	10.6	**Third Basemen**			
Thomas F, ChA	1406.0	13	12.0	Jefferies, KC	1288.1	26	5.5
Murray E, NYN	1308.1	12	12.1	Martinez E, Sea	869.2	17	5.7
McGriff F, SD	1334.2	12	12.4	Williams MD, SF	1247.2	23	6.0
Clark W, SF	1229.2	10	13.7	Palmer De, Tex	1272.0	22	6.4
Joyner, KC	1262.1	10	14.0	Gruber, Tor	1021.2	17	6.7
Sorrento, Cle	1016.2	8	14.1	Ventura, ChA	1395.1	23	6.7
Karros, LA	1201.1	9	14.8	Boggs W, Bos	993.2	15	7.4
Kruk, Phi	958.0	7	15.2	Gomez Le, Bal	1221.2	18	7.5
Milligan, Bal	1061.0	7	16.8	Leius, Min	1025.1	15	7.6
Olerud, Tor	1095.2	7	17.4	Magadan, NYN	755.0	11	7.6
Martinez Tin, Sea	663.2	4	18.4	Buechele, ChN	1240.1	17	8.1
Merced, Pit	834.1	5	18.5	Pendleton, Atl	1389.0	19	8.1
Stevens, Cal	738.0	4	20.5	Jacoby, Cle	731.1	10	8.1
McGwire, Oak	1181.2	6	21.9	Hollins D, Phi	1367.2	18	8.4
Palmeiro, Tex	1382.2	7	21.9	Wallach, Mon	700.2	9	8.7

Name	Inn	E	G/E
Sheffield, SD	1247.2	16	8.7
Zeile, StL	1079.0	13	9.2
Livingstone, Det	841.1	10	9.3
Sabo, Cin	790.0	9	9.8
Hayes C, NYA	1211.2	13	10.4
Caminiti, Hou	1140.2	11	11.5
Hansen D, LA	832.1	8	11.6
Seitzer, Mil	1265.0	12	11.7
Lansford C, Oak	963.1	9	11.9

Shortstops

Name	Inn	E	G/E
Offerman, LA	1290.0	42	3.4
Lewis M, Cle	1017.1	25	4.5
Thon, Tex	678.2	15	5.0
Weiss W, Oak	859.2	19	5.0
Rivera L, Bos	732.0	14	5.8
Listach, Mil	1279.0	24	5.9
DiSarcina, Cal	1376.1	25	6.1
Fryman T, Det	1202.2	20	6.7
Belliard, Atl	860.1	14	6.8
Stankiewicz, NYA	696.0	11	7.0
Gagne, Min	1146.1	18	7.1
Bell Ja, Pit	1411.1	22	7.1
Velarde, NYA	606.1	9	7.5
Clayton, SF	787.2	11	8.0
Howard D, KC	616.0	8	8.6
Grebeck, ChA	728.2	8	10.1
Owen S, Mon	972.0	9	12.0
Larkin B, Cin	1207.2	11	12.2
Smith O, StL	1156.1	10	12.8
Ripken C, Bal	1440.0	12	13.3
Fernandez T, SD	1348.1	11	13.6
Lee Manuel, Tor	1079.1	7	17.1
Vizquel, Sea	1152.0	7	18.3
Schofield, NYN	1153.2	7	18.3

Left Fielders

Name	Inn	E	G/E
Reimer, Tex	840.2	11	8.5
May D, ChN	667.2	5	14.8
Hatcher B, Bos	701.2	5	15.6
Gilkey, StL	814.0	5	18.1
Maldonado Can, Tor	1123.0	6	20.8
Anderson Br, Bal	1330.0	7	21.1
Polonia, Cal	841.0	4	23.4
Henderson R, Oak	883.1	4	24.5
Gladden, Det	754.2	3	28.0
Gant, Atl	1096.2	4	30.5
Bass K, NYN	603.2	2	33.5
Mack S, Min	1265.0	4	35.1
Clark Je, SD	958.0	3	35.5
Vaughn G, Mil	1147.0	3	42.5
McReynolds, KC	818.0	2	45.4
Bonds Ba, Pit	1240.2	3	46.0
Gonzalez L, Hou	859.1	2	47.7
Hall M, NYA	860.0	2	47.8
Raines, ChA	1118.1	2	62.1

Center Fielders

Name	Inn	E	G/E
Sanders R, Cin	600.2	6	11.1
Gonzalez Jua, Tex	1023.1	8	14.2
Wilson W, Oak	903.0	7	14.3
Lofton, Cle	1256.1	8	17.4
Kelly R, NYA	877.1	5	19.5
Felix, Cal	1076.2	6	19.9
Cuyler, Det	733.2	4	20.4
White D, Tor	1307.0	7	20.7
Grissom, Mon	1402.1	7	22.3
Dascenzo, ChN	634.2	3	23.5
Johnson Lan, ChA	1364.0	6	25.3
Johnson H, NYN	713.0	3	26.4
Dykstra, Phi	750.2	3	27.8
Van Slyke, Pit	1373.2	5	30.5
Devereaux, Bal	1396.0	5	31.0
Martinez Da, Cin	718.2	2	39.9
Nixon O, Atl	826.0	2	45.9
Puckett, Min	1274.2	3	47.2
McRae B, KC	1283.1	3	47.5
Finley S, Hou	1352.1	3	50.1
Yount, Mil	1196.0	2	66.4
Butler, LA	1318.1	2	73.2
Jackson Darrin, SD	1338.1	2	74.4
Lankford, StL	1369.0	2	76.1
Griffey Jr, Sea	1187.0	1	131.9
Lewis D, SF	720.1	0	-

Right Fielders

Name	Inn	E	G/E
Pasqua, ChA	622.0	6	11.5
McGee, SF	721.0	6	13.4
Carter Jo, Tor	1043.2	8	14.5
Justice, Atl	1198.0	8	16.6
Anthony, Hou	900.1	5	20.0
Sierra R, Oak	1269.1	7	20.1
Whiten, Cle	1278.1	7	20.3
Jose, StL	1117.1	6	20.7
Brunansky, Bos	784.1	4	21.8
Gwynn T, SD	1127.2	5	25.1
Hayes V, Cal	681.2	3	25.2
Deer, Det	919.0	4	25.5
Canseco J, Tex	766.2	3	28.4
Orsulak, Bal	812.1	3	30.1
Munoz P, Min	920.1	3	34.1
Bichette, Mil	846.0	2	47.0
Bonilla B, NYN	988.0	2	54.9
Dawson, ChN	1182.1	2	65.7
Walker L, Mon	1216.2	2	67.6
Buhner, Sea	1325.1	2	73.6
O'Neill, Cin	1209.2	1	134.4

HOW IMPORTANT IS AN EFFICIENT DEFENSE? (p. 230)

The first section of the tables below lists the team's Defensive Efficiency Rating (**DER**), which is the division of the Plays Made (**PM**) by the Balls in Play (**BIP**). The second section shows that team's traditional defensive statistics: Total Chances (**TC**), Errors (**E**), and Fielding Percentage (**Pct**), the latter being the division of (Total Chances minus Errors) by Total Chances.

American League

Team	BIP	PM	DER	TC	E	Pct
Milwaukee Brewers	4766	3354	.704	6201	89	.986
Toronto Blue Jays	4566	3164	.693	6006	93	.985
Chicago White Sox	4830	3344	.692	6292	129	.979
Baltimore Orioles	4791	3312	.691	6193	93	.985
Oakland Athletics	4718	3252	.689	6042	125	.979
Minnesota Twins	4656	3201	.688	6230	95	.985
Kansas City Royals	4786	3268	.683	6212	122	.980
New York Yankees	4759	3239	.681	6211	114	.982
Boston Red Sox	4652	3158	.679	6356	139	.978
Detroit Tigers	4971	3355	.675	6189	116	.981
California Angels	4691	3167	.675	6283	134	.979
Seattle Mariners	4735	3190	.674	6210	112	.982
Cleveland Indians	4835	3237	.669	6278	141	.978
Texas Rangers	4646	3090	.665	6189	116	.981
AL Average	**66402**	**45331**	**.683**	**86930**	**1656**	**.981**

National League

Team	BIP	PM	DER	TC	E	Pct
Atlanta Braves	4611	3221	.699	6192	109	.982
Chicago Cubs	4679	3272	.699	6455	114	.982
Montreal Expos	4552	3172	.697	6302	124	.980
Pittsburgh Pirates	4837	3363	.695	6471	101	.984
St. Louis Cardinals	4867	3384	.695	6311	94	.985
Philadelphia Phillies	4684	3223	.688	6029	131	.978
San Francisco Giants	4671	3206	.686	6278	113	.982
Houston Astros	4659	3194	.686	6113	114	.981
Cincinnati Reds	4486	3070	.684	6110	96	.984
San Diego Padres	4702	3189	.678	6218	115	.982
New York Mets	4573	3090	.676	6173	116	.981
Los Angeles Dodgers	4629	3110	.672	6315	174	.972
NL Average	**55950**	**38494**	**.688**	**74967**	**1401**	**.981**

WHICH OUTFIELDERS HAVE THE CANNONS? (p. 234)

Both Leagues — 1992 — Listed by Hold Percentage
(minimum 25 baserunner opportunities to advance)

Left Field				Center Field				Right Field		
Player, Team	Opp	XB	Pct	Player, Team	Opp	XB	Pct	Player, Team	Opp	XB	Pct
Braggs, Cin	33	6	18.2	Sanders D, Atl	41	16	39.0	Snyder C, SF	26	8	30.8
Bass K, NYN	59	11	18.6	Van Slyke, Pit	144	62	43.1	Abner, ChA	31	10	32.3
Bonds Ba, Pit	110	23	20.9	Lofton, Cle	140	64	45.7	Hayes V, Cal	48	16	33.3
VanderWal, Mon	27	6	22.2	Hamilton Dar, Mil	32	15	46.9	Martinez Ch, Bal	45	18	40.0
Curtis C, Cal	44	10	22.7	Grissom, Mon	132	62	47.0	Incaviglia, Hou	42	17	40.5
Cotto, Sea	56	13	23.2	Finley S, Hou	141	67	47.5	Walker L, Mon	115	48	41.7
Gilkey, StL	69	17	24.6	Martinez Da, Cin	67	32	47.8	Whiten, Cle	122	51	41.8
Winningham, Bos	36	9	25.0	Winningham, Bos	27	13	48.1	Webster M, LA	28	12	42.9
Clark Je, SD	84	21	25.0	Griffey Jr, Sea	145	71	49.0	Anthony, Hou	95	41	43.2
Hill G, Cle	51	13	25.5	Nixon O, Atl	82	41	50.0	Brunansky, Bos	91	40	44.0
Coleman, NYN	51	14	27.5	Lewis D, SF	76	38	50.0	Buhner, Sea	138	61	44.2
Hatcher B, Bos	85	24	28.2	Johnson L, ChA	175	91	52.0	Curtis C, Cal	51	23	45.1
Gonzalez L, Hou	70	20	28.6	Sosa S, ChN	57	30	52.6	McGee, SF	64	29	45.3
Vaughn G, Mil	97	28	28.9	Zupcic, Bos	73	39	53.4	Phillips T, Det	30	14	46.7
Alou, Mon	61	18	29.5	Jackson D, SD	179	96	53.6	Hamilton Dar, Mil	42	20	47.6
Maldonado C, Tor	105	31	29.5	Lankford, StL	149	80	53.7	Cole A, Pit	25	12	48.0
Howard T, Cle	60	18	30.0	Dascenzo, ChN	68	37	54.4	Dawson, ChN	110	53	48.2
James C, SF	39	12	30.8	Butler, LA	169	93	55.0	Jose, StL	97	47	48.5
Boston, NYN	42	13	31.0	Javier, Phi	47	26	55.3	O'Neill, Cin	88	43	48.9
Roberts B, Cin	31	10	32.3	Puckett, Min	144	80	55.6	Thurman, KC	51	25	49.0
May D, ChN	65	21	32.3	Yount, Mil	143	80	55.9	Bichette, Mil	77	38	49.4
Henderson, Oak	98	32	32.7	Devereaux, Bal	119	67	56.3	Carter Jo, Tor	113	57	50.4
McReynolds, KC	88	29	33.0	Gonzalez J, Tex	123	70	56.9	Deer, Det	112	58	51.8
Hall M, NYA	84	29	34.5	Pettis, Det	54	31	57.4	Eisenreich, KC	52	27	51.9
Javier, Phi	26	9	34.6	Wilson W, Oak	87	50	57.5	Canseco J, Tex	73	38	52.1
Mack S, Min	125	44	35.2	McRae B, KC	156	90	57.7	Justice, Atl	96	50	52.1
Davis E, LA	53	19	35.8	Dykstra, Phi	107	63	58.9	Gwynn T, SD	117	61	52.1
Anderson Br, Bal	132	48	36.4	Sanders R, Cin	73	43	58.9	Chamberlain, Phi	32	17	53.1
Belle, Cle	49	18	36.7	Kelly R, NYA	119	71	59.7	Pasqua, ChA	56	30	53.6
Gladden, Det	100	37	37.0	White D, Tor	133	81	60.9	Strawberry, LA	39	21	53.8
Daniels, ChN	32	12	37.5	Burks, Bos	67	41	61.2	Benzinger, LA	29	16	55.2
Polonia, Cal	104	39	37.5	Felix, Cal	112	69	61.6	Munoz P, Min	67	37	55.2
Gant, Atl	88	33	37.5	Thompson R, NY	27	17	63.0	Plantier, Bos	50	28	56.0
Duncan, Phi	42	16	38.1	Cuyler, Det	104	66	63.5	Bonilla B, NYN	80	45	56.3
Raines, ChA	133	51	38.3	Johnson H, NYN	79	54	68.4	Rodriguez H, LA	29	17	58.6
Mitchell Kev, Sea	76	30	39.5	Felder, SF	54	37	68.5	Sierra R, Oak	112	66	58.9
Kelly R, NYA	48	19	39.6	Williams Be, NYA	48	33	68.8	Orsulak, Bal	87	52	59.8
Greenwell, Bos	29	12	41.4	Curtis C, Cal	44	31	70.5	Amaro, Phi	38	23	60.5
Calderon, Mon	33	14	42.4	Amaro, Phi	27	20	74.1	Tartabull, NYA	62	38	61.3
Incaviglia, Hou	25	11	44.0				55.1				49.2
Smith Lo, Atl	29	13	44.8								
Reimer, Tex	118	56	47.5								
Carreon, Det	67	32	47.8								
			50.0								

About STATS, Inc.

It all starts with the **system**. The STATS scoring method, which includes pitch-by-pitch information and the direction, distance, and velocity of each ball hit into play, yields an immense amount of information. Sure, we have all the statistics you're used to seeing, but where other statistical sources stop, STATS is just getting started.

Then, there's the **network**. Our information is timely because our game reporters send their information by computer as soon as the game is over. Statistics are checked, rechecked, updated, and are available daily.

Analysis comes next. STATS constantly searches for new ways to use this wealth of information to open windows into the workings of baseball. Accurate numbers, intelligent computer programming, and a large dose of imagination all help coax the most valuable information from its elusive cover.

Finally, distribution!

For 13 years now, STATS has served over a dozen Major League teams. The box scores that STATS provides to the *Associated Press* and *USA Today* have revolutionized what baseball fans expect from a box score. *Baseball Weekly* is chock full of STATS handiwork, while ESPN's nightly baseball coverage is supported by a full-time STATS statistician. We provide statistics for *Strat-O-Matic Baseball, Earl Weaver Baseball, Tony La Russa Baseball, Rotisserie Baseball* and many other baseball games and fantasy leagues all over the country.

For the baseball fan, STATS publishes monthly and year-end reports on each Major League team. We offer a host of year-end statistical breakdowns on paper or disk that cover hitting, pitching, catching, baserunning, fielding, and more. STATS even produces custom reports on request.

Computer users with modems can access the STATS computer for information with STATS On-line. If you own a computer with a modem, there is no other source with the scope of baseball information that STATS can offer.

STATS and Bill James enjoy an on-going affiliation that has produced much of the STATS product catalogue. We also administer *Bill James Fantasy Baseball*, the ultimate baseball game, designed by Bill James himself, which allows you to manage your own team and compete with other team owners around the country. Whether you play BJFB or another fantasy game, our new STATSfax report can show you what your players did the previous night as soon as you can get to the fax machine in the morning. STATS also offers a head-to-head fantasy football game, *STATS Fantasy Football. BJFB The Winter Game* is a brand new, totally unique, historically based fantasy baseball game for those who can't wait for Spring.

For more information write to:

STATS, Inc.
7366 North Lincoln Ave.
Lincolnwood, IL 60646-1708

. . . or call us at 1-708-676-3322. We can send you a STATS brochure, a free *Bill James Fantasy Baseball*, *Winter Game* or *STATS Fantasy Football* information kit, and/or information on STATS On-line or STATSfax.

For the story behind the numbers, check out STATS' other publications: *The Scouting Report: 1993* combines the observations of baseball's top analysts on the skills and potential of each player with the state-of-the-art statistics of STATS, Inc. Over 800 player scouting reports are detailed. John Dewan and Don Zminda edit this book that fans, players, sportswriters, broadcasters, and general managers can't be without! *The STATS 1993 Major League Handbook* and *STATS 1993 Minor League Handbook* will provide a complete 1993 reference library, especially important for the coming expansion season. Last, but certainly not least, the new addition to the STATS Publishing family, the *STATS 1993 Player Profiles Book*, is full of breakdowns and situational stats for every Major League player, for those fans who need more than just wins, losses, home runs and RBI.

Index

=? (Bill James)